A Search for Love and Power

WOMEN, SEX, AND ADDICTION

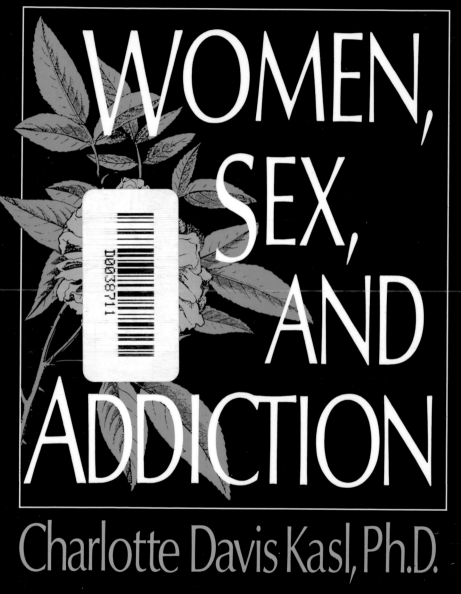

Charlotte Davis Kasl, Ph.D.

"This is one of the most sane, warm, wise books I've ever read....
a chance for rebirth."
—Gloria Steinem

Chris McKay

WOMEN, SEX, AND ADDICTION

A Search for Love and Power

CHARLOTTE DAVIS KASL, Ph.D.

PERENNIAL LIBRARY

Harper & Row, Publishers, New York
Grand Rapids, Philadelphia, St. Louis, San Francisco
London, Singapore, Sydney, Tokyo, Toronto

First PERENNIAL LIBRARY edition published 1990.

Library of Congress Cataloging-in-Publication Data

Kasl, Charlotte Davis.
    Women, sex, and addiction : a search for love and power /
Charlotte Davis Kasl.—1st Perennial Library ed.
        p.   cm.
    Includes bibliographical references.
    ISBN 0-06-097321-8
    1. Sex addiction.   2. Women—Mental health.   3. Codependents.
4. Love—Psychological aspects.   5. Control (Psychology)   I. Title.
[RC560.S43K37   1990]   89-46229
306.7'082—dc20

---

95 RRD-H 20 19 18 17 16 15 14 13 12 11

Written in the hope that a time will come for
all people, that whenever they see a body, they
will also see a sacred soul.

———————

Acknowledgments

Throughout the process of writing, I was touched again and again by the willingness of so many people to give of themselves, often in very personal ways, in the interest of helping this book come to life.

My heartfelt gratitude goes to the more than ninety women who completed lengthy questionnaires or took part in interviews on some aspect of sex addiction and sexual codependency. Your words — the result of your struggles and growth — are woven throughout the book, bringing a warmth and immediacy to the material. Many thanks also to the men from a Sex Addicts Anonymous group who so openly told their stories and provided the foundation for the chapter on men.

A bouquet of roses to Kate O'Keefe, who provided steadfast help throughout the process by organizing materials, editing drafts, providing content input, giving much needed support, and being a friend.

I am deeply grateful to Katrina Kenison, my editor at Ticknor and Fields, for having faith in this project, giving support, and gently leading me to write in a relaxed, personal style. Edite Kroll, my agent, went beyond the call of duty in every aspect of our collaboration. Along with her impeccable professional help, I was delighted by her sparkling sense of humor and tremendous warmth. I would also like to thank Gerry Morse for her meticulous manuscript editing.

Many thanks also to Lenore Davis, my sister, for the drawings, and to Pat Rouse for the diagrams. It was magical to watch you translate the images in my head into actual designs. I appreciate your willingness to keep at it until they were just the way I wanted them.

Two very special people who helped this process were my dear friend Joy Huntley and cotherapist and friend Shirley Carlson. Joy cheered me on as she read every draft of every chapter. Shirley willingly responded to my frequent phone calls asking for her input on codependency. Her wisdom and wit shine throughout the book.

Several people read numerous chapters and kept me going with continued enthusiasm, interest, and helpful feedback. They are cousin Marilyn Shope Peterson, Peggy Machen, Kit Dahl, Jennifer Holt, Lori Kainulainen, Beth Dahl, and Cheri Honkala. People who focused on specific chapters are cotherapist and friend Sigurd Hoppe, Shoben Floyd Weincoff, Allen Gibas, and Peter Dimock on men; Judy Smith, supervisor of the Family Renewal Center, Edina, Minnesota, on eating disorders and multiple addictions; Craig Nakken on the nature of addiction; and Gail Thowen on violence and masochism.

Louann Kleppe played an important role as personal secretary and typist for the project. I enjoyed her warm company, delightful responses to the manuscript, and dedication in helping us meet deadlines.

A very special group of people who gave personal and spiritual guidance were my Quaker Clearness Committee — Fran and John Martinson, Wayne and Mary Kassera. On two separate occasions when I was stuck in the process of formulating the book, they came to my house and spent an evening helping me regain my vision and faith.

Other people who have been part of the journey leading me to write this book are members of the Upper Midwest Sexual Abuse Consortium, grandma Charlotte Davis, my father, Kenneth Davis, Kay Detweiler, Rus Gregory, Anita Muth, Margaret Wickes MacDonald, Torry and Ernie Harburg, Pat Dewees, Peg and Ed Stevens, Bette and Stanislav Kasl, Elspeth Colwell, and Deb Wasilowski. In addition, I have great appreciation for Jungian dream analyst Ruth Goodwin and my only writing professor in college, Arthur Eastman. He would go over something I had written and ask, "Now what are you *really* trying to say here?" I would say what I had *meant* to say and he would respond enthusiastically, "Just say that. Just write it down. Say what you mean."

CONTENTS

Introduction

SEXUALITY. When does its expression bring us closer to ourselves and other people, and when does it tear us from our ability to love ourselves and others? When is sexuality a source of love, power, and spirituality, and when is it a source of pain and self-destruction? This book focuses on the immense impact of sexuality on our lives: how it is intertwined with cultural values, childhood conditioning, and self-esteem, and how sex itself can be used addictively. The book also explores the process of changing sex from a genital body experience to a rich human experience, one that honors the soul as well as the body.

Most women have struggled at some time with various aspects of sexually addictive or sexually codependent behavior, ranging on a continuum from short-term concerns to feeling overwhelmed and out of control with sex and relationships. In most instances, traits of sexual codependency and addiction are interwoven.

Sex addiction and codependency are directly related to childhood sexual abuse and neglect. One of the most insidious and confusing beliefs that result from sex abuse is that a woman's value and power are associated with her sexuality. Sex is at once what men want and what they despise. As one woman said, "I've always had this feeling that sex is bad and sex is my salvation." Since the middle 1970s the taboo against talking about childhood sex abuse, which affects roughly one in four females and one in eight males in this country, has gradually lifted. Explicit discussion about sex has also become commonplace, as concern about AIDS, prostitution, and pornography have had an increasing impact on our lives and our communities. As a result, we are gaining new understanding of the concept of addiction as it applies to our destructive use not only of chemicals, food, shopping, gambling, and pornography, but also of relationships and, most recently, of sex.

I see strong connections between the epidemic proportion of addictive behavior in this country and a spiritual breakdown that seems to be causing a progressive deterioration of human values and our commitment to care for one another. On the other hand, I also suspect that our current widespread attention to addiction reflects a massive awakening that will help heal individuals and positively affect our values and our culture.

For this book I drew on my twelve years of experience as a psychologist/healer working with abuse survivors, and from my own spiritual journey. In addition, I created an extensive questionnaire for women from SAA (Sex Addicts Anonymous) and CoSA (the codependents or partners of sex addicts) groups. I also conducted a series of group interviews with a wide range of people on topics from multiple addictions, to prostitution, to successful relationships, to spirituality and recovery.

A series of seemingly isolated events led me to write this book. In the fall of 1975, while cooking soup and reflecting on a sexual relationship that had recently ended, I found two thoughts flashing through my mind: "This wild romantic stuff just doesn't work," followed by, "There is something I need to learn before I get sexually involved again." I was acutely aware of how my own intense romantic relationships were alternately emotionally exhilarating, then exhausting and depressing, draining my energy and distracting me from my work. At the time I was in my final year as a piano instructor at Ohio University and taking classes in the counseling department, preparing for a career change. I was passionately involved with my studies and didn't want to let a romance get in the way. But, I thought, "Couldn't one have both?"

Since then the concept of addiction has become increasingly important to me, to the point where I now find in it a basic model for understanding human suffering and spirituality. My graduate school training included a course in alcohol addiction, which included working at a weekend intervention program for people (mostly men) charged with driving while intoxicated (DWI). They could choose between the weekend program or jail. It was a great place to cut one's teeth on addiction. Most of those who attended the program were long-time alcohol abusers, usually with a ton of problems and two tons of denial.

After I completed my course work, I moved to Minneapolis to work in a women's therapy collective. The women had a strong consciousness about addiction and made frequent references to the Twelve Steps of AA (Alcoholics Anonymous) and Al-Anon, a support group for families and partners of alcoholics. Slowly, I assimilated the meaning of the steps. At the same time, I started working with survivors of childhood abuse in individual and group therapy. Many of these women had been through treatment for chemical dependency or drug abuse. More than once when

I decided to start a therapy group for incest survivors, I ended up referring nearly half of the women who interviewed for the group for chemical dependency evaluations.

As a result I became familiar with various treatment programs and began to be invited to give in-service training sessions. The networking was fundamental in heightening my awareness that childhood abuse, along with poverty and oppression, underlie numerous addictions, addictions that may operate alternately or simultaneously. In many instances, misuse of food, sex, alcohol, work, and money either occur together or interchangeably as an individual desperately tries to quell an inner emptiness created by some form of childhood abuse or neglect.

Ken Keyes's book on addictive behavior, *Handbook to Higher Consciousness,* and a three-week personal growth workshop at the Ken Keyes Center helped me internalize the concept that nearly all people are prone to addictive behavior and that spirituality is the only cure for addiction. What I learned there had the single greatest impact on my spiritual life and on my own work as a therapist.

In the meantime, I struggled with work, single motherhood, settling into a strange, flat, northern city, and intermittently researching and writing my doctoral dissertation on the oppression of minorities in psychotherapy. The writing did not come easily. During that painful period I would take a week off to write and end up pacing around, cleaning out drawers, eating chocolate and junk food, and writing nothing. When I finally finished the dissertation in June of 1982, I swore I would never write again if it made my life so crazy.

After a couple of years with no projects, no workshops, and no conferences — *unless I felt like it* — I attended an Association of Women in Psychology conference in Boston, where I presented a day-long workshop on addiction and codependency. Several weeks later, one of the organizers called, asking me to submit a chapter based on my workshop for an anthology. Although the subject seemed too broad for a single chapter, I agreed to consider the idea.

The next day a woman in my therapy group spoke about her addictive use of sex. She had brought along a book on male sex addiction that was only marginally relevant to her experience as a woman. Lamenting the lack of a similar book for women, a member of the group grinned at me and said, "Why don't you write one?"

Two days later, seemingly from nowhere, I received a call from a woman member of a Sex Addicts Anonymous group. In the course of our conversation I said that I was thinking of writing a piece on women and sex addiction. "This is like a gift from the blue," she said excitedly. "We really need something written for women who come to SAA groups, or women who are thinking about the issues." Swept along by her enthusiasm, I asked, "Do you think you could find some women in SAA who would be willing to be interviewed?" She was sure she could.

Two weeks later, seven women from an SAA group came to my home for a four-hour interview that left me deeply moved and with the beginning of a rich body of knowledge that complemented my observations as a therapist.

As I started the project, it was as if two of me were writing. The part that guided me most strongly was the voice of the woman saying, "We really need something for women coming into the program." The other part pretended to be writing a chapter for the anthology. When I finished, as a gesture of gratitude, I sent bound copies with a red cover to the seven women I had interviewed and the one who had helped with editing. Several days later she called to say that forty women wanted copies. At that point I knew I had tapped into something more far-reaching than I had imagined. From then on it felt like a grass fire. In a few months' time I had sold over a thousand copies through local bookstores, at workshops, and as a result of requests from around the country. I refer to the article as my monograph or the Red Book, a name bestowed by SAA and CoSA women because of its cover.

Another synchronistic event left me feeling guided by a force far greater than myself: the conference committee for the anthology suggested that I omit all the sections on spirituality; then, a day later, a local therapist called to say she loved what I had written on spirituality and wanted permission to make copies for members of her therapy group. This gave me the courage to cease trying to adapt the article to fit the anthology and accept that it was not meant to be included there. Meanwhile, the growing response to the article convinced me that subject and author had met and that I should write a book. Yet I was still torn, because maintaining my peace of mind had become my highest priority.

I decided to go to a Jungian dream analyst. My dreams repeatedly suggested an immense struggle between my ego, demanding to know exactly how to write a book in advance, and the other part of me, seeking faith that I could simply plunge in. After nearly a year, simultaneously with my signing the contract for the book, my ego started to relinquish its hold and I started having very peaceful dreams about finding what I need when I need it.

As I was writing this book, events constantly affected my thinking and analysis. Up until the last possible moment, I kept returning to chapters to make changes. So if something doesn't fit for you, I hope you'll remember that I am saying only what I see for today. Please take this book in the spirit of twelve-step groups, which encourage people to "take what you like and leave the rest behind."

■

I have attempted to avoid therapy jargon in my writing, but some background information and a few definitions may help the reader.

Sex Addicts Anonymous groups are modeled after Alcoholics Anonymous. These peer support groups follow a twelve-step recovery program similar to that of AA's Twelve Steps, which involve acknowledging the power of the addiction and its harmful consequences; finding a source of spirituality; restoring one's relationship to oneself and others; maintaining a "sober" lifestyle; and finally, reaching out to others in need.

The first SAA groups were formed in 1978 in Minneapolis, Minnesota, by a group of men. Some time later, a brave soul of a woman recognized her own sex addiction and asked to join, but the men did not feel secure enough in their recovery to include a female member. However, through therapists and friends they helped her locate other women with similar concerns. The week before Christmas of 1980, assisted by two men from SAA, four women held their first SAA meeting. Since then it is estimated that more than a thousand women have attended these groups in the Twin Cities area.

Recovery groups for Codependents of Sex Addicts (CoSA) — women who tend to pick sexually addicted partners — also originated in Minneapolis. CoSA is to SAA as Al-Anon is to AA.

The expression *acting out* means that a person — against his or her wishes — is operating from his or her addictive side. If a woman says, "I won't be sexual with him again, it's bad for me," then is sexual anyhow, she is "acting out." Some people call this being "in their addiction."

I use the term *modus operandi* in talking about women who may operate primarily from an addictive mode but are not necessarily addicted in the classic sense of the word. The term simply means a mode of operation.

Chemical dependency includes all drug, alcohol, and substance addictions, which are now routinely treated together in many treatment programs. A person addicted to any mind-altering substance is referred to as chemically dependent. Sometimes I use the term *alcoholic* interchangeably when the person is addicted to alcohol.

Since this book includes stories of both heterosexual and lesbian women, sometimes the partner in a relationship will be a she. Unless the reader is prepared for this, it might appear to be a mistake or be confusing. And because so many people are coupled but not officially married, I use the word *partners* as well as *husbands*.

I use *parents* and *caregivers* interchangeably, since many children do not live with their biological parents and many people take care of children they did not originally bring into the world.

About the word *God*. I use it interchangeably with Great Spirit, Goddess, life force energy, Creator, Source, the Wise One, Universe, or light energy. For me it refers to the mystical power at the source of creation. It is the energy that flows through all living things.

There are various references to Reiki or Reiki healing, a system in which practitioners, through the use of symbols, channel healing energy through their hands into themselves or others. I teach classes in Reiki healing and often use it as part of therapy. *Reiki* is the Japanese word for "life force" or "light energy."

I take a bit of literary license in presenting the stories throughout the book by exchanging various incidents. I have at times drawn composite pictures in order to protect the identity of the women, but in essence and spirit, the stories are entirely true.

Charlotte Kasl
Minneapolis
December 1988

PART I

LOST IN THE SEARCH

CHAPTER 1

Sexuality and Spirituality

S EX IS SEX. Sex is simple. Unfortunately, when our minds and egos become involved, sex becomes complicated. While the desire to be sexual with a partner can be spiritually motivated, because we love and care for that person and desire to feel connected, it can also come from feelings of hate, anger, fear, need, sadness, or insecurity. It can come from a desire to feel important or a need to alleviate tension. It can come from wanting to fill a big empty place inside. But, sex is still sex.

We forget that sex is sex. And that

> sex is not proof of being loved;
> sex is not proof of loving someone;
> sex is not proof of being attractive;
> sex doesn't make anyone important;
> sex doesn't cure problems;
> sex is not nurture; and
> sex is not insurance against abandonment,
>> even if you're terrific in bed.

In the long run sex will not shore up a shaky ego. Sex will not fill the emptiness left from childhood wounds or abandonment. Sex will not save a failing marriage. Being able to seduce attractive partners does not mean a person is important, attractive, smart, virile, or sexy. It means she or he is good at seduction.

Having a fulfilling, sustained sex life does not depend on being cute, sophisticated, handsome, rich, charming, cool, seductive, well educated, owning a fabulous car, or being spectacular in any way. I have interviewed some very ordinary people who have had long-term, sustained, satisfying sexual relationships. In contrast, some very exciting, good-looking, financially successful people told me that they feel an emptiness associated with their sexuality. Many have never experienced a lasting enjoyable sexual relationship even though they may have had numerous sexual partners and are able to seduce nearly anyone they desire.

When sex is used for the wrong reasons a spiritual problem is created — we feel a void within us and in our relationships. The underlying hunger remains unsatisfied. We start wondering what went wrong, or we get irritated or depressed. While the misuse of sex may result in a short-term high, it ultimately creates distance between oneself and another person, or, in the case of compulsive masturbation, distance within oneself. Using sex for the wrong reason, as a substitute for what we really need, also leaves us feeling increasingly frustrated, angry or hopeless.

If a woman needs a shoulder to cry on when she is feeling sad, and she has sex instead, she does not satisfy her need for comfort. If a woman is mad at her lover for leaving town without her, sleeping with his best friend will not assuage her anger or fear of abandonment. If a woman is unhappy with her husband, spending endless hours fantasizing a romantic interlude with a man she once met on a beach in Florida will not improve her marriage. If a woman uses sex as a reward or punishment to control her partner she loses the joy of her own sexuality.

Sex does not solve problems. Being sexual with a partner or picking up a one-night stand at a bar will relieve loneliness only momentarily. When we mistakenly use sex as a substitute for nurture, love, power, or anger, sex is no longer a wonderful source of connection between our deepest selves and a beloved partner. It becomes a commodity used to avoid intimacy and mask needs that should be addressed directly. As the Buddhists say, When you are sleepy, sleep; when you are hungry, eat; when you are sad, cry. I would add, When you need comfort, find someone to comfort you; when you are lonely, learn to experience your loneliness as one of many human emotions. Don't flee from it, don't grab on to it, don't label it *bad;* just let it be.

For some people, sex and relationships become the primary way of attempting to fill their emptiness. Paradoxically, in the process they get hungrier and hungrier, and often more angry or hopeless, because sex does not quiet the nameless yearning. Still, since they don't know what else to do, they intensify their attachment to a relationship and it becomes addictive. At this point, all aspects of their lives are affected — work, friendships, health, and peace of mind. Some people use sex addictively for a while and then stop. For other people, it's as if they are on a train with no brakes, and they can't get off. At this point sex becomes the primary force driving them, a full-blown addiction.

Our culture encourages women to attach all sorts of erroneous meanings to the sexual act. Women are taught that sex is a commodity for trade, something that "belongs to men," and that women "have to give." It is not surprising that, as a result, many women associate shame with sexuality. Instead of its being a natural part of themselves, sexuality becomes a dishonest act associated with duty, security, or a means to have power over someone. Think of the woman who submits dutifully to her partner for dreary, unfulfilling sex without orgasm, year after year; the partnered woman who remains technically monogamous, yet spends hours in a dream world of romance and sexual trysts with other men; the woman who destroys her relationship through her compulsion to flirt and have affairs; the woman who frequents singles bars and picks up men, risking disease and violence; the woman who wants a long-term relationship but feels compelled to leave her partners when sex loses its high; and the woman who is totally out of touch with her sexuality and tells herself she is asexual.

In all these cases sexual activity is out of balance, unfulfilling, and not about genuine pleasure and satisfaction. Paradoxically, a positive intention underlies such behavior. Each of these women is searching for something to help her feel complete, but she doesn't know how to find it.

Sex is tremendously distorted by our culture. Our preoccupation with sex reflects an underlying uneasiness and discomfort with it. One of my favorite ways of putting sex into perspective is to imagine looking through a kaleidoscope at all the color particles making up a mandala. Imagine each color representing a part of your life. One color represents friends, one color is work, one color is family, one color is hobbies, and only one color of the entire maze of particles is sex. As you turn the kaleidoscope the particles change, constantly recreating the design. The picture is never the same. Sexuality, as the kaleidoscope imagery suggests, is simply another part of life, sometimes more in the forefront than other parts, sometimes relegated to the background. It provides color and beauty. When it is kept in perspective with the rest of life, sex is not to be wrestled with as a devil, not to be idolized as a god, but to be accepted and embraced as a natural and integral part of the whole.

SENSUALITY AND SEXUALITY

Sensuality and sexuality are elusive concepts that can be broadly defined. Sexuality is not always about partners and orgasm. It is also about how we live in our bodies. It is about being alive to our senses, yet not being controlled by them. It is about taking pleasure in stroking velvet, smelling bread baking, walking barefoot in sand, and gazing with wonder at a beautiful sunset. The paradox for women is that what we are told makes our bodies look sexy — high heels, flat bellies, makeup, tight skirts, and a passive demeanor — are often the opposite of what helps us feel alive in our bodies. Sex without sensuality is a dry, mechanical experience.

We have many experiences, particularly physical activities, in which the parallels with sexuality are strong. I often illustrate this concept in sexuality workshops by drawing what I call the "human jogging cycle" in a way that corresponds to Masters and Johnson's human sexual response cycle. As women begin to see that much of what happens during running — the production of endorphins in the brain that bring feelings of peace, the changes in heartbeat and blood pressure, the wonderful sense of exhilaration, release, and satisfaction — is analogous to the sexual act (if this isn't true for you, we'll get to that later), they smile in recognition of the similarities. This is not to say that a run around the block is a substitute for sex, but the comparison helps broaden our concept of physical enjoyment. It also gives us validation for the good physical feelings we get from sports, and acknowledges the natural connection between sexuality and sensuality.

I also like to quote Billie Jean King's description of hitting a great tennis shot: "It's a perfect combination of a violent action taking place in an atmosphere of total tranquillity. My heart pounds, my eyes get damp, and my ears feel like they're wiggling, but it's also just totally peaceful. It's almost like having an orgasm — it's exactly like that. And when it happens I want to stop the match and grab the microphone and shout, 'that's what it's all about.' Because it is. It's not the big prize money. . . . It's just having done something that's totally pure and having experienced the perfect emotion."

Sexuality is something we each possess and have available for our pleasure whether or not we are with a partner. Being alive to one's sexuality and being at ease with one's own eroticism is part of being a fully integrated person and having free-flowing energy. It is not *dependent* on having a sexual partner, or even on being sexually active. In fact, as a woman becomes integrated with herself, having a primary partner loses its "do-or-die" importance. She realizes that a partner would be nice, but that a mate is not crucial to a fulfilling, harmonious life. The erotic can be associated with living fully, being guided by our greatest wisdom, and ultimately having an ecstatic love affair with the miracle of life.

SPIRITUALITY AND SEXUALITY

The experience of spirituality is indescribable. When it is felt, words are not necessary. We use words to tell our stories, hoping they will ignite the experience. Spirituality is at once a complete mystery and a simple reality. It is about living a life of minute-to-minute honesty that springs from an internal source of wisdom. It brings feelings of power, joy, fullness, and contentment. Spirituality is, above all, about love. It is what transforms sex into a rich, life-affirming experience.

As we tune in to our spirituality we become alive to the world and feel awe at the miracle of our own existence. We make a commitment to working toward self-love and acceptance that is inseparable from our love and acceptance of others. Sexuality is a profound, powerful part of this.

One aspect of being alive to the spirit within us is to be alive to our wonderful bodies, to be in tune with their rhythms, and to treat them with care and love. Physically, for women, spirituality includes acknowledging our sacred capacity to create and nurture life. When we shame, hide, hate, or misuse all that is associated with reproduction, including our sexuality, we damage our love of self and diffuse our power to love, create, celebrate, and feel joy. When our sexual and reproductive organs are relegated to being called "them privates" or "down there" or "it," we externalize our sexuality and disown a part of ourselves, compounding feelings of shame. If the body is created by a spiritual force, then to disown the body is to feel separate from that spirit. Such an imbalance results in our having unloved and unnurtured parts. And unloved and unnurtured parts are prone to becoming sick.

Each of us is on a spiritual journey. We may not call it that, but we are all seeking something. What are we *really* looking for? I call it a sense of internal personal power — that is, the ability to identify, acknowledge, and act on our own inner feelings, needs, and wants, fulfilling them when possible, and accepting with grace when we cannot have what we want. It also means being secure in the knowledge that we are essentially good, loving, and lovable people, knowledge that is not easily shaken by what others around us say and do.

The search for this sense of self, for harmony between oneself and the world, for a sense of personal power, is a spiritual journey because it inevitably results in the discovery that our greatest wisdom lies within. We may learn from teachers and read great books, but ultimately each of us must learn to trust our own inner wisdom.

My favorite expression of this simple but elusive idea comes from the story of a Navajo woman who, when asked for advice by her daughter, said, "Put it in your holy middle and sleep on it." Wisdom comes from that quiet center, our holy middle. This is not a new idea; Buddhists, Sufis, Christians, native Americans, and other groups throughout the world have taught it. Peace of mind, self-acceptance, and knowledge of God come from living in tune with one's inner self, experiencing the spirit within.

SEX AND CULTURE

We are a culture obsessed with sex, yet we talk very little about sex in a positive way. JoAnn Loulan, who frequently writes and speaks on lesbian sexuality, brought this point home in a talk to over two hundred women. She said, "All those who know their best friend's favorite type of restaurant, raise your hands." Up went most of the hands. She then asked, "How many of you know how often your best friend has sex? Raise your hands. Come on now, let's see them." Great giggling rippled through the audience, and eyes met eyes as everyone twisted and turned, scanning the room. A few hands went up. Faces turned red.

Why are we so afraid to talk specifically about sex and why does everyone giggle like a bunch of adolescents when we do? Maybe because the last time we had permission to talk about sex was when we were adolescents. We may have had a couple of hours of sex education (mostly reproduction and plumbing) in high school, if we were lucky. Think about it. Aren't you at least a little curious to know what other people really do sexually? Don't you wonder about your women friends?

We are taught to feel shameful in talking about most of our body functions. A Catholic friend told me that, as a child, she was amazed the first time she saw a nun go into a toilet stall because it had never occurred to her that nuns would have to pee. When she actually heard the sound of the nun urinating she was mortified.

Confusion about defining healthy and unhealthy sexuality is natural enough in a culture that is immensely confused about sex. We are at once bombarded with sexual images, yet prohibited from talking about sex, and we live in the midst of many paradoxes that add to our confusion.

Children are surrounded by sexual images, yet shamed when they ask questions about sex. Reading through a women's magazine is enough to confuse anyone. An article on keeping slim faces a page with recipes for chocolate raspberry torte. An anorexic-looking high-fashion model, depicting themes of sadism and battering, is across from a soap ad portraying a woman conquering "ring around the collar." These are all caricatures that do not really exist. Yet they are the models before us. They leave women feeling that they are never enough — not smart enough, not stupid enough, not tall enough, not sexy enough, not sweet enough, not Mom enough, not wife enough, not passionate enough. Instead of being encouraged to be themselves, women are taught to try to assume an endless list of roles.

There are very few models of healthy sexuality in the culture. Instead, there are images of Kitten Woman, slightly out of focus in a gossamer nightgown sipping coffee on a sunny marble veranda; or Tiger Woman, sophisticated and slender in black satin with a macho hunk on her arm. I don't know any such women. In addition to these images, we are besieged with ads urging us to remove "unsightly hair," to have fat sucked out of our thighs, or to have the age lines under our eyes removed. No wonder so many women hate their bodies.

Seductive or pornographic images of women abound on television, in advertising, in family-oriented catalogues — in short, everywhere. Increasingly, young children are presented in seductive, "charming" advertising poses. Is it any wonder that pornography has become, at minimum, an $8 billion a year business, trafficking in the brutalization of women? Something in our society is clearly out of whack.

SEXUALITY AND INTIMACY

Intimate is defined in the *American Heritage Dictionary* as "1. Marked by close acquaintance, association, or familiarity. 2. Pertaining to or indicative of one's deepest nature. 3. Essential; innermost. 4. Characterized by informality and privacy. 5a. Very personal, private. b. Of or having sexual relations. Noun. A close friend or confidant."

When is sex an intimate experience? This definition spells out the sequence beautifully. Intimacy begins as familiarity and close acquaintance. The next step is sharing deep innermost feelings and creating a sense of informality. Only then do we get to sex.

Intimate sex connects us inwardly to our selves as well as to another. We touch both spirit and soul. If spirituality involves mind, body, and spirit operating as one, it follows that sex is life affirming only when one is truly present within oneself. Other forms of sex separate us from ourselves. How do you know if sex is spiritually centered? For starters, it is *not* dependent on being married, being heterosexual, or being a particular age. It *is* dependent on feeling clear, honest, and in tune with yourself and having the best interest of yourself and your partner at heart. It is not a substitute for another need that is avoided or being kept secret.

Sex can be understood as energy. Physiologically, sex opens up the energy in the body at every level of your being, if you are emotionally and physically alive to the experience. In order for sex to create positive energy, you need to be completely honest with yourself about whether or not you feel right about engaging in sex (either by yourself or with a partner). If, for example, you block out the knowledge that you are being sexual because you are angry, part of your body will be numb, walled off from the positive energy sex can bring. And the partner of someone who is having sex to release anger often feels heavy, drained, or ashamed afterward.

When you open yourself to the kind of inner knowing and honesty that goes with intimate sex, you open yourself to all that you feel, to a deep knowledge of yourself. Sexual energy may trigger anything that is stuck inside — joy, sadness, or anger. Many women cry after a truly intimate sexual experience, because they are overwhelmed by a wonderful flow of energy and love. Sex may also trigger sadness, memories of past sexual experiences, or memories of abuse.

If a woman has a history of incest or sexual abuse, intimate sex may bring up the profound pain of that abuse, for intimate sex will give her the experience of being loved, as opposed to being used. This gives her a perspective on her past, and her rage and grief may come to the surface when the reality of the early betrayal is internally experienced full force. This is, in part, why so many women who have been abused flee from potential partners who have a capacity to love them.

ADDICTIVE SEX

When sex is separated from love and care, it can become addictive. Rather than bringing us close to someone, it becomes a block to intimacy. This kind of sex frequently involves secret agendas. Addictive sex does not open up feelings but is carried out in an attempt to hide them. Participants are not alive and present to themselves or their partners.

Addictive sex is time spent attempting to have orgasm with another's body, often while fantasizing someone else. It objectifies oneself and another person. It is skin touching skin in search of a "high." After the high, participants feel lonely, empty, and, often, disgusted. While money may not cross palms directly there is often a covert bargain: "I'll be sexual if you pretend to care"; "I'll be nice to you and buy you things if you're sexual with me"; "I promise not to notice that you're ripping me off if you'll be sexual"; or "I promise not to leave you if you're sexual with me."

Is this the way people want sex? I don't think so. Why, then, do we continue this loveless, exploitive form of sex? Because of a profound, long-standing conditioning in our culture that says sex is love, sex is power, and sex makes us important.

I believe addictive sexual behavior reflects a great spiritual malaise. Addictive sex goes with our belief that things outside us can make us happy. Addictive sex goes with our belief that more, bigger, richer, and faster are better. Addictive sex is a flight from self-knowledge and from the knowledge that we are exploiting others.

It is important not to see addiction as "bad," but rather to understand that the underlying intention of addictive behavior is to find love and to feel good. Such behavior actually comes from a desire to fill a profound inner emptiness, anesthetize pain, and stay away from feelings.

Looking at sexuality is scary, because our sexual beliefs and practices are tied to culture, religion, and socialization. Much of our earliest programming about touch, closeness, and bonding lies hidden in our unconscious, and has a profound impact on the comfort we have with our bodies and sexual relations. We often have deeply felt "opinions" that emanate from unconscious programming. Sexuality and spirituality are deeply personal, often problematic areas in our lives. Many people are reluctant to talk about them, fearing shame and embarrassment, or being called deviant or strange.

When I start talking about addictive ways people use sex, both men and women have "hot" reactions: "Are you telling me I have to quit sex?" "What do you mean, flirting can be addictive? You mean it's *wrong* to flirt?" Because people don't realize that their "hot" reactions usually mean they have touched an uncomfortable inner place, they often become hostile or defensive — and I sometimes feel like a messenger about to be shot.

The purpose is to raise *awareness* about sexuality so that people can make conscious choices that affirm their highest selves. I encourage people to learn to look underneath their behavior. If a woman can't be comfortable at a party without flirting, she may want to know why. If her life is controlled by sex and sexual fantasies, a woman may want to cease being sexual for a while, or talk to someone about the fantasies to discover their source.

SEX, ADDICTION, AND RELIGION

I believe that patriarchal Christian religious practices — not necessarily reflecting the true spirit of Christianity — have had a profound, and mostly negative, effect on female sexuality. At its worst, traditional Christianity teaches that evil comes through a woman's body, which is born into sin and shame. At its best, traditional Christianity teaches that sex can bring a woman pleasure if she is married and heterosexual. At other times, traditional Christian teaching can be confusing. One woman I interviewed was taught that to be attractive and alluring was to be the temple of the Holy Spirit. However, if a man looked at her with lust, she was considered seductive, and deserved to be punished. When I asked a Jewish friend to describe Christian girls' attitudes toward sex as she perceived them growing up, she said that sex seemed so austere and serious. Then she laughed and said, "Kind of like, sex is dirty and you do it with the one you love."

Jewish women also struggle with the trappings of sexism. However, while virginity has traditionally been considered important in Judaism, women are encouraged to enjoy sex after they are married. Sex is also associated with Friday night, Shabbat eve, a time for rejoicing. In other words, sexuality is less associated with sin and shame and more integrated into life. Yet several Jewish women have commented in interviews, with some sadness, that the current generation of Jewish children in the United

States are taking their cues about sexuality more from the culture than from their families or from Jewish teaching.

The fact is, the Bible was written by men, from a male perspective, and translated into English by men. In it, women have routinely been charged with responsibility for men's sexuality or lust. Could it be that men, who believed *their* feelings of lust for women were shameful and evil, projected their feelings onto women, branding them as shameful, instead of grappling with the complexities of their own sexuality and taking responsibility for their own feelings?

The church has created and perpetuated a false dichotomy between female sexuality as both "in her" and "out of her." Physically a woman's sexuality is in her body. At the same time, its use is dictated outside of her, by men, from the Pope to her husband. Her virginity is an "it." The church, instead of tackling difficult issues, has for the most part hidden behind simple external rules, dictating what constitutes "good" and "bad" sexual behavior.

The results are ludicrous. A man can rape a woman, yet his behavior is in the "good" category if the couple are married (and live in certain states). A woman can be sexual in the context of a loving, committed relationship, but her behavior is in the "bad" category if her beloved is another woman. In short, the church has set up external codes that have nothing to do with the internal experience of love, care, respect, and commitment to one's partner. *The Gnostic Gospels* by Elaine Pagels discusses gospels — accounts of Jesus' life and times — that were written by early Christians but denounced as heresy by the controlling church "fathers" in the middle of the second century and buried. Rediscovered in 1945, they lend a different tone to many traditional teachings and reflect the years Jesus spent studying Eastern religions.

In the Gnostic Gospels, conversations are reported of Jesus talking with disciples who were both men and women. The serpent in the garden is shown as a symbol of wisdom and knowledge. Knowledge of self is seen as the starting point for discovering knowledge of God. Most of all, the feminine is seen as divine, with no duality between sexuality and spirituality. The following poem from the Gnostic Gospels is in the voice of the feminine divine:

> For I am the first and the last,
> I am the honored one and the scorned one,
> I am the whore and the holy one,
> I am the wife and the virgin [*virgin* is a wise
>   woman unto herself] . . .
> I am the barren one, and many are her sons . . .
> I am the silence that is incomprehensible . . .
> I am the utterance of my name.

There are no dichotomies here. To be a wise woman unto herself is compatible with being a wife. To be a "whore," a sexual being, is compatible with being a holy one.

What would it have been like to grow up with the idea that the feminine divine includes being both a woman unto herself and a wife? Clearly, a large part of what was suppressed in early Christianity was the idea of the feminine as holy, and sexuality as compatible with enlightenment. Unfortunately, we have a few images of powerful, loving, wise, sexual women. One fine exception is *Resurrection,* a movie starring Ellen Burstyn. It portrays the life journey of a rural woman who, following a near-death experience, discovers she has the power to heal. She is portrayed as strong *and* gentle, healer *and* healed, spiritual *and* sexual, wise *and* earthy. In the movie, she evokes the reaction that strong, sexual, spiritual women traditionally receive in this culture. Her father rejects her for having sex without marriage. Her sexual partner loves and fears her and is unable to accept her powers of healing without believing she is either the resurrection of the Christ or the devil. When she rejects both his ideas and says she doesn't know where her power comes from besides from love, he tries to kill her.

Given the dearth of role models, how are we to develop a notion of healthy sexuality? We are all trying to find ourselves somewhere between vapid virgin and whore. We are supposed to be vapid virgins prior to marriage and then secretly be hot stuff in bed, returning in daylight to the role of "nice wife."

We need to collectively internalize the belief that we can be both powerful and gentle, radical and loving, sexual and spiritual. A way to begin is by questioning everything we have been taught about our sexuality, and by starting to listen to our own inner wisdom, a source available to us all.

SEXUAL ENERGY AND JOY

During a retreat for women psychologists, I spent an evening receiving instruction in, of all things, belly dancing. Belly dancing, I learned, is an ancient women's rite that was never intended for men's eyes. (So much for the harem movies of my childhood.) It was a way for women to enjoy their bodies, to be spiritually alive and close to one another, to create energy. I felt happy amusement in seeing us all, a bunch of highly educated grown women of all shapes and sizes, decked out in scarves, silks, bangles, and beads, swinging our hips and torsos, letting ourselves delight in our own sensuality — what is often negatively called seductiveness. It was wonderful. Everyone was laughing, everyone was trying. "One, two, three, swing." It was okay to "look" at one another's bellies, breasts, and hips, and to enjoy the erotic feelings that many of us experienced. I had no sense of needing to act on any of those feelings but simply enjoyed the power and energy they created.

After the lesson, our teacher did a breathtaking dance that was beautiful, powerful, and erotic. It was also satisfying to many of us that she was a woman of ample proportions who, some might say, was definitely overweight. Preconceptions about her size melted into the beauty of her dance. How she could undulate, vibrate, and control her belly! And oh, the shamelessness of her dance. Nothing was held back. We watched, we giggled, we laughed, we tingled, we were in awe. It was as if she controlled and enjoyed every part of her body. We cheered with delight when she was done.

In the conversation that followed, our teacher said that some feminist women who had taken belly dancing classes wanted her to get the sexy stuff out of it. She stated that the whole point is for women to get in touch with the power of their sexuality and to feel alive in their bodies in every respect! We need to love, not be afraid of, our sexuality and sensuality.

The evening resulted in an explosion of energy. When it started we had been a group of polite women professionals. By its end we were energetic and glowing in the midst of a celebration. There was a bonded feeling, a warm sense of intimacy. With our wordless dance we had come closer to one another and to ourselves.

Sexuality is a part of all of us. Being alive to our sexuality is part of being alive to who we are. We have been taught to disconnect from our sexual feelings, to hate, only secretly enjoy, or feel ashamed of them, thereby blocking much of our creative capacity. Many women walk in frozen bodies, holding back energy in their reproductive and sexual areas. Women's sexuality and our capacity to create life within us is both mysterious and powerful, and when a source of power is shamed, hated, or denied an outlet, it can turn on itself and become a destructive force.

Women all too often channel their sexual shame back into their own bodies, like poison contaminating their spirits. Repeatedly, studies show that perpetrators of sexual abuse have been taught an oppressive double standard about their sexuality and their sexual organs. Sexuality becomes at once shameful, dirty, secretive, and terribly important. They learn to channel anger, hurt, and fear into sex.

You do not need to be active sexually to experience healthy sexuality. In far broader terms, being a joyful person means being alive to and not ashamed of your sexuality. True ecstasy comes from having a love affair with life and living in harmony with your inner wisdom.

CHAPTER 2

The Nature of Addiction:
Seeing the Body but Not the Soul

THE CONCEPT OF ADDICTION has given us a relatively new approach to understanding some fundamental aspects of spirituality — what creates suffering in life, and what brings peace and love.

Addiction has become a popular term because it gives us a concrete way to describe an experience most of us recognize — an obsessive dependency on people, substances, money, material goods, or situations. Most of us have at one time or another been "hopelessly devoted" to someone or have experienced some kind of obsessive attraction. Most of us also know what it feels like to believe "I've just got to have that whatever"; and most of us have felt hysterical or upset because someone didn't agree with us or give us what we wanted. If you have ever violated your values and ignored responsibilities to pursue an overpowering desire, then you understand the feeling of addiction.

In the first century A.D. the Greek thinker Epictetus suggested that all unhappiness arises from attempts to control events and people we have no power to control. Cancer surgeon Bernie Siegel supports this notion in *Love, Medicine & Miracles,* in which he says that to unblock the fountain of love we must give up our fears, for fear is essentially the flip side of control.

A basic belief of Buddhism is that *attachment* is the cause of human suffering. We can become attached to substances, wealth, ideas, opinions, theories, beliefs, sense pleasures, and even the concept of nonattachment — virtually anything and everything. When we become enslaved by our "thirsts," we lose our connection to our spiritual center. Buddhism also holds that people create suffering because they don't accept certain truths about life, namely, that there is pain, sickness, constant change, aging, and that death is inevitable. When people attempt to escape these aspects of life — which is exactly what they attempt to do with addictions — they end up suffering.

Peace and contentment come when we relinquish enslaving attachments. In the gentle, noncombative teachings of Buddhism, we are advised not to purge our desires from our lives, but to let them pass through our awareness and to observe the experience of them, without madly seeking them or becoming bound to them.

Mother Teresa arrives at the same idea with a different approach. In the movie about her life, she repeatedly uses the words *accept* and *surrender* when she speaks of being free. She talks about being where God wants you to be. She sees surrender as accepting whatever God hands you — whether it is to lose everything you have and end up on the street, or to be given a palace. The important thing is not to put yourself on the street or in the palace, rather to accept what is given and to give what is asked of you. Her words echo the Quaker teaching that joy and inner peace result from being true to the light within and following one's calling.

Epictetus, Buddhism, and Mother Teresa all focus on an individual's internal experience. Serenity is lost when one attempts to control anything outside the realm of what can actually be controlled. The early Roman Catholics moved from the simple, nonjudgmental notion of attachment to a list of specific sins considered to willfully "violate the divine law, destroy the friendship of God," and cause the "death of the soul." They were pride, covetousness, lust, rage, gluttony, envy, and sloth.

When these attachments were labeled sins, many people looked on them as imperfections to be cast out. Flog them, beat them, starve yourself, give up sex (except to create babies) — or live without possessions. These sins were not considered part of human experience, to be balanced and grappled with; rather, they were seen as desires to be cast out in the interest of becoming "holy." Losing sight of the fact that lust and covetousness are not the same as joyful sex and having enough to be comfortable, sex and possessions were often viewed as the enemy. And so models of "pure" people were set forth: priests and nuns, sexually bound by vows of celibacy and poverty, along with vapid female Catholic martyrs who glorified suffering and chose death over impurity. It all set up a terrible message about sex. As a former priest said, "Why can't I serve God and love a woman too?" Essentially, no sex was best; sex to produce babies who would be raised Catholic was okay; and sex for pleasure was bad. As a result, sex, shame, and confusion became synonymous.

Today, we have begun to regard these "sins" as potential addictions. Instead of gluttony, we say compulsive eating. Instead of lust, we say sex addiction. Covetousness becomes compulsive spending, and envy is an essential component of codependency. In other words, we are learning to recognize the unconscious forces that lead us to what were once considered "willful acts." Thus we can see these urges in a more gentle, less shaming light, an approach that is infinitely more healing because it accepts natural human experience.

Alcohol was officially recognized as an addiction in 1937. Alcoholics Anonymous, or AA, was the first successful model for treating addiction, and it started a new trend. Begun by Bill W., AA established a model composed of twelve steps intended to support abstinence from alcohol and lead to spiritual recovery. The wisdom underlying the steps draws from Eastern teachings as well as Christianity and is profound in its understanding of the process of healing. The wording of the steps, however, carries a definite patriarchal Christian tone, using the image of an all-powerful, external male God and implying that one's goal is to get rid of "character defects" rather than balancing, integrating, accepting, or transforming them. Even so, the development of the steps, and of the model for support groups, was a landmark that has had profound effects in affirming the healing power of a community of peers who are committed to recovery and to each other.

As recognition and treatment for alcoholism evolved from the 1940s through the 1960s, the notion of addiction was attached primarily to alcohol and drugs. Originally, alcoholism was regarded as a sign of weakness and lack of moral character. Eventually, professionals moved toward the definition of alcoholism as a pathological or sick relationship of a person to a mood-altering chemical substance that begins as a search for pleasure. It was seen as an escalating, progressive disease that eventually culminated in death. Not only was alcohol considered the primary form of addiction, the focus was more on the actual drug than on the individual's attachment to it: a person was an alcoholic rather than an addictive personality. Recovery was largely measured by one's ability to give up the drink or the drug, and connections were not made between alcoholism and other addictions. The recovering alcoholic would say, for example, "I've been sober for five years."

As treatment programs competed and got territorial, many resisted the notion that other things could be addictive as well. On one occasion, a chemical dependency counselor became quite irritated with me for saying that sex could be an addiction. After I told him how people's behavior with sex fits all the criteria of addiction, he said with some hostility, "Well, then anything could become an addiction," to which I replied, "Yes, more or less, that's true."

He responded, "But that takes away from the seriousness of alcohol addiction," which is not true.

In 1975, Stanton Peele and Ken Keyes both published books on addiction. In *Love and Addiction,* Peele challenged the notion that alcoholism is about alcohol and drug use per se, suggesting instead that drug addiction is about an individual's subjective experience in relation to the substance. Peele demonstrated that addictions to people have exact parallels to the experience of drug addiction, including the physical symptoms of withdrawal. While I agree that the subjective experience is crucial, and that it is, for many people, core to the addiction, I also believe that in cases of substance addictions — to food or drugs — body chemistry plays a part in making some people more susceptible than others.

Peele also observed that addiction is the norm for our society. This idea, which is only now gaining wide recognition, leads the way to our understanding the nature of addictive attachments and how they permeate our lives. As a society we have become addicted to a particular way of life, to things: money, power, status; in other words, to external forms of gratification.

In *The Handbook to Higher Consciousness*, Ken Keyes describes *addictiveness*, rather than the classic progressive disease model of addiction. Like Peele, he returns to the Buddhist notion that addiction can be an attachment to virtually anything. Keyes sees people as "running addictions" anytime they get upset because something is not going their way.

He writes, "Addiction is *any* desire for something that, when not fulfilled, leaves a person experiencing feelings of frustration, anger, unhappiness, or emptiness." If you are extremely upset when your partner says no to having sex, you are "addictively demanding" that your partner be sexual with you. If you change your addiction to a preference, you won't be upset for long. In that case, you would *like* your partner to have sex with you, but you'll feel all right if she or he doesn't want to. (The notion of changing a demand to a preference is taken in part from the Albert Ellis's Rational Emotive Therapy model.)

Keyes describes the inner experience of being addicted to something. I will use sex here as an example to illustrate some of his points. Addictions bring:

- "Fear of nonfulfillment": I'll never be happy if I don't have a lover.
- "Jealousy that someone may steal our source of fulfillment": I get jealous when my lover looks happy to see someone else.
- "Anger when someone thwarts us": how dare he say no to having sex with me.
- "Paranoia if constantly threatened": she must not love me anymore, she's so excited to see her other friends.
- "Boredom if we're making no progress toward satisfying our addictions": life's a drag without a lover; gotta get me a lover.
- "Worry if we can't see a steady supply": what can I do if he doesn't always want to be sexual with me?

- "Unhappiness when the outside world does not supply us with whatever it is we are addicted to": I'm so unhappy not having a lover, something must be wrong.

What is important in Keyes's approach is that a clear distinction is made between *preferring* to have something and being *addicted* to having something. Thus food, sex, lovers, money, and things can all be congruent with a spiritual path *when* you have them preferentially, without the addictive fear of losing them, and without believing that you *have* to have them.

I believe that addiction is a misguided search for self-love and spiritual fulfillment. It's as if people knock on many different doors in the hope of finding happiness and fulfillment. You may try money, drugs, status, work, or sex and relationships, all in the mistaken belief that these will make you happy or give you personal power. You may reach for a bottle instead of quietly listening within. You may have sex rather than learning to open your heart to others and create genuine intimacy. There is nothing wrong with the goal of being happy or powerful. The question is, How do you attain it? Our culture has sold us a bill of goods, so to speak, about what constitutes happiness. Corporations spend billions of dollars trying to convince us that possessions and sex and a classy image will make us happy. And — forgive the pun — we've bought it.

In reality, the momentary euphoria brought on by sex, fame, money, fantasies, or drugs will never quell the inner emptiness that comes from forgetting how to love, how to live in community, and how to care for one another. In our addictive state, we forget that the poet, the lover, the healer, the Wise One is within us.

ADDICTION AS A DIS-EASE PROCESS

When the American Medical Association and the American Psychological Association recognized alcoholism as a disease, they acknowledged that people are powerless over chemical addiction. As a result, the accusations of weakness and moral deficiency that had been hurled at alcoholics began to diminish. Our image of the falling-down slum drunk slowly changed to include businessmen, professionals, and finally women, all of whom had a disease.

Unfortunately, for many the term *disease* was interpreted as solely physiological. While research indicates that some people do have a physiological predisposition to alcoholism, this definition precludes considering alcoholism as a way people attempt to escape suffering from oppression, poverty, incest, and abuse. If we consider alcoholism generically as a dis-ease, something that tears a person from inner peace, the concept applies in both cases.

The question then becomes, Can addiction to sex be called a disease? If we apply the definition of disease as "lack of ease," or an "impairment of normal functioning," then, yes, it can be called a disease. Likewise, alcoholism can be called a disease no matter what the cause — biological predisposition, poverty, abuse, or oppression. The point is, once a person becomes truly addicted to anything, a common progression will occur.

Five basic criteria are used to determine addiction:

> Powerlessness to stop at will
> Harmful consequences
> Unmanageability in other areas of life
> Escalation of use
> Withdrawal upon quitting

To illustrate each of these in the context of sex addiction and sexual codependency, I will go through them step by step, using Ellen as an example.

Powerlessness. Ellen is sexually addicted. She promises herself that she will not go to a bar and pick up strangers. She manages to keep her promise for several weeks, but when, after a rough Friday at work, a friend breaks a date for that night, she feels an overwhelming emptiness. Feeling *powerless* to stop herself, she rationalizes by saying, "This one time won't matter." And she goes to a bar to pick up a man.

Harmful Consequences. To blot out knowledge of her self-betrayal and to cover her anxiety about finding a man, Ellen has too many drinks at the bar. Eventually she gets into a conversation with a man and goes home with him. The following morning, hung over and tired from staying up late, she oversleeps and misses a breakfast appointment with a friend. Feeling guilty and too ashamed to tell her friend what happened, she picks a fight with her on the phone instead of apologizing for missing breakfast, thus harming the relationship. By late afternoon she is feeling terribly lonely and rotten about herself. In her desire to escape her despondency, she talks to a lot of friends on the phone, but not about her pain, and fails to complete the homework for a course she is taking to improve her job skills. As you can see, the harmful consequences add up quickly: too much alcohol, a hangover, not eating, being tired, breaking an appointment, picking a fight, and dishonesty with friends.

Unmanageability. The harmful consequences multiply, eventually making life chaotic and unmanageable. To cover for being late to work and not being prepared for a meeting, Ellen says she was ill. This happens more and more often. Her boss, unimpressed, passes her over for a promotion. At this point depression sets in and Ellen loses her appetite and can't get motivated to exercise. Her inertia results in deeper depression, increasingly poor job performance, and more feelings of emptiness. She escalates her sexual acting-out to escape the reality of the situation.

Escalation of Use. As time goes on, Ellen becomes increasingly desperate to fill the emptiness that overwhelms her. She becomes virtually terrified of being alone and goes to the bars more and more often. What once created a high now feels like survival. If she can't find someone to be with she starts to take it out on herself, sometimes scratching her arms or breaking her possessions in desperate frustration. Her job performance deteriorates further, and she builds a wall between herself and her friends. She is less able to concentrate, her memory slips, and the web of lies she creates to hide her sexual obsession causes others to avoid her. She gets sloppy about paying her bills, and runs up a huge long distance phone bill with calls to an old friend. On several occasions she goes on shopping binges to soothe herself and charges far more than she can afford. She gets involved with a married man at work and, when the affair is discovered, loses her job. Panic sets in. Engulfed in what feels like a nightmare, she is afraid and desperate from morning to night. She starts fantasizing about suicide.

On a continuum, the motivation for acting addictively progresses from pleasure, to relief of pain and tension, to maintenance (just getting through the day), to a desire for oblivion. It's akin to the old proverb: "The man takes a drink, the drink takes a drink, the drink takes the man."

Withdrawal. Ellen eventually goes to a therapist and enters an SAA group. When she forces herself to stay home alone and not use sex as an escape from herself, she is restless, has heart palpitations, panic attacks, and difficulty sleeping. Although members of her SAA group encourage her to call them when she feels bad, it is very difficult because she can't believe anyone will like her when she feels this way. Most of all, a huge emptiness wells up in her and she wonders if she can stand the pain. See Figure 2.1.

Ellen's story illustrates the disease process over a period of time. Now we'll look at the stages of a single addictive episode and the inner struggle that accompanies it, still using Ellen as an example.

Stage One: A bruise to the ego causes shame. Ellen is having a fairly good day at the office until her boss calls her in to say that she has made some serious errors on a report. The minute he says the word *errors,* she translates it to mean she is bad and starts to feel ashamed. She goes back to her desk thinking, "I'll probably get fired." Unable to stop her negative thoughts, she starts to sink into intense self-hatred. "I've screwed up again. I'll never get it together. I'm so stupid." She has experienced a bruise to her ego, and she is unable to cope with it.

Stage Two: The cue. Ellen's addict side starts the cycle by using a cue — much like a hypnotic cue — to shut down her healthy self, create a trancelike state, and take control. The addict part slips Ellen a fleeting image of Bob, a man she recently met. It feels as if the cue comes from outside of her; Bob just popped into her mind. Thinking about him makes

Figure 2.1.

THE ESCALATING ADDICTION CYCLE

Early stage of addiction

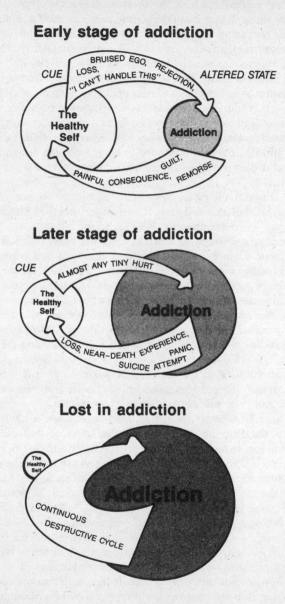

Later stage of addiction

Lost in addiction

her feel better; it is enticing and takes her mind off her feelings of incompetence at work. The image dances around in her mind, slowly coming to the forefront. At first, her healthy self vaguely protests: "No, I shouldn't call Bob; he's just on the make." But wanting to escape the rotten feelings, she permits herself to toy with the idea for a moment. She lamely tries to push it out of her mind, but when she does, the rotten feelings surface again, so she lets the image of Bob drift back. She imagines talking with him over drinks. Once she starts toying with the idea, she is already well into her addiction. The control from her healthy side is slipping and it is just a matter of time before she acts out. If a friend who knew what Ellen was thinking were to say "You shouldn't see Bob; you get in a lot of trouble with that kind of guy," Ellen would protest. "Oh, come on, I'm just going to call him and say hi. What's the big deal?" When a person is this far into an addiction, trying to intervene is like talking to a wall.

Stage Three: The trance is induced. The trance takes hold. Ellen moves into action. She feels an adrenaline rush as she looks for Bob's phone number in her wallet, at the same time conning herself by saying she will call him just to chat. But that is the addict's con. She has already crossed the threshold of powerlessness. She reaches him at his office. Instead of honestly telling him that she is having a bad day, she sounds cheery and casual. "I'm fine, just wondered what you're doing. You said to call sometime." Her palms start to sweat as her mistaken search for love and power depends on Bob's availability.

Bob, also addicted, reads between the lines and reciprocates with a similarly dishonest reply: "Great. Want to get together after work?"

Ellen, still lamely using denial, thinks to herself, "I'll go for just one drink." She says to Bob, "Oh sure, just for a little while."

Stage Four: In the addiction. Ellen hangs up the phone and is "in her addiction." All memory of pain and trouble vanishes as her mind is occupied with thoughts of being with Bob. Her adrenaline is rising. She can hardly wait until work is over. In the meantime, she acts cheerful and is rather distracted. She has trouble concentrating in a meeting because she is thinking about Bob. She leaves work a few minutes early to check her makeup. Twenty minutes later she meets Bob at a cozy bar. They chat over drinks, both acting very cool and casual, and decide to get some supper together. Ellen's adrenaline is reaching a fever pitch when, three hours later, they arrive at Bob's apartment. After another drink, some soft music, and a lot of superficial talk, they engage in sex. She has an orgasm, which feels good.

Stage Five: The hangover. Within moments after orgasm, the hangover begins. Bob turns over and goes to sleep. The intimacy, the illusion of love, vanishes as an empty chasm quakes open inside Ellen. The original problem, hidden by the trance, reappears as reality strikes. Life again looks bleak. Ellen lies there worrying about her job and knowing she should go home and feed her cat. She looks at Bob asleep and feels a sense of disgust for him and for herself. But not wanting to be alone, she decides to spend the night. Bob is strangely cool when they wake up in the morning, adding to her emptiness. Her fantasies of an ongoing relationship dwindle away. She leaves early to rush home, feed the cat, and change for work. When she walks into her apartment, the emptiness rips through her again. She pounds her fist on the wall.

The cycle is complete. To escape her shame, Ellen will soon look for another sexual partner to fill her need for love.

A person in the addictive state can become very sneaky, dishonest, and hurtful to others. Once the addict part takes over, anything goes; the only thing that matters is achieving the goal. At best, the person is detached, her mind clearly elsewhere. At worst, the person is dishonest, ruthless, and violent. The addict part becomes tyrannical, demanding to be appeased at all cost.

As the disease reaches the oblivion state, the first stage of the addictive cycle disappears, the shame is constant and the person operates from her addictive side from morning to night. Virtually no cue is necessary. Positive parts of the person's life are crowded out by the all-consuming appetite of the addict for a fix.

It takes increasingly serious consequences to pry the person out of her addictive state. It is as if she goes into a deeper and deeper sleep, requiring a more and more powerful alarm to wake her up. This is why addictive people tend to have dramatic lives.

Associated Traits

Traits that escalate with the disease process as I have described it include blame, fear, rigidity, delusion, denial, minimization, rationalization, outbursts of hostility, negativity, obsession, and shame.

- Blame signals the increasing sense of powerlessness. When we decode blame statements, we find powerlessness and dependency. For example, when a person says, "You make me unhappy because you won't have sex," what is really being said is "I feel powerless to create feelings of happiness inside myself. My happiness depends on your being sexual with me."
- The fear accompanying addiction represents both a fear of touching the inner pain and a fear of having the addiction exposed. People protect their addiction because it feels like the source of life.
- Rigidity is a sign of how fragile an addicted person has become. People hold on to an external framework because their insides are crumbling.
- Delusions can take the form of misinterpreting the signals of others, or making unrealistic, grandiose plans.
- Denial and minimization are expressed in statements like, "There isn't

a problem" or "It's just a little thing." To an outside observer this can seem crazy because the problems are so obvious.

- Rationalization is a sure signal that someone is lost in an inner struggle. We don't rationalize when we feel comfortable about something. Using a rationalization such as, "It's okay to go to the bar just this once. Everyone does," is a means of giving the addict part permission.
- Outbursts of hostility occur when someone challenges the addiction or upsets the fragile, rigid inner world the addict has created.
- Negativity starts permeating all of life. "People are jerks; life is stupid; no one understands me." The addicted person becomes unable to experience or receive kindness, love, and compassion and dwells instead on how bad everything is. This is a projection of feeling bad inside.
- Obsession and fantasies of addictive ventures increasingly take over, reducing the ability to concentrate, to be present with others, and to attend to daily tasks.
- Shame, a feeling of unworthiness, escalates at the core but is denied.

ADDICTION AND COMPULSION: WHAT'S THE DIFFERENCE?

In an article on sex addiction in a Minneapolis paper, several professionals debated whether certain sexual behavior should be called addiction or compulsion. A person from a Sex Addicts Anonymous group, who had nearly died from out-of-control use of sex, responded by saying that to those suffering from the misuse of sex, the label didn't matter. The important thing is for professionals to educate themselves so they can help people. Overall, I agree with this stand. When we bicker about words, theories, and concepts to the exclusion of a deeper generic understanding, we lose sight of the purpose of our work, which is to help alleviate human suffering.

On the other hand, I think it is important to have some criteria, so that the word *addiction* doesn't get bandied around in a meaningless way. As I was struggling to clarify my own ideas on the differences between compulsion and addiction, I learned about a model that therapist Craig Nakken uses in workshops to explain the distinction.

Nakken breaks behavior down into a four-part continuum: Patterns, Habits, Compulsions, and Addictions. As with any continuum, categories are not always discrete and the line between them can be fuzzy. The progression, however, as we move across the continuum from pattern to addiction, is increasing discomfort if the impulse is not obliged and far greater effort to cease the behavior.

Patterns help us organize our lives so they are not chaotic. Most of us sleep at roughly the same time within a twenty-four-hour period and eat two or three meals a day at roughly the same time. Patterns can be social or cultural norms. A pattern in this culture is to stress monogamy within marriage. Men and women use numerous behavior patterns to indicate that they are interested in getting acquainted or being sexual. A couple may develop a pattern of having sex about once a week, on no given day.

Habits are more specific, and more individual, than patterns. *Usually* and *always* are words associated with habits. I *usually* masturbate after bathing. I *usually* eat popcorn when I go to the movies. We *always* make love on Friday night. I *always* flirt when I'm nervous at a party. I *usually* eat oatmeal for breakfast. Some people are in the *habit* of thinking that all dating involves seduction, flirting, and sexual innuendo.

Habits can be broken with effort and a bit of will, usually without a great deal of insight. Dolores can go to a party and not flirt if she decides to. She may feel a bit uncomfortable for a while, but the feeling fades. If Jane does not have enough money to buy popcorn at the movies she may feel momentarily uncomfortable but can quickly forget it and still enjoy the movie. If Rebecca does not have time to masturbate after taking a bath, she may feel tense for a few moments, but the feeling passes.

Compulsions. Compulsive behavior is rooted in a need to reduce tension, often caused by inner feelings a person wants to avoid or control. One does not derive pleasure so much from the actual behavior itself, but rather from the tension release it provides. The *Diagnostic and Statistical Manual of Mental Disorders* describes a compulsion as "repetitive and seemingly purposeful behaviors that are performed according to certain rules or in a stereotyped fashion. . . . The activity is not connected in a realistic way with what it is designed to produce or prevent, or may be clearly excessive. The individual generally recognizes the senselessness of the behavior (this may not be true for young children) and does not derive pleasure from carrying out the activity, although it provides a release of tension." A compulsion could be washing one's hands repeatedly or having to sweep the kitchen floor after each meal. One woman said she counted stop signs as she was driving to meetings she feared. Many women recall compulsive behavior that started while they were being abused. They would count, think of patterns, or have fantasies to blot out the reality of being violated.

Can't and *must* and *I've got to* are words associated with compulsions. "*I've got to* get the house cleaned." "I *can't* sleep without masturbating." "I *must* have pornography to get sexually aroused." "I *can't* have orgasm without a vibrator." "*I've got to* be with Charlie tonight." "I *can't* relax without knitting." As you read these statements you can feel the intensity. If you ask people why they "have to," they can't always give you a reason beyond, "If I don't, I can't relax," or more strongly, "If I don't, I go nuts."

A compulsion may be ritualized with time of day, certain objects, or as a way of doing something. A person may go into a trancelike state when doing it. In any case there is often a frantic feeling associated with the task until it is completed. When a person is unable to carry out a compulsion, feelings of agitation and distress may continue for hours or days, until the compulsive urge is met. Compulsive behaviors are more set than habits and more difficult to stop. It often takes insight into underlying unconscious conflicts or buried feelings, which may require psychotherapy or counseling. People may not like their compulsions but they do not usually hide them, deny them, or feel dreadfully ashamed of them. They can live with and manage them. Compulsions generally do not escalate or change over time. They are fairly fixed. Aunt Rosie must have her knitting along so she can relax. We always have to keep Aunt Judy's house tidy or she gets upset. Margaret has been masturbating every day for twenty years.

There are some harmful consequences to compulsive behaviors, for they can limit one's emotional life, can be physically harmful, or restrict a person from participating in a wide range of activities. One person may not be sexual on hot days because sweat repulses her; another rarely eats out with friends, because he feels anxious eating in front of others; someone else won't travel because she can't sleep in strange beds. Compulsions may intrude on relationships with family and friends when a person can't connect with someone until the compulsion is satisfied. Compulsions tend to limit rather than destroy relationships.

Addiction. When a person becomes addicted, the personality splits into two distinct parts, each denying the existence of the other. Addiction involves the words *powerlessness* and *unmanageability,* both of which the person *denies.* It is as though the person has two sets of dreams, two kinds of values. Addiction is like having two sides — the addict side and the healthy side — engaging in a life-and-death struggle to control the inner world. In an interview on "60 Minutes," Liza Minnelli described her addict part as "Slick." It's an apt name, for the addict part is a terrific con. Its goal is to avoid pain, achieve euphoria, and have control. It wants immediate gratification. As the addict side progressively gains control of the personality, the denial and delusional state escalates. A woman says to herself, "All these men want to sleep with me because I'm attractive and likable." She is denying that when people want to be sexual with her, it's probably because they want sex and are turned on by her, not that they like her. She is also denying her lack of power to say no to them. A woman having a secret affair with a man at work tells herself that it is helping her feel alive. She denies that she is sacrificing her self-respect, that she may lose her job, that her powers of concentration are waning, that she drinks too much when she is with him, that she is losing weight, losing sleep, threatening her marriage, and lying to her daughter. In other words her life is becoming *unmanageable.*

While people derive temporary feelings of pleasure through their addictive behavior, harmful consequences are sure to follow. They may be almost imperceptible at first, but once the addiction takes hold of the personality, the individual's ability to order her life slowly disintegrates and she falls more and more under the control of an unknown force within. The progression may take years or happen rapidly. Health, relationships, work, play, parenting, creativity, and peace of mind slip away as the person slowly builds a wall around herself and becomes increasingly difficult to reach with either love or reason. Eventually the addicted part sees other people out there, but does not see other souls.

The addict's friends increasingly tend to be addiction buddies who enable the disease by colluding in the denial. "Hey, we're cool. This is fun. Those other people are so square and old-fashioned."

Addiction usually occurs within a social system that colludes by denying the problem. Someone once described it as living with an elephant in the house but no one saying, "There's an elephant in the house." All those in the addict's close circle — family, friends, and colleagues — are affected to some degree. An addiction cannot be stopped without either extremely painful consequences or an intervention that involves other people. It takes great effort and a social support system to recover from an entrenched addiction.

THE GENERALIZED ADDICT

Some people are "generalized addicts." They may use something addictively for a period of time and then shift to a different addiction, or they use a lot of things addictively on a regular basis. They avoid meeting life straight on by medicating themselves with too much food, cigarettes, coffee, sugar, inappropriate involvement with their children, spending, alcohol, or dependent relationships. No single addictive behavior takes on a life of its own and becomes a full-fledged addiction, but the general addict is always mucking around in a slightly depressed soup.

"I AM AN ADDICT" VERSUS "I HAVE AN ADDICTION"

There is considerable controversy over the use of labels. Since AA started more than fifty years ago, it has been considered crucial to the process of recovery to declare "I am an alcoholic" at the opening of meetings. Since that time we have added, "I am a codependent," or a compulsive eater, a compulsive gambler, a compulsive spender, a workaholic, a sex addict, or a sexual codependent, to name a few.

The positive reason for using labels is to cut through denial and help the ego surrender to the reality of an out-of-control problem. "I am an addict. I have a big problem. I'm out of control. That's why my life is such a mess." The addiction usually has a person convinced that it is the supreme power. Saying that one is an alcoholic puts the ego in its place, so to speak, and makes room for a spiritual power. Another reason for the label is to establish a common ground and a sense of community between otherwise divergent people. "I'm an alcoholic. Oh, you're one too." We suddenly know a lot about each other.

On the negative side, labels can be limiting or shaming and can obscure the knowledge that we are essentially spiritual beings. Our addictions come out of our socialization, our genetic makeup and programming. They are *part* of us, but not our identity. The same is true with all aspects of ourselves. I am not a psychologist; rather, I play the role of psychologist. I am not a pianist; I play the piano. In some situations we make the distinction. A person who has cancer doesn't say, "I am cancer," but rather, "I have cancer." The cancer is kept separate from the person's essential identity.

Labels tend to make artificial distinctions. With labels, there are only alcoholics and non-alcoholics, sex addicts and non–sex addicts, rather than numerous people with varying degrees of alcohol use or abuse or sexual concerns. Our minds tend to jump toward stereotypes when we hear labels and scare us away from looking at ourselves. Our egos get caught up with labels, believing they make us important or unimportant.

We are all prone to addictive behavior to one degree or another. We all cover up pain by using things outside ourselves to make us feel better. It is part of the struggle of life. One trouble with labels is that we start thinking of ourselves as the label. *"I'm* a sex addict. Argh, yuk! How dirty and disgusting. I don't want to think about it."

When you label any part of yourself — your body, thoughts, or behavior — as bad *or* good, you end up being judgmental and shaming. Instead of thinking, "Using sex addictively is bad for my soul," you think, "I'm a defective soul for being a sex addict." Ram Dass, a spiritual teacher and writer, talks about labels as "the ephemeral rings around our essence." They are part of you, but not your essence.

I consider the following sexual labels destructive: nymphomaniac, impotent, frigid, asexual, sadist, and masochist. No one is a nymphomaniac. Rather, women use sex to varying degrees in a misguided search for love and power. By the same token, it is destructive to label a man impotent because he cannot have or maintain an erection. A man is not an impotent person simply because he is unable to have an erection. A woman who is unable to have intercourse is not a frigid person. Her inability to become aroused may be a signal from her body that it is time to examine her feelings.

Shame is, essentially, the degree to which you mistake your labels for your identity. If you draw your labels into the core of yourself (what I often call the holy center), you can no longer see the center. The following represents the fallacy of mistaking your labels for your identity.

MY LABELS ARE ME

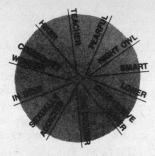

When you pull the labels away from your holy center, they aren't so serious because you remember your essential divinity. This relieves shame.

MY LABELS ARE SEPARATE FROM MY HOLY CENTER

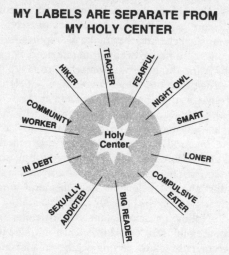

It is far different to feel simply lonely as opposed to lonely and ashamed. If we flee from our shadow side, judge it, or hate it, it will come back to haunt us in mystifying ways. Under every addiction is a longing for self and for love. Addictive behavior is simply one way we fall off the path. All that really matters is that we get up and keep traveling.

CHAPTER 3

The Nature of Codependency:
Who Am I?

CODEPENDENCY, which is women's basic programming, frequently underlies addiction. For many women there is no clear distinction between the two because they play off each other. For example, a woman may be sexually codependent within her relationship and become addicted to alcohol as a way to numb her pain and maintain her denial system. She may be sexually codependent with her partner, and have sexually addictive flirtations at work. Addiction is often an escape from the powerless feelings of codependency.

I describe a codependent person as someone whose core identity is undeveloped or unknown, and who maintains a false identity built from dependent attachments to external sources — a partner, a spouse, family, appearances, work, or rules. These attachments create both the illusion of a "self" and a form from which to operate. Codependency is a disease of inequality in that any minority person who has to survive in a world defined by others will know more about those in power than about himself or herself.

The word *codependent* (or coaddict) was originally created to describe a person, usually female, who is the partner of an alcoholic, usually male. It was often said that the codependent *enables* the addict to stay in his addiction. The term came into use as people realized that partners of alcoholics usually suffer with a parallel set of destructive symptoms, and that they need their own support system. Al-Anon was thus created as a twelve-step program for partners of alcoholics.

I take exception to the traditional notion of defining a codependent solely as the partner of an addict. Because the word is associated with women, this definition tends to reduce the codependent's identity to that of Mrs. Addict. I prefer to regard her as a woman with a unique set of problems that may go hand in hand with those of the addict, just as the addict's unique set of problems go hand in hand with those of the codependent.

Addictive and codependent personalities come into full bloom in adult relationships, but are rooted in early childhood experiences in the family and the culture. Whatever is lacking in the individual comes roaring to the surface in the addict-codependent interplay. An old diagnostic category, *folie à deux,* is used to describe two people who share one psychosis. Essentially, it refers to two people who seem to trigger all that is crazy in each other, which is how I see the interplay between a co-dependent and an addict. Whatever was buried becomes magnified in the relationship, and as long as the two are together, the craziness escalates.

Another reason to expand on the Mrs. Addict definition is that co-dependency in women can be fully understood only in the context of women's socialization, not just in relation to a particular addiction or addict.

Some professionals have gone so far as to say that you can't have an addict without an enabler, or a codependent. To me, reading between the lines, this suggests that women are to blame for addicts' behavior. I've never heard it said that you can't have a codependent without an addict. In fact, the latter seems closer to the truth because, as you will see, traits of codependency are usually associated with those who have less power in the system — women — and have to figure out how to live in someone else's — men's — world.

Traditionally, addicts and codependents have been regarded as two separate breeds. But this oversimplifies a complex issue. While in a broad sense addiction reflects the norm for men, and codependency the norm for women, addiction and codependency often mesh within one person. To complicate things further, some people consider codependency in its extreme form an addiction, an all-encompassing destructive force controlling a woman's life. If we are to better understand both men and women, we need to see the complex web addiction and codependency weave in both of them. Otherwise we will continue to reinforce stereotypical assumptions about men and women that are harmful to everyone.

As I see it, one significant harm that has come from the Mrs. Addict label is that the addict gets most of the attention. There are many treatment programs for addicts and few for codependents. Typically, the addicted person may receive a month of intensive treatment, while the codependent is included for a week of evening family therapy groups, if that. Another pitfall is that the codependent usually receives help only if she is in a relationship with an addict, although this is starting to change. In reality, a person with codependent traits experiences them whether or not she is in a significant relationship. Therefore, treatment programs for codependency would be helpful regardless of the relationship status.

As children we all experienced feelings of powerlessness. Dependency is inherent to childhood. That's why the use and abuse of power in families has such a profound effect on children. Children who grow up in dysfunctional families spend all their energy dancing to the tune of the parents in the hope of being loved or to avoid shame and abuse. As a result, they don't learn to know themselves.

Because a codependent woman has not developed a sufficient sense of self, she can't really tell you how she is; she can only tell you how her husband, children, and cats are. She can't tell you how she *wants* something to be, but she can tell you the rule for how it *should* be. Not having a center to resonate from, she takes her cues from the outside. Her greatest fear is that if she loses or lets go of the external forms — the house, the husband, the rules, the status — she will fall into a terrifying emptiness. She fears she could not exist on her own. Developmentally part of her is like a tiny child who has not left her mother's arms, so she clings to forms, to people and things representing security, as if they were life itself. Because her spirit and soul have been profoundly neglected, she neglects her own inner self; indeed, it is unknown to her.

Some people define codependency as an addiction to a destructive relationship. This is usually a fundamental symptom of codependency, but the codependent is not so much addicted to the particular person as to what he (or she) represents, namely, security in the form of a partner and a provider. Essentially, she is programmed by the culture to model herself after the images portrayed in countless women's magazines. Addiction takes the form of wanting someone to take care of her financially, provide a beautiful home, and confer on her the status of being Mrs. Someone.

Codependency represents an attachment to *all* those things that give a woman the security of knowing she exists. It follows that, at its deepest level, codependency is essentially an addiction to security. This definition took shape as I listened over time to the countless reasons women gave for not leaving a painful relationship or job, for not saying no, for not moving, for not taking risks. At the bottom of every response was a need for security: "I might never find anyone else." "I don't have other friends." "I wouldn't have enough money." "I couldn't live alone." "I might not find another job." "Something terrible might happen." Underlying all these statements is a crippling sense of powerlessness.

A predictable pattern emerges in conversations with codependent women when they discuss their abusive or neglectful partners. Marsha came to therapy and recited the reasons why she should leave her husband, Hank, who was "just awful." She couldn't stand him. The marriage had been miserable for twenty-five years. She had been massively depressed, suffered from chronic compulsive eating, and was feeling hopeless. Sex was just awful. As she described it, "He would get on me and do his business."

I listened for a while and then asked her if she told him what she wanted sexually or ever said no if she wasn't in the mood. She prickled a little at my nudging her to take some responsibility. Well, no, she couldn't say no to sex. "That's a man's right." I pressed her a little more. When she looked beyond her righteous reason, she admitted that she was afraid he might get upset or even leave her if she said no.

"Are you really saying that, after twenty-five years of marriage and bringing up five boys, if you said no to sex one night he would pack his bags and walk out of the house?" I blurted. While I wanted to challenge her delusion of power, I also knew that if her husband was sexually addicted, her fear had some basis. To say no to sex would be to threaten his identity, which was tied to sex. If he was addicted to sex, her sexual availability was to him like alcohol for an alcoholic. Her saying no would threaten his stash and his anger.

Throughout our early sessions it was very difficult to get Marsha to talk about herself. It was always what Hank said and did. She rarely stayed focused on any one subject and she showed no anger. When I tried to direct her to talk about herself, she would do so for a few minutes, then continue the litany of Hank stories. Finally I said, "Well, then, if it's so bad, why don't you leave him?"

In a reply typical of codependent women, she said, "Oh, it's really not so bad. He's better now. The kids need a father."

Just as she was psychologically cornered into facing up to the fact that she wanted to leave her partner, she would pull out a familiar list of rationalizations to cover her fear. When we delved into the underlying fear, Marsha, like many women who remain stuck in a destructive relationship, reached a terrifying awareness. She came face to face with her fear that she would die if she left him. In a very real sense, in her mind, her identity was more about him than about her. If she left him, who would she be? It slowly emerged that her fear of death was related to childhood abuse and lack of sufficient early bonding with either parent. She had never formed a sufficient sense of self to make possible the thought of being on her own. But I get ahead of myself. I worked with Marsha for over four years, and her story will emerge throughout the book.

Codependency is difficult to describe because it is often about what a person does *not* do, which is basically to live her life. She doesn't follow the path of her own interests or let her passions flow through her. She is afraid of strong feelings and power. If the addict overindulges in sensory pleasures, the codependent starves herself of them. Of if she does indulge, she immediately feels guilty and can't enjoy them because at her core she feels undeserving.

Think of the stereotypical female and how people praise her: She never thinks of herself. She is a devoted mother. She'd do anything for you. She is a saint. She always puts her husband first. She is patient, kind, and never complains. What her admirers omit is that she probably acts like an angel out of fear: fear people won't like her; fear of financial insecurity; fear her partner will leave her; fear of a fight. Notice that no mention is made of what she feels like inside. That's because to fill this role, you aren't allowed to feel inside; you have to be nice all the time.

CODEPENDENCY AS AN ADDICTION

The five aspects of addiction also apply to codependency. Remember that individuals differ, and not all traits apply to all people, but this list gives the general picture.

Powerlessness The codependent woman feels powerless to

- accept that she has to create her own sense of achievement and purpose from within.
- stop taking personally all the words and actions of those around her (her self-esteem is determined by what other people say).
- get angry directly when she doesn't like something or when someone violates her rights.
- say no to requests for help, service, and sex.
- let people suffer their own problems and take responsibility for themselves. (It is difficult for anyone to watch another person suffer or make destructive choices, but the codependent feels it is her job to stop them, which is, of course, impossible.)
- stop feeling responsible for her children's self-esteem. (She constantly tries to improve them, which only increases their low self-esteem, because the children get the message that they are never good enough.)
- stop trying to change her partner, family, or children. She tries to impose her standards, often with such indirect statements as, "Wouldn't you like to . . ." "Don't you think you should . . ." "Wouldn't it be nice if you . . ."
- stop worrying about her partner, family, friends, and children.
- give up hoping something will magically change her partner or take away life's problems.
- face life on her own.
- see herself as a separate person.
- tune in to her own internal world and operate from self-knowledge.
- stop imagining scripts for how events *should* take place and what

people *should* say. (She doesn't tell people the script, but when they don't follow it she is hurt, angry, and thinks they don't care about her.)
- give up putting on a good external front to present to the world.

Harmful Consequences   The harmful consequences for codependents are far more subtle and insidious than those for an addict because they usually happen within the woman. Because part of the disease is to keep up a good front, she hides her suffering from herself and others. As the saying goes, she is "laughing on the outside, crying on the inside." This intensifies the pain.

Harmful consequences may include

- depression, which can show itself as either agitated activity, lethargy, or the two alternately.
- anxiety, a constant sense of foreboding that veils her emotions.
- profound loneliness of the soul because she keeps her pain hidden and shares her truths with no one, including herself.
- out-of-control, abusive, shaming outbursts when her partner does not do things her way. This often happens when their bond gets shaky; she feels abandoned and it touches on her unconscious fear of dying.
- chronically telling little lies, such as I'm fine; Everything is great; I'm not upset; I'm not angry.
- body tension — tight jaw, shoulders, neck, mouth — from holding in anger.
- chemical dependency, compulsive eating, physical illness (often a long history of medical problems, including headaches, stomachaches, tumors).
- failure to develop her talents, or if she does, abandoning them if her partner feels threatened.
- living in constant fear of losing her partner or not finding or maintaining close friendships.
- feeling terribly separate from herself and from her sexuality.

Unmanageability   Again, the unmanageability is difficult to see because the codependent keeps it so well hidden. Because maintaining the form of her life is core to her addiction, she keeps at it until she nearly drops. Unmanageability is most likely to manifest itself in accidents, sickness, severe depression, or anxiety. She usually doesn't reach out for help until she no longer has the energy or ability to keep up the external form — the perfect house, the perfect looks, the dinner on the table every night, the unfulfilling sex, and so forth. Eventually, she may cease to function in nearly all areas of her life.

Even then the codependent does not always ask for help for *herself* per se. She wants to get rid of the depression and anxiety, so she can continue the relationship, be a better sex partner, tolerate the emotional desert she lives in, and keep the external forms in operation. Repeatedly women come to therapy wanting to learn how to be calm and happy in an abusive home. While there are certainly ways to detach from negative situations, I usually tell women that my work is not to increase their tolerance for suffering but to help them become powerful individuals.

Often a codependent woman becomes dependent on prescription medication, over-the-counter pills, alcohol, or drugs, or develops eating disorders or other compulsions. The unmanageability may also manifest itself in her children, who act out her inner rage or become a problem for her to deal with.

Escalation The intensity of the situations just described increases, until they permeate her life. She increasingly disassociates from her genuine self in the interest of maintaining external security. Some women die to get out of a bad relationship. They get cancer and other diseases: "I'll make this relationship work if it kills me." Others become clinically depressed and require hospitalization; still others become addicted to Valium, antidepressants, or other medications. It may take years to reach a bottoming-out point because the codependent has an immense tolerance for suffering, never having known that anything else is possible. Most of all, she wakes up daily with fear in her belly, having lost any ability she had for pleasure and enjoyment and not feeling in control of her life. She may attempt or commit suicide.

Withdrawal If the woman embarks on a course of recovery, she initially experiences profound guilt and shame as the primary symptoms of withdrawal. She feels awful if she says no to sex with her partner or to listening to her mother complain on the phone for half an hour. She thinks she is selfish, whiny, and fussy if she starts asking for what she wants, sexually and otherwise. She has an immense fear of abandonment. She is afraid of rejection and retribution every time she says I want, I feel, or I think. She also starts to have fleeting moments when she feels a surge of power within her as she takes on an identity that belongs solely to her. Her fear abates and her body starts to relax as she discovers herself and lives more in tune with her inner truths.

THE CODEPENDENT HIGH

In listening to accounts of codependency I frequently wondered whether there was an adrenaline high parallel to the addiction high. When I asked my friend and colleague Shirley Carlson, she laughed and said, "Oh, yes." She described it for me as follows:

The adrenaline high comes from functioning impressively in a crisis. Everything is falling apart and you are going to be the one who copes, the one who rises to the occasion. This is not to be mistaken for coping as a healthy sign of being able to function. What makes it different is that the energy is fueled by resentment, self-righteousness, and feelings of superiority. There is a secret self-satisfied smugness rather than the feeling "I want to do this because I care about these people." It's more, "I've got to do this because no one could do it as well as I could, and anyone else would mess it up. I'm superior." It's like cleaning out the garage while feeling resentful and pissed as hell because your husband is away screwing someone, and you want to make him feel guilty when he returns. This is quite different from simply wanting to clean out the garage and feeling good about the accomplishment.

When I asked codependent women to describe their "highs," they responded:

"Having the partner blow up and look out of control so people would think he was a jerk and look at me and say, 'Poor you.' "

"Righteousness. Making plans for him. 'What a fool you are; how wise I am.' "

"My self-esteem would rest on being better than him. Watching him fall apart makes me an angel, a savior, and powerful."

"Watching him grovel and beg for sex would make me feel pure and see him as disgusting." (Another version of groveling is for the partner to be superhelpful and buy presents to atone for his misdeeds.)

"I developed skills of telling people about him with great sighs. I'd get them to criticize him, then I'd say, 'It's not as bad as all that.' "

Many double binds and paradoxes related to codependency reflect the basic double messages about being a woman. For example:

She feels powerless to live her own life, yet is deluded in thinking that she has the power to change another person's. Historically, women have not been given power within the culture, yet have been told they are responsible for (i.e., have power over) the welfare and behavior of their husbands and children.

She is praised for being the perfect, subservient wife and mother, yet this role destroys her sense of self and leaves her sick and depressed. Traditional mental health professionals have colluded in the repression by treating her resulting depression with pills, thus helping her to sustain the role of "good" subservient wife. (Designating codependency a recognized mental disorder is under consideration. While I understand some of the arguments for the diagnosis — the codependent is indeed dysfunctional — I propose that the culture be diagnosed as repressive for teaching women that sweetness and saintliness are good for them.)

Her sexuality is sacrificed for the benefit of her partner, yet she is called frigid or a prude if she does not enjoy what he wants. And if she starts asking for what *she* wants sexually, her partner, if he's a sex addict, will get angry.

She is not given power or responsibility in the culture, yet when she chatters about what she is doing — fixing up the house, buying new drapes, what she is cooking for dinner — she is called superficial and boring. Because she receives little sustenance and nurture for her inner world, she nurtures the only forms she knows — her house, her looks, the rituals of eating, socializing, and being a partner and mother.

Codependency is women's basic training. That is, in order to be acceptable in the male system a woman is taught to set aside her knowledge, her hopes, her dreams, and her power by playing the role of wife, secretary, maid, cheap laborer, mistress, prostitute, and so on. She is taught that her identity comes through her partner. If he or she has status, she has status. If anyone in the family is in trouble, she worries. If her children are nice, she is successful. If they get bad grades, she is a failure. It follows that her overidentification with her partner's addiction, whatever it is, is an extension of her overidentification with her partner's life, successes, failures, and all. They all go together.

While a woman's symptoms of codependency may intensify as the addiction of her partner progresses, the seeds of her behavior were planted when someone first said, "It's a girl." While times are changing, and women are increasingly encouraged to develop their talents and skills, the fundamental message is still that men come first and that they have the power. And there are many women today who are terrific in their careers, climb mountains, are savvy about financial planning, yet turn to mush in their personal relationships.

Codependency is a devastating disease. If we remember that the codependent woman is really a tiny child living in a woman's body, trying desperately to hide from the terrible emptiness at her core, her behavior becomes more understandable. Clinging to an abusive relationship feels preferable to letting go and falling into a terrifying abyss.

In *Women Who Love Too Much*, Robin Norwood accurately portrays the experience of codependency. The fact that this book was a major best seller indicates that women are still trying to find their meaning and worth through relationships and believe that they simply "love too much." I differ with two of Norwood's major points. I would like to see the word *love* reserved for its real meaning, which is to care for another person without dependency or possessiveness. Love comes from a state of surrender to the deepest part of ourselves. Codependency is not about *loving* too much. It is about being extremely dependent on another person, about women who control too much, seek their identity through others, and pay for care with self-sacrifice. Learning to love, particularly oneself, is the antidote for codependency.

Regarding Norwood's list of traits that a woman will achieve once she has recovered, I question suggesting a concrete notion of "being recovered," because it reinforces the delusionary thinking of the codependent — that there is a model of perfection to be reached. I differ with Norwood's suggestion that a woman will be "in touch with her feelings and attitudes about *every* aspect of her life, including her sexuality," or that *"all"* the struggles, drama, and chaos of the past have lost their appeal." This is simply not realistic and leaves us striving for an unobtainable goal rather than learning to accept our humanness and watch with humor and a sense of perspective as our life drama unfolds. It also fails to recognize the whole notion of impermanence, the fact that we will always grapple with life and sometimes fall into the soup. What's important to learn is to fall in gracefully and enjoy the noodles.

WHAT CODEPENDENCY IS NOT

Sometimes people mistake the milk of human kindness for codependency. Thus, when codependent women start to recover, the pendulum swings the other way and they become determined not to "caretake" or to give away too much. They don't want to offer care unless someone asks. This is fine, and for some a necessary part of the recovery, but some distinctions are in order.

Empathy, sensitivity, care, compassion, and tenderness are wonderful traits. Being deeply involved and nurturing in a relationship can reflect a woman's wonderful capacity for intimacy. The ability to protect and care for children is a skill to be highly valued. When you comfort someone in need, you bestow a precious gift. Tuning in to the needs of others is beautiful. A woman does not need to get rid of these abilities; she needs to learn both to recognize her motivation and to bestow these gifts on herself.

Her behavior becomes codependent only when carried out with a hidden agenda — to look good, to have her partner indebted, or to feel superior. Then it is not love and nurture.

Calling up someone whom you know is hurting and saying, "How are you doing?" is a caring gesture. Too often women attempting to recover from codependency think that they shouldn't reach out, that the other person is always supposed to ask first. The easiest way to distinguish between codependency and genuine care is to examine your own motivation. If you are about to do something because you think you should, or because you need to reinforce your image of yourself as a good person, or you are keeping score and expect something in return, you might experiment by not doing it and see how you feel. If, on the other hand, you are acting out of simple caring and concern, without negating your own needs, by all means reach out. That's what love is about. That's what will heal the world.

I would like to see the term *love addiction* dropped from the vocabulary. People may be addicted to euphoria, romance, people, security, but they can't be addicted to love. It's like saying one is addicted to breathing clean air: that can't be, for there's enough and it's right there and there are no side effects. Similarly, there are no harmful consequences to love and there can't be too much of it. We don't find love by chasing after it; we simply open our hearts and find it within us. We don't have to work hard to breathe deeply; we just relax and it comes. We find love by learning to tell the truth, by surrendering to our calling, by having discipline in our lives, by operating from faith. No one loves too much. Love is the ultimate joy.

CHAPTER 4

Sex Addiction and Sexual Codependency: *What Are They?*

I MAGINE A GROUP of famous women, real and fictitious, coming together in a support group to talk about their sexuality and relationships. Anna Karenina reports that she is feeling less obsessed and paranoid about the count's abandoning her. She has taken up riding and is making friends so she won't be so dependent on him. Juliet decides to put the brakes on her infatuation with Romeo, realizing it is a bit melodramatic to think of killing herself if they can't be together. Marilyn M. talks about going through treatment for chemical dependency and her decision to stop wearing seductive clothes. She is struggling with a major decision to stop making movies that portray her as a sex object. Although terrified, she realizes that this is the only way to gain confidence in the belief that she is lovable for herself. Grace K. G. asks for support in summoning her courage to tell the prince she's upset about his affairs and wants him to see a marriage counselor with her. She is so angry at him that she's been having fantasies of renewing an affair with an old lover. Lady Di lets her hair down and cries on Elizabeth T.'s shoulder about her loneliness at the palace, admitting that she has translated her anger at Charles into flirtations with other men, and that she has filled her emptiness by buying clothes. Ingrid B. talks about her powerlessness to leave her abusive relationship with Roberto and her realization that falling in love was not necessarily a sound basis for marriage. Jackie O. describes the isolation and pain she experienced while her first husband played around with other women. She felt she couldn't talk to anyone about it because of their status, especially not to her mother-in-law, who turned her cheek when her own husband did the same. Elizabeth T. is discovering that being sexual with a man doesn't mean she has to marry him.

Far-fetched? Not really. In the last decade we have seen a president's wife, Betty Ford, openly seek treatment for chemical dependency. That, too, would have been unheard of twenty years ago. As a woman married to a man of status and power, she would have been expected to suffer or die in silence, keeping up the illusion of the American Dream. We have entered an era in which many taboos about women are finally breaking down. One of the greatest taboos is talking about the unhappiness of women who attempt to find their identities through men, particularly rich and powerful men. When famous women open up about their pain, they help crack the myths that govern our sex role socialization. We grow up believing that one must be the "right kind" of woman to attract a prince, president, or millionaire. And it goes without saying that this is a goal for little girls to aspire to. When women open up and talk honestly, they start to move beyond the myths and illusions fostered by a culture that equates female success with the power, wealth, and status of a woman's partner.

In the following section we will examine how individuals move from victimization to a self-destructive belief system to addiction, and we will see that underlying sexually addictive and codependent behavior, there is always a primary drive for survival.

ADDICTIVE SEX AND SEX ADDICTION

It is important to distinguish between addictive sex and sex addiction. Addictive sex occurs when a woman mistakenly uses sex to express anger, to feel powerful, to be held, to relieve tension, to hide from feelings, or to create a false bond of intimacy. Sex addiction is when the mistaken use of sex for love or power fits into an escalating pattern of behavior that the woman feels powerless to control. A full-fledged addiction inevitably leads to harmful consequences, unmanageability, obsessions, and a decreasing ability to function. Sex addiction in women reflects an internalization of male norms of sexuality involving power, aggressiveness, and control.

Sex is used codependently when a woman has sex she doesn't truly desire, excluding rape, in order to maintain a relationship or placate a partner. She has sex out of fear, obligation, or to prevent abandonment rather than out of love. Sexual codependency becomes an addiction when a woman feels powerless to stop letting her body be used by someone else in order to maintain a relationship. Sexual codependency also leads to an escalating pattern of harmful consequences, unmanageability, obsessions, and a decreasing ability to function. Sexual codependency is, in many ways, only a slight exaggeration of the culturally prescribed norm for women: the passive, sweet, servile female who believes that she must be sexual to receive love and care. Having been taught this basic partnership bargain throughout the ages, women learn to detach from their sexuality, believing it is a thing to be "saved" and "given" to men, and the means by which to control men. Women are also taught to mistake sexual attraction as a sign that they are valued as a person. Both addictive and codependent forms of sexual behavior are limiting and both are dysfunctional. It can be said that sex addiction is mistaking sex for God, while sexual codependency is sacrificing one's sexuality in the mistaken belief that one's partner is God. Because women are traditionally socialized to be codependent, very few women fit solely into the role of sex addict. Codependency and addiction are interwoven for many women.

DEVELOPMENT OF SEX ADDICTION AND CODEPENDENCY: A MODEL

Sex addiction and sexual codependency have their roots in survival skills women adopt to cope with childhood wounds — neglect, abuse, loss, sexual shame, and negative sexual programming about being female. Although I always feel uneasy about models and theories — mostly because I resent other people imposing a fixed formula to explain "how I am" — I present the model shown in Figure 4.1 to provide a description that may help people understand themselves. If it doesn't quite fit, it's probably because I didn't think of something, not that anything is unusual about you, the reader.

The model for sex addiction and codependency proceeds through the following stages:

> Victimization
> Development of core beliefs
> Cultural, family, and genetic filter
> Beliefs to reduce anxiety
> Operational beliefs
> Sex addiction and sexual codependency as modus operandi

Victimization involves any form of neglect, abuse, or betrayal that leaves a child's basic needs unmet or that violates the child's body, mind, or spirit. It can be willful abuse or result from ignorance, death, accidents, war, catastrophe, early hospitalization, or isolation. While all parents make mistakes, victimization involves a parent's continued inability to understand and respond to the emotional and physical needs of a child, as well as overt abuse of the child. Over time, victimization and neglect leave a basic emptiness, an unmet longing or hunger that becomes the driving force underlying addictions.

Development of Core Beliefs. The child who is abused, neglected, or abandoned feels terrified, angry, or sad. She fears she will die. When no one responds to her feelings, she assumes that they must be bad. Unable to separate her feelings from her identity, she translates "My feelings are

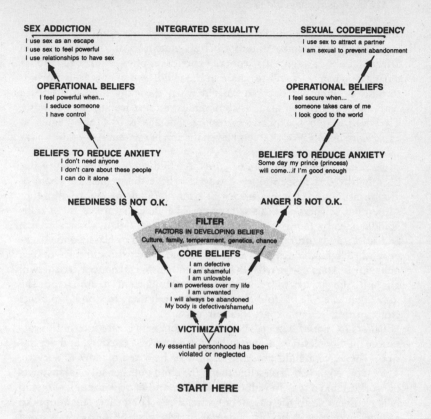

Figure 4.1.

FROM VICTIMIZATION TO SEX ADDICTION AND SEXUAL CODEPENDENCY

SEX ADDICTION   INTEGRATED SEXUALITY   SEXUAL CODEPENDENCY

I use sex as an escape
I use sex to feel powerful
I use relationships to have sex

I use sex to attract a partner
I am sexual to prevent abandonment

OPERATIONAL BELIEFS
I feel powerful when...
I seduce someone
I have control

OPERATIONAL BELIEFS
I feel secure when...
someone takes care of me
I look good to the world

BELIEFS TO REDUCE ANXIETY
I don't need anyone
I don't care about these people
I can do it alone

BELIEFS TO REDUCE ANXIETY
Some day my prince (princess)
will come...if I'm good enough

NEEDINESS IS NOT O.K.   ANGER IS NOT O.K.

FILTER
FACTORS IN DEVELOPING BELIEFS
Culture, family, temperament, genetics, chance

CORE BELIEFS
I am defective
I am shameful
I am unlovable
I am powerless over my life
I am unwanted
I will always be abandoned
My body is defective/shameful

VICTIMIZATION
My essential personhood has been
violated or neglected

START HERE

bad" to "I am bad." Eventually she becomes a "shame-based" person, meaning that she feels defective at her core. Her core beliefs about herself are negative, and her script in life will be written based on these beliefs. She may go through life believing herself guilty of a nameless crime, for which she deserves to be punished. Because her emotional and physical needs are not met in childhood, even if her parents were physically present, she believes that she will always be abandoned.

The negative core beliefs most often articulated by the women I interviewed include

· I am defective. I am shameful. There's something wrong with me.
· I'll never be loved for myself.
· I am powerless over my life.

- I am unwanted.
- I will always be abandoned. I will always be alone.
- My body is damaged/defective/shameful.

Messages about a child's worth are conveyed in a multitude of ways, beginning in the womb. A mother's stress, nutrition, and chemical use all affect an unborn infant. If a woman experiences physical or sexual abuse during pregnancy, it will resonate in the child. A parent who is uncomfortable holding her baby, disgusted when the baby drools, messes a diaper, or explores her genitals communicates those feelings to the infant. The child develops a nameless feeling that she is bad. She begins to experience her body as shameful, even though her parents may never have said anything negative.

Cultural, family, and genetic filter. A child whose vulnerability has been betrayed is desperate for a way to relieve the tremendous pain of victimization and devise a means of control. That the child will adopt some kind of survival skills is a given. The exact nature of these skills is influenced by family experiences, innate temperament, chance events, education, and cultural messages that are influenced by class, ethnic background, religion, education, and the media. When she stumbles onto a behavior or stance that relieves pain or gives power, chances are she will adopt it. She may try to be cute, competent, tough, smart, athletic; or she may adopt the role of troublemaker, or loser, hoping to stop her parents from hurting her and to get their attention.

Beliefs to reduce anxiety. Negative core beliefs create internal devastation and hopelessness along with tremendous fear, anxiety, and depression. They give a child no sense of how to be loved or how to survive. They have no payoff. To escape them, the child puts her survival instincts to work to find a way to reduce the anxiety and pain. The goal is to stop being vulnerable to the parents or caregivers. The beliefs she adopts to reduce anxiety will be fundamental in whether she moves toward a primary role of sexual codependent or sex addict. The anxiety-reducing beliefs most likely to lead to an addictive modus operandi include: I don't need anyone; I don't care about these people; I'm tough; I can do it myself. It is far less painful to believe that you don't need someone than to have your longing for love and care constantly denied.

The woman headed for codependency is more likely to say, just as in the fairy tales, "If I am good enough, someday my prince will come to take care of me." The essential difference between the two paths is that the potential addict denies her neediness and seeks power, while the potential codependent denies her anger and searches for security.

Of course, the child does not deliberately choose these beliefs; they are formed at all levels of consciousness. The beliefs feel like the truth, and they keep the devastating pain of victimization at bay.

The anxiety-reducing belief "I don't need anyone" submerges the child's need for nurture. However, this denial creates tension, for somewhere deep inside, the wounded child continues to cry for attention and care. The need, like an underground stream, is ready to spring up whenever there is an opening. The codependent's anxiety-reducing statement "I will find someone to take care of me" also creates an internal tension, for it takes her search outside herself, causing her to lose control over her life.

Operational beliefs are created by transforming core beliefs into a course of action. Developed over a long period of trial and error, operational beliefs lead to actions that will provide illusory escapes from the dreaded feelings associated with core beliefs. The goal is to feel wanted, powerful, attractive, and lovable, or, for the codependent, secure.

In order to achieve these goals, the child transforms the core belief by adding a conditional clause that provides a course of action. For example, "I am powerless" becomes "I am powerful when I seduce someone, someone is hopelessly in love with me, I am sexual," and so forth. For the codependent, who seeks security, the core belief "I am powerless over my life" becomes "I'll find security in a partner." These operational beliefs become important survival tools. They create a pathway out of despair. Once she clicks into action, the woman feels more like a survivor and less like a victim; she now has a behavioral recipe for survival. Paradoxically, this recipe may eventually lead to devastation, for it is almost always a faulty foundation for living.

The translations from core beliefs listed below are the ones I most frequently observe. You may have different core beliefs and translations. One basic variable between the addict and codependent is that when the addict feels powerless she looks for ways to feel powerful; when the codependent feels powerless she tends to look for security.

Addict Translations of Core Beliefs to Operational Beliefs

Core Belief	Operational Belief
I am powerless.	I feel powerful when I flirt/am seductive (cool, tough, innocent, etc.).
	I feel powerful when I get someone turned on to me.
	I feel powerful when I get an important person into bed.
	I feel powerful/good when I masturbate.
	I feel powerful/relief when I have a fantasy of romance or sexual conquest.

Core Belief	Operational Belief
I'll always be alone or lonely.	I'm not lonely when I masturbate.
	I'm not alone when I have sex with someone.
	I'm not lonely when I fantasize romance.
I'll always be abandoned.	I won't be abandoned if I never get close to anyone.
	I won't feel abandoned if I'm good at seduction.
	If I'm sexy and attractive, I can have all the sexual partners I want.
	I'm not afraid of abandonment when I have sexual fantasies.
	I won't be abandoned if I become successful in my work, achieve status, or get rich.
My body is shameful/defective/repulsive.	My body feels good when I have sex.
	My body feels good when I look sexy.
	My body feels good when I get people turned on to me.
	My body feels nothing when I block out my feelings.

Codependent Translations of Core Beliefs to Operational Beliefs

Core Belief	Operational Belief
I can't take care of myself.	I'll feel secure if I have a husband or partner (preferably with money and status) to take care of me.
	I'll be secure if I have a nice house, enough money, pretty children.
I'll always be abandoned.	I won't be abandoned if I'm good enough in bed.
	I won't be abandoned if I do whatever he or she wants sexually.
	I won't be abandoned if I'm nice, helpful, kind, and do everything my partner wants.
	I won't be abandoned if I am indispensable to him or her.

Core Belief	Operational Belief
I am unlovable.	I am lovable when someone wants me sexually.
	I am lovable when someone flirts with me, sends me flowers, and pursues me.
	I am lovable when I give to others.
	I am lovable or important in my fantasies (which may include fantasies of fame, dramatic illness, rescue scenes, being pursued romantically).
I am powerless over my life.	I feel powerful when I get attention for being good.
	I feel powerful when I get people to feel sorry for me.
	I feel powerful when my partner begs for sex.
	I feel powerful when people see me as good and my partner as stupid/helpless/bad/out of it.
	I feel powerful when I imagine dying and people feel guilty about how they treated me.
My body is shameful/defective/repulsive/imperfect.	My body is attractive when someone wants me sexually.
	My body feels good when I think of myself as pure and not sexual.
	My body is acceptable when I am thin.
	My body feels good when I am beautifully dressed and made up.

As a woman puts her operational beliefs into action, they become her reality and her painful core beliefs are increasingly forgotten and repressed. Painful childhood memories are relegated to the unconscious or kept at bay. She might even say, "Oh, I had a wonderful childhood," or "It wasn't so bad," or "Underneath it all I know my parents loved me. They did the best they could." The pain associated with the core beliefs is triggered only when life brings disappointment, rejection, or loneliness. That's where addiction and codependency enter. When the pain associated with the core beliefs is triggered, the woman uses her operational tactics to fend off the feared feelings. Thus, the panic response to rejection, hurt, and disappointment can be stopped with the addictive or codependent behavior. Upset and lonely? Seduce someone. Your lover rejects you? Sleep with his or her best friend. Feeling neglected? Get sympathy by telling someone what a jerk and a sexual bore your partner is. Feeling powerless? Make a subtle dig at your partner about his sexual inadequacies and watch him blow up or feel hurt. Feeling empty? Redecorate your house and buy new clothes.

SEX ADDICTION AND SEXUAL CODEPENDENCY

Sex addiction and sexual codependency may manifest themselves either as true addictions or as the modus operandi in a woman's life. Women are socialized to value relationships strongly, and sexually addicted women are no different. Therefore, underlying sexually addictive behavior in most women there is a desire for an ongoing relationship.

Very few women set out to have as many sex partners as possible. Sexually addicted women get caught up in a cycle in which their primary source of power is sexual conquest, and they fulfill their need for tenderness and touch through the sexual act. Beneath their addiction is a burning desire to escape feelings of worthlessness and shame. These women become addicted to seduction, to the hunt, and to the feeling of having made a conquest. They long to bond but they don't know how.

Codependent women, on the other hand, derive a sense of self-worth from being pursued. And, as noted earlier, the codependent's need for security usually takes the form of an addictive relationship. Women in both groups may become addicted to romance — candlelight dinners, flowers, living out the illusion of love. For the addicted woman, romance is part of the high and usually the prelude to sex. For the codependent woman, romance is proof of being loved and sex the price she pays.

THE ADDICTIVE SEXUAL EXPERIENCE

The stories women tell of their sexually addictive behavior vary externally, but the themes of pain, fear, loneliness, and desperation cut through superficial differences. Some women have many partners, some very few. For some women compulsive masturbation is the primary form of the addiction; others have never masturbated.

One woman, who had had only one partner, described her addiction as a fear-filled preoccupation with sex. For most women it is a combination of many factors — sexual acting-out, fantasies, obsessions, and an escalating pattern of driven compulsive behavior that permeates their lives. Some are attracted to older authority figures, others to younger people with less power.

For many women there is a binge-and-starve quality to the addiction, periods of intense sexual activity followed by periods of sexual numbness during which they worry about their sexuality and ability to have a relationship. The pendulum may swing over a period of months or even years. Either way there is no process of bonding. See pages 52 and 53.

Self-abuse and violence are part of the pattern for some women, particularly in the later stages of relationships. Some are in sadomasochistic sexual relationships; some use pornography to become aroused; others become addicted to it. Some women engage in prostitution for short periods of time, others for a period of years. A few women had fantasies of sex with animals. Some women had at one time, usually as a child or adolescent, sexually used a younger child. One woman I interviewed had sexually abused a child when she was an adult.

Women rarely engage in exhibitionism the same way that men do. However, dressing with the blinds open, dressing to be seductive, stripping, and knowingly flaunting their sexuality in an attempt to seduce are forms of self-exposure that are part of the addiction.

Overall, with sex addiction, sexuality is not an integrated and balanced part of life. Whether or not a woman is actively sexual, sexual behavior and thoughts of sexual relationships play an inordinately large role in her life at a tremendous cost to her inner spirit.

When I ask sexually addicted women to describe the internal experience of addictive encounters, they describe it as a performance-oriented, genital experience focused on the high of orgasm, bringing a momentary escape from pain. It is a metaphor for an emotional longing to be connected to another person and escape feelings of alienation. As one woman said, "There is a feeling that nothing else matters but being sexual, even though it's always followed by emptiness."

The high for a sexually addicted woman often starts long before the sexual act. The adrenaline buildup can precede the sexual encounter by hours or days as women turn on the future fantasies of romantic encounters, which get their sexual juices flowing. Women may sustain a high for days in anticipation of an upcoming sexual encounter, or they may drift into a euphoric recall of a past experience hundreds of times. At first the sustained high may help them function well in other areas of their lives. However, this will eventually fade as the addictive cycle runs its course.

For many women, the high is in the feeling of power and control that comes with seducing a partner, or as some women call it, the hunt. One lesbian woman described the hunt as electric, saying, "I thought I was the queen of the world. All I had to do was turn on the energy. I could always find somebody. Women would fall for it. I always thought they were dumb asses because of it. As soon as I got them I despised them, because all they wanted was my body. It's funny how things get turned around." Other women express the high of living on the razor's edge, playing with danger, risking being sexually victimized. There is a paradox in this behavior. At a subconscious level the women are reexperiencing their childhood abuse; the dangerous situation keeps the psyche tuned in to the

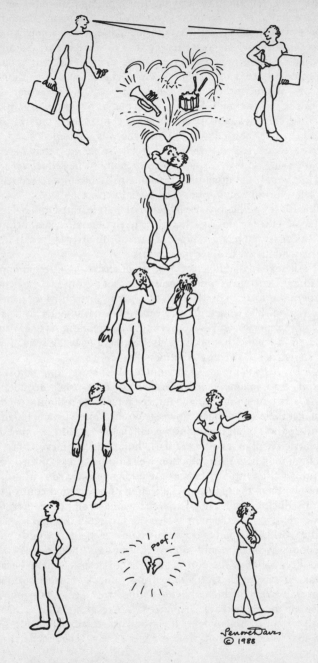

AN INTIMATE BONDED RELATIONSHIP

original violation. At the same time, drama and danger keep their focus turned outward, away from buried feelings.

Women often describe taking in the body-level physical experience of sex, yet feeling emotionally disconnected from their partners. In a sense, this is a form of masturbation with the use of a partner. One woman said that even when she was high from sex she was still lonely. Many others express a profound sense of loneliness following the sexual act. I believe this occurs because somewhere within us we feel shame when we use ourselves or another person. In our souls, we know the bargain we have struck, and to quell our shame we distance ourselves from our partners.

Some women clearly understand that their sexually addictive behavior is a direct expression of rage at an abuser: "I wanted to get even, to screw them and leave them and let them know how it feels." Women also describe the high of fooling people by appearing good and sweet on the outside and having, as one woman put it, "a secret sleazy part of me on the inside." These women are acting out the virgin-whore dilemma.

THE CODEPENDENT SEXUAL EXPERIENCE

Codependent women's descriptions of sex ranged from enjoyment to pure drudgery and detachment. Women said they enjoyed sex because it was the most important sign of being loved and assured them that their relationship was all right. "Because sex meant he loved me, I would forget the fights, the infidelities, and the neglect." At the other end of the spectrum a woman said, "Sex feels like something to be done, like a task, like the dishes. Inside I feel like I am going crazy." Another woman said, "I'm emotionally gone because I am trying so hard to please him." Another said the experience was "mentally abusive." After sex she was unable to sleep, and would feel herself emotionally disintegrating inside. Another woman, describing the essence of the codependent experience of powerlessness, said, "I feel kind of like a trapped animal." Although several women also told of experiencing physical pleasure and orgasm during sex, they spoke with little emotion.

A codependent woman may be upset when her partner does not want sex, but that's because having sex reassures her of her desirability and provides proof that her partner cares about her. In her mind she may also be sexual to assure herself her partner is not acting out addictively. She has internalized the cultural myth that if she "gives her husband enough" he won't run around. Nothing could be further from the truth. His acting out is about *his* addictiveness. One woman said she got high from getting her partner sexually excited. Another said she could feel superior, more pure and righteous, when he got sexually aroused and she stayed cool and detached. "I could loathe him and feel powerful when I saw him all turned on and excited and wanting me."

Another woman caught in the double standard of sex said, "I got to secretly enjoy sex because he made me do it. I did it because 'I'm a dutiful wife.' I didn't have to own that I wanted sex. I could stay the victim that way." Another way to interpret her statement was that she was groping to find a way to let herself overcome her own negative programming and enjoy sex.

SIMILARITIES AND DIFFERENCES

One thing struck me repeatedly as I gathered information for this book. The differences between sexually addicted and codependent women were manifested more dramatically in direct interviews than in the written questionnaire. During interviews, the sexually addicted women checked me out by asking questions, were more energetic, cracked more jokes, had a greater sense of camaraderie, and generally seemed more at ease than the codependent women. They would tell me when they didn't want to answer a question. They also had an easier time staying on track with the questions and were more able to talk about underlying personal and relationship dynamics.

There was a greater undercurrent of fear in the codependent women, at least initially. After I got to know some of them, we developed a warmth and ease similar to what I had with the SAA women. This fits with my sense that codependent women in general have more difficulty building trust. It may have to do with their lack of bonding and the extreme amount of stereotypical female programming many have internalized, particularly about being stupid and inferior. Several women confided that they felt uncomfortable at interviews because they couldn't imagine that anything they said would matter or make a difference.

Women in both groups project an image that hides significant parts of themselves. Codependent women tend to let their dependent, frightened side show and to keep their powerful part submerged. The addicted women show their bravura and hide the frightened dependent side.

The addicted women were far more articulate and angry about childhood abuse and sexism in the culture, yet the questionnaires revealed as much childhood abuse in the lives of codependent women, who seemed less conscious of their oppression and abuse. The addicted women tended to appear competent and independent, yet when asked, most said that underneath all the acting-out they were really looking for someone to take care of them. The codependent women appeared to spend far more time on their appearance and dress, conforming to the female stereotype, but addicted women revealed that they spent hours in ritualistic trances, fostering the image they wanted to project.

The CoSA women tended to talk about their long-term relationships, yet I was surprised to learn from the questionnaires that they had had nearly as many sex partners as the SAA women. Moreover, while CoSA women rarely spoke about themselves as lesbian or bisexual, the questionnaires revealed that many of them had had sexual relationships with other women.

When I brought the women from CoSA and SAA together to talk about these seeming disparities, I asked why those from CoSA appeared to be so uneasy with me. "That's easy," one woman responded. "As the interviewer and the one writing the book, you're in the role of an authority person, and we never question authority or talk back. You're known as a feminist, and many CoSA women associate that with hating men, and they don't want to face their own hatred for men." When I mentioned that my data from the questionnaires showed that numerous women in CoSA had been sexual with other women, a woman explained that sexual relationships with other women are rarely discussed in CoSA because there is a great deal of homophobia. Codependent women are often afraid to be in touch with their powerful side, which they attach to being lesbian, and they don't want to be seen as "unfeminine."

We talked about differences in feelings of camaraderie. One CoSA woman said, "We have a hard time celebrating each other's victories because there is an underlying sense of competition. There's also a feeling that there's not enough love or joy to go around, so we are cautious about handing them out."

When I asked why CoSA women rarely talk about their affairs, one woman grinned and said, "We don't talk about anything that dispels our image as angels." One woman summed up the codependent's view of multiple affairs and sex partners by saying, "The codependent hates the addict so much, she doesn't like to acknowledge any way she might be like him (or her)." We discussed how denial becomes a major block to a codependent woman's psychological reintegration. Unless she confronts her shadow side and gives up the high of being superior to others and appearing to be a saint, she will not be able to love herself. It is a great struggle because she is convinced that no one could love the angry addicted part of her. To her, giving up that image of the pure and innocent female often feels like losing her total identity. And showing her powerful angry side triggers fear of total abandonment.

RATIONALIZATION

Rationalization is a big part of addiction and is core to codependency. The mind wants to figure out a way to make something work that doesn't work, like trying to fit a square peg into a round hole. Rationalization is a cue signaling that you are off center, that you want something to be the way it isn't.

Codependents live in a world of rationalizations, forever trying to shut off the internal signals they don't want to hear. They dwell on the hope that things will magically get better tomorrow or be like they were in the initial romantic period. "He was nice the first four months we were together. I'm trying to find a way to have it like that again." A codependent woman will exaggerate any indication of "improvement" on the part of the partner, while denying blatant daily abuse. She has great difficulty seeing the "big picture," namely that, overall, she is suffering, lonely, and tremendously unhappy with her relationship. The codependent's mind works nonstop, often causing her to wake up in the night or have insomnia.

Common rationalizations used to maintain a dysfunctional relationship or avoid confronting it include: It's better than it used to be; But he's (she's) got so much potential; It's really not that bad; Everyone has problems; No relationship is perfect, so why leave; This is all I deserve; He couldn't survive without me; I'll never have anyone if I lose this one.

The sexually addicted woman is generally less busy with rationalizations, and more likely to be focused on her addictive encounter. She needs *just one* permission-giving statement to jump into her addiction. For example: Just one more time won't hurt anyone; Who'll ever know? It's my right; Life was made for fun.

The relative length of these two lists makes a significant statement about the differences between addiction and codependency. The codependent woman spends an enormous amount of time "in her head," rationalizing her life, trying to figure out how to make an impossible situation work.

Many codependent women think that if they admit a relationship is not working, they will have to leave. This was clear to me in working with Esther. At one point I asked her, "If you came out and said, 'My marriage is rotten,' do you think it means you automatically have to leave?"

"Of course," she replied.

"Why couldn't you just say, 'I don't like my marriage but I'm not ready to leave'?"

She looked startled, then thought it over for a moment. "Well then, I'd feel like a jerk for staying." She smiled broadly and said, "Then I wouldn't be perfect."

"Hallelujah," said I.

USE OF PORNOGRAPHY

Pornography plays a role in the lives of sexually addicted and codependent women. On this issue, perhaps more than any other, women in codependency groups expressed strong feelings. Their reactions to pornography included gross, terrible, harmful, insulting, unprintable. They despised it, felt degraded by it, and felt it was a form of violence. One woman said simply, "I hate it."

By far the majority of CoSA women had been with partners who used some form of pornography, ranging from "girlie" calendars, to *Playboy*, *Penthouse*, and X-rated videos, to hard-core porn, magazines of sex "tools," and suggestive lingerie. One woman said her husband wanted her to wear her high heels to bed. Others had been asked to pose for pictures like those of women in porn magazines or to act out scenes from sexual videos or even make videos themselves. They were asked to put various objects in their vaginas, and to submit to a variety of sexual practices their partners discovered through pornography, including sadomasochism, bondage, and violence.

Most of all, these women felt affronted at having pornography around them. Many believed that their husbands were addicted to it — they spent a lot of money on it and were more emotionally involved with pornography than with them. When I asked women if they confronted their partners' use of pornography some of the replies were: "I never thought I had the right to do anything like that"; "I had many philosophical debates about the ethics of women posing in *Playboy*. Conversations were on an intellectual level (his) and from a feminist's perspective (mine)"; "I would throw it out of the house or hide it when he was away."

CoSA women rarely mentioned using pornography themselves. However, quite a few SAA women said that pornography played a role in their sex addiction or sexual behavior. Some used it while masturbating and some patterned their sadomasochistic behavior or methods for arousal with a partner on it. Others became addicted to it.

Many women said that pornography, like a hypnotic cue, triggered their addiction. One woman spoke of the arduous process in recovery of training herself not to let her eyes linger on seductive makeup and clothing ads, because those were such strong cues to her addiction. For many, sexual "abstinence" included *not* looking at pornography, X-rated movies or videos, or magazines sexually objectifying women, which for some women meant most magazines. Women also felt disturbed by their attraction to pornography because they knew it violated their innermost values. As one woman remarked, "There I was using pornography to get high. How's that for feminist values?"

When I asked women about the relation between pornography and sex addiction, one summed it up by saying, "Pornography is about disconnected, violent, abusive sex, so it's basically bad news for anyone who wants a healthy, spiritual sexuality."

FEAR AND ANGER

Two pivotal differences between the two groups are the way women deal with fear and the way they deal with anger. Codependent women tend to be controlled by their fear, which keeps them stuck in their security addiction. The addicted women leap over their fear, often getting into extremely dangerous situations. What women in both groups lack is an ability to determine when fear signals a dangerous situation to be avoided, and when they need to push through fear to make changes. Paradoxically, codependent women who are afraid of taking emotional risks often remain in dangerous situations with an abusive partner, while addicted women flee from partners who genuinely care for them.

The codependent woman attempts to keep her anger buried, acquiescing to sex on her partner's terms. If that is intolerable, she may set up her addicted partner to blow up, hoping to distract him from wanting to be sexual. That may also provide a vicarious tension release for her. Or sadly, to avoid being the object of her partner's negative sexual energy, she may look the other way when he sexually abuses their children.

Over a period of years her resentments swell into a seething rage that takes enormous energy to control. In her effort to keep her lethal rage in check, she becomes more and more entrenched in her "nice woman" role, creating an even greater chasm between her inner and outer self. Imagine having sex year after year, holding in rage and disgust, the prime motivation being to hang on to your partner and the security he or she provides. No wonder codependent women so often describe their experiences of sex as numb, detached, and dead. If a codependent woman were to be emotionally present during sex, and let her sexual energy flow through her body, it could well open up a Pandora's box of her most dreaded emotion, rage, along with her buried grief and emptiness about the life she has not lived.

She frequently expresses her anger in a passive-aggressive way, sweetly making digs below the belt, then disowning their impact. "I only said that to be helpful. You don't need to get so upset." Some codependent women displace their anger on their children. Others become sarcastic or blow up, but usually in a torrent of bitter complaints, outright screaming, or a shaming attack on their partner. Because the anger is not directly attached to a specific situation, it does not lead to resolution of a problem. For others, anger stays forever inside, eating away at the gut.

Addicted women are more likely to express anger with affect. It might be overstated or aimed at the wrong person, but at least it is being turned outward. As a result, they tend to have more energy than codependent women. With some, the anger becomes dysfunctional, taking the form of blaming or shaming others or simply blowing up. Some sexually addicted women use anger as a cover for hurt or sadness. Because many are ashamed to feel sadness or dependency, they become hostile or rageful toward people who trigger those emotions.

Many women in both groups confuse anger with rage. They have not learned the difference between dumping rage on someone inappropriately and expressing one's anger respectfully. In the families of many of these women, anger meant that someone got a black eye, a beating, an emotional battering, or was sexually abused. Few had adult models who were able to be appropriately angry and to resolve conflicts.

THE CONTROLLED ADDICT

Many women, in an attempt to bury their sex addiction and the chaos it creates, bury their sexuality. In essence the addiction goes underground and wreaks internal havoc in the woman's body, mind, and spirit. She is usually unaware of her addictive impulses. They remain hidden as doctors and therapists continually treat such cover-up symptoms as depression, anxiety, compulsive eating, compulsive smoking, alcoholism, ulcers, migraines, digestive difficulties, and so on. In therapy she rarely reveals her pain and anxiety over her physical isolation. A woman may attempt to make sense out of her sexual numbness by saying that she is "asexual." But that doesn't solve the problem. Her sexual shame remains an unresolved dilemma churning away inside.

All too often, these women are taunted in the back of their minds by thoughts of being defective. "I'm destined to be alone; I'll never have a sexual relationship. Something is wrong with my sexuality." It is like constant self-flagellation, a hateful tape-recorded message that runs nonstop. Trapped in the emotional desert of their own lives, these women long for a partnership, but sex and intimacy are so fraught with fear that they withdraw whenever a potential partner comes on the horizon. Usually they tell themselves they haven't met the right person yet, not realizing that they flee from healthy people who could genuinely love them. Instead, they tend to try to attract and flirt with people who are physically or emotionally unavailable.

In therapy it often emerges that these women have deeply buried pain and anger, and they fear it will be released if they open up their hearts to another human being. Many are survivors of insidious covert sexual abuse, which is difficult for them to identify. This leaves them feeling worse, because they can't link specific events to their sexual fears. Many are children of alcoholics, but addressing that issue alone doesn't help to solve the puzzle.

When I first met Ida in my waiting room, her eyes flashed a momentary fear, which she rapidly averted by chatting politely. Usually I reach out and shake the hand of a new client, but below her surface amiability I picked up a strong signal not to touch her. Eventually, she revealed that she feared touch because it nearly always aroused sexual feelings, which in turn brought profound feelings of shame. In the first months of therapy her story unfolded slowly while I continually had the uneasy feeling that she might bolt at any moment. She had the symptoms of an incest survivor, but no memories of sex abuse as a child. At one time in her life Ida had been in a series of addictive sexual relationships, often getting into triangles with friends or close relatives. Later she had been in a devastating and emotionally abusive relationship in which sex had been dead for nine out of the eleven years. She had almost no close friends and was incredibly compulsive at any task she undertook. A friend once told her, "If you were washing the kitchen floor and the house was burning down, you wouldn't leave till you finished the job." She smoked and had migraine headaches and a recurring ulcer.

Whenever I brought up the subject of sex I was politely made to feel that I was snooping or acting inappropriately. When I said this to her, she laughed and replied, "Sex is private."

"Just like your pain," I said.

It was months before Ida was willing to do a sexual history, and even then her shame was enormous. It was over a year before she let me know that she had a continuous sexual fantasy of a person she knew. It occupied her mind daily and was a huge part of her life. She resisted seeing it as anything significant, saying "Don't all people have fantasies?" For a while we took the focus off sexuality and talked about her family. Even though she could list numerous ways her parents had neglected her, she was never able to feel angry at them. Or if she was momentarily angry, she would immediately counter her feelings, saying "They had a hard life themselves."

I tried many approaches with Ida, but she never followed through on her work. We did cognitive therapy for depression. For a while we worked at a behavior plan to improve her diet, which included enormous amounts of sugar and caffeine. She tried to quit smoking unsuccessfully, despite a couple of programs and many sessions of hypnosis. It seemed that every door we knocked on in an attempt to jar her system loose was securely closed. She had the defenses and emotional symptoms of a sexually addicted woman, but she could sidestep that notion by saying she wasn't being sexual with anyone.

Ida grew frightened of becoming dependent on me. She told me she thought about me a lot and had recurring fantasies of my being her friend. Much later, she admitted with shame that she was sexually attracted to me. At first I treated this as normal transference — displacing and sexualizing the longing for an all-caring mother on the therapist. But no discussion, limit setting, or insight helped her move on. She was at once obsessed with pleasing me and underneath, I suspected, building up a great rage at me. I realized that her sex addiction had become directed at me and was being played out in her fantasies. I told Ida that I did not want her to have sexual fantasies of me, pointing out that they prevented her from forming a trusting alliance with me that would enable us to work together to help her feel better.

I also started feeling uneasy in our sessions, wondering if the rage beneath her dependency would somehow explode. Finally it did, in a way typical of sex addiction. Ida made friends with a lesbian couple I was working with in therapy, and proceeded to discredit me to them. Because she felt helpless to conquer her dependency on me, she wanted others to collude in making me the villain so she would have an excuse to leave. At first the couple believed her negative comments, which created difficulties in our work together. When they finally set limits and told Ida that they did not wish to discuss me, she seduced one of them. In her mind, as she later revealed, she wanted to ruin their relationship so I would feel like a bad therapist. She was also jealous of them because they spoke of feeling close to me and she didn't believe I liked her. Eventually she admitted she was angry with me and wanted to get me back.

At that point, I made going to SAA a condition of her continuing therapy. She went a couple of times, then quit after again becoming sexually involved with a client of mine in the SAA group, breaking the rules for my therapy and those of the SAA group. A month later, seeing that we were making no progress, I suggested that we stop therapy, saying I simply didn't know what else to do and that she clearly hadn't accepted the terms of the therapy relationship. I offered to refer her, but she was not interested.

Ida and women like her often resist facing up to possible sex addiction because their shame is so intense. They may have a huge amount of buried grief and rage, stemming from severe emotional deprivation in childhood, which they steadfastly deny. Many had severe ruptures in early bonding and are unable to trust as a result. They also have well-formed defense systems and usually survive through their work. In fact, many are successful professionals.

Some of these women do eventually get into SAA groups. Frequently, however, their pain is so great and their defense systems so well entrenched that they find reasons to leave: they are different from the other women who act out sexually; nothing in their life is so out of control (they pay the rent on time); they are successful at work; and, well, who needs a relationship, anyway?

In some ways a controlled addiction can be more detrimental to a person than an active one, where the harmful consequences can be readily seen. With sexually addicted women there may be periods of sexual inactivity, but there is less denial of sexual difficulties than with the controlled addict. The controlled addict may also appear to be sexually codependent, for this is a more acceptable role and serves to keep her addiction buried.

FANTASIES

While I don't use the term *love addiction,* I think romance addiction is a major component for many women who identify themselves as sexually addicted. A huge part of sex addiction and codependency takes place in a person's head, often in the form of fantasies and obsessions. Women may walk in front of cars, make mistakes at work, be unable to concentrate or to focus on their lives — all because they are so totally preoccupied with fantasies related to sex, romance, and relationships. If you have ever fallen in love, you probably know what it is to be absorbed in thinking about another person, longing to see him or her, hungering for their touch, and experiencing symptoms of withdrawal when they are distant or unavailable. In functional relationships the initial high gradually gives way to reality — you relinquish the high as a tradeoff for comfort, stability, and the desire to turn the focus back to your own life. For addicted and codependent people, the romantic illusion becomes an unrealistic goal that can never be attained. Many people, not wanting to leave an addictive relationship, say, "I want to find a way to get back to the feelings of the first few months." What they don't realize is that the high of the first few months is simply a beginning phase of a relationship and it is unrealistic to expect it to last.

The most frequent types of fantasies for sexually addicted women involve pursuing someone, the hunt; a passionate sexual encounter; euphoric recall of a sexual experience; finding the perfect relationship; and being cared for. Slightly less frequent are fantasies of being special, having someone falling madly in love with them, being passive during sex, dreamy or romantic scenes, being violent with someone, and masturbation. Some women have fantasies of being sexual with children or with animals and often feel tremendous shame about it.

Codependent women present a somewhat different picture. Their most frequent fantasies revolve around being taken care of, being special, and being romantically pursued. Slightly less typical are fantasies of romantic scenarios, dreamy romantic scenes, or euphoric recall of a sexual experience. Rarely do they have fantasies of masturbation.

Fantasies take many forms. For most women the fantasies are as much about the flirtation, the hunt, seduction and romance, as about sex. Some women never fantasize explicitly about sex. Others have violent or masochistic sexual fantasies associated with masturbation or sexual encounters.

Fantasies serve many purposes for the addicted woman. Fantasies about someone else can keep a relationship going, although the fantasy lover often becomes more real than the actual partner. Keeping a fantasy alive for years is like keeping a little booze in the closet, to be pulled out to ease the pain. One woman said, "I fantasized a sexual/romantic encounter with a man almost daily for two years after one date with him."

People often ask me whether all fantasies are bad. Of course not. Fantasies are a way to create an altered state of consciousness. They may be useful or damaging, depending on the content and how they are used. A person may drift into them or start them at will; they may provide a reverie or a pleasant interlude. Creative people often find inspiration in fantasies. They can provide relief during a difficult day — a brief reverie to imagine a coming vacation on a beach can reduce stress and help someone get through the day. In fact, people are taught to image warm, comforting scenes as a strategy for relaxation.

Fantasies can also be a road to the unconscious, a source of information about yourself. You can drift off into an altered state and let the images come; it is a trip into your inner world. Fantasies are a way of staying connected to yourself. Unfortunately, for many children in abusive or neglectful homes, what starts as a survival tool eventually becomes an addiction.

For children in abusive families, fantasies may become the only means to escape the harsh realities of pain or neglect. While being abused they may count repeatedly, hear music, fantasize being rescued, imagine the abuser dying — anything to get the body to detach from physical or emotional pain. But, like so many survival tools forged during a painful childhood, the fantasies that once served as a core to survival eventually become a destructive addiction and a block to intimate relationships. They become a way to get through the day and start to be more real than life itself. Fantasies play a huge part in the addictions of most women and for some they become the primary addiction.

When I asked women if their fantasies had helped them in any way, some responded that fantasies had kept them from going crazy or committing suicide. Fantasies hold out hope of something better, giving comfort and a feeling of control.

When exploring fantasies it is important to consider both the *nature* and the *use* of the fantasies. The nature or content of a fantasy can tell you how comfortable you are with your sexuality. Are your sexual fantasies set in dark rooms with faceless, mysterious strangers who are very different from you, or are you comfortable with sexual fantasies of familiar people more like you? Do you pair violence, masochism, or being in control with sexual arousal, or do you imagine warmth, love, and tenderness? The nature of your fantasies reflects not only what happened in your family but also the culture you live in. The fact that so many women use masochistic or passive sexual fantasies to get sexually aroused reflects the cultural norms that women have absorbed. If we lived in a country where women were never sexually abused, had equal rights, and were never portrayed as sex objects, I do not believe we would associate passive fantasies of being tied up or abused with sexual arousal.

Can fantasies lead people into acting out addictively? Absolutely. Remember the cycle of addiction. The first stage is a fleeting image of an addictive sexual encounter; it means the addict part is going into operation. A person who pulls the fantasy in and gives it attention is apt to be overpowered by addictive impulses.

In order to come up with your own definition of sexual sobriety, you must determine what types of fantasies trigger your addiction or are themselves addictive. Most often addictive fantasies pair sexual arousal with seduction, control, power, violence, masochism, or thoughts that some man or woman will come "and take me away from all this." Others vary according to individuals.

Most women in recovery can sense in their body when fantasies take them across a line into an addictive world. One woman described it as crossing a line into euphoria, where all her troubles melted away and she felt safe. In this context, any type of fantasy can be used as an escape. When there are harmful consequences to having fantasies, when the fantasies start to be more real than life, when they represent a secret world of escape, the questions to ask are: What am I running away from? What don't I want to feel? One obvious signal that a fantasy is addictive is when you can't make it stop; it takes control as if it has a life of its own.

Addictive fantasies used as an escape from reality often have dire consequences. They also perpetuate the addiction because as women spend more and more time in a fantasy world, they neglect such responsibilities of life as paying bills, caring for children, and, in general, patching leaks before they become floods. This creates more problems to run from. For some women, fantasies lead to the use of alcohol, for others they function as a substitute. In any case, they are part of an escalating cycle that renders life more and more out of control. The content of the fantasies also changes over time for women, particularly if they involve violence or masochism. As one fantasy loses its euphoria-inducing ability, one tends to adopt a more intense or violent fantasy, or simply spends more time in fantasies.

The following are some of the ways fantasies operate in women's lives.

As a high between sexual encounters: Fantasies can be used as a bridge between addictive sexual encounters to keep a person from connecting with reality. A woman may keep herself high from one sexual encounter to the next with euphoric recall of the past encounter or images of the one to come. She recreates the adrenaline high as she recalls getting dressed for the encounter, eating out, romantic glances, conversations, kissing, and the sexual act. She keeps a vibration of sexual energy running constantly, drifting through her days totally detached from what is happening around her. She may also maintain her high with a variety of other fantasies to ward off unwanted feelings. These fantasies not only act as an interim high, they set the stage for the next addictive encounter with the partner.

To avoid confronting a dead or dying relationship: Fantasies can be used as an escape from a dead relationship and cause a relationship to die. One woman said that while she was in a dysfunctional relationship she would constantly have sexual and romantic fantasies of another woman that were more real than her actual relationship. She avoided confrontation with her partner by drifting off into a fantasy world. By not dealing with the conflict, she created more and more distance in the relationship. People in troubled relationships may also imagine a day when everything will be rosy, just as it was in the euphoric beginning, rather than facing the reality of the present. In this situation fantasies are used to relieve pain, just as some people use alcohol or drugs.

Women also survive painful marriages by having constant fantasies of other men. One woman said that when she was angry at her husband, she would have a sexual fantasy about another man, perhaps her partner's boss or best friend. Such behavior represents the fantasy level of sex addiction. She didn't literally have sex, but she did in spirit and out of spite.

For sexual arousal: A woman addicted to sex panics when the sexual high in a relationship starts to wear off. To her, good sex means that the relationship is working. Therefore she has a large investment in keeping the sexual aspect of the relationship alive and maintaining the romantic connection. Her fantasies may be about other people and may involve masochism or violence. They may occur during sex or between sexual encounters. As the fantasies become the connection to her sexuality, she creates greater distance from her partner.

As a bridge between relationships: After a period of time — be it a few weeks or a couple of years — the stuff of everyday life starts to interfere with the romantic high. The partner is no longer the fabulous prince or princess of the woman's dreams. Because the intense feelings are gone, she thinks the relationship is no good. Panic sets in and she looks for a solution. All the people she meets become potential sexual partners, and she starts fantasizing about them until her addictive radar connects with another person. She knows deep within her that she is planning to leave her partner, but she doesn't mention it for fear of a fight or of having the partner leave first. She may have unrealistic fantasies in which she, her current partner, and her new lover all become good friends. This helps her deny both her own dishonesty and the pain her partner will feel. When she has her new partner emotionally on the hook, she abruptly leaves her old one. The fantasies may then wane, because the unrealistic, illusory fantasy of true love is again fulfilled — for a while. If a woman goes through a period without a relationship, she may indulge in fantasies to stave off the knowledge of her inner emptiness.

OBSESSIONS

Most of us are occasionally preoccupied with a person, a job situation, or children. Obsessions go a step beyond preoccupations. A person who is preoccupied is distracted or engrossed in thoughts about something — often a current situation or a coming event. With effort, however, she can shake it off and engage in her daily thoughts and activities, sometimes drifting back to the troublesome thoughts.

An obsession occupies the mind and is often experienced as a painful intrusion that can't be shut off at will. It feels like an inescapable presence, another person in your head. It takes you out of the present, out of control, sometimes for months or even years. One woman described an obsession about a woman she was attracted to as "a knife in my head I couldn't shake off. It was with me every minute. I started to feel physically sick, I couldn't eat, and I prayed it would go away."

An obsession with someone or something over time signals that you are unclear about the situation. You are obsessing rather than facing some important truth about yourself or the other person, feelings or knowledge you want to avoid. When you know and accept the truth about a relationship you will cease to obsess about it. If the relationship itself is fulfilling and satisfying, there is no need to create an imaginary relationship. When you are away from your partner, you are free to be absorbed in other people and in other aspects of your life, because deep down you know you are committed, and that your partner will be there when you return.

An obsession may signal that you are not being honest with yourself. Obsessive thinking is often the difference between what we *know* to be true and what we *want* to be true. If you want to get over an obsession, you may need to look within yourself. Are you hanging on to a person out of fear? Do you know that a relationship is destructive, but don't want to leave? Are you obsessed with plots to change your partner rather than change yourself? Are you picking up danger signals about the person you don't want to face? Are your feelings a transference of a childlike longing for the all-loving parent? One way to start cracking an obsession is to speak the truth. You may need to say, "I am afraid you will leave me," "I suspect you are not being honest," "I am angry," or "This relationship isn't working for me."

Carried to an extreme, obsessing about an unobtainable person can become an addiction. This means that a woman never has to deal with her own sexuality or a down-to-earth relationship. The *National Enquirer*, a favorite source for stories on sex addiction and codependency (although the paper doesn't call it that), ran an article about a woman who began obsessing about *Miami Vice* star Don Johnson on her honeymoon. She subsequently collected every article she could find about him and started sending him "Dear Don" letters and romantic poems ending with the phrase "Just to be with you, Don." She ultimately spent $4,000 and destroyed her marriage to go to Florida, where she was able to visit the *Miami Vice* set on two occasions. She didn't speak with Don Johnson, but she claims that he glanced at her twice and smiled. "If he had asked me to come over to his place I would have responded, 'Sure I'll go.' "

While most adolescents engage in obsessions and fantasies to some extent, SAA and CoSA women recall that their obsessive adolescent fantasies of unobtainable movie and rock stars led to their spending money on rock magazines and putting themselves to sleep with illusions of living with "him" or "her," thereby avoiding going through the uncomfortable, experimental, vulnerable stages of adolescence. The fantasy world evolved to cover the loneliness of not fitting in and not having friends. Because it is accepted and promoted for young girls to have teenage male heroes, frequently no one noticed the addictive and codependent implications of their obsession. They needed to talk about sex, to understand themselves, to be encouraged to find power within themselves.

Whether a woman acts out her sex addiction or sexual codependency, in her mind, body, or spirit she creates a chasm that separates her from what she is seeking — her internal power and capacity to love. Instead of increasing self-knowledge she loses herself. Instead of experiencing intimacy she finds loneliness. She becomes dependent rather than powerful, empty rather than full, barren rather than creative. Paradoxically, when a woman integrates her sexuality with knowledge of herself, when it is a source of energy, it becomes a force in the expansion of her love and power. When a woman ceases to use sex as a bribe, escape, or weapon of power, it can become one with her Source, her spirituality. Kundalini yoga regards the body as a microcosm of the universe: when one is alive and at one within the body, one is likewise at one with the universe, with pure consciousness. Kundalini stands for female sexual energy, represented by a coiled serpent in the form of a flower resting at the base of the spine. When the serpent uncoils, energy rises through the body, awakening pure knowledge and a state of bliss, and sexual energy is transformed to cosmic consciousness.

The purpose of suffering the pain and struggle of identifying sexual codependency and addiction in ourselves is to clear the path for a whole new concept of sexuality, one that includes a free flow of energy in the body, thereby increasing our personal power and ability to love.

By addressing this core issue, we gain new insight into our programming, our socialization, and many of our faulty beliefs. Many women can't imagine feeling good about their bodies or enjoying their sexuality for themselves. They know that sex as they experience it is not satisfying or life affirming, but they have no idea how to change it. Part of the journey is to accept the fact that when we give up misusing sex, a long period of personal awakening may be necessary before we can experience it in a new way. We make the journey toward truth as an act of faith, because for those who seek inner peace, it is the only way.

CHAPTER 5

Will Someone Please Help Me?
Gerri, Martha, and Anita

G ERRI, MARTHA, AND ANITA were the first women who responded when I solicited an SAA group for volunteers willing to be interviewed for my book. Their stories are poignant and varied, illustrating many of the aspects of sex addiction and codependency that we have already touched on. The stories focus on childhood origins as well as the events that led each of them to join a recovery program for sex addiction. If their stories sometimes seem overwhelming, you have connected with how their lives felt for them.

I interviewed Gerri and Anita again three years later, when I was nearing completion of the book, so they could bring me up to date on their lives and recovery. You will read about them again in the last chapter. Martha's story is told in its entirety here since she was nearing the end of her healing journey when we first met.

GERRI: NAMING THE ADDICTION

My request for women subjects was delivered on a Saturday morning, and I figured I'd be lucky if I received a response sometime during the ensuing week. Much to my surprise, Gerri called half an hour after the meeting ended. She sounded young and had a warm, vibrant voice. She told me a little about her background — she grew up in a violent abusive family — and said she would like to be interviewed. As we discussed convenient times to meet, I felt pulled by an urgency in her voice when she said, "This afternoon would be okay." Something inside of me said cancel your plans for the afternoon and see her.

An hour later the doorbell rang. Before me stood a very beautiful young woman with tawny skin, long brown hair, and dark eyes. Having heard some of her painful story on the phone, I found Gerri's casual demeanor a surprising contrast. An underlying vulnerability was barely perceptible, like a shadow of fear that showed occasionally in her eyes. We settled into my sunroom with a pot of tea, my notepad, and a tape recorder.

Gerri told me that she had read my Red Book. She had been in SAA for only a couple of months and was having an extremely difficult time getting herself to meetings and keeping in contact with people. On that particular Saturday her lack of plans for the whole weekend loomed like a frightening abyss that left her feeling vulnerable to acting out. When she had heard the request for volunteers in her group that morning, she immediately thought, "Oh good, something to fill the time." Gerri also hoped that telling her story might help her recovery.

Before joining SAA, Gerri had been leading a double life. She was a teacher's assistant in an alternative school by day, and when she wasn't taking women's studies courses at night, she frequented singles bars and juggled relationships with as many as four different men, each of whom thought he was "the only one."

Gerri's moment of truth had come several months earlier, when she discovered her twelfth case of venereal disease. She described compiling a list of men she dreaded to call, sinking deeper and deeper into despair as she ended up with fourteen names. As she sat there wishing the horror would go away, memories of her previous experiences with VD haunted her. "I didn't want to call them, I felt so terrible."

A year earlier she had ignored a pelvic infection until her temperature hit 104 and she nearly collapsed at work and had to be rushed to a hospital, where she was told she was lucky she hadn't died.

When I asked her what it was like to be so sick, she said with some embarrassment, "I would lie there imagining the infection eating away at my insides, scarring and closing off everything." She looked at me to check my reaction. "I know it sounds crazy," she said, "but I wanted something to take away my desire for sex, to kill my sexuality so I could be free."

Gerri's longing to lose her sexuality reflected the powerlessness intrinsic to addiction. If she couldn't stop her sexual acting-out, maybe some twist of fate would kill her sexual desire and free her from the bondage of her addiction.

Gerri continued talking about her life before she joined SAA. She was in the advanced stages of addiction in which the addictive agent, in her case sex, had lost its high and was necessary for mere survival. This had left her trapped in her pain with no escape from a drive that felt totally out of control. It was a terrifying time.

"My life had become a nightmare," she told me. "I felt as if I had a big, empty hole inside. I couldn't get high from anything — not from fantasizing about sex, not from romance, not from cocaine, not from seduction, not even coke and sex together. My whole world had turned to plastic. Everything and everybody was unreal. And there I was in the middle of it.

"My five-year-old-son was acting out, hitting me, crying a lot, and misbehaving. I'm sure it was because of the stress of living with a mother as messed up as I was. He followed me around like a shadow. I hated the terror I saw in his face every time I left him. It reminded me of how I was constantly afraid of being alone as a child. And would you believe, two years ago an agency named me teenage parent of the year? If they only knew! I was also in trouble at the university. My grades were bad, and my counselor said I had only one more chance or I'd flunk out. Then, when I got another case of VD I started fantasizing suicide. That's one thing I vowed I'd never do. My brother killed himself when he was twenty-one. I thought it was a cop-out. But there I was, thinking about killing myself. I can't describe how terrified I felt."

The emptiness, which was the breeding ground for Gerri's sex addiction, was set in motion at her birth. She was the oldest of four girls. Her mother was passive, alcoholic, and emotionally vacant. Her father was alcoholic and violent. Gerri had no memories of feeling safe and secure as a child. Some nights her father would come home drunk and beat all four girls; other times he would rape them. Gerri learned that if she was "nice" to him when he got home, he was more likely to be sexual with her and leave her sisters alone. One can imagine her rage when a counselor later told her that her seductive behavior with men meant that she *wanted* to be sexual.

At one point, when she was eleven, she decided to kill her father and be sent away rather than endure more rape and abuse. "I broke the end off several green wine bottles until I had one with sharp edges. Sometime around ten at night, I hid in the bathroom, standing on the toilet seat waiting for him to walk in. After what seemed like an eternity — probably a half hour — I heard a noise. I heard footsteps coming, the door opened, and I was about to take a swing when I realized it was my sister. She stood there at the door looking up at me standing on the toilet, first with terror, then as if I was crazy. We just stared at each other for a while. I was afraid she would tell Dad about it, but I didn't say anything and neither did she. We just walked away from the bathroom. I was so exhausted I fell asleep."

Alcohol and drugs often become early refuges for abuse victims. The human psyche, under siege, reaches for anything that brings relief. Gerri was an incredible survivor from early on. She started drinking anything she could get her hands on around age nine. She dropped hints to the neighbors about the abuse, and even reported her father to the county on one occasion. A social worker visited the family and Gerri sat helplessly by as her father conned the professional. Afraid of his retribution, and desperate to escape her home situation, she went to school high on marijuana and danced on a lunchroom table, in an attempt to alert the school social worker. Hoping that the juvenile authorities would place her and her sisters in foster homes, she was instead assigned to chemical dependency treatment.

In the treatment program, a male counselor asked a few casual questions about her childhood, but no one thought to ask why this child was acting out so much. This is a problem with traditional forms of chemical dependency treatment which, based on a medical model, treat alcoholism as the problem instead of going beyond the symptom to treat the wounded soul that so often dwells in battered children. Gerri recounted, "One time when I did bring up the incest in a treatment group, the male counselor said, 'That doesn't belong here. We're here to deal with your alcoholism.' Later he told me my sexual acting-out was just part of my drug use. If I stayed sober it would go away."

In Minneapolis in the middle seventies, women founded treatment programs that took a more holistic approach. Among other things, they realized that chemical dependency was often linked to childhood abuse and neglect. Early data revealed between 50 and 80 percent of women coming for treatment were survivors of abuse. One program instituted a separate program for incest survivors; another began an educational program for awareness and made referrals for continued therapy following treatment. Gerri, who was assigned by the county, attended a more traditional program. When she completed treatment, no follow-up care was provided and she was sent home. Within two days her father abused her and she started drinking again. This pattern continued for years, with the focus remaining on her alcohol and drug addiction.

Gerri resumed describing her life prior to joining SAA. "Nothing worked anymore," she lamented. "I was always sneaking around, lying to everybody, and feeling paranoid that one of the four guys I was seeing would bump into another one and there would be a big scene. On top of that, I had broken one of my sacred rules. My sister and I have a pact that we'll never mess with each other's boyfriends, but I had flirted with her boyfriend and we started making out." Again Gerri was describing the powerlessness her addiction created. Her inability to keep her promises to herself left her panicky and ashamed, particularly since she had had so much "help."

"I had been in treatment and halfway houses for alcohol and drugs nine times, nearly half my life, yet the pain had never gone away." Gerri paused for a moment and looked at me. "Can you understand how awful that made me feel?" she said. "It was as if I was beyond repair, a hopeless case. I am so angry that they never asked me questions about my sexual acting-out or my childhood abuse! *Do you know, I flirted with every male drug counselor I ever had, and there was not one I couldn't get to flirt back with me?*" she said, the anger rising in her voice.

Many women express the same frustration of repeatedly going for help but never getting to the core problems of sex addiction and childhood abuse. Gerri felt as if there was no way out because no one named her sexual behaviors as an addiction, an escalating force beyond her control that she used to protect herself from inner pain. Professionals either didn't notice, said she just had a strong sexual appetite, or else, like the male counselors, became part of the problem by engaging in addictive behavior with her. Gerri knew that something was wrong, but without a label, a diagnosis, she was powerless to embark on a path of recovery. This reflects our blindness to sex addiction and codependency. Because such behavior is essentially the norm of the culture, few people see it as a problem.

"Didn't anyone notice, not even the women?" I asked her, easily imagining the male counselors being charmed by this attractive young woman.

"Some of the women counselors saw what was happening," she continued, "but the men, who were always in charge of the programs, wouldn't back them up. One time I overheard a woman counselor telling a male supervisor that he shouldn't flirt with me. At first he acted bewildered, as if he didn't understand what she was talking about. When she pressed him further, he suddenly got angry and said that flirting had nothing to do with drug treatment.

"I'd known for five years, deep inside, that at some level I was using sex addictively," Gerri recalled, "but I never heard the expression 'sex addiction' and I had no idea there were groups where you could talk about it. Then, one day after school, I went out to the parking lot to get my car. There on the windshield was a weekly newspaper with SEX ADDICTION written in huge print on the cover. When I saw it, I was really indignant, but I rushed home to read it. The article was mostly about men and didn't fit too well for me. But then I read the twenty questions of Sex Addicts Anonymous printed at the end. Some of them really got to me: 'Do you sense that your sexual appetite or sexual images, either real or fantasized, are controlling you? Do you use sex to escape from worries or troubles or to relax? Do you use sex to hide from other troubles in your life? Do your sexual activities include the risk of contracting disease?' I was socked in the gut. They were talking about me. It was like a door opening inside of me. Something finally connected with that empty place inside.

"The article said there was a local treatment program for sexual dependency, the first one in the country. The thought of going there to talk to someone passed through my mind, but I just sat on the couch for a long time. Then I called up a guy and asked if I could come over."

A Life-and-Death Struggle

The thought that glimmered for a moment in Gerri's mind about reaching out for help set off her tyrant addict part, causing her to phone a man instead. But Gerri also started having thoughts about doing something about her "problem" . . . sometime.

In the past, her addict part had kept her from taking further steps. However, the recent crises had caused a momentary crack in her denial system, putting her in touch with her painful situation. A series of such little awakenings can lead a person to get help. For Gerri, the repeated cases of VD, thoughts of suicide, and breaking promises to herself awakened her to her terror, creating an openness to the information in the sex addiction article.

When Gerri was "socked in the gut" and felt a connection with "that empty place inside," she touched the truth about herself. But the pattern of thinking about getting help and then being assaulted by the addicted side continued in full force for a long time. A life-and-death struggle was truly taking place. The important thing was that she persevered.

Many people are confused in believing that because they *want* to stop doing something addictive, they should be able to "just stop." Others around them often comment, "She's so stupid for doing that again. She's just weak. She has no moral character." Addiction has nothing to do with weakness. An essential part of addiction is that we are powerless to stop it alone. And it usually takes a painful consequence to jolt a person from her addictive side into awareness. Because Gerri didn't yet understand this, she often assaulted herself verbally whenever she acted out. "How could I have had sex with him when I knew he had herpes? How could I have flirted with my sister's boyfriend?"

It took another crisis to make Gerri take the next step. "For quite a few days I 'forgot' to call the treatment program. Then, one night, my sister and I went to a bar and picked up two guys. God, what a horrible night. The man I was with was attractive, wealthy, and totally drunk. Driving back to my house, we got into an accident. I was in a state of shock when we got home. Even so, I wanted to be sexual. Usually with sex I can make everything go away, but I couldn't that night. During sex I felt dead and sick to my stomach. I was relieved when the guy went home during the night. I had no interest in seeing him again, but my ego was outraged that he didn't call me the next day. I pride myself on getting men to chase after me. I felt panic at the loss of control.

"The next day I called the treatment program, part of a local hospital. I could hardly talk when this cheery-sounding secretary answered. I couldn't say the words Sexual Dependency Unit, so I asked for the Chemical Dependency Unit. When they answered I said, 'Oh, someone must have made a mistake, could you switch me to the er . . . ah . . . Sex . . . ual (whispering) Dependency Unit.' When somebody answered, 'Sexual Dependency Unit, Julie speaking,' I just froze. In a voice I hardly recognized, I said, 'I'd like to make an appointment.' When she said they had an opening for the following day, my heart started pounding. I paused for a minute, then said, quickly, 'I'll take it.'

"I don't remember driving myself there. I was completely numb. I walked into the building and headed for the elevator. I cringed walking past the receptionists in the lobby, hoping they wouldn't ask me where I was going. Julie had told me it was on the third floor. Just as I got near the elevator, I saw an old counselor of mine right in front of me. 'Oh, God,' I thought, 'this is awful. He musn't see me here!' My throat tightened up. I turned around and headed for the stairway across the hall. I got through the door unnoticed and stayed in the stairwell until my heart stopped pounding so hard. I walked upstairs and slowly opened the door on the third floor. He was there again. Feeling totally exposed and wanting desperately to be invisible, I hid again before I walked up to the desk and told the receptionist I had an appointment to see Wilma. I couldn't believe I hadn't backed down. It was a miracle."

"I guess!" I exclaimed, realizing I hadn't said a word in a long time, so engrossed was I in Gerri's vivid story. "Getting yourself to that interview sounds like a journey through a land of demons." She agreed.

"I liked the way Wilma looked as she walked toward me. She was relaxed and friendly and said hello without gushing. I hate gushy counselors. She led me to a nearby room and I hurried in behind her. I started breathing again when the heavy door shut and we were safely inside. Then I thought, 'Oh, my God! This is it. No way to get out of it now.'

"With Wilma, I was totally on guard, ready to discount her at any minute. I was also trembling inside." Gerri paused and looked at me again. She laughed. "I don't mean to sound arrogant, but remember, I've been in seven treatment programs, two mental wards, had six social workers and probably a dozen different counselors, so I know a lot about treatment programs and therapists. If a counselor is uncomfortable, or faking it, I pick it up right away. I also know whether or not they know what they are talking about. So I was checking her out.

"I can't remember exactly what happened, but at some point Wilma started telling me about sex addiction — the desperation, the inability to say no, the terror underneath, the relationship to childhood sex abuse. Suddenly I realized I had let my guard down and was really listening to her. She seemed to know what she was talking about, and she certainly knew about me. I trusted her because she called me on my bullshit. I remember thinking I could no longer tell myself I was unique. Other people apparently had the same problems with sex as I did.

"Her attention didn't falter, even when I told her there was no way I could afford to come to the program. It was then I started to believe she truly cared about helping me. I told her some of my story, leaving a lot out, always checking out her reactions as I talked. Toward the end of the interview she suggested a couple of therapists, gave me the phone number for SAA, and explained a little about their program. Then she showed me a red handbook about women and sex addiction." Gerri suddenly looked at me and said with a grin, "Well, you know, you wrote it." She continued, "I practically grabbed it out of her hand. While I was looking at it, she told me I could buy it at the hospital bookstore.

"After the interview, I hurried downstairs to buy the book. The hospital bookstore didn't have it, so I went to my car and headed for one of the other bookstores she had mentioned. Then the thought, 'Aw, you can wait a while,' popped into my head. So I drove home and called one of my boyfriends. A week later I had contracted a painful case of VD and realized I had to call four guys. I was chatty with them, saying it was from a long time ago. I had just discovered it. Inside I felt sick. I suddenly remembered the name of the bookstore and drove over to buy the handbook.

"When I got home I set it down on the table and thought of a zillion things to do. I changed the Kitty Litter, put away dishes, and generally messed around while that little red book sat on the coffee table and stared at me. Finally I started to read it." She paused. "It really hit home."

"What connected for you?" I asked curiously.

"Saying that sex addiction was 'mistaking sex for God!' really stopped me. I thought of all the awful sex in my life and realized my spirituality was dead. Another part was where you said addiction was the antithesis of spirituality. That really got to me, too. My favorite part was where you said spirituality had a feeling of fullness and hope."

As Gerri talked I couldn't tell if my ego or my healthy side was feeling happy inside. It's one thing to write such an article thinking it might help someone; it's quite another to have someone tell you how it affected and helped her.

"I realized that the secret dream world I kept hidden in my head was exactly what you were talking about. It was right there on those pages — a world where you could make mistakes, where you knew what you wanted, where you felt connected to other people. It wasn't just my isolated dream world. It could exist. It made me want to cry. It gave me hope."

Many women echo Gerri's experience. They maintain a belief that life could be better, despite much life experience to the contrary. That hope, like a semiconscious dream, drifts around in their minds as they yearn for something to confirm their belief.

Gerri proceeded to describe getting into her first SAA group, again a competition between her addict and her healthy sides. In trying to set up a twelfth-step call, in which someone from an addiction recovery group meets informally with a prospective member to share stories and help the person decide if the group meets his or her needs and whether to join, she called and hung up before anyone answered, canceled two appointments to meet with two SAA women — SAA and CoSA traditionally have two group members make the call — acted out several times, and nearly got hit by a car before she finally made it to an interview.

The Twelfth-Step Call

Gerri described the call in which her healthy side overpowered her addicted side and got her to the meeting. "The last time when a woman called me back, she suggested we meet at a local vegetarian restaurant. "Oh yuck,' I thought, 'a bunch of health nuts. We'll never relate.' I started to tune her out on the phone, but a voice inside of me yelled, 'Go!' So I set a time to meet her.

"Two weeks and one more cancellation later, terrified, I headed for the restaurant. I'd made a date to meet a guy afterwards at the bar across the street. I kept wondering if he would see me going to the restaurant. And then I wondered how I was going to get from the restaurant to the bar after our meeting without the women seeing me."

Her description sounded like two people bargaining. The healthy side says to the addicted side, "You let me go have the interview with the women and I'll take you to a bar to meet a guy afterwards." In a sense her healthy side had started conning her addict side.

"When I walked in and looked around, I saw two women in a booth facing the entryway. I could tell they were looking for me. My legs were numb, but I managed to get to the booth and sit down with them. I was relieved to see that one of them was drinking coffee. They introduced themselves. Their manner was gentle, unassuming and friendly, not pushy. They didn't promise me the universe if I joined SAA, which was good. I'm cynical about people who come on like they're 'born again.' When these women talked, I identified with lots of what they said. I told them part of my story. They listened knowingly, nodding their heads. They were like Wilma. They didn't seem surprised, grossed out, or particularly floored by anything I had to say. I knew at that moment I would eventually attend an SAA meeting with these women.

"I got nervous as we walked out of the restaurant together. I wanted them to leave so they wouldn't see me cross the street to meet my friend at the bar. I figured it was okay to be with a guy today since I intended to join the group. I pretended to be going back to my car, but instead stood behind a tree until they left. Then I went over to the bar, feeling very sneaky and hoping no one I knew would see me.

"A week later, the night before going to my first SAA group, I lay awake thinking of all the times I had been through treatment and lived in halfway houses. I lay awake a long time. I had this feeling my life was going to change. All the drug treatment I had been through had never touched the empty feeling in my gut. But the talks with Wilma, and the other women, and reading about spirituality had awakened something. I felt warm inside and I knew I wanted more."

The First SAA Meeting

"A week later, at age twenty-two, I went to my first SAA meeting. There we were, nine women in a grubby church basement lounge. They all looked like normal people! I don't know what I was expecting, but when they laughed and talked just like anyone else I felt better and less weird. I was pretty numb during the first part of the meeting, but when women began to talk personally about their lives and how they were struggling with their sexuality and relationships, I was amazed, I thought to myself, 'They're really talking about this stuff openly. If they can sit around and do this, maybe I can too.' I liked some of the women a lot — they seemed genuine and honest.

"As I looked at them and listened, a thought flickered through my mind: *'I'm willing to give up everything to be well. Everything.'* I'd never thought anything like that before. This was the first time I'd ever felt I could let it all go. *All of it.*"

As Gerri said those words, I looked out the window and realized that dusk was settling in. Over four hours had passed without my realizing it; I was simply overwhelmed by her story. It occurred to me that Gerri had revealed these painful details with little emotion, which was not surprising considering that she was in the beginning stages of recovery. For most people, the story comes first; feelings are connected later. We sat and talked a little longer, giving ourselves time to return to the reality of the day. When she was ready to leave I asked, "Would you be willing to come back and talk to me again when I get to the recovery part of the book, probably about two years from now?" I remember hearing my words, sounding casual and confident as if I wrote books all the time.

"Sure," she said. "Anything I can do to help."

MARTHA: THE DULL ACHE THAT WOULDN'T GO AWAY

I interviewed Martha in the late fall on one of the last warm, sunny days we had before winter set in. She had been in SAA for over three years and was just about to leave. Because of her extensive therapy she was able to reflect quite eloquently on the dynamics of her addiction and its origins in an emotionally neglectful and covertly incestuous family. While Gerri told her story almost as if she was talking about someone else, Martha spoke from within, her face reflecting her feelings.

Martha had a wonderful sense of style and was a comfortable person to be around. She said she wanted to be interviewed because "I feel I need some sort of graduation ritual from SAA, so when I heard you wanted women to interview it felt just right." She added, "I also think it is important to talk about covert incest because no one pays much attention to it. I had all the symptoms of an incest survivor and no 'evidence,' no memories, no words. It made me feel absolutely crazy and took years of therapy to uncover."

Martha used sex both addictively and codependently but it never became a full-fledged addiction as it had been with Gerri. She did not experience the powerlessness of being unable to stop her sexual behavior once she decided to. Even so, her sexually addictive behavior had a profound effect on her life.

To the world, Martha appeared to be someone who had "made it." At thirty-nine, she was an attractive, successful woman, a criminal defense lawyer. She came from a "nice" middle-class professional family and projected the image of a successful, liberal single woman, in charge of her life and confident of her future. She earned a good salary, handled money well, traveled, and had a large circle of friends. But, for thirty-five of her thirty-nine years, Martha struggled alone, concealing the cracks in the picture.

"It was so confusing for me. I did all the right things, but I always had this ominous feeling that something was terribly wrong with me, and I couldn't figure out what it was. I felt as if I had an undiagnosed internal deformity. When everyone was praising me for my success, I felt more and more crazy on the inside. Sometimes, with certain people or in meetings, I would experience a paralyzing fear. Other times I would feel incredibly furious at someone for doing some little thing. I hated myself for doing that. Until I was thirty-six, I never thought my problems had to do with sex or my childhood, which I thought was fairly happy."

Martha described the illusion of control she felt in her sexual relationships during what she called her addictive period. "During the seven years after my divorce, when I had over forty different lovers, I always felt in charge. I was only sexual when I wanted to be. If I met a man I wanted to be lovers with, I'd just let the juices flow and it would happen. I always liked the men; in fact, most of them had high-status positions. I always hoped the relationships would turn into a committed relationship, but they never did. That was what felt so terrible."

She described numerous romantic meetings, highly charged evenings accompanied by candlelight dinners, when the adrenaline started flowing and the evening culminated in passionate sex. The problem was that she could never sustain the high and would lose interest in her partners once she had conquered them. Or if she maintained her interest, she would start feeling her dependency. Not wanting to expose it, she would become cool or indifferent or just plain freeze up and go away, bewildering her partner and herself.

"I was uneasy that none of my relationships resulted in a committed partnership or marriage, but I would tell myself, 'I'm too powerful for a man, I'm too intelligent. Any man would be threatened by me.' Looking back, I realize that getting a man into bed with me was an angry conquest, a way to get him down to my level, whatever that was! If I couldn't be as powerful as a man, then I could have power over his sexuality. The angry part was the cover for how terribly needy I felt and how much I wanted someone to take care of me and love me."

I asked about her childhood.

"I was lonely. I don't have any conscious memory of being held by my mother, and I have vivid memories back to the age of two and a half. I was also raised on a lot of double standards. As a child I always heard comments about when I would get married and 'make some man a nice wife.' At the same time my father adored my competency and treated me like a bright intelligent woman. Even during my horribly depressing marriage, I managed to maintain a dance studio, have elegant dinner parties, and do most of the home repairs." She paused for a moment and sighed. "You know, I did everything I had been taught would make me happy, yet I was miserable.

"It was the same thing when I was little. My parents did all the right things. They took us on picnics, celebrated holidays, and took vacations together. Yet they never gave me what I wanted most." She paused for a moment.

"What was that?"

"Actually, several things come to mind. I was very gifted for dance, yet they sent me to the cheapest teachers once a week when I wanted to go twice. They did enough so they could say they cared about me, but I never felt they *really* cared. I remember when I was seven I wanted a big teddy bear for Christmas. I wanted it in the worst way. I remember scheming to get it because they'd never give me what I asked for. They'd 'surprise' me. I decided that if I asked for only one thing I would have the best chance. We put our Christmas lists on the fridge door. Mine said 'Teddy Bear,' with the page and order number from the Sears catalogue. I remember that my mother kept saying, 'Wouldn't you like a doll?' I kept saying, 'All I want for Christmas is a teddy bear.'

"I still have the picture of myself on Christmas morning standing with my bear, grinning because I got what I asked for. But there was an emptiness, too." Martha sighed and looked down as if contemplating something. "You know, when you have to scheme to get something, you never feel that you really got it."

The teddy bear episode was a metaphor for Martha's childhood. At a basic level it was not all right to ask for what she wanted, emotionally or physically. One way children learn to feel powerful is for parents to believe what they say, and within reason give them what they want. Because direct requests were never honored, Martha came to believe that it was greedy and bad to ask for what she wanted, so she became used to scheming or being vague in asking for things. Moreover, she became deeply ashamed to want anything.

Martha could use her competence to protect herself from the pain of parents who never addressed her emotional needs. She remembered by age three deciding that she would never let her parents see her cry again. Of course, it was a double bind. Children need to cry when they hurt. By holding in her hurts and never crying, she built up tremendous anger, which she attempted to repress. The wall she built around her feelings paralleled the wall she put between herself and other people.

"When I look back it's as if my parents saw me having no needs. They also neglected me. When I was eleven I bet my dad I could swim across the lake we were staying at. He just said, 'Go ahead.' So my sister, who couldn't swim, rowed our little boat and I jumped in and swam across. At the time I felt very proud of myself. It was only later when my therapist looked shocked at that story that I realized you don't let kids swim across a half-mile lake without life preservers and someone competent in a boat.

"Another way I learned to feel crazy inside was that my mother would deny what she had said to me. I'd ask her if I could go to the Saturday movies and she would say yes. Then later, my father would say he wanted me to do something, and I would say Mom had said I could go to the movies. Then, right in front of me, she'd say, 'I never said that,' and I would stand there frozen on the outside but feeling hysterical on the inside. When I'd protest, my father would say, 'Don't talk to your mother that way.' I ended up having all the symptoms of an abandoned child even though my mother was home every day. I still feel hysteria inside when someone blatantly lies to me, but I've learned to say 'That's about my mother; I don't have to get crazy!'

"It took me a ton of therapy to understand that their not noticing my needs — physical, emotional, you name it — was a form of emotional neglect that created a rage inside. I finally understood it full blast when my mother started making out her will.

"My mother asked me what I wanted. The only thing I asked for was her silverware, which had great sentimental value for me. When we read the will after she died, and I found out she'd given it to my brother, I was devastated. At the same time all the major stuff was divided up equally, so I felt like a fool for complaining. Still, I was shattered. During the following year, I bought silverware whenever I got depressed. I remember telling a friend how stupid I felt to be buying silverware to get over my mother." Martha laughed. "A friend said to me, 'If it helps you get over your mother, it's cheap at twice the price!' "

"Really!" I said, laughing with her. "Tell me about your father."

"My father's influence was equally confusing. He was an engineering professor. He was very rational and logical. The only way he knew how to talk was to debate and argue. If I said I learned something exciting in school, he would bring up reasons to question it. He had no idea of how to talk to me as a child. He would explain things in detail, as if I were an adult. When I was nine I asked him about his slide rule. He explained it as if I were one of his college students. I was flattered at the attention and respect for my intelligence, but I couldn't follow his explanation, so I stood there and pretended to understand." Martha stopped herself. "I just realized something as I'm saying this. Until very recently I would get that same feeling of paralysis when I didn't understand something. I'd feel as if I should always know the answer, just as I should have understood the slide rule explanation. I'm still afraid to say I don't understand something because someone might think I'm totally stupid, or yell at me, or tell me to get out of here."

"Can you tell me about the sexual stuff with your father?" I asked.

"It's hard to put it into words. He had this friendship with a sexy, flamboyant woman named Rose who worked with a circus. We joked in the family that she was Daddy's girlfriend, just as if it was normal. I know it bothered my mother, but she never said a word. My father lit up when he talked about this woman and I was immensely flattered when he told me I was 'quite a trouper, just like Rose.' When I met her I thought she was neat. She wore real bright clothes, put her arm around me and called me honey, gave me a present, and talked to me like a real person. I felt so special. I wanted to be just like her."

Martha had been confused in trying to take on the mixed family values. Like all sexually addicted women, she developed a dual sense of herself. Although the surface message in the family was to be a nice woman and wife like her mother, the underlying message was that you put the light in your father's eyes if you act like Rose, a tough, sexy woman with a lot of pizzazz.

The role fathers play in the development of female sex addiction cannot be overstated. Little girls take their cues from their dads. They want that special energy, the light in Daddy's eyes, to be directed toward them. The ache for a warm and affectionate dad who did not sexualize the relationship is deeply etched in the hearts of most women.

Martha attempted to reconcile the dual messages. "I got all A's, excelled at dance, and imagined myself as Rose or as a prostitute. At about age twelve I got obsessed with drawing women in stripper costumes. Once a page of them fell out of my books in school and some boys got hold of it. I was freaked out inside, but then one of the guys said, 'We know it isn't you, but just tell us who it is.' I was totally relieved. Whew! Pretending to be an intensely loyal friend, I dramatically told them I just couldn't tell who had drawn the pictures and I insisted they give the drawings back. I felt a great sense of excitement in fooling those boys. It really fed into my secret addictive world of the high of being sneaky and fooling people by looking nice and innocent."

"Did you have any other signs in your life at that age of the sex addiction stuff?" I asked.

"From ages twelve to fourteen I put myself to sleep at night with fantasies of being ordered to be still by several women who would sexually fondle me. I remember some nights I just couldn't wait to get into bed and start the fantasies. I could feel myself cross over a line to this intense pleasure. It was like a click to another place and all my loneliness was gone." She paused for a moment. "It is so amazing how that works."

The click that Martha recalled is that of crossing the addictive line, out of pain and into euphoria. People experience the same relief by shooting heroin, slugging down a drink, or buying an unneeded article. It is so seductive because it works immediately. In recovery from sex addiction and codependency, people learn to define their addiction by recognizing when they cross over that illusive line of escape.

Martha continued talking about her father. "I often felt uncomfortable with my father touching me or wanting hugs. One time when I was backstage after a dance concert I was in, I turned around and saw him with a glazed-over look in his eyes. He was staring at my body in my leotard. I immediately felt scared and wanted to hide my body. He said, like a puppy dog, 'Do I get a kiss?' It made me feel sick. If I didn't kiss him he would act wounded. He loved me when I was his darling daughter, but if I pulled away or asserted my independence from him by arguing with his beliefs or refusing him hugs or kisses, his ulcer would bleed. Then my mom would say, 'Can't you be nicer to your father? He gets so upset about you!' "

This dynamic gave Martha an exaggerated sense of her power. She could make her father's ulcer bleed. She could render her father despondent or upset for days by refusing him a hug or disagreeing with him. That made hugs awfully important. It created the role reversal that typically takes place in chemically dependent family systems. While there was no apparent alcoholism in her family, Martha recalled that her father had chronic headaches and ulcers for which he constantly took aspirin and stomach acid pills. While it is a moot point whether this would be diagnosed as chemical dependency, her father ran from his feelings with headaches and stomachaches as surely as an alcoholic runs away with alcohol.

As in chemically dependent family systems, neither of Martha's parents maintained a parental role. While a father wanting to give his daughter a hug after a performance could be a wonderfully loving gesture, his wanting the hug for his own needs was what made it feel so awful. As an adolescent desiring autonomy, Martha had learned to wield her power over her father to create distance. "I would alternate between not speaking to him or setting him off. I would poke fun at the uncool engineering students who wore slide rules on their belts. He couldn't see that I was just an adolescent pushing his buttons. He would be absolutely obsessed with me. Our bedrooms were separated by a thin door. Night after night I would hear him lying in bed talking to my mother about me. 'Why does she have to argue with me? Why can't she be nice to me?' I lay there hoping my mother would tell him to shut up. She never did. Then I would hear them have sex. I would feel sick. How I wish he could have laughed at me, or not taken me so seriously."

The sexual implications here are obvious. Martha's father was obsessed with his daughter during sex with his wife. If we accept that mind, body, and spirit operate as one, Martha's mind and spirit were being abused as surely as if he had come into her room and abused her body. In some ways this was more crazy-making, because her feelings could easily be discounted — as they were by several therapists until Martha found one who understood. When a therapist responded, "That's terrible; I can just imagine how awful that must have felt," Martha's sick feelings were finally validated.

Martha's mother also played her role inappropriately. A typical codependent, she acted the good wife at one moment and mocked her husband the next, with a wink to Martha behind his back. Martha remembered the winking as being fun — she felt close to her mother. But when her mother winked at her that way during a family therapy session, the therapist later remarked to Martha that it was cruel of her mother to do this. It set Martha up against her father and made her a peer of her mother's. It was like pulling Martha into the crossfire of the marriage relationship, which was never confronted directly. It was not surprising that Martha commented that, growing up, it had never occurred to her that married people actually loved each other.

Because her parents' actions were sins of omission and just "little things," Martha was thoroughly perplexed about her inner rage and her fear of talking directly with people. She was therefore actually relieved when her father was more overtly sexual with her. She told the story.

"One time when I was sixteen, I was playing bridge with my parents. My father suddenly ran his bare foot up my leg and on to my thigh. He had that same glazed look in his eyes as when he asked me for a hug years earlier. I felt my face burn and said loudly, 'Daddy, don't do that.' My mother asked, 'Don't do what?'

" 'He's putting his foot up my leg.' I remember feeling righteous, as if

I'd caught him in the act. Now I had proof. Mother said real loud, 'Robert!' He said in a kind of foggy way, 'You don't want her to be frigid, do you?' Her eyes bugged out and she said, 'Robert!' again. Then we went on playing bridge as if nothing happened. No one ever mentioned the incident again.

"These memories were in the distant reaches of my mind before I began my therapy. My therapist once described my parents as nurturer-violators. Those are people who appear to care, but are actually concerned with their own needs. They see everything from their own point of view and have difficulty tuning in to other people. The problem in my family was that to the world it looked as if my parents cared. In any case, when I finally crashed into my anger in a therapy group, there was rage that could kill."

We sat quietly for a while. She didn't offer a further explanation of the "rage that could kill," so I asked, "How were your relationships with men?"

"Oh, God," she said with a sigh. "I ran away from good, kind men and went for men who gave me nothing. They were usually exciting, bright, playful, or adventuresome, but totally unable to be involved." Martha smiled as she added, "A little bit like me. I have had some terrible regrets about the men I turned down or left. I also learned in therapy that the reason I froze up sexually was that when I started to get emotionally intimate with a man, memories of the childhood abuse would start to surface and to avoid them I would leave the relationship."

"What was your marriage like?"

"I feel as if we were never *really* married. There was an underlying care for each other, but no communication. I lost interest in sex shortly after the marriage, and had sex with my husband fewer than ten times throughout our four-year marriage, all of it after drinking and all of it pretty awful. It was as if once I had succeeded in marrying a man who would give me security and status, I lost interest in sex. He kept saying things would get better, and I believed him. I had no idea how to ask for anything or how to work on anything. Looking back, I think I got married to please my mother. She was always talking about when I'd get married, and some of it sunk in and I felt I just had to get married. As if something was really wrong with me if I didn't."

"What happened during the marriage?"

"I died inside. I got so depressed, I could barely move. I'd have periods of activity, teaching dance and going back to school, but the minute I stopped, I just fell asleep all the time. Sometimes I'd sleep fifteen hours a day, but I'd still get up and have a nice dinner on the table and pretend everything was all right. I even got a job as a Kelly girl for a while, just to stay awake. My husband quietly had affairs, which he denied even though one of his girlfriends called me.

"When I was twenty-eight, on an evening when my husband didn't show after calling to say he'd take me to the movies, I made a suicide attempt with alcohol and sleeping pills. I know it sounds awful, but it didn't feel like a big deal because I felt so dead inside. And partly I didn't want to really die, I wanted my husband's attention. I remember waking up late the next day on the couch in the study feeling indescribably horrible, as if a truck had run over me. I was still in my dress and cold from having no cover over me. Yet I had this feeling of calm. And then this thought went through my head like a light turning on. I could have actually killed myself. It was *me* I was hurting. It had felt like someone else.

"I remember thinking, 'What a desperate thing to do for somebody's attention.' And of course it didn't work. That suicide attempt really jolted me. I told a friend about it a couple of days later and ended up crying for the first time in years, realizing how painfully unhappy I was to want to kill myself. I know that may sound strange, but it was as if I had sunk into a big, dark hole little by little and I didn't even realize it was happening. It took that suicide attempt to shake me loose."

Martha fit the stereotype of a codependent woman during her marriage. She expected her happiness to come from filling a certain role — wife, nice home, enough money, parties, and looking good to the world. The only thread tying her to a sense of self was teaching dance. Her other behaviors were all directed at getting her husband to talk to her, be nice to her, give her what she wanted. The suicide attempt was another way of saying, "Notice me." Fortunately, it acted as a wake-up alarm to her profound codependency, which had led her to abandon herself.

"I went to a therapist. He was very direct in telling me that I had lost myself in the marriage. He said I was attractive and talented and a nice person, and the marriage had made me neurotic, which didn't help me understand my part, but it was nice to hear him say that anyhow. He had been a professor of my husband's in graduate school. He said my husband was incapable of giving me the love I wanted and that he was abusing me and that the longer I stayed, the more it reinforced his doing it. That word *abusing* totally shocked me. I had thought my husband was perfect and that there was something wrong with me. It only took three sessions for me to accept that I needed to leave the relationship. I was scared, but I remember thinking to myself, 'I'd rather work in the dime store and live in a single room than be so unhappy.' I can't tell you how happy I felt to have that thought. It was like finding the lost me inside. It was wonderful."

What separates Martha from the more deeply entrenched codependent women was that it took only three therapy sessions for her to gather the courage to leave her marriage. She was also willing to give up the external trappings of a privileged life and take what came without guarantees of security, which is what locks most codependent women into their suffering. The other part, paradoxically, was her profound depression, which belied a knowledge of her self-betrayal. While depression is often anger turned inward, and that was certainly true for Martha, it is also a symptom of loss of self. But Martha had a self to return to, unlike women who have never developed a career or experienced a passion for some type of endeavor in their lives. I have seen many women who stayed in miserable marriages for years — through depression, illness, and death of the spirit — rather than face life on their own.

Shortly after her separation, Martha fell in love with Philip. Feeling exhausted and weary, she was extremely surprised when Philip called her after learning she had separated. He had seen her perform at dance concerts and they had met at a recent party. It was through this relationship that she discovered the power of her sexuality, both for herself and for her ability to attract men. While there were many positive healing aspects to the relationship, she also switched from a codependent role to more of an addictive role.

"We had a tremendous sexual attraction for each other. It was the first time I enjoyed sex. He talked so easily about sex and feelings. It was a tremendous change. He was fun, creative, and playful. I felt loved. We would look at each other when we made love, hold hands in the movies, take walks, and just hang out together. Knowing him was very healing. He was both a friend and a lover. My depression vanished, life was full of excitement, my creativity returned, and I felt free."

Martha thought she had discovered a cure for the depression that had nearly killed her. In reality the source of the depression had not been healed. The tip-off to her switch of addictions was the instant disappearance of her chronic depression when she and Philip became lovers. You can't get over depression that easily. On the positive side, being cared for and feeling the power of her sexuality brought energy back to a body that had felt lifeless. It rekindled Martha's love of dance and ignited her passion for life, even though she was still looking for validation outside herself. Then, even though she and Philip were still lovers, an event occurred that signaled Martha's addictive part was crystallizing.

One night after a dance performance in a nearby town, Martha went home with a musician, had sex with him, and spent the night. He, too, was attracted to Martha, and once again she found the sex pleasurable. She was also surprised that she didn't feel guilty. She remembered telling a friend, "Now I understand how men feel. It didn't mean anything about not loving Philip, I just enjoyed being with him and having sex."

While she maintained her euphoria for a time, within a few months depression crept in. Meanwhile a significant step in Martha's spiritual awakening took place. "Something else very important happened to me. It was how I learned to listen to my gut. I had this feeling deep inside me that there was going to be a big change in my life. It was through that experience I learned that when I have a question or want something to happen, I just say, 'I want it to happen' and put the thought on the back burner like a pot of stew and live my life as honestly as I can. Anyhow, the change came when I was visiting some friends in New York. One of them mentioned an opening in a dance company. On a last-minute lark, I auditioned and was accepted. It all felt just right."

Leaving Philip was difficult, but some of the high was fading, and Martha was ripe for a change. While she enjoyed her work as a dancer in New York, she experienced a series of dead-end relationships that reinforced the ominous feeling of being defective. Most of the time her denial system would take hold after a disappointment, and she would immediately become involved with someone else. Often the relationships overlapped. But after four years she could not keep her buried depression at bay with sexual relationships. Without consciously understanding why, she decided it was time for another change. Having earned a master's degree in dance before her marriage, she qualified for a teaching job at a midwestern university.

"The university was a good atmosphere for me. It woke up a part of me that had been lost while I was in New York. Feminism was blossoming and I started making friends with several active feminists. I decided to stay out of sexual relationships for a while. At first I felt nervous about it, but there was tremendous freedom in it, too."

"What role did avoiding relationships play in your recovery?"

"As I look back, I think it was two things. First, it was a very healthy way of stopping a pattern that was obviously not working. It also freed me to get immersed in other things, particularly the feminist movement and my work. The other part was that without having help to understand what was going on, there was still this nagging voice in the back of my mind: 'You're defective. You're destined to be alone. You'll never have a sexual relationship that works. People will always abandon you.' As much as I tried not to think about it, these thoughts felt like truths. A couple of years later I put on extra weight for the first time in my life, felt the depression creeping in, and, once again, went to see a psychologist."

It was then that Martha started, for the first time in years, to think about her childhood and to consider changing her career. Her interest in dance was waning, and she wanted her work to be more powerfully integrated with women's struggles. She thought of studying law, something that had appealed to her as an undergraduate but had seemed out of reach.

After considerable preparation and thought Martha left her dance career and went to law school. As she talked about this I remembered Sandra Butler's description of childhood abuse as a psychological time bomb. Martha's career change was certainly an important step in her recovery, but it was also once again a way to submerge her depression, which was the cover for her abuse. Because she was so well equipped to use work as an escape, the cycle continued for many years before the ravages of her childhood neglect caught up to her.

While at law school, Martha was a volunteer at a women's resource center. Its workshop on incest turned out to be the catalyst for the time bomb of Martha's pain to explode. "It seemed totally out of the blue that I felt compelled to go to that workshop. But the urge was so strong, I changed several appointments so I could make it. I still remember the beautiful May day I waltzed into the workshop that changed my life.

"Right from the first lecture I started recognizing patterns in myself and my family. It was like bam, bam, bam. This fit, that fit. They talked about shame, pain, secrets, neediness, isolation, fear, being the family scape-goat, the competent cover, sexual acting-out. In a lecture on victim behavior and incest-family systems I became overwhelmed with dizziness and thought I might pass out. I left the lecture room, stumbling over a chair on the way to the door. I headed to the women's bathroom, sat down on the floor, and leaned against the wall. A torrent of tears broke loose and I cried as never before in my life. I was just amazed at the power of the feelings. Evidently my tripping over the chair alerted one of the presenters, who came into the bathroom. She sat down at my side, put her arms around me, and held me while I cried. It was the first time that I could remember ever crying in someone's arms. After I stopped crying, she looked at me kindly and said, 'Are you a victim?' 'I don't know, but it feels like it,' I said, feeling like a little girl.

"She brushed the hair out of my eyes and said, 'Yes, it does.' "

As a result Martha joined an intensive incest treatment program. The warmth and care she received provided a striking contrast to the emotional starvation of her family, and she began to understand her rage and emptiness.

"I felt completely safe saying anything. I can't tell you what a relief it was to let down that competent exterior. The women instinctively understood my pain. When I read my first step later in an SAA group — a history of my family and how I had used sex addictively — I remember the women putting their arms around me while I cried. It was so wonderful. Tears were really sweet for me because I had so rarely cried in my whole life. I had held in so much and it again was a relief to let go."

"And the depression?"

"It's barely visible now. Sometimes it lurks just outside the window, but it's like I can blow it away if I work at it. I've learned a lot of skills for easing depression. I don't live in fear of it overwhelming me anymore. I feel as though the source of the emptiness is no longer there. Before, it used to descend on me and I felt absolutely powerless to do anything about it except work. And sometimes even that didn't work. What's best is that the ominous feeling — sort of like this nightmare demon inside of me, this feeling of being defective — is gone."

"What do you think it was?"

"It was the pain of my childhood and not feeling loved. I had buried a lot of pain and anger, and I finally got it out and someone listened . . . and put her arms around me. All my addictive sexual stuff, and the drinking that went with it, faded away as I healed the incest wounds."

ANITA: NO LANGUAGE FOR LIFE

Anita, who belonged to the same SAA group as Martha and Gerri, sounded painfully shy when she called. She betrayed her uneasiness by a nervous laugh and her frequent question, "Do you know what I mean?" following a statement. Over the three years that followed, I watched with great amazement Anita's perseverance and tenacity in the face of her fears and uneasiness. There was a tremendous will to heal beneath her self-effacing exterior. She participated in a lengthy individual interview and three group interviews, always saying in advance, "I don't know if I'll know what to say, but I'll probably learn a lot and it's good for me to keeping talking about this stuff." Like most of the women who contributed to this book, she also hoped her story of her pain and struggles would make a difference to someone else.

After our first talk Anita called a couple of times to find out if I had written it up yet. She didn't want to bother me, but she was curious to see it. She came to get the pages as soon as they were typed. A couple of days later she called and said, "Gee I feel so sad for me after reading about me. This stuff is really big, isn't it?"

"Yes, it is," I replied. "Your story really touched me, and I'm impressed with what you've done to change your life."

There was something paradoxical and delightful about the process with Anita. She'd tell me her story, I'd write it, she'd read it, and then could better believe her own experience. For Anita there was magic in the written word, providing a mirror that brought reality to her experience. I liked being part of the process.

Anita and I talked on the phone fairly often. She kept me updated on what was going on with her, and we occasionally had breakfast together, sometimes including Gerri. When I heard that I had a publisher for the book, she was the first person I thought to call. She had been rooting for the book with such warmth and had already given so much time. Most of all, I wanted her to know that her story would probably make a difference in someone's life.

Anita did not experience overt sexual abuse or physical violence as a child. The source of her addiction was an emotionally impoverished childhood divided between her mother's obsession with her physical appearance and her father's aloofness coupled with his use of pornography. To begin, I asked her to tell me about her family background.

"My parents gave me no words. There was nothing," she stammered, trying to find an explanation for a nameless experience.

"Kind of like . . . no language for life?" I offered.

"That's it," she said. "No language for life. My father had the air of someone important, and he was very distant, very unconcerned. He always seemed preoccupied and my mother was always saying not to bother him. He was a high school counselor. My mother was preoccupied with the way I looked. She would tell me to gain weight, lose weight, exercise my calf muscles so my legs would be more attractive. She thrived on buying me cute clothes."

"How was that for you?" I asked.

"Awful! It was like my body was never okay. I just hated myself. When I was about twelve, I came home from school one day and found a bag on my bed with two padded bras in it."

"She just left them on the bed?" I groaned inside.

"I felt sick and so ashamed. But I was afraid not to wear them for fear of hurting her. The first time I wore one of the bras under one of my 'cute' dresses, my father suddenly noticed me and looked at my breasts in a way that made me squirm."

Because nothing was ever discussed in her family, Anita could not find words to refuse to wear the bras. Although it felt noxious to wear them, it was preferable to threatening her tenuous relationship with her fragile mother. This is typical of children in emotionally impoverished homes. They deny knowledge of their needs and wants in a frantic search for the food of life, namely, love and approval. Their inner thoughts center around what they can do to get their parents' attention, which is basic training for codependency.

Anita continued to describe the emotional desert of her childhood. "There was no music in our house. No one told stories, made jokes, or fought. No one ever argued. I remember, day after day, coming home from school, standing at the door of my home, and feeling sick. I didn't want to go in. I didn't know why. I only knew I hated to be home."

It is not surprising that she stopped at the door, not wanting to enter the abyss that lay within. There is a terror in the silence she described. (I thought of Gerri's house, the flip side of the coin, households with constant chaos, violence, and overt abuse. While Gerri's home life sounded like a war zone, Anita's sounded like the morning after the bomb had dropped.)

"Did you talk when you ate together?" I asked, fishing for something positive.

"Not *with* each other. They only said things like, 'Why did you get such bad grades?' And then they would never wait for an answer or really sit down and talk about it. I had this fantasy of my mother putting her arm around me and saying, 'Seems like you're having trouble in school, dear; any idea what's wrong?' But my mother was a shadow of my father. If he wanted to drink, she'd have a drink. If he wanted to talk, she would sit and listen. It's like she didn't really exist. The main thing I got from her was the message that I was *only* a body and that you always do everything a man wants. I was so hungry for their approval."

Anita's mother was profoundly codependent. I asked various questions about her, but Anita couldn't find anything that gave her mother an identity. She seemed like a ghost. I imagined how frightening it must have been for Anita as a child, having this person called Mother, a body walking around but with no energy or warmth emanating from it.

"Did they teach you about sex?" I asked.

"I didn't know anything about my body, about having periods, nothing. The messages I got about sex were that it is important and disgusting. One time, when I was nine years old, kids were getting in trouble at school for writing f-u-c-k on the bathroom walls. I felt left out because I didn't know what it meant, so I asked my mother. For a split second, her eyes flashed with terror; then, in a shocked voice, she said, 'Wherever did you hear a word like that?' I wanted to die inside. I felt like the dirtiest person in the world. I was also mad because I wanted to know what the word meant. I never again asked my mother anything about sex."

Knowledge is power for children. Not knowing about sex or the language used by their peers sets them up to be victimized by schoolmates, who have an uncanny knack for picking out vulnerable children to scapegoat.

Dad's Inner World

"Tell me more about your dad," I said.

"My dad stayed away from home most of the time. He had lots of evening school gatherings to attend. When he was home, he sat around drinking or went up to his attic room to work. His 'work' was something of a mystery to me until I was thirteen years old."

Anita finally discovered the nature of Dad's "work." "One day, my older sister, Mary, came into my room with a funny grin on her face. 'Do you want to see something?' she asked. 'Sure,' I said. She took a book from behind her back and showed it to me. It was a pornographic novel. 'Daddy wrote this,' she said. 'Geez. How cool!' I thought, 'My dad writes dirty books!' I was impressed. I already idolized him for being intelligent and working with kids.

"I asked Mary if I could keep the book. She said, 'Yes, but don't tell Dad.' After she left my room, I started to read it. I was fascinated. Something very exciting welled up inside of me. I devoured the descriptions of women."

"What were they like?"

"It was soft porn about women turned on for hours, having blissful, endless, ecstatic orgasms." Anita finally had some information about her father and about sex. Here at last was information about relationships, sex, and life. As she said later, "It molded my belief that relationships *are* sex."

Anita had found the solution to her emptiness. "One day I sneaked into my dad's study upstairs when he was gone and started looking through his bookshelves. I remember a delicious turn-on from my secret search through his study. I would pull out the pornographic books he had written and look through them one by one. It soon became a ritual to sneak into his study, pick out a book, creep back to my room, get on my bed, and read the book while masturbating. There would be a kind of click as I got started, and then I felt very close to my father and very happy inside. It also had a kind of neat, dirty feeling to it. Here was Dad at last. This is what he was thinking about. This was what he was doing all day Sunday in his study! What I learned from reading my father's books was that the answer to everything is sex. So of course I wanted to try it.

"At thirteen, I asked this guy to have sex with me. The sex was icky and I didn't have the wonderful feeling my father described in the books. I was terribly disappointed. I got obsessed wanting to have those feelings. I slept with a lot of guys at school and got a bad reputation. I felt so bad about it I started smoking dope every morning at the bus stop.

"During school I was so preoccupied with fantasies about getting home and masturbating that I started failing. By the time I was fifteen, I was going to parties every night, and by sixteen I dropped out of school and had slept with a ton of men. I always thought if someone asked I had to say yes, just like my mother. I never thought someone might find out, or I'd get a disease or get pregnant. By then I had a reputation all over town. I would wake up late in the morning, smoke dope, go to a friend's house, shoot speed, go to a party, and drink at night."

"And your folks never said anything?" I thought about Anita's father as a high school counselor.

"No. At seventeen, I was busted at a party for shooting speed. After I spent the night in jail on drug charges, my father came to the police station to pick me up. He was friendly and took me to lunch and never said a word about the arrest or the night in jail. Two hours after we got home, I left to go partying again. My parents didn't even try to stop me!

Can you believe that? There were no rules in my house. None! Their behavior made no sense to me."

Anita's sexual relationships were a combination of sexual codependency and addiction. In her search for love she sought men to be sexual with, but the codependent part left her unable to have any control over whom she slept with. While Martha controlled the relationships — "I'd turn on the juice and they'd come" — Anita had no sense of control.

"At nineteen I left home and moved to a nearby city to live with my sister. In the midst of all the parties, I trained as a typist and secretary. I don't know how I ever got through. When I got a job, I had no idea of how to behave appropriately. I always ended up having an affair with someone in the office. I'd smoke dope in the morning, go to work, and spend the whole day fantasizing about being sexual with my lover or flirting with him. When one of the guys at work told me to stop flirting with him, I couldn't understand, and I'd ignore his requests to stop. Weekends were a blur of drinking and sex. Needless to say, my attention on the job was lousy. Besides that, having those affairs at work created so much tension all around that I would eventually get fired.

"Then I met a guy named Mike. I really fell for him. He'd flatter me when we first went out and bring me roses. I thought for a while that maybe this affair would work out, that I'd be happy forever. He liked to read pornography when we were about to have sex. At first it was *Playboy*-type stuff. I was relieved to know other people used pornography for sex. Sometimes we'd read it together. Then he started bringing home pictures of women in weird positions. I didn't want to do what was shown in the pictures, but I was desperate not to lose him, so I went along with it for a while. The only reason I did *any* of that stuff was because I so desperately wanted to be loved. I feel sick when I think of it now."

Again Anita, once involved in a relationship, rapidly moved from addiction to codependency and would do anything to keep a partner.

"The more crazy stuff we did, the more attached I became to Mike. I wanted to be with him all the time. But, like all the other guys, he started getting impatient with my constant demands for his attention. He started avoiding me. I would drink before I saw him and then grovel for his attention and beg him not to leave me. I was depressed when he wasn't around. Finally, he broke up with me and married my roommate soon afterwards. God, that hurt!

"I felt ugly, worthless, defective, and abandoned. I had done everything sexual he wanted, so I couldn't understand why he left me. After that, waking up in the morning was torture. Inside my head I screamed that I hated men. I told myself that I'd never have sex again. But what else was there in life? I had no idea. I wanted to get back at him so bad that I went on a four-day drinking binge and slept with five different guys. I got crabs and gonorrhea. Then I felt even worse and got terribly depressed.

"Nearly every night after work I wandered into a bar. If I found someone to sleep with, the filled-up feeling after sex would only last a moment. If I couldn't find anyone, I would come home and cry. I had more and more difficulty finding men to sleep with and my crying jags got longer and longer. On top of that, I started having difficulty getting high on sex."

The addiction moved into the advanced stage as the high of sex wore thin and Anita was no longer able to fend off the pain. It is not unusual in the addictive cycle that unmanageability in all aspects of life escalates at this point.

"My life got even worse after that. I started being late for work, and I was exhausted much of the time. One night I spent a lot of time fixing myself up for a party. Right after I got there, a guy made an ugly remark about my makeup. I picked up a bottle of vodka and drank nearly half of it. On the way home, I was arrested for drunk driving. A few days after that I got arrested on a second drunk driving charge. That night, after I got home, I felt terrible. I clawed at my arms until they bled. Two days later I found out I was pregnant. My life was utterly desolate. I remember screaming to an unseen power, 'Please take this pain away. I don't know how much longer I can go on.'

"I was sentenced to fifteen days in the workhouse, to be followed by chemical dependency treatment. In the two days before I went to the workhouse, I had an abortion and was fired from my job. Every inch of my body ached. I cannot describe the loneliness and terror I felt. Those fifteen days in the workhouse were the low point in my life. I felt hollow and ate sweets the entire time. I wandered around hopeless, staring out the windows. Every hour without drugs or sex was excruciating. No one visited me — not my parents, not my friends, not anyone. I occasionally said hello to the women there, but I had no idea what else to say. I'd never really talked with women before. I thought of my friends. Why didn't they come to see me? I went straight from the workhouse to an in-patient chemical dependency treatment program.

"When I got into treatment I was ready to be helped. But the program addressed alcohol and drug abuse only. No one ever asked questions about sex, so I never talked about it. In fact I started having sex with a man going through the program. I didn't ask the counselors if it was okay, but since they didn't say anything, I didn't worry about it. Mostly they kept saying that if I stayed off drugs I would be okay. All my other problems would go away."

It was a familiar story: the narrow vision of the treatment program, the counselors' inability to recognize sexually addictive behavior, and their lack of knowledge about childhood abuse. Some treatment programs do prohibit sexual relationships with other people in treatment, but the one Anita attended did not.

Sex and AA

"After completing treatment, I joined an AA group and started having sex with a couple of men in the group. But without alcohol sex didn't work, so in a few months I started drinking again. I told myself it was just a little slip. Within a few weeks I was back to partying and having sex every night.

"Over the next two years I would be sober for a while, abstain from sex for a while, lose jobs, try different AA groups, live with different people. At one point I stayed in one AA group for a year and a half. I call that my shame group. At first the men would be real friendly and tell me what to do. When I didn't follow the program their way, they would start making icky comments about me and ask me a lot of questions about my sex life."

"In a predatory way?"

"Yes. One time, after I told my story in front of the whole group, a bunch of them started saying things like, 'You're seductive, you're a whore, you're just after sex all the time.' They whacked away at my self-esteem. I remained sober, sure, but came to hate myself as a woman, even more than before! But I figured that since the group was keeping me sober, they must be right. I didn't realize then that I kept *myself* sober."

Anita's story of her AA group is one I have heard repeatedly in various forms. Women like Anita go to AA and, feeling vulnerable and desiring guidance, they are easy marks for predatory men who, needing to shore up their own self-esteem, play the role of all-wise mentors. Many women who go through treatment are survivors of abuse, and with their protective shield of alcohol or drugs removed, they are very close to their pain and longing for someone to take care of them. For this reason I suggest that women attend all-female recovery groups, at least in the beginning of recovery and until they can hold their own and recognize when they are being seduced.

"How did you get into SAA?" I asked her.

"One day, I bumped into a woman I had met in treatment. She asked me out for coffee. I told her about sleeping with the men in my AA group who called me a whore. She was so nice I couldn't believe it. She asked me if I had ever heard of SAA, a twelve-step group for women who felt out of control with their sexuality. I remember saying, 'No kidding, a group of women who talk about sex.' Something inside of me clicked.

"A couple of weeks later, on my birthday, I met with two women from an SAA group and went straight from there to my first meeting. It was very scary to go to the group, but I was ready. I was lonely and in terrible pain. It was completely different from the 'shame' group. The focus was on loving yourself and filling up the emptiness. They often said things like, 'Be gentle; everyone has slips along the way.' I didn't feel judged about anything. That's when I finally started to heal."

These stories may bring instant recognition for some of you and leave others confused or overwhelmed. You may have found assorted pieces that connect. It is important to know that you don't have to understand immediately. If something touches you, I suggest you trust those feelings. Many people have the experience of being touched by something before they have a cognitive understanding, that is, before they find words or memories to validate the experience.

Many women who join SAA groups are completely unaware of anything having been amiss in their families. But as they listen to other women's stories, memories of childhood abuse or neglect surface. Their acceptance of what they believed was normal behavior gives way to rage and sorrow as they recognize what they missed during childhood.

While the stories of Gerri, Martha, and Anita have some striking differences in terms of background, family, and experiences, these three shared a profound desire to find the kind of love that would fill the terrifying emptiness left from the ravages of childhood abuse and neglect. All three mistakenly used sex and relationships to fill that emptiness, until they found other, more genuine sources of love and power.

CHAPTER 6

From Grace Kelly to Prostitution:
How Sex Addiction and Codependency Intertwine

> *My addict developed to take care of my codependent feelings, particularly her victim feelings of being empty, having no personal power, and being unlovable.*
> — Kim, a recovering SAA member

YOU MAY have noticed that each of the women described in Chapter 5 had some traits of sexual codependency and sex addiction. Gerri's primarily addictive behavior was a cover-up for her deep dependency, which surfaced when she started to recover. Martha's modus operandi was codependency during her marriage, followed by a period of sexually addictive behavior. Anita's codependency and addiction intertwined, operating almost simultaneously.

Prostitution, as you will see, is, in many ways, a microcosm of the interwoven nature of sex addiction and codependency in women. Our society's attitude toward women engaging in prostitution gives us yet another mirror for reflecting on our own internalized sexual values and our double standards about sex.

On pages 100 and 101, I refer back to the continuum at the top of the model in Figure 4.1 on page 45, showing addiction and codependency at opposite extremes, with healthy sexuality between them. The following illustrations show what happens when we bend that continuum into a circle. Sex addiction and sexual codependency now appear closely related and opposite to spiritually integrated sexuality.

What do the two modes of behavior have in common? Both are dysfunctional uses of sex in a mistaken search for love and power. The addicted woman uses sex to feel in control, to feel attached to someone, and to hide her pain. The codependent woman allows herself to be used sexually to maintain a relationship that brings the illusion of security and provides structure in her life.

The switch that flips a woman from codependency to addiction is usually anger. "You've been pushing me around long enough. I'm going to get back at you. I can screw somebody too." A woman may go out and sleep with her partner's best friend, start flirting in front of him, or make hurtful comments — anything to inflict on her partner the pain she has felt for so long. This kind of acting-out may feel like sweet revenge even if the feelings are momentary.

These newfound feelings of power and control can seem lifesaving. Remember Martha: falling in love after her divorce took away the depression that had led her to a suicide attempt. Because romance and sex addiction generate a lot of energy and usually lead to meeting new people, for many women they come as a welcome relief from the passivity and hopelessness of codependency. That's not to say sex addiction ultimately works, but it does create the illusion of control.

Some women act out the codependent and addictive aspects of their personalities differently with men and with women. For example, one woman had sexually addictive relationships with numerous men, always leaving them before she became attached or vulnerable. However, when she fell in love with a woman, she became dependent. She was sexual when she didn't want to be and found herself compromising her values to keep her partner involved with her. Several women have told me it was

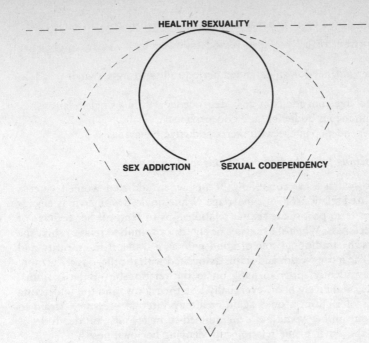

HEALTHY SEXUALITY

SEX ADDICTION   SEXUAL CODEPENDENCY

easy to be detached with men, but that a bond was more likely to develop in sexual relationships with women.

IF I CAN'T GET LOVE, I'LL TAKE SEX

Nearly every woman I interviewed expressed an unfulfilled longing to be loved, a longing that flowed like a river back to childhood. As lonely, unhappy, and sometimes desperate teenagers, they were left casting about for something to make them feel good. Slowly, by trial and error, patterns evolved. A young woman felt euphoria the first time a date touched her sexually and soon had many sexual partners at an early age. Another woman discovered that men pursued her when she was aloof, so she cultivated a cool demeanor. Another drew attention by being outrageous.

Inborn temperament, family programming, and internalized cultural messages combine to form patterns of codependency and addiction. Because neither attitude generates a feeling of power from within — precisely because both are *roles* as opposed to genuine expressions of self — women shift from one to another.

Some of the basic patterns women describe include

- addiction for an extended period followed by a switch to codependency.
- codependency for an extended period followed by a switch to addiction.
- switching from addiction to codependency within a single relationship.
- simultaneous addiction and codependency.
- codependency image with secret addictive behavior.

Switching from Addiction to Codependency

This switch most commonly occurs when addicted women enter a committed relationship or a marriage. While single, a woman may engage in short-term passionate sexual relationships to fend off her feelings of powerlessness. When she marries or enters a committed relationship, she accepts the traditional role of good wife as a tradeoff for security and form. The more wealth and status associated with the marriage, the more she may silently suffer to hang on to the relationship. But the status, security, and lovely home eventually lose their glow, and the underlying feelings of emptiness once again create an internal pressure. Afraid to strike out on her own, and programmed to believe in "till death do us part," she clings to the relationship, denying her own needs.

The woman's need to control may become directed toward her partner and her children. Her sexual interest may wane or she may go numb during sex. She may keep the addictive side buried with compulsive or addictive attachments to clothes, redecorating, cultivating a community image, romantic fantasies, romance novels, TV, medication, alcohol, drugs, or food. She may also develop numerous physical symptoms.

James Spada's best seller, *Grace: The Secret Lives of a Princess*, portrays Grace Kelly as a woman whose search for love and power took her down a difficult path of self-sacrifice, leading to loneliness, isolation, struggles with alcohol, and possibly suicide. The glitter aside, her story reads like the unenviable stories of countless sexually addicted and codependent women.

Openly rejected by her father, and taught by a mother that appearances are everything, Grace experienced a profound emptiness at an early age. While her father rejected her emotionally, he apparently thought he owned her sexuality, a common trait among fathers of sexually addicted and codependent women. According to Spada, when Grace became sexually involved with her acting teacher, Don Richardson, nine years her senior, her outraged father first offered to buy him a Jaguar and then threatened to break every bone in his body if he didn't stop seeing Grace.

The following is Richardson's description of the actress in Spada's biography.

She rebelled against the heavy-handed moral strictures forced upon her and became sexually promiscuous. . . . I began to see the other side of her nature, which was that she was cold as steel. She was like a Patton tank on her way somewhere. . . . She screwed everybody she came into contact with who was able to do anything good for her at all . . . agents, producers, directors. . . . It wasn't that she was a nymphomaniac, in any way at all. I saw no signs of that.

She was a normal girl. *But she just had a terrible need to have someone put his arms around her. What she needed, constantly, was reassurance that she existed.* She was starved for affection because of the family. She was afflicted with a great sense of emptiness, terrible loneliness, and this was her way of alleviating it. (Emphasis added)

In her marriage to Prince Rainier of Monaco, Grace replaced the intensity of steamy passion and stardom with a codependent's dream of security and form — a prince, a palace, and numerous rituals to fill her life. Spada's description depicts many traits of codependency. According to Spada, "Rainier frequently vented his anger and frustration on his wife. She, characteristically, remained calm, allowing him to let off steam. But the pressures built up in her too, and household staff members often saw her wandering the palace corridors in the middle of the night, unable to sleep."

Rainier's difficulties as leader of his country placed great strain on Grace and often left her isolated from the wives of the opposition leaders. As is so common for codependent women, the strain took its toll physically. After the birth of her first child, Grace had two miscarriages and was hospitalized for an intestinal problem that was reported as appendicitis. On returning from her last visit to her dying father, Grace was met by rumors that her husband was having an affair, and she began to suffer from depression. When she received an offer to make a movie (paradoxically, playing the part of the Virgin Mary), she deferred to her husband's wishes that she stay home. They fought continually over her desire to resume her career. When a second opportunity arose he *permitted* her to make the film, provided it did not interfere with her official duties. This time she succumbed to pressure from her subjects to remain in her role of princess. At this point, Grace worked to convince herself, as Spada says, of "the correctness of sacrifice and unselfishness," the perfect motto for the codependent.

The years rolled on. Struggles with her children often mirrored her own rebellion. Her husband withdrew from her when, once again trying to nourish her own identity, she went on a poetry reading tour. She drank more heavily and gained weight toward the end of her life.

The mystery of the fatal car accident has never been solved, but some suspect suicide. The driver of the truck behind her said no brake lights went on when she came to the curve in the road. Instead of slowing down she sped up and sailed off the cliff. She may have had a stroke, as some suggest, but that, too, could have been at least partially a result of great unhappiness and stress. (There has also been speculation of murder, by Mafia members who tampered with her brakes, but Spada stands by the original story.)

When I think of Grace Kelly I can't help thinking of women's magazines. The women who appear most frequently on the covers are those who have elevated their status by marrying wealth and power — Princess Di, Jacqueline Kennedy Onassis, and most recently, Sarah Ferguson. Before her death, Grace Kelly was high on the list. These magazines are largely devoted to articles about homemaking and keeping sex alive. The ads, with few exceptions, reinforce the idea that women should be sexy or create an image that attracts rich and powerful men — a message that blocks passionate, sustained, loving sex. They teach women that power is achieved through appearance and marriage to important men, which in reality leaves women feeling internally powerless. Staying sexually responsive and alive depends on feeling powerful within.

I believe we are fascinated with these women because their lives magnify the dilemmas all women face. We are told that marrying status and wealth will make us happy. Yet somewhere inside of us, we long to know it isn't true, because few of us could make it even if we tried. Moreover, somewhere deep inside, we know that the only true source of power lies within. So when we read of family discord in the palace — Lady Di and Charles sleeping in separate bedrooms, Princess Grace being unhappy — a part of us feels relieved; their suffering helps us cast off false beliefs that wound our spirits.

Switching from Codependency to Addiction

This shift frequently occurs when women leave devastating marriages or partnerships in which they had played a sexually codependent role, often to a sexually addicted partner. Martha followed this pattern. This switch may also occur when a woman discovers feminism and gives herself permission to be more in control of her sexuality and relationships.

Calley's case is typical. She grew up with a "nice guy" father who was very flirtatious with her. He loved to have her sit on his lap and repeatedly reminded her that she was "Daddy's favorite girl." Her mother, having given up her dreams of a career for a financially secure but hollow marriage, secretly disdained her husband's spinelessness and sexual demands, but kept a tight grip on her feelings. She found sex distasteful, but never protested or stated her desires. She was at once relieved to see him enjoy their daughter, which lessened his demands for sex with her, and jealous of the intensity of their relationship. Her ambivalence surfaced in her relationship with Calley. She spent a great deal of energy focusing on

Calley's appearance, but paid little attention to her daughter's feelings and talents.

Because Calley derived her self-worth from being her father's favorite girl, she was easy prey to sexual abuse by her uncle. When he visited, he, too, would hold her on his lap. When her parents were out of view he would sometimes slip his hands up her thighs and rub her genitals. His sweet talk and "gentleness" left Calley thoroughly confused. She simultaneously felt pleasure and shame.

At nineteen, Calley became involved with a sexually addicted man who originally seduced her with presents and charm. She rushed into the relationship without looking beneath the surface. Soon after their marriage he became domineering and possessive. She quickly learned that if she was seductive with him, he was less likely to get violent, be verbally abusive, or withdraw emotionally. For several years, she acquiesced to his sexual demands, never complaining, even when sex was physically painful. She greeted him after work wearing sexy clothes and usually had a lovely dinner on the table. She maintained this seductive role as the best means of protecting herself from his violence.

Calley gave up her job as a legal secretary, which she loved, to placate her jealous husband. Even after she made this sacrifice, he continued to be repressive and abusive. He persisted in putting her down and calling her a bitch, even though she made a great effort to fit his image of a sexy woman. As so often happens to women who are sexually codependent, Calley came to hate sex, herself, and her life. Unaware of her rage at both him and her father, she became extremely depressed, and eventually went to a therapist to find out what she was "doing wrong."

From codependency, Calley moved to sex addiction. Eventually she filed for a divorce and immediately after the separation went back to work and joined a singles group, where she made an important discovery: when she attracted a man sexually — and it was easy for her to do if she dressed right and was flirtatious — she instantly felt powerful. Being in charge of a sexual encounter was a great rush. Her depression vanished. Calley's therapist colluded in the addiction by supporting the relationships because they made her feel so good. She soon had numerous men friends in her life and was involved in several sexual relationships. All were reminiscent of her relationship with her father: the alliances were based on using another person sexually; little genuine interaction was demanded of her; her role was to look sexy and be charming; there was no emotional intimacy.

Codependency and Addiction within a Single Relationship

This was Anita's pattern. To cover up her victimization, Anita attracted her partners by assuming the role of addict, appearing competent, in charge, and independent. At first she was able to maintain her assumed identity within a relationship. Little by little, however, her neediness would rise to the surface: the competent persona would slip away, revealing a dependent child clutching for security. Within days or weeks after the initial meeting she slipped into the codependent role, becoming preoccupied with future fantasies — a happy marriage, a home, and a family — thinking they would make her happy forever. Her need would overwhelm her partner, who would leave.

Many addicted women, like Gerri, leave a relationship before this can happen. Others, like Anita, stay with their partners, sliding into a hopeless dependency, doing anything to prevent abandonment. Anita continued to initiate sex because she believed that as long as sex was wonderful, her partner would never leave her. Partners of women like Anita often love the sex at first, but they soon feel consumed by it. Even if they are not conscious of it, something inside rebels. Several men told me that they never thought they would refuse to be sexual with a woman, and were surprised to find themselves pulling away, feeling drained or swallowed alive by sexually addicted women.

When Anita was operating from a codependent role she would become obsessed with her partner, calling him at work, at home, or in the middle of the night. She was also exquisitely sensitive to any signals that he was withdrawing. When she perceived them, she panicked.

Unconsciously, the withdrawal of her partners triggered long-forgotten feelings of the tiny child inside her who longed for a parental bond. That was why she felt as if she would die when someone left her — she was reexperiencing her childhood abandonment. To escape this pain, Anita would say to hell with him, flip back into her addiction, and find a new sexual partner.

Simultaneous Addiction and Codependency

Marilyn Monroe was miraculously able to combine the codependent and addictive roles. She could project the needy vulnerable child, and at the same time play the elusive, desirable sex goddess. She could at once elicit men's need to feel protective and fatherly and their desire for a sexually exciting woman. No wonder she still evokes such a powerful response in our collective imagination. She epitomizes what women are supposed to be — dependent, vulnerable, soft, sweet, innocent, and at the same time sexy, enticing, and challenging. I believe our cultural obsessions reflect our collective dilemmas, both conscious and unconscious. Marilyn Monroe is still alive in our memories because we are still caught up with the essence of what she represented — the image of a woman men desired.

When Marilyn Monroe died, many stories surfaced about her sexual involvements with famous men. It seemed it was an accomplishment to have had sex with Marilyn. Did she, too, like addicted women, keep score of her sexual conquests? Was she, like all codependent women, silently enraged about being used sexually? Did her tendency to be temperamental, late, and difficult to work with result from hangovers from medication or repressed anger? Or both? Or was her reputation for being "difficult" really about the unmanageability resulting from her struggle with advanced stages of sex addiction and sexual codependency?

Outwardly Marilyn appeared to be sexy, yet naive and innocent. She had no difficulty attracting men, but as soon as she was in a sexual relationship, the facade cracked and the lonely, dependent little girl emerged. She would cling to the relationship, hoping it would fulfill her, and in doing so, she would push her partner away.

We all know the story of the love-starved Norma Jean. She married young and struggled with depression much of her life. The seductive appearance she cultivated — her enormous sexual energy — gave her, like Anita, a sense of power. It brought attention, an illusory sense of fitting in. Yet her underlying vulnerability left her easy prey for sexual exploitation. And, like Anita, she did not know how to protect herself.

Where were her women friends? Did she have any? How did she feel when she was alone? The role of sex object carried her from a poverty-stricken childhood to fame and fortune — and to isolation, depression, and death.

Codependency with Secret Addictive Behavior

Some women play the role of perfect wife and mother while having a secret affair. (One variation is having an addiction to romantic sexual fantasies or romance novels.) After years of playing a role that leaves them spiritually empty, they fill their longing for care and warmth with a secret affair. They want to maintain their security while still having the passion of a love affair. I have seen very responsible women who have done all the right things — maintained a beautiful home, gone to church, cared for children, held responsible jobs — lead this sort of double life. They are usually desperate to recapture a nearly forgotten feeling of passion that faded away over the years as their spirits became imprisoned in the good-woman role. Some women who have affairs are ripped apart with guilt, yet fear giving up the lover who awakens their heart. Women with a strict religious background often berate themselves terribly. For many, the affair feels like emotional survival, a way to keep the heart and soul alive.

WOMEN IN PROSTITUTION

Prostitution combines aspects of sex addiction and codependency. If we think of prostitution in the verb form *to prostitute* — to sell oneself or one's talents to an unworthy cause — we can see that all sexual codependency and addiction are really forms of sexual prostitution. Sex is a commodity used for trade, barter, or bribe.

I would like us to stop using the term *prostitute* as a noun. By using prostitute as a label, we artificially separate a certain group of women and obscure our understanding of prostitution as a cultural institution that maintains the sexual double standard for men and women. I use the expression "women in prostitution" because I would like us to think of these people simply as *women*. And, like most of the women described in this book, the vast majority were sexually abused or emotionally neglected as children, and left vulnerable to men who wanted to control and exploit their sexuality.

I interviewed a number of women from a group called PRIDE — *People Reaching Independence, Dignity, and Equality*. As I listened to these women recovering from prostitution tell their stories, I kept looking for a pattern to distinguish them from women who did not engage in prostitution. The theory suggested by several therapists that their childhood abuse was more severe than that of women in SAA and CoSA simply didn't hold true under careful scrutiny.

Before describing the interweaving of sex addiction and codependency in prostitution, I will digress slightly to relate some of the women's stories, which take us behind the surface image of "prostitute."

Ann was raised on a farm in a family that lived a life of silent drudgery, never sharing feelings or talking about sexuality. As a child she was quiet, had few friends, and experienced little joy. At fifteen, scared, shy, and vulnerable, she attended a summer Bible camp. A man who was unlike anyone she had known visited the camp. He was spirited, talked kindly to her, and put his arm around her. She had never heard anyone laugh so much. He asked her to visit him in "the city," and several weeks later, telling her parents she was going to visit a friend, Ann went to see him. After two more visits, he persuaded her to stay with him. Mesmerized by his charm and attention, she felt loved for the first time in her life, and their relationship soon became sexual. Three weeks later he "sold" her, and she was on the street.

Julie grew up with an alcoholic mother and a father who ran a bar frequented by people in an "escort service," chiefly pimps. The father often showed off his cute daughter to his friends at the bar when she was young. Julie learned how to turn on the charm and get attention at an early age, and she took it for granted that having sex was part of having a date. This idea soon evolved into the notion that, as she put it, "if you have to have sex to have a date, you might as well get paid for it." When she was seventeen, her father "fixed her up" with a pimp friend of his. She spent the next six years in prostitution.

Allison is an attractive, well-dressed twenty-four-year-old who was entered in numerous beauty contests and taken to modeling school as a young child. She had been sexually abused by her father since the age of nine, while her socialite mother looked the other way. In high school, Allison found out that her father had several women "on the road" and frequently hired prostitutes. She spent seven years in prostitution, working in an escort service.

Rowena is a tall, strong, big-boned, yet shy woman in her forties. The oldest of six children, she took care of her siblings in place of her parents, who were both alcoholic. Her father was also violent, continually berating and abusing her mother. When Rowena arrived home after her first date with a boy, her father beat her, screaming that she was a whore, a slut, and a bitch. Desperate to escape her home, she ran away many times but was always sent back by social services people. Eventually she found a way out: she spent twenty-one years in prostitution.

Pimps know how to spot insecure young women, and to flatter and seduce them. They tap into a woman's longing for the loving parent who will take care of her. When women from PRIDE described their start in prostitution, their portrayals of their pimps echoed the codependent women's descriptions of the charming, seductive men who brought hopes of security, money, or prestige. The basic exchange was the same; one was just more covert. In both cases, the women believed that the price of security and care was sex.

To me the women from PRIDE were no different from other women who didn't know they had a right to their bodies and a right to say no. They were no different from women who had sex with the landlord to avoid losing their apartments, or from the woman who was pushed down the stairs and broke her arm when she wouldn't have sex with her rich husband, or from the woman whose husband threatened to kill her or take away the children if she left him. They were no different from drug-addicted women who were sexual to get drugs.

The difference between women in prostitution and other women is chiefly in safety and society's reaction to them. We treat women who have engaged in "official" prostitution as another species. These women epitomize the sex-for-sale norms of the culture, yet they are shunned because they sell sex openly and take money. They make overt the covert standards we wish to obscure. I believe the only thing separating women in prostitution from women involved with sexually addicted men is differences of degree.

Women in prostitution do experience a higher level of danger. It is extremely dangerous to be on the street, controlled by a pimp, to have no choice over who uses your body for sex. There is potential for abuse every time a woman is alone with a john. Women in prostitution are regularly battered and killed when they try to escape. The vast majority of them become addicted to drugs or alcohol. Women partnered with sexually addicted men may experience less violence overall, but they, too, suffer terrible physical abuse when they try to leave or show signs of autonomy. One forty-year-old woman who returned to school described how her professor husband would walk up to her at her desk while she was studying and, without saying a word, haul off and slug her, knocking her to the floor. Women involved with sexually addicted men, be they pimp or professional, have been hospitalized as a result of battering. Some are hurt during sexual acts. In the mildest cases, these women suffer daily assaults on their intelligence and sacredness as a soul.

I believe the institution of prostitution provides a way to hide from our internal conflicts about sex. As long as we can point a finger at someone else and say "prostitute," we can avoid looking at the ways we prostitute ourselves sexually, both individually and as a culture.

In family systems therapy, psychologists call the person in the family who *appears* to be sick the "identified patient." In reality, this person often takes on the pain for the whole family, acts it out, and provides a target for everyone else's troubles. I think that, at a cultural level, we do this with women who engage in prostitution. They are the necessary scapegoats, the scorned ones, the ones who carry the shame for us all. And the extent to which we need prostitution is reflected in our refusal to help women leave prostitution by providing rehabilitation programs and transitional facilities. Practically no professionals are trained to understand the socioeconomic factors involved in prostitution, and few institutions are attuned to their needs. Women attempting to leave prostitution are often rejected or treated insensitively at battered women's shelters, treatment programs, or halfway houses. As one woman remarked, "There is all this sympathy for battered women and incest survivors. Why not some sympathy for us? I'm a battered woman and an incest victim too."

With this in mind, we can better understand the sexually addictive and codependent aspects of prostitution. The addictive part may include rituals of dressing, putting on makeup, fantasizing about the hunt, and the moment of capture. "To know you could go out there and they would come running. What power! Men would actually pay for sex — something I've got." For women in prostitution, like women in SAA, that feeling of power, along with the excitement of living on the edge, is one of the hardest things to give up. Terrifying as it is at times, prostitution provides intensity, a high, and a distraction from buried pain.

The PRIDE women share with codependent women a feeling of being disconnected from their sexuality. When I asked them about the actual sexual experiences with johns, they said they were awful — something to get over with. While engaging in sex, they would detach emotionally, disconnect from their bodies, and think about other things. Sex is something you put up with to get what you want, namely, money and the "protection" of a man. Like the CoSA women, those in PRIDE also express disdain for their partners: "What fools the johns are to pay for sex."

As I listen to these women tell their stories, my first thought is "There but for the grace of God go I." Going one step beyond, I am challenged to look at the ways I have falsely engaged in sex for security, power, or nurture at cost to my soul. While there may not be a direct exchange of money, there is a covert exchange nonetheless. And if mind, body, and spirit are one, there is no difference. No matter what the packaging, the inner wound is the same. Whether a woman sacrifices her soul for a classy marriage, is a swinging single, or engages in prostitution, she is acting out of the mistaken belief that sex is the way to secure what she needs.

CHAPTER 7

Relationships:
Bonded with Love or Addiction?

Preparation for adult intimate sexual relationships begins with conception. In *High Risk: Children Without a Conscience,* Dr. Ken Magid states, "It is estimated that half of all our knowledge — our *life's* knowledge — is locked in during the first year of life. During the second year we learn half as much as we did during the first year." By the end of a child's first year, the basic underpinning for intimate relationships — trust — is set in place. And the establishment of that trust depends on the child's bonding with a caretaker during his or her first year.

Dr. Magid's list of symptoms of children who suffer from a lack of bonding echoes the difficulties addicted couples experience. They include an inability to give and receive affection, self-destructive behavior, cruelty to others, superficial warmth and attractiveness, problems with food, control problems, lack of long-term friendships, and abnormalities in eye contact. These children pull away when you want to hold them, hurt you when you try to love them, and lie and deny reponsibility for their actions.

Many people suffering from severe forms of addiction and codependency experienced ruptures in bonding and nurture in their infancy, or even during the gestation period in the womb, and it is this initial lack of care and bonding that results in some of the negative core beliefs we discussed earlier. In general, the earlier and more intense the rupture in bonding, the more deeply embedded are the negative core beliefs. Lack of an early primary bond is the great hidden crippler of the soul. It leaves a child feeling isolated and separate from others. This in turn affects the development of spirituality, the ability to experience a sense of oneness. Very often children create their image of a god or the Universe based on their relationship with their parents. Cruel parents, cruel gods. Reestablishing an ability to trust and bond in an adult is extremely difficult, but, as you will discover in the recovery section, it is possible.

■

In initial bonding, a child forms a trusting attachment to a primary caretaker who is warm, sensitive, and responsive to the child's needs. Through deeds, looks, and words, the adult attends to the child's needs and well-being, which is, of course, the definition of love.

The more infant bonding is studied, the more we learn about the devastation experienced by children with inadequate or nonexistent bonds. I believe sex and relationship addictions have their roots in an unconscious desire to create or mend this primary bond. One reason addict-codependent relationships get so out of hand is that those involved in them fail to realize that they are using sex and security to create or supply a missing bond. *Sexually addicted adults are essentially children hiding out in grown-up bodies, hungrily seeking parents to love them unconditionally.*

Another manifestation of insufficient bonding is the total merging of people under the influence of psychopathic leaders of cults and communities, who demand unswerving loyalty from their followers. Like tiny children seeking a parent to guide their lives, these disciples surrender all self-knowledge to a leader who exploits their vulnerability for self-aggrandizement. A chilling example of this phenomenon was Jim Jones, who, in what came to be known as the Jonestown massacre, led several hundred of his followers to commit suicide in Guyana in 1978.

In some cases bonding ruptures occur later in childhood. Usually, however, the pattern of bonding established in the first year continues into childhood. In some cases, deficient bonding stems from a parent's relating to a child as an object: a baby doll to dress, a possession, a cute object without a soul. If a parent is interested primarily in appearances and coerces the child to fit into a preconceived mold, the child may become very successful yet feel essentially empty and unlovable. Some parents feed emotionally off their children, creating a symbiotic tie that leaves the children feeling both dependent and furious.

In other cases, bonding ruptures occur as a result of emotional, physical, or sexual abuse or neglect. If a parent is alcoholic or works long hours and appropriate child care is not available, inadequate bonding may result. A combination of a symbiotic tie coupled with neglect and abuse can have the same effect. Sometimes bonding is thwarted because of separations and neglect due to natural catastrophes, war, or illness of the primary caregiver or child. In the United States, problems of bonding are exacerbated by a system that deprives children and their caretakers of basic care, including paid maternity leave, medical care for children and their mothers, support payments for single parents and low-income families, and subsidized quality child care.

As children grow, they learn to apply positive traits of bonding — trust, love, and care — to themselves. Adult relationships are related to people's ability to feel safe in the Universe, to believe in the essential goodness of others, and to care for themselves. With this foundation people are able to form bonds based on cooperation and a "we're in this together" attitude: "I feel safe with myself, so I feel safe with you." Those in codependent and addictive relationships operate from a "you versus me" stance. Everyone is defending her or his turf. Not knowing oneself and not feeling bonded is like living alone in an empty house. Neglect of children leaves us with a legacy of millions of people who are empty inside. The result is nothing less than a national crisis of loneliness and isolation, covered over by violence, addiction, and dependency. As a result we live in a society in which increasing numbers of people have difficulty caring for each other and creating supportive communities.

RELATIONSHIPS CAN HELP US GROW

What can we do with our negative childhood programming when we want to create a healthy adult relationship? My approach is to think of friendships and intimate sexual relationships as opportunities for growth. They are not the goal; they are a means to learn about oneself. In general, the more emotionally intimate a relationship, the closer we get to our own negative programming or "unfinished business." Many people, lacking childhood bonds, start the process of forming a relationship with a therapist, a spiritual teacher, or a peer support group. Fears of abandonment or rejection and beliefs that we are unlovable roar to the surface as we dare to care and to be cared about. Our fears lead us to either damage our relationship or to grow within it.

Many people comment that so long as they are not in a sexual relationship, they feel perfectly "healthy." That's why some sexually addicted or codependent people avoid primary intimate relationships. However, when you avoid intimacy or sexuality you simply set aside a whole segment of your negative programming and submerge an important part of yourself. You may feel more comfortable, but you also feel less complete. This doesn't mean that you need to be in a sexual relationship. It means that you need to create a feeling of harmony with your sexuality in order to feel at one with yourself.

When your goal is a nonaddictive relationship, the focus becomes changing your own attitudes and perceptions rather than changing things you don't like about your partner. You can dislike certain traits in your partner, but you remember that they result from programming, and are separate from his or her essential sacred self. You can prefer that your partner change without insisting on change. You learn to ask directly for what you want without flying into a rage or losing self-esteem if you don't get it. You don't measure your partner's love for you by things he or she gives you. You work to give up your preconceived model of what your partner *should* be and try to cherish him or her, foibles and all. Paradoxically, you don't hide your thoughts and feelings; you learn to tell your partner the little things that bother you in a nonshaming, nonblaming way to clear the air and keep unspoken gripes from turning into buried resentments, which are the bane of intimacy.

A note of caution for codependent people: many people suffering terribly in painful relationships say, "I just have to learn to love my partner more." What they are really saying is "If I'm nicer my partner will change" or "I have to learn to put up with his emotional or physical abuse, because I'm too scared to leave." In these cases the motivation is still a desire for the partner to change and to find a way to hang on to a relationship that doesn't work. Nonaddictive sexual relationships, by contrast, are built on honesty that requires self-knowledge and a willingness to let go if one is being harmed.

Loving sexual relationships require equal vulnerability and equal risk taking. Inequality in roles is reflected in inequality in vulnerability and risk taking. The person in the dominant role will be less vulnerable than the one with less power. To offset this imbalance, people, often unconsciously, engage in covert compromises and manipulations.

In the United States, we place extraordinary emphasis on sexual relationships, yet we create a system of exploitation and inequality between the sexes that makes real equality almost unattainable in intimate heterosexual relationships. Maybe that is why we are so obsessed with relationships — we *want* intimacy but our social setup makes it very difficult to achieve. Men and women are taught different values and roles from the day they are born. Sexual relationships are overemphasized, while friendships, working relationships, community relationships, and spirituality are underemphasized. By putting so much emphasis and value on all forms of sexual relationship, our culture unwittingly promotes sex addiction and codependency.

Many women enter therapy hoping to "work on" being able to have intimate sexual relationships. I always try to assess four things: How much is that person committed to living her own life according to her inner truths? Does she see herself as responsible for supporting herself financially? Does she create excitement and passion in her life from things she does for herself? What is the level of her involvement with a support system? Without self-awareness, a strong support system, and a sense of personal responsibility, a person is far more susceptible to addictive or codependent sexual relationships.

A woman who lacks a sense of purpose about her life will identify with her partner's life and, therefore, try to control it. People who lack friends for support and care and do not have a sense of spirituality usually place overwhelming expectations on their partners. A woman who does not feel financially responsible for herself will automatically assume a dependent role, casting her mate in the caretaker role. The relationship then takes on an inappropriate parent-child quality. Trying to have a primary, intimate sexual relationship before you know how to care for yourself and sustain friendships is like trying to climb a mountain before learning to walk.

Think back to the messages you received as a child about "adult" relationships. Did the "real" relationships always involve sex, marriage, and babies? Were they always heterosexual? According to the messages I received from my mother as a teenager, the most important thing was to have a date — with a boy. And, of course, it was always okay to break a date with a girlfriend if a guy called. The script for life read: Find a man, preferably one with a good career, marry him, have children, and . . . well, no one talked about anything beyond that. I remember a teacher in junior high who had the class make lists of what we wanted in a mate. Girls were looking for cool dancers, good dressers, a man who was friendly and on his way to a good job, preferably with high status.

A young woman of the eighties might be more sophisticated, seeking a partner who will help at home, be able to talk about feelings, and support women's rights. Yet we have only to look at the current crop of teenage movies and rock videos to see that the old foundation has not yet cracked. Males are still center stage, controlling the show and dominating women, who readily submit. Males are also portrayed as demigods, in a form of male objectification. They are responsible for supporting women and giving them status. And teenage girls still have posters of male rock stars, rather than models of successful females, hung on the walls of their rooms. Ads in teens' and women's magazines still carry the message be beautiful so you can attract a man. I'm still waiting for the ads and commercials that encourage young women to be strong, to develop their skills and intelligence so that they can support themselves, have fun, and feel powerful.

Reminiscing about my early models of womanhood, I have to laugh. They started with Cinderella, Sleeping Beauty, and Snow White, those passive, inordinately sweet and perfect models of femininity waiting for their princes to come. Next came the Virgin Mary; my greatest hour as a teenager was playing her in a Christmas pageant at church. Chorus girls, like Betty Grable in *Mother Wore Tights,* shared the Virgin's spot. There were other movie stars, and also circus women — I especially admired the acrobats and loved their costumes. At least they *did* something, but never with another woman; it was always a man throwing them around and catching them. Then there was Pauline and her perils, rescued from the train tracks at the last moment by a handsome man. There was the wonderful, noble, all-loving wife, the kind played by Myrna Loy in *The Best Years of Our Lives*. How could anyone be that understanding? But the strongest image I carried with me was that of the young married woman, played by Olivia De Havilland, going crazy in *The Snakepit*. So strongly did I identify, both with her and with the male psychologist who worked with her, that I saw the movie seven times. So there I was, rather confused, as I tried to sort out my heroines and decide who to be: virginal-good-girl, chorus-line-bad-girl, noble-martyr-woman, or woman-losing-her-mind. Your role models may have been equally confusing. And if you are like me, models of people with interesting careers were usually men.

If your self-image is equally confused and you don't feel able to explore all your interests because you don't consider them feminine, you will find it very difficult to know yourself fully. As a result you may pick a partner who fills in the gaps for you, thus creating a symbiotic relationship. Like so many women of my generation, instead of pursuing the career I really wanted, I married it — a social psychologist — and felt the loss until, at the age of thirty-five, as a single mom, I took the plunge and went back to school. Knowing what you want in a partner or a friendship inevitably starts out with knowledge of self, and with a willingness to *be* yourself.

STAGES IN RELATIONSHIPS

It is important to bear two things in mind with regard to primary relationships. For people who come from dysfunctional families, *the underlying goal of the psyche in choosing partners is often to address unfinished business left from childhood.* We pick people like our parents and try to change them. If you haven't realized that you're not to blame for having a father who was cold and distant, and you still hope he will change, you may pick a cold and distant partner and try to change *him*. If you have buried your anger at a parent who beat you, you may pick a partner who can readily have you on your knees with fear. If you accept that you can't change a cold person and give up trying, two things will happen. You will feel the grief for the loss of the father who was so cold, and you will be freer to choose a more loving partner. If you haven't expressed your anger for being beaten as a child, you may not be able to get angry at an abusive partner. If you don't learn the lesson involved, you will probably repeat the pattern. Some family therapists suggest that we all marry our image of our mother. I believe that we often form relationships in which we replay our relationships with various members of our family, until we recognize that the negative programming we learned from these people has nothing to do with our true worth and lovableness. Only when we stop trying to change other people are we free to truly explore our own identities. When someone gets on our nerves we learn to realize that the person is mirroring some aspect of ourselves we reject.

The second crucial principle of primary relationships is that *self-esteem levels attract*. When there is a wide discrepancy in self-esteem between partners in a relationship, one person will leave fairly soon. Women sometimes have a hard time believing this because they are so conditioned to see all men as superior to themselves. They are unable to see that a man who acts as if he has it all together and is continually handing out advice is really covering up his own lack of confidence by assuming the role of a teacher.

Let's look at three relationships and how they vary at different stages, depending on whether the woman plays an addict role, a codependent role, or a healthy role. As you read about these three couples, keep in mind that healthy couples operate from an "us" stance, while dysfunctional couples operate from a "you versus me" stance. Paradoxically, functional couples maintain their separate identities and dysfunctional couples tend either to merge or to avoid merging by keeping a lot of distance between them. Often they seesaw between enmeshment and distance.

STAGE ONE: THE HUNT

Most people want to find an intimate partner at some point in their lives. The problem for many addictive people is that they tend to have fixed images or rigid scripts for their partners to follow. The ad for a female date reads: Handsome professional male, age 46, seeks thin, tall, shapely, dark-haired, exceptionally classy lady, age 36 to 42 for elegant dining, romantic evenings. . . . He's probably already written the script for her clothes, dinner conversations, and their first sexual encounter. More successful couples allow the relationship to evolve out of the attributes of each partner. They have the idea for the play but not a specific script. A more open ad might read: Woman seeks confident, compassionate, sensitive man with a spark in his eyes. In other words, *in addictive relationships, the partners attempt to fit a given form, and in healthy relationships the form evolves from the characteristics of the individuals, and it changes as they change.*

When a codependent person meets an addicted person they begin with two different sets of dreams. Instead of recognizing their incompatibility, they delude themselves into thinking that their dreams could fit together. This was illustrated marvelously in a cartoon that appeared in the *Utne Reader,* a Minneapolis-based alternative magazine. It presents a below-the-surface dialogue in a singles bar between a man and a woman who fit the description of an addict and a codependent. Their dialogue epitomizes the different agendas that men and women often bring to relationships.

MAN: Hi, there.

WOMAN: Hi ya!

MAN: Looking good.

WOMAN: Thanks.

MAN: Name's Rex.

WOMAN: Mine's Judy.

MAN: You sure are stacked, Judy.

WOMAN: You sure look like good husband material, Rex. Do you have a good job with a solid future?

MAN: Do you have anything on under that dress?

WOMAN: I'm 32 years old and I want to get married and have babies.

MAN: I'm 36 and I wouldn't mind getting it on with you, but hey, no commitments. I bet if I'm really nice to you, I bet if I'm really charming, you'll take me home with you tonight.

WOMAN: I bet if I'm really good in bed you'll want to have a relationship.

MAN: You're on. Shall we?

WOMAN: Let's.

While people are rarely this blatant, the conversation accurately reflects the basic bargain struck by many sexually addicted couples. One wants sex, the other wants a relationship, and they both delude themselves about their real motivations. Yet underneath, they really *do* know the truth, and the relationship gets crazy because they collude in denying what they know.

In all relationships, the tendency is to show one's strongest, healthiest side first. On the outside we see the cool, gutsy (addicted) person or the sweet, all-caring (codependent) person attempting to find a partner. Underneath lurks the inner needy child, looking for someone to fill her emptiness or make her feel whole. When a relationship deepens, partners build trust as they reveal their less adequate, frightened sides in small doses and check out each other's reactions. In other words, they are honest, and they share their uneasiness and fears as part of the initial bonding period.

Bonding in an adult relationship echoes qualities of infant bonding except that the attachment is made between equals. The infant develops trust by being lovingly held, being looked at with love, and having her needs met without too long a wait, particularly in early infancy. In adult relationships trust is built when two equal partners openly show affection for each other, are reliable, keep appointments, make plans together, own up to discomfort and fears, and refrain from pressuring each other to do things against their will. Eye contact and nonsexual touch are also an important part of bonding. Unbonded children avoid eye contact. Addicted people may make eye contact, but it is likely to be starry-eyed and seductive rather than open and honest. Genuine eye contact is unaffected, gentle, and steady. Bonding includes genuine eye contact while talking and making physical and sexual contact. Bonding also occurs as partners include each other in various activities with friends and family. In addictive relationships, both partners are ashamed of their needy side, so they keep it entirely hidden and play the role of the person they think they should be. Most of all, they avoid showing the awkwardness and uncertainty that is part of getting to know another person. Instead, they simply jump into bed. But the hidden child will not be silenced forever and will eventually start controlling the relationship, unbeknownst to the people involved. Eventually the relationship becomes that of two children in adult bodies, slugging it out, unaware that they are transferring all their anger and hurt about their parents onto their partner. The point is graphically made in the illustrations on pages 122 and 123. Only when adults accept the child within can they be relaxed and playful.

Sexual Chemistry and Flirting

Flirting is basic to the hunt of the sexually addicted. The lingering look, the shining smile, and the kind of teasing that turns people on are used to entice a partner. Our culture accepts flirting as a given, but I doubt that flirting is based entirely on genetic instincts. I suspect that some flirting is an attempt to compensate for feelings of fear, awkwardness, and inadequacy. It is born of inequality and the fear of being honest and direct. If you want to gain insight into your own flirting, go to a social gathering or a party and *do not* flirt or act cool. Ask yourself, "What do I really want to have happen at the gathering? What do I expect or think should happen? How do I feel when I don't flirt? Is there a more direct way to get what I want? What would it feel like to go up to a person and simply start a conversation by saying, 'I feel uneasy here'?"

When Elana — who, in her tough, addictive role, was easily the female counterpart to Marlon Brando — tried this experiment, she said she had never felt so lonely and inadequate in her life. She stood around at a party with no idea of how to start a conversation. After forty minutes she went home, struggling against a desire to drink. Without the crutch a flirtatious role provided, the frightened child, unsure of how to be with people, appeared. But by allowing that child to surface, Elana could start to heal herself. The important thing is to recognize the motivation underlying flirting.

In the addictive mode, there is always a hidden agenda, and flirtatious behavior serves as a substitute for such honest sentiments as "I want you to like me." "I enjoy being with you." "I'm afraid you will leave me if I don't flatter you." "I feel I have to earn your love."

When I ask women about the feelings that lie underneath their flirting, their responses range from a longing to be touched, to a need to feel wanted, to feelings of anger. One bisexual woman said, "With men I was motivated by anger and by a desire to control their sexual energy. With women it was more neediness." Another woman, voicing a common refrain, said, "Internally, flirting was done out of a need to have a man desire me and find me attractive. It boosted my sense of self-worth and made me feel powerful. Generally I made references to sex immediately. I would say things that hinted at my sexual prowess. Often it was very blatant. I talked about past sexual experiences without hesitation. I had no verbal boundaries." Other women described their flirting as disrespectful, angry, powerful, or a means of releasing tension.

What people communicate to each other when they first meet often sets the stage for their relationship. In addictive relationships there is usually an unspoken bargain. Flirting, indirect signals, and hidden emotional bribes are the norm. Functional relationships generally get under way with far more honesty. In therapy, I track back with troubled couples to the very beginning of their relationship, for those first few meetings often encapsulate the nature of the relationship. Together we assess the basic bargain they struck, either overtly or covertly. I then suggest that they renegotiate their relationship by stating openly and honestly what they want from each other and what they are prepared to give. Addicted couples have great difficulty doing this because they are so ashamed of their needs. Bringing expectations to the surface makes people vulnerable; it also takes away the ambiguity, often the source of misunderstandings and arguments that those in addictive relationships need to keep the drama alive.

I urge you to keep in mind that underlying the addictive behavior in the following examples is the *positive* intention of creating an ongoing, satisfying relationship. All these couples were seeking love and happiness. Unfortunately, their longing conflicted with a need to avoid intimacy that would open their hearts and touch off buried pain.

Arlene and Barry: An Addictive Approach

A psychological conflict arises for the sexually addicted woman who wants a long-term relationship but is unable to be emotionally vulnerable. Of course, she can't have it both ways, for intimacy and vulnerability go hand in hand. But she will struggle to find a way. To do this she covertly seduces the unconscious part of the codependent by "promising" to take care of him, to be protective or provide him with the status of having an attractive woman on his arm. She may also provide the bravura and

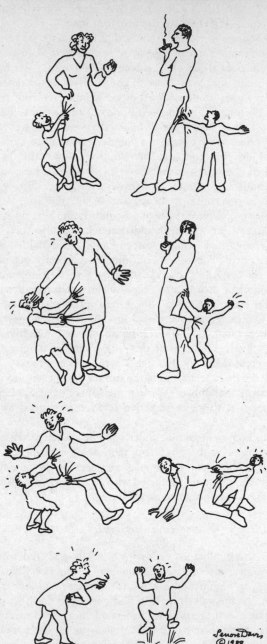

pizzazz he lacks. She presents herself as fearless and assured, which provides a feeling of security for the partner longing for a parent to take care of him. This "hooks" the codependent, who, in turn, becomes "hopelessly devoted" to the addict and, like a child needing a parent, will not leave, at least for a long time. The basic bargain is struck: the addict plays the role of wise and dominant parent, the codependent, the needy child who is too insecure to leave.

Arlene is a successful, competent, and hard-working real estate agent, admired by everyone in her office. When Barry came on staff as a new broker, she was delighted. He was single, and she was looking for a mate. From the first day, she dazzled him with her competence and quick-witted charm. She began to pay extra attention to the way she dressed. On Barry's second day she wore an "uplifting" bra and a soft white sweater with a V-neck that just ever so slightly showed her cleavage, along with a pendant necklace sure to focus attention where she wanted it. On Barry's third day, she offered to take him to see a particular house to help him "learn the territory." His ego was flattered; he was being pursued.

There is nothing wrong with helping out a new colleague, but this was not Arlene's motivation. Like a spider weaving a web, she was gaining control over Barry. She arranged to show him the house at the end of the workday, and after their tour she casually mentioned that she was hungry. Barry, picking up the cue, suggested they stop and have dinner. As they went into the restaurant, Arlene "accidentally" brushed his hand with her fingertips, ever so lightly. He flushed at her touch. Soon after they settled in with a drink, Arlene made a reference to a past lover and how wonderful their sex was: an invitation to Barry to enter the competition.

Arlene maintained control by speaking abstractly about what she hoped to find in a partner, thereby further challenging Barry to prove himself. Their conversation was like one of those dry "relationship" discussions that Woody Allen has made his stock in trade, full of phrases like "meaningful," "not controlling," "letting each person have power," and "being really supportive." Arlene dazzled Barry with her smile, a smile that said, I like you. She also let her gaze linger just a few seconds beyond what Julius Fast refers to in *Sexual Chemistry* as the "moral looking time limit." Arlene intended to turn on the sexual juices.

Barry was smitten, thinking, "Gee, this exciting woman wants me." Within two days they embarked on a highly charged, "this-is-it" sexual romance. They were both "in love." Once Arlene had control, she could allow him to ask *her* out and bring her gifts. But make no mistake, she stayed in charge.

The scenario would be slightly different if Barry were also an addict. The opening lines would be the same, but Arlene might adopt more of a smart-ass attitude. She would one-up him with jokes and sassy retorts that would subtly put him down. She would appear unobtainable, thus challenging him to overpower her. She would still put out the sexual energy, but he would do the asking. If he got "out of line," she'd seduce him back by withdrawing and acting cool. They would both know they were playing a game, but would never say so. In this addict-addict encounter, both would engage actively in the seduction. In this scenario, the relationship is far more likely to be very short-term because each of them will feel disdain for the other and pull away. The first scenario is more likely to result in an ongoing relationship because Arlene and Barry were playing the complementary roles of addict and codependent.

Mary and Jack: Codependent Seduction

The codependent at some level, usually unspoken, hooks the addict's inner child by promising to love him as he's never been loved before without his having to give anything in return. In other words, the codependent covertly promises mother love. The addicted partner interprets this as a guarantee of sex anytime he wants it and a caring partner at no emotional cost. Of course, the codependent actually wants a lot in return. Her unspoken hope is that her addicted partner will become completely dependent on her for care and will never leave. In addition, he will provide status and security. The addicted one is hooked when he realizes he can get the care he unconsciously seeks, and maintain his power, without having to own up to his insecurity and neediness.

Mary was also a real estate broker. Jack was a supervisor in her office, a man on the way up. Without consciously owning up to what she was doing, Mary started to seduce him by building up his ego. While she can appear very competent out in the field selling houses, she changed her demeanor around Jack by holding back her thoughts, opinions, and ideas — her power — and acting childlike. She talked to him sweetly and flattered him by listening intently to his every word. She was exquisitely tuned in to his every move, often anticipating his wants. Her clothes were subtly sexy, innocent and pretty, but also sheer and close-fitting. When there was extra work at the office she offered to stay late and help Jack. "Oh, it's no trouble," she would say sweetly. "I don't mind."

From her first day on the job, Mary was obsessed with Jack, thinking about him from morning to night. When she walked past a bridal shop, she imagined herself getting married to him in a beautiful dress. When she walked past a kitchen shop, she imagined her bridal shower. She imagined what their children would look like.

Jack, who at some level was both angry at and afraid of powerful women, found himself thinking about Mary. She obviously adored him. She never complained, worked long hours, and always deferred to him.

He was unconsciously drawn to the safety of being sexual without being overwhelmed by a strong woman or having any demands placed on him to be vulnerable. He thought he was experiencing an attraction to a good mate, but in reality it was a form of dependency. He was adored, free of charge, and she promised to take care of him unconditionally. His buried feelings could remain in check.

One night when Mary was working late at the office, Jack said, with casual indifference, "Maybe we should go out for a bite to eat." Note the carefully planned invulnerability of Jack's language: "We *should* go out to eat" (so we can get more work done), rather than "*I would like* to go out with *you* and eat." But Mary, unable to read such subtle signals and lost in her fantasies, practically jumped out of her skin thinking, "Oh, this means he likes me!"

Her adrenaline was pumping as they left the office. At the restaurant, she sat with a pasted-on smile on her face, absorbed in his every word. After dinner, they returned to work.

Michelle and Ben: An Honest Couple

I've known Michelle and Ben, the youngest couple I interviewed, for a long time. They have been together for seven years and are about to have a second child. While they clearly have separate identities, I have always felt that there is a special connection between them. When they told me their story, it became clear that they had weathered their share of difficulties. What struck me most as they talked, however, was their commitment to truth, which had repeatedly brought them through hard times.

At eighteen, Michelle was a university student, working part time in a hospital. She was very pretty and had been popular in high school, especially with the boys. Ben, twenty-two, also worked part time at the hospital while working toward his master's degree. A mutual friend, Janet, introduced them one day at the hospital. A week later, when Michelle and Janet moved in together, Janet asked Ben to help them.

Ben was immediately drawn to Michelle but thought to himself, "She's too attractive for me. She'd prefer someone less awkward." Ben recalls that he was very shy and sexually inexperienced. Michelle's attraction to Ben came to life somewhat later, when she saw him carrying a technical book on electromagnetic energy. Intrigued, she thought, "I really like the person reading that book." At first, they went out with a group of people, going to movies, plays, and talks at the university. Sometimes Ben went home with Michelle and they would talk late into the night.

"We'd talk about dreams we had, the nature of the world, what we did when we were kids." After a couple of months, Michelle suggested that they go out together, just the two of them. Notice that Michelle took the lead and did not leave it up to Ben to play the typical male role of aggressor. A few weeks later they discussed the possibility of a more serious relationship. During this period their relationship was not sexual.

Michelle told me that she loved Ben's shyness. "He was inexperienced and not demanding. He didn't try to conquer me. I had felt used sexually by my first boyfriend. It was refreshing to have a man so sensitive. He was real enough to be shy about sex and not put on an act. He would tell me about his insecurity. I would say it was okay with me."

As I reflected on her words *he was real enough to be shy*, I thought of the sexually addicted men I have worked with. Beneath their surface bravado, most of them, like Ben, feel awkward and inadequate about sex and relationships. The difference is that Ben didn't fight the feelings. He suffered the pain of his shyness and sexual uneasiness and overcame his fears by talking about them and daring to be his authentic self. Michelle was able to see the strength in a man who didn't run from his fears. She was also secure enough not to need the tough, strong father image many women seek. She had dreams of her own for a meaningful career. She was interested in Ben as a companion and friend, as well as a lover.

STAGE TWO: IN LOVE, IN LUST

At this stage in a relationship we often believe that we've found the perfect person and that all our problems are solved. In reality it is a kind of symbiosis. Partners in addictive relationships truly believe they have found "the one" who will "make" them happy. Less addicted people may feel the high of love, but they don't usually expect the high to last forever or for marriage to bring happiness ever after. They are also more honest, talking about fears, uneasiness, and discontent. Some of the successful couples I interviewed had experienced an "in love" period, feeling light-headed, seeing each other daily, and feeling high. Even so, they weren't necessarily sexual right away. Others, like Ben and Michelle, knew each other very well and bonded on numerous levels long before becoming sexual.

The unfair catch in falling in love is that our radar goes out to people who remind us of our parents. If we come from a fairly functional family, we tend to pick functional partners. Unfortunately, people from dysfunctional families often are attracted to dysfunctional partners, so falling in love can prevent them from recognizing a dangerous or abusive person.

Getting to know someone you are sexually attracted to can be very uncomfortable. Taking time, getting acquainted, managing your sexual energy and fantasies, and staying honest are not easy. It's so much easier to create an instant bond with sex.

It has often been said that love is letting go of fear, and that's exactly right. A new relationship is a bit like a trip to a foreign country. You can stay alive to it, accepting the hard days, the uncomfortable moments, along with the newness and excitement, or you can get lost in your fears of losing your way and never savor the experience.

Addictive relationships are enticing precisely because they avoid the pain, fear, and vulnerability that are part of getting to know someone and letting yourself be known. Of course, what is also avoided is a genuine loving relationship, but people brought up without good models of intimacy don't know that. They experience sexual relationships as the only kind that feel real. It's so easy to hop into bed, have sex, feel good, and pretend all your troubles are gone.

Feelings in this stage are intense. Couples often start acting married within a week or two of meeting each other. Instead of going through the challenging process of getting to know each other, they form a bond that feels close but that doesn't really have any foundation. Any depression and emptiness they felt prior to meeting instantly disappears. In this phase, the focus is on similarities. The difference between addictive and healthy couples at this stage is that addictive couples delude themselves into thinking their euphoric feelings will last forever if they do everything right. Healthy couples are more likely to know that there will come a time when the high subsides.

There is something wonderful to be learned from falling in love. Even though it isn't true ecstasy or unconditional love — it gives us a taste of it. We float on gossamer wings and wait breathlessly for our beloved to appear, mistaking the source of our ecstasy. We think our beloved causes those euphoric feelings in us, rather than realizing they originate within ourselves. The presence of the partner *awakens* feelings of love that we cannot reach on our own. When that happens, we feel that we have touched the divine. Mistakenly, we attach ourselves to the partner as if he or she were the Divine One.

For people who are emotionally starving, this euphoria is very seductive. It brings instant relief and a promise of fulfillment. Unfortunately, it can lead down the mistaken path of addictive relationships. If we acknowledge that in-love feelings in a relationship are transitory and not about the partner, we won't get lost in them. Instead, we can learn to realize that they have given us a momentary taste of the bliss that comes from being spiritually alive.

Falling in love has another little catch. Physiologically, it produces a chemical high similar to an amphetamine high. The muses of creation must have had a good laugh when they arranged for chocolate, sex, aerobic exercise, and meditation to all release endorphins from the brain, causing feelings of pleasure and calm. Fantasizing about a sexual encounter can also create an adrenaline high in the body, similar to the rush you get from eating a lot of sugar and chocolate. It is no mystery why so many people lose weight when they fall in love: they switch from a sugar high to an "in love" high.

Sex, romance, and feelings of being in love are extremely powerful, emotionally and physically. Along with the physical high, sex kindles all that is primitive and vulnerable in us related to touch, nurture, care, and bonding. It is not surprising that sex can so easily become an obsession and an addiction. Let's rejoin our three couples at stage two in their relationships.

Arlene and Barry spent a lot of time together. They had sex every day, often more than once. They glowed when they saw each other. They went to lovely restaurants and took walks together. But much of their time together was spent fantasizing their next sexual encounter. It was like two plays running simultaneously in the same theater. On one stage, the characters were going through the motions of doing what people are supposed to do in relationships; in the other, they were preoccupied with sex. As Arlene recounted, "There was often this fleeting feeling that something wasn't real. I'd find myself asking, 'Does this relationship really exist?' " That uneasy feeling comes when no genuine bond exists because each partner is following an addictive script.

In a manner typical of a sexually addicted relationship, Arlene attempted to make her relationship with Barry feel real by having more sex. When they woke up each morning, she put her arms around Barry and aroused him sexually. One morning he had to attend an early meeting and said, "No, I have to leave." Arlene sulked and pulled the covers over her head. For a moment a disturbed feeling crackled through him, but he pushed it away by thinking about work. Even so, his need to be needed — the little child within — was not about to give up Arlene. As Barry worried throughout the day about Arlene's response, his fear of abandonment started to take hold. Instead of discussing his concern with her, he was especially "thoughtful" of Arlene and acquiesced to sex whenever she wanted it during the next couple of weeks. They continued to act "in love."

But more problems began to surface. Arlene started snapping awake at 4:00 A.M., an early symptom of depression. She was often preoccupied at work and had difficulty concentrating. She forgot an important appointment and felt ashamed. To hide her pain she invited Barry to a romantic dinner that night, and after a couple of drinks "forgot" to tell him about her error at work. After dinner, they went to Arlene's place and had sex. To keep their "in-love" feelings, Barry and Arlene continued to sacrifice the truth. That's the core of addiction.

Being addictively in love has many parallels to manic depression. Indeed, several women I interviewed believed they had been mistakenly diagnosed as such. Reflect, for a moment, on the symptoms of falling in love: alternating with the euphoria is an inability to sleep, difficulty in eating, feelings of spaciness, difficulty concentrating, obsession with past or future encounters, mood swings (often determined by availability and mood of the love object), distortions of reality ("This is the most wonderful person in the world"), and unrealistic expectations ("Now I'll live happily ever after; my worries are over"). With the exception of euphoria, these are also symptoms of depression. Arlene repeatedly traded depression for the high of new relationships and a fantasy world. The pattern of her behavior over the years was a mild version of a manic-depressive mood swing: the manic side was dominant when she was in love, the depression creeping in when the high wore off.

Why do depression and addiction go hand in hand? Falling in love is an altered state of consciousness only partially grounded in reality. It may signal that the person you have met is a kindred spirit, and it may also be a more visceral chemical reaction. Your warm, wonderful feelings are based not on real knowledge of that person but rather on what you project onto him or her. The feelings satisfy the unconscious yearning for the safety and security you felt or craved in infancy, the sense that you were unconditionally nurtured and protected. Falling in love satisfies the unconscious desire to return to a dependent state.

Paradoxically, when you tell yourself that another person can make you happy, you are also telling yourself that somehow you are incomplete. In feeling less than whole, you seek out and become dependent on another person for your sense of wholeness and self-worth. Thus, you also give up power over your own life because you cannot control the other person. He or she will not always do your bidding, fulfill your fantasy images, or come at your beck and call. It follows, then, that if you believe another person's love makes you happy you will want that other person to stick around. The fear of losing that person escalates, which reinforces dependency, powerlessness, and depression.

It is depressing to feel that you are incomplete in yourself. It is depressing to feel that you can't control your self-esteem. It is depressing to constantly fear the loss of a person who becomes a source of life, to feel utterly dependent on that person for your survival. Dependency and rage always go hand in hand. The depression also comes from buried rage. Dependency triggers rage at the person who holds power over your self-esteem. Yet, to prevent abandonment, dependent people bury their rage. Buried fears of abandonment hold sway over your behavior when you haven't internalized the belief that you are indeed an adult, free to make choices.

Various theories suggest that depression comes from learned helplessness, anger turned inward, loss of self-esteem, lack of connectedness to others, and negative, inaccurate, self-defeating beliefs. All these theories fit with the depression so often associated with addictive relationships. We believe we are helpless to love ourselves, we hate our buried feelings, we hide our rage at the partner, and we move from intimacy to interpersonal detachment as we attempt to control another's life. We increasingly operate on a faulty belief system, thinking that our self-worth rests on being loved by another person and that love is measured by sexual activity.

Let's return to Mary and Jack. When Jack finally showed an interest in her, Mary was in seventh heaven. She had found "him." She told all her friends about him. He's good looking, he's on the way up, he has sent her flowers and taken her to a very expensive restaurant. She showed them the new clothes she bought for a Saturday night date.

Like most codependents, Mary measured Jack's feelings for her by the things he gave her and the money he spent on her. Never having experienced genuine love, she mistakenly believed that these outward signs were true indicators of it. Society tends to disdain women who think this way, but in fact it conditions women to do so. Mary typified the tragedy of being programmed as a stereotypical female. Rejected on a deeper level, as a person with a soul, she counted up the gifts she was given to convince herself she was loved.

Mary continued to be extra helpful at work and Jack's ego felt secure. When he asked her out, he never put his vulnerability on the line: "My friends are having a barbecue and I thought you might like to go." When they went to social gatherings, he sometimes acted indifferently toward her. This left her feeling desperate to regain her connection to him, so she always readily consented to go home with him afterward and have sex. Buried from her awareness was her anger at him for being so powerful and for acting indifferent. Conditioned to believe she was essentially unlovable, she settled for what she could get: sex. In her mind she repeatedly said, "He must really love me to want to have sex with me." On one occasion Mary confided in Annie, a friend from the office. Annie quickly perceived what was going on and warned Mary of Jack's history of chasing women. Mary immediately assured her that this was different. To herself she said, "If I love him enough he won't want another woman." When Annie mentioned Jack's indifference to her in public, Mary geared up her defense system, finding rationalizations. "Oh, I think he's shy. He doesn't want it to be too obvious we're together. I know he really cares." But in her gut, a sinking feeling took hold. She immediately buried the feeling by talking more about Jack and dismissed Annie's observations by saying, "You know, no relationship is perfect."

As Mary's addiction to the security of having an "important man" grew more intense, her ability to see reality faded and the rationalizations increased. Her mind became a beehive of activity, but she ignored the bee stings in an attempt to prove that everything was honey. Her very sense of self disappeared into the quagmire of her frantic desire to be Mrs. Jack.

When I interviewed Michelle and Ben, and other stable couples, the discussion never stayed on sex for long. They spoke more about the wonderful, warm feelings they get from talking to each other, spending a special evening together, or the fun they have doing things as a pair.

Ben's early uneasiness about sex didn't prohibit the relationship from forming, because they found so many other ways to be close. It was the third month before they started "making out," and two months more before they spent the night together, snuggled up, hugging and caressing each other. Although Ben thought about sex quite a bit, he didn't attempt it when he felt uneasy. It was awkward for him because he believed that Michelle was more sophisticated, having already had a sexual relationship.

After a couple more months, they agreed to "let it happen" when the time felt right. Nine months after they met, they had intercourse for the first time. While it didn't have the superelectric charge of the first-time addictive sexual encounter, it was a warm experience that felt good to both of them. This is not to say that nonaddictive sex doesn't have a wonderful feeling, but it often starts out with less of a high. The electric charge of addictive sex is the incredible release from the adrenaline buildup as well as the ego's feeling victorious at having made a conquest. More typically in healthy relationships, sex improves with time and shared experiences. Addictive sex, on the other hand, wanes with increased knowledge of the other person because it no longer provides escape from buried feelings.

By the time they finally had intercourse, Ben and Michelle knew each other very well, emotionally and physically. They had created a strong bond that would carry them through some difficult times together.

STAGE THREE: WARTS AND DIFFERENCES

In stage three the differences between healthy and addictive relationships intensify dramatically. In healthy relationships, because a multifaceted bond has already been created, coming down from an "in love" high is usually a gradual process, as the first rush is slowly replaced by deepening intimacy. Addictive relationships, on the other hand, simply crash or go numb.

Because healthy couples usually have strong friendships outside their relationship, they have other sources of emotional gratification as well. One hallmark of a healthy relationship is that both members bring to the partnership excitement and energy they find outside it, giving added depth to the passions they share. Addictive couples tend to drop their friends and interests when they begin a sexual relationship.

It's hard for addictive couples to settle conflicts openly because they experience differences as both shameful and a terrifying threat to feelings of oneness. Because the relationship is built on a false foundation it becomes increasingly difficult to tell the truth. As the high starts to fade, panic sets in, and the couple musters all its addictive resources to keep the relationship going. This requires a lot of denial, which becomes an energy drain on each partner, particularly the codependent, who gives her all without thought for herself. Each partner suffers from fear of abandonment, fear of reconnecting with painful buried feelings, and fear of connecting with the lonely inner child. Although they both genuinely want to love and be loved, their past negative programming, lodged deep in the unconscious, like a monster in a dream, overpowers them. They never genuinely open themselves to each other.

Arlene and Barry had sex every night for four months, and Barry was starting to feel exhausted. Psychically, Arlene had been feeding off him through the sexual act. Neither of them understood it, but Barry knew that he wanted some breathing room. He told Arlene, with hidden fear and trembling because unconsciously he knew he was treading on tender addictive territory, that he was going to see his parents in a nearby town for a couple of days.

His words "I want to go alone" struck terror in Arlene's heart. Her shame-based mind-set, which told her she was inherently defective, made her jump to the worst conclusion: "He doesn't love me anymore. He'll go away and never come back. I'll be all alone." Afraid of saying these things, she attacked him verbally, saying, "You're afraid to be committed. This isn't what I want in a relationship."

Despite her protests, he left for the weekend. On Friday afternoon, facing her first night alone in two months, Arlene felt extremely anxious and depressed. She was slipping into a state of withdrawal. Her heart pounded; she broke out in a sweat. She was embarrassed to call friends because she had not kept up contact over the past three months. She did go out for a drink with some colleagues after work, but the emptiness was only a hairsbreadth away. Her stomach was tied in knots and she drank more than usual. When she got home her apartment seemed like an empty cave about to swallow her up. She tried to read a book but couldn't concentrate. She made a long-distance phone call to an old friend and ran up an immense bill. Oh, how to get through the lonely night! She eventually distracted herself by watching TV.

She thought of Barry and felt betrayed. The child in her wanted to be the center of his universe, but his universe extended beyond her. Her feelings paralleled those of a two-year-old upset to discover that her mother loves other people, and that she is expected to do some things on her own.

On Saturday morning, Arlene woke up with a slight hangover. While making breakfast, she burned her hand and accidentally spilled cold cereal on the floor. It felt as if her insides were spilling out. As she surveyed the mess, her feelings of emptiness increased. She had a hard time getting mobilized or approaching any task. She felt exhausted. But on Sunday, as the time of Barry's return neared, her adrenaline started to lift her energy and she chose something nice to wear. Sex with Barry that night was all right, but it lacked some of the old euphoria. The truth is that Arlene was angry at Barry, and she was holding the anger in.

All this was buried as Arlene and Barry proceeded with their relationship. However, Arlene started to get critical of Barry. He made a great effort to be nice and swallowed his fear of her leaving. He felt powerless to talk back to her or get angry. They avoided all direct conflict because telling the truth would shatter the whole system. Arlene would have to say "I'm using you sexually to feel I matter." Barry would have to say "I'm being used by you sexually so I have a woman in my life and to feel sexually acceptable." Both of them would have to admit they were afraid.

Partners in an addictive relationship usually are ill equipped to talk about "warts" when they appear. Everyone has moments of disillusionment in the early stages of a relationship. Talking about them helps ease the discomfort; when they're not openly discussed they can turn into little monsters.

A short time later, Arlene suddenly began to feel contempt for Barry. He looked different, like a stranger. She noticed the hair growing in his nose. She didn't like the clothes he was wearing. This was how she displaced her fear. It was as if a mist had suddenly swept away, and her beloved appeared with glistening clarity — all the faults, vulnerability, imperfections, and warts.

Arlene's experience is a painfully common one. What happened, of course, was that the image that suddenly came into focus was not her partner's face but her own. There she stood, alone, naked with the rawness of a self that does not accept the imperfections of her humanness. Genuine acceptance of humanness of oneself or a partner is frightening for most people. For those who are sexually addicted, it is impossible. They do not have the capacity to see beyond the body and into the soul. They are looking for some nonexistent notion of perfection.

When reality begins to set in, they experience a terrifying flash of loneliness. Arlene felt rage at Barry for coming out of the romantic mist and being an ordinary mortal. Along with being a mirror of herself, it was a transference of rage at her parents, who starved her emotionally and imposed unrealistic standards of perfection on her. Barry started to withdraw, finding various reasons to stay alone at his place for the night.

He also spent more time out of the office, where they had once managed to bump into each other regularly. Arlene, sinking into her dependency, felt an inner panic. She called Barry to suggest that they go on a camping trip for the weekend. Barry, not wanting to be trapped alone with Arlene, said he needed to stay home to get some work done. Arlene hung up the phone, was overwhelmed by shame, picked up a dish sitting on the table, and smashed it into the wall.

She had a couple of drinks, and then called an old friend to see if he was free for the evening. He was. She put on some makeup and took off. Like a lost child searching for a mother, she would do whatever it took to feel attached to life, to another human being. Too ashamed to talk about her emptiness, she snuggled up to her old friend and seduced him. Her infant hunger for love was once again translated into "making love" sexually.

Barry, afraid of losing Arlene, called the next morning and went on the camping trip after all, but it became a drama-filled weekend. By the time they got home they were either fighting or not speaking.

The web of lies between Barry and Arlene expanded from inner lies about feelings to lies about behavior. A few days later when they got together, they acted as if things were normal. Arlene didn't tell Barry about her sexual encounter, but he sensed that something was wrong and asked her what was going on. She replied, "Oh, nothing." That evening they had another fight. Arlene tested the waters with another man she knew. He seemed interested in her, and she started to use her wiles to seduce him.

When the woman in the relationship is sexually codependent, the scenario at this stage is somewhat different from Arlene and Barry's.

Mary and Jack continued to see each other. Mary attempted to be an acquiescent sexual partner, but she started having difficulty becoming aroused. She bought Vaseline to use as a lubricant, but hid it because she didn't want Jack to feel like a bad lover.

A new secretary, Margot, started working in the office. On her first day there, Mary noticed that when Jack handed Margot a letter, he gave her a warm look. On the second day she saw him take off his glasses when he talked to Margot. Mary felt a sense of uneasiness, but tuned it out, blaming herself. "I need to work on trusting more. I don't know what's wrong with me that I get so jealous." By making it all her fault, she denied the reality that Jack was flirting with Margot. Rather than confronting Jack directly, she sweetly asked him what he thought of the new secretary, commenting casually that Margot was a slow typist. Jack defended Margot, and he and Mary got into an argument. Throughout, they related to each other in code. Even when Mary finally told Jack that he seemed to be flirting, they debated whether in fact he was, instead of getting to the real issues between the two of them: "Do you really want to be with me?" "What's going on here?"

In addictive relationships people typically argue over the surface content and avoid saying what their behavior really means and feels like in the gut. If Mary were to trust her true feelings and perceptions, she would know that Jack was not being honest with her, and possibly not with himself, and was playing with her emotions. She would realize that the jab in her gut was a red flag saying, "This relationship causes you pain." But having been raised in a family where denial of pain was the norm, Mary knew no other way of thinking.

Jack continued to flirt with Margot, and Mary started waking up nights and having violent dreams. Looking back she said, "It was complete denial. It's like I was determined to believe that he cared about me and nothing, absolutely nothing, could change that." Mary masked her depression and continued to be cheerful in the office, at least most of the time. But her migraine headaches made it increasingly difficult. One day she saw Jack and Margot getting into a car together after he had said he was leaving town. Mary's denial snapped. The next day she told Jack that she was not going to see him anymore. He panicked and asked Mary to marry him, promising that he would not see Margot anymore. Mary accepted.

Mary threw all her energies into planning their elegant wedding. "He'll be different after we're married," she told herself. Fear, anger, and hurt were all denied. So was the truth. Neither of them had ever witnessed a relationship in which people were honest instead of acting out roles. People from dysfunctional families learn to lie chronically as a survival tool. For some, the pattern becomes a habit, takes over, and life itself becomes a lie.

Michelle and Ben had struggles but found the resources to work through them. In their first few years together, several men pursued Michelle, and she spent time with a couple of male friends from work. When she went out with her men friends for coffee, saw them for an evening, or spoke to them on the phone, Ben felt a lot of pain. He felt possessive, nervous, and jealous. He tried not to act on the feelings but they persisted. "I didn't know how much of it was in my head, but I was afraid she would leave," he said. He did occasionally tell Michelle that he didn't want her to see these friends. Once they broke up for a week. A turning point came when Ben met a woman he liked and told Michelle he was planning to date her.

At that point Michelle realized how much Ben meant to her. "I felt so deeply the pain of having Ben say he'd date another woman. I thought, 'This is how it feels to be on the other side of the fence.' And I felt such love for him and so terrible for how I'd hurt him. I realized I had been very insecure. I was making myself feel powerful by causing Ben pain. It hit me how dishonest and trashy and immature I had been. I really stopped to think about where my sense of self-worth was coming from" — she laughed — "outside of me and from men." Not long afterward, Michelle moved in with Ben "temporarily." She never left.

Both Ben and Michelle were able to delve inside themselves and own up to their unconscious motives. I was moved as I listened to them talk warmly, simply, without extraneous words, pausing to reflect and consider their statements. Nothing was glib or formulated. Their ability to reach for the truth and their willingness to share it with each other had been what kept the relationship going.

STAGE FOUR: RESOLUTION

Once another man became attached to Arlene, she began to feel safe again. She felt bad about Barry and the way she had treated him, but her addicted side, looking for a way out, switched everything around in her head so that it was all Barry's fault. He didn't satisfy her sexually, he was not attentive enough. He, he, he!

Focusing on Barry's failings gave her addicted side permission to leave him. Arlene sent him a letter, a tipoff to her shame, ending the relationship. This kind of brittle ending is typical of addictive relationships. It is as though the addicted partner, having exhausted the resources of the codependent, discards the person like an empty milk carton. Barry wanted to get together to talk about it, and Arlene agreed out of guilt.

At their meeting, Arlene never talked about her inner feelings. Her addicted side maintained control; she subtly blamed Barry and, in an effort to get his sympathy, talked at length about her suffering.

Mary and Jack did get married, but each one suffered terribly. Jack continued to flirt with women at work. Mary left her job and busied herself creating the house of her dreams and taking care of their two children. For fifteen years, her addiction to security kept her from confronting the reality of Jack's affairs, his use of pornography, his drinking, and his occasional involvement with women in prostitution.

In the first four years of the marriage Mary made herself available to Jack sexually, but she found little pleasure in it. As she slid into depression, she continued to show a brave front to the world, but the increasing intensity of her chronic headaches made it difficult. But they also gave her a reason to refuse sex. Her psychological pain began to show itself in physical symptoms. She was hospitalized for an ovarian tumor. At thirty-one she began taking Valium to help her relax. At age thirty-two she had a hysterectomy. Later she saw a doctor about her insomnia and he prescribed medication. By age thirty-four she was addicted to pain medication and alcohol. At thirty-five she was hospitalized for severe depression. On discovering her alcohol and medication addiction, a psychologist transferred her to a chemical dependency treatment program within the hospital.

It was there that Mary learned about codependency as well as drug addiction. When she left the hospital she was referred to a therapy group and Al-Anon. A year later she heard about CoSA from a friend in Al-Anon and eventually joined. Two years later, after continuous therapy, she moved out of her house to live alone. When Jack felt the emptiness of losing his fix, he started asking Mary to move back. The attention and kindness she ached for were suddenly forthcoming. When she maintained her refusal he said he would go with her to see a psychologist. This is when I met them.

When Jack discovered that the goal of therapy is not to "fix" their relationship so that it would be the same as it once was, but to get to the truth and help them both be more honest, he balked. *His* goal was to restore Mary to her former role. I explained that there was no guarantee that the relationship would work out, but that if they were able to get past their shame and talk more honestly, they would both feel better and that it would no longer be so crucial for them to stay together. I brought in a male cotherapist in the hope that Jack would join a men's group, gain some awareness of himself, and ease his isolation.

Today, Jack and Mary are still separated. Jack has had sporadic therapy, but he is having difficulty seeing that he is part of the problem and that things can never be the same as they were. Mary is feeling happier with each passing month, yet still wavers in her resolve to create a life of her own and not go back to Jack unless things change. She has reactivated her real estate broker's license and has started working. Her health has improved considerably and she is learning to take better care of herself. No matter what happens, they both have behind them fifteen very unhappy years and two adolescent children who have never seen their parents engage in a genuine, honest interaction.

Michelle was twenty-seven and Ben thirty-one when she became pregnant with their second child. They were married a couple of years earlier, after their first child, Katie, turned one. I asked them what precipitated the marriage. Ben's unmarried sister, who had been living with a man in a committed relationship, was killed in an automobile accident. In Ben's words, "When I saw how the family excluded him, and his lack of any legal rights to their things, I thought Michelle and I should probably get that piece of paper."

They had a simple wedding with members of the family and a few close friends in attendance. According to Michelle, marriage did not change their relationship at all. When I asked them how they handle conflicts,

Michelle said, "The big stuff is no problem. Our values are alike. It's the petty things we still don't deal with too well. They kind of build up. But we eventually get to the root of things."

Typical of functional couples, she didn't paint the perfect picture. She didn't say things were "just fine," the way a codependent woman often does, nor did she make a big drama out of their problems. Her tone implied, "We're still struggling with some things, but they don't get out of hand."

"Here's an example," she said. "Right after I got pregnant with Katie, I got impatient with Ben and was at his throat all the time. I didn't quite know it was fear. I knew I was thinking a lot about what would happen to my body and about giving birth. We decided we'd better take an evening to go out to dinner and talk. [Notice the "we" stance.] As we entered the restaurant, my fear suddenly flashed through me and I turned to Ben and said, 'Ben, I'm really afraid of having this baby.' The fear just washed away and the love came back."

When I asked them to describe how they talk things over, what came across most clearly was that when one of them is getting picky or difficult, or withdrawing, or having difficulty with sex, they see it as a problem for the two of them to deal with. It's "Let's talk about *us*" or "*We've* got a problem." It isn't, "What's wrong with you?" Michelle said, "We don't say things like, 'You did that.' " She went on to explain that they help each other by asking questions about what's going on, but the questions are in the form of speculation, not analysis. No one plays the wise one or teacher. Together, they try to find a solution. This trait is typical of every successful couple I have seen. Paradoxically, they don't get overly caught up in each other's individual problems or tough times. For the most part, they accept that problems do exist, and they take note of them without laying blame or getting emotionally enmeshed.

I also talked with Ben and Michelle about commitment in their relationship. Ben said, "You should read our marriage vows. We were very noncommital. We haven't promised each other the moon, so we don't have to deliver." Yet my sense is that they have a strong commitment. They explained that, above all, both of them are deeply committed to honesty, which requires continued soul searching. Michelle commented, "We know what a mess things get to be when you aren't as true as you can be. It's so important to take time out and talk about the little stuff hanging around in your gut."

While addictive couples often profess great commitment to keeping the relationship and to loving each other, their behavior, the real sign of commitment, often belies their words. Michelle and Ben, by contrast, were very cautious not to promise anything they couldn't deliver. Yet their behavior demonstrates a profound love and commitment to each other.

I asked Michelle and Ben if there was anything else important that I should say about their relationship. Ben paused for a moment. "Ummm. I'm glad we took it slow. I've seen lots of people go fast and crumble." Michelle echoed his words. "It's wonderful to go slow. And it's nice to share life with a man who has thoughts . . . and feelings."

My interview with Michelle and Ben left me with a quiet, warm feeling. They had said so much in so little time. Addictive couples can go through three months of therapy before either one makes one of those simple from-the-gut statements that cuts through the rattle of coded words.

TRAITS OF ADDICTIVE RELATIONSHIPS

The following are some characteristics of addictive and functional relationships. The pitfall in making such a list is that people tend to take it too seriously and categorize themselves. In reading these lists you may recognize pieces of yourself in both categories. Some traits may not fit at all. This is as it should be, for few things are clear-cut, particularly relationships. My hope is that you will take these lists with a grain of salt, remembering that no relationship is perfect and that few are all bad. A list is just a list — the real truth resides inside you.

As you read this section, note the frequency of the me-versus-you stance typical of people who have been abused or neglected. Never having felt attached in a trusting way, they slug it out all alone, always jockeying for power. They both fear and expect lies, betrayals, and pain. Fear of abandonment looms largest of all.

Addictive people hold on to many of these seemingly useless attitudes so tenaciously because they were developed early in childhood as a means of surviving pain. As adults, they harbor a great, sometimes unconscious fear that giving up a protective behavior will mean losing control, for example, that they might cry forever or be so angry they could kill. If you have never experienced trust, it is hard to believe that you will not be torn open and left bleeding if you *show* how afraid or hurt you really are (and I mean *show* rather than *discuss* your feelings). As we have seen, the intention behind addictive behavior is to protect oneself from buried feelings that are experienced as shameful and overwhelming.

It takes trust to cooperate, to solve problems, to say this is "our" problem, to express feelings clearly, to laugh together, cry together, to expose one's flaws, to get close. The first lesson that those who are sexually addicted have to learn is that vulnerability can be safe with the right people. And they need to start by creating intimacy without sex through a community of peers who accept them, warts and all.

■

Sexually addicted and codependent people sometimes suffer from the following problems.

A pattern of alternating between enmeshment and detachment: The addict and the codependent are attracted to each other, as two halves forming an illusory whole. At first they merge together and feel afraid of being apart. Eventually the closeness becomes suffocating and someone wants breathing space. Afraid to say what they want, their feelings build up until they explode inside. Then they cut and detach from the partner. To avoid merging again they keep tremendous distance. After a while, isolation becomes painful and they attempt to get close; but having no boundaries they again merge and feel unable to operate autonomously.

Attraction to people who reinforce their negative core beliefs: Addictive people attract partners, friends, and often work situations that reinforce their negative core beliefs that they are unlovable, undeserving, and that nothing will ever work out. As children they learned to detach or disengage from their feelings when they were abused or the family erupted. Numbing out in the face of abuse and exploitation is so natural that they don't see the craziness of their relationships or their work situations. Once they start connecting with their underlying abuse they often recognize the dysfunction of relationships or work situations.

They are ashamed and afraid to say "I'm sorry, I made a mistake, I was being sneaky, I lied": The ability to acknowledge mistakes is central to any successful relationship. If mistakes threaten one's sense of self-worth ("I'm bad to have made a mistake"; "They'll hate me for lying"; "Nobody could possibly love me if I make a mistake"), they tend to deny that they made them. If that doesn't work, they may try blame: "I was late because of the weather"; "It's your fault; if you hadn't . . ." If their partners won't accept the blame, they may rant and rave or become violent — anything to avoid feeling ashamed and imperfect.

Keeping score, fighting dirty: Again, this comes from feeling separate and ashamed. If one partner makes a mistake, the addictive or codependent one gains a sense of power. "See what you did!" The thought is, "Well I may be a jerk, but my partner is even stupider than I am." In unhealthy relationships, both partners keep score. That way, if one partner makes a request, the other can always respond, "But last year you didn't do X for me, so why should I have to do Y now?"

Right-wrong/good-bad thinking: Most of the time, getting into right-wrong/good-bad thinking is destructive. The feeling beneath the surface often is, "You've hurt me so much I want you punished." Or "I want you

to admit you know you've hurt me." Or "I'm angry at you." The preoccupation with being right pervades shame-based people. Being "right"
may be momentarily satisfying, but it doesn't bond people. The question
to ask yourself is, *"Do I want to be right or do I want to be close?"* The
approach to problems that works is, "Does this work for our relationship?
And, if not, what can *we* do to change it?" The key lies in developing
problem-solving skills and learning to cooperate: *We* have a relationship
problem. What are *we* going to do about it? It's not good, it's not bad, it
just is.

Freezing emotionally when someone is caring or loving: Over and over
again, addicted people talk about running away in terror when people
show them kindness and love. Many sorrowfully recall times that they
pushed away someone who genuinely cared for them. Once again the
buried core beliefs are running the show. "I don't deserve him. Love will
always cause you pain"; "It's just a matter of time until he leaves me so
I'd better leave first." People describe the experience of "freezing up"
inside or feeling terribly ashamed and exposed if someone is kind and
caring. They think, "I don't deserve this. Don't you know how rotten I
am?" They fear that if they open their hearts to people who care, all their
buried pain will surface. (Which is right, but that's how we heal.)

Passive-aggressive sabotaging of relationships: This is an indirect way to
express anger. It can take many forms: "forgetting" appointments and
agreements, breaking dates, leaving dirty dishes in the sink, tearing the
cold cereal box so it can't be closed, picking fights, being late, not showing
up, flirting with others, and, of course, through it all, denying what you
are doing and denying that you are angry. When the partner then blows
up in frustration you can say righteously, "Don't be so hysterical."

Causing hurt out of unrecognized fear: Many people have been trained
through early abuse not to recognize fear. Instead of expressing their fear,
they pick at their partner, freeze up emotionally, start fights, are exces-
sively good, withdraw, or simply get bored. Until they are able to recognize
their fear and look beneath it, the relationship stays at a superficial level.

Fear of initiating relationships: Because "nice girls" don't initiate relationships, holding hands, or sex, they transmit indirect messages for their
partners to decode. This leaves women in a victim role. If women want
genuine intimacy, they must take an equal part in initiating contact with
a partner at all stages of a relationship. (Try it sometime and you'll
understand more about what men go through and why they steel themselves emotionally against rejection.)

■

Having to control a relationship: Addictive people are usually well versed in power plays. They may want to initiate everything in a relationship in order to be in control at all times. They may withdraw to punish their partner. They may gain control by giving presents and being warm and caring just as their partner is about to walk out. Their goal is to stay in control, keep the focus outward, and feel nothing inside.

Being the teacher or wise one in a relationship: One feels secure in that position because it gives the illusion of control. But the teacher role is really a cover for insecurity and fear of an intimate peer relationship.

Feeling powerful by causing pain: If you feel unimportant, one way to prove your partner cares is to cause him pain and see the hurt or anger on his or her face. It is also a way to have the partner feel all the pain. For example, when a man neglects to pick up a couple's child at day care, the wife, the child, and the child-care worker all feel the pain while the partner is righteous: "I was busy. Don't get so angry." This is one of the most devastating aspects of addictive, low-self-esteem relationships. The relationship has a pattern — I hurt you, then you hurt me. This is all about power and control, the opposite of love and intimacy.

Partners alternate crises: Couples often take turns having emotional crises. That way, someone is always too busy being upset to be intimate. The crises seem very real, and it is easy to become caught up in them. When the pattern of rotating crises continues, it is time to look at the behavior in the context of the relationship and to learn to recognize it as a distance-keeping device.

WHAT SUCCESSFUL COUPLES SEEM TO KNOW

If it seems unfair to you that some people just appear to know how to be in an intimate relationship, I agree with you. It is incredibly unfair. If you can remember that our earliest childhood conditioning is the luck of the draw, and that with effort we can *learn* to have more intimate relationships, then it may not hurt so much.

When I asked couples I considered functional and reasonably content for their insight into good relationships, they laughed. "Are you talking about us?" None claimed to have created a panacea. "We're not perfect by any means. We've had lots of ups and downs." Overall it is their genuine acceptance of their ups and downs, their humor, along with their reasonable expectations, that enable partnerships to withstand the test of time.

Like Ben and Michelle, functional couples seem to have communication skills they don't even know they possess. So often during an interview a couple would describe the way they'd handled a problem, and I'd think, "It took six months of therapy for another couple to be able to do that!" When I showed my amazement, they would look at me in puzzlement, as if to say, "What's the big deal?"

The following are some traits of reasonably successful couples. (I use the word *reasonably* to avoid creating an unrealistic image of a perfect couple, the emulation of whom can become a false goal.) The couples I interviewed were in committed relationships — some married, others not; some heterosexual, some lesbian. Much of the material in this section comes from a group of Quaker women I interviewed. While some of the people came from functional families, others came from dysfunctional ones and had done tremendous personal growth work with a variety of resources, usually including psychotherapy, treatment programs, and twelve-step groups.

Functional couples had adult models of caring relationships (this applies primarily to those who didn't require a recovery program): While these people were not exempt from troubled or difficult times during childhood, most had parents who obviously cared about each other and were able to weather hard times. The children adopted a similar attitude. One woman spoke of the two years her mother was hospitalized for emotional problems while she was a teenager. "It was a real growing-up time for me. I had to carry a much bigger load at home than before. What I remember is how much my father cared for my mother, visiting her often. He also told me he appreciated all the work I did around the house." It was clear from her story that while she helped around the house, she did not become the wife surrogate; her father did not make her his intimate other.

Successful couples maintain separate identities: The women are conscious of their separate journeys. When you ask how they are, they are far more likely to talk about *their* jobs, *their* thoughts, and *their* lives than about their partners, their children, or their families. Within the relationship, each partner is more likely to be able to listen to the other's struggles as a caring friend with some sense of detachment. They are able to care for their partners, have compassion for each other's struggles, yet avoid becoming emotionally entangled.

They view their marriage or partnership in terms of "us": This may seem contradictory to the preceding paragraph, but a sense of personal identity is a prerequisite for an "us" relationship. It takes two people to go beyond a me-versus-you stance. In an "us" relationship, if one person is hurting or there is conflict, it is approached as something to talk about, to work out *together*. Ideally, each partner tries to understand the other's position before seeking a solution. A solution is more likely to be arrived at by consensus, something both can live with. They realize that it is important to resolve problems in such a way that they maintain their personal integrity and respect for each other, rather than adopting a win-lose attitude. In some cases, when a solution is not forthcoming, they find a way to live with the differences without trying to smooth them over.

Although they do everything they can to make the relationship work, they know they can survive without it: This is a key difference between addictive and nonaddictive relationships. All the women I interviewed knew that they would go to the wall to keep their partnerships together; they also knew that if their partner repeatedly violated their values in some basic way — abuse or dishonesty, for example — and resolution was not forthcoming, they would separate. All of them knew they could survive. Codependent women tend to avoid confronting a relationship because they fear that if it comes apart, they would be unable to survive on their own.

They accept change in themselves and in their partners: As one woman put it, "We've had many marriages over the last twenty-five years. Neither of us is the same as when we first got married, but we've managed to renegotiate as we change." Addictive couples resist change, the addicted partner insisting that the codependent always be the same: "I want you to be the way you used to be [a doormat.]"

They maintain basic trust: Successful couples know that their partners will stick by them when the relationship is tested. Jan's husband, Steven, conducted his consulting business from their house in the early years of their marriage. With two young children, it was more than Jan could handle. "I finally got my courage together and said to him, 'Now, this isn't about you. I love you. But I can't stand the disorganization this causes here. Either it's got to go or I've got to go, because it's driving me crazy.' When he moved the office out of our home, I knew I was truly wedded." Another woman said, "When I was really sick and he brought me a bedpan, I knew we were married."

Healthy couples are not jealous of friendships outside their marriage. Both Miriam and Martin, who have been married for thirty years, are my friends. Miriam has spent a night at an out-of-town conference with me; Martin helped me frequently when I bought my word processor and once drove me to a party when Miriam was away from home and I had an injured knee. Miriam's only comment was "I'm glad Martin could help you out. How's your knee?" Such trust comes from a valuable core belief that "people will hang in with me and my partner is committed to me."

They have a sense of humor about themselves: I have heard women laugh uproariously as they told stories about mistakes and natural disasters that had occurred in their relationships. They were also able to laugh at themselves. Laughter, a sign of not taking things too seriously, is crucial. Many addictive couples treat everything as a do-or-die situation.

Healthy couples listen to each other, think about what their partners tell them, take what they've heard to heart, and make changes: Addictive couples may talk a blue streak, but neither partner seems to hear anything or make changes as a result. Miriam told of a time early in their marriage when she was criticizing Martin for this and that. Eventually, he countered, "Did it ever occur to you that you're not the easiest person to live with, either?" Miriam laughed. "That really changed my perspective." In addictive relationships statements are repeated time and again, but they seem to fall through a sieve, as if no one is listening.

They have the ability to say "I made a mistake. I'm sorry": Because they are not ashamed of being human and making mistakes, both partners can own up to their foibles, again a factor of basic trust. They know that no single mistake will pose a serious threat to their relationship.

They expect and weather hard times: Nobody looks for trouble, but healthy couples accept that sometimes the going gets rough. They are able to weather hard times because they have a sense of perspective and, as individuals, they trust their ability to survive. Therefore a problem in the relationship is not experienced internally as a threat to either person's survival. No moment, no event, no year, is seen as catastrophic.

The partners also have the ability to bond together in hard times and support rather than take out their frustration on each other. If they do vent their frustrations they can usually step back, gain perspective, and apologize for their misplaced anger. They can also draw support from outside the relationship, so that one partner is not overwhelmed with the other's needs. There is an easiness in their reminiscences about hard times when they make such simple statements as, "Those first few years with the babies were really tough"; "I went through four tough years trying to figure out what career I wanted to follow"; "It took me a long time to stop worrying when Janet got depressed."

Sex flows from a caring bond: Couples have different rhythms and different sexual patterns in regard to frequency, time, and ways they like to make love. What is most important is that sex reflects each individual's warmth and care for the other. It affirms, but is not relied on, to create their bond. It is a way to feel close and express care for each other. It is not used as a substitute for solving problems or as a way to create closeness that is otherwise lacking.

Sex is the barometer, not the thermometer, of the relationship: When sex isn't hot, addictive couples view it as a sexual problem. When sex isn't going well, successful couples believe that the problem lies in the climate of the relationship. In one woman's words, "When sex doesn't feel right, we stop and say things like, 'What's going on here? Is there something we haven't been saying to each other?' It's a signal that it's time to talk." Notice once more that it is always "*We* have a problem," not "What's wrong with you?"

Paradoxically, many loving couples experience "dry spells" in their sexual relationships, but they consider them to be natural. Jeanne told of a six-month period when she just didn't feel like being sexual. "I don't know why, but I just wasn't in the mood."

"What did you do about it?" I asked.

"Nothing. I just told him I wasn't in the mood. That it wasn't anything about him."

"What was his response?"

"Well, I suppose he didn't like it, but it was no big deal. We have so many other ways to feel close."

"Then what happened?"

"I started wanting to be sexual again, so we were."

I told this story to some CoSA women, who were amazed. When I asked what would have happened in their relationships they described far different scenarios: "He would have told me I was a prude"; "He would have said, "What's wrong with you?"; "She would have said it meant I didn't love her"; "I would have gone to therapy for being frigid"; "He would have hit me or threatened to have an affair."

These responses underscore the mistaken role sex plays in unhappy relationships. Of course, what is missing is not sex, but the genuine honesty that comes from airing problems and trusting each other with feelings.

Sex books and props are not generally used: Because warm and caring sex evolves from a warm and caring relationship and does not have to be artificially created, it is not surprising that few successful couples had much interest in books about sex.

Jan laughed when she told about her husband bringing home *The Joy of Sex*. "Well, Steven's that way; he likes instruction books. But I said to him, 'I'm not going to follow some damn book. I'm not going to keep track of how often. Our relationship comes out of who we are.

Sex is going to come or not. It's either real between us, or forget it!' "

Miriam commented that she and Martin had glanced through the same book. "It was interesting but no big deal. It didn't really have to do with what sex is about for us."

The relationship gets priority time: All these couples make time to be together, even though there are periods when external pressures create conflict. They are aware of the need to make choices. Carrie said, "Several times we had to decide to limit some external activities in order to have time for us."

They try to make decisions to please both partners: In making purchases or decisions about trips, movies, and so on, healthy couples try to find solutions both can live with. Instead of saying, "You picked the couch so I get to pick the dressers," they say, "If we can't both be satisfied with this couch, we'd better wait until we find one we both like." The love between them, the relationship bond, takes precedence. Instead of having a fight that only one person can win, they generally make decisions by consensus. This process can take a long time, but it eventually pays off. It reinforces the belief that feeling connected to each other is the most important thing.

They are involved in some form of service to others: Couples who achieve a deeply bonded, loving "us" relationship usually have a basic belief in service to others. They see the whole world as an "us" situation and themselves as having a place in it. Their commitment to serving others emanates from their enjoying and valuing life. They don't do it to look good; they do it to feel good.

SOME CLOSING THOUGHTS

Communication skills are core to any satisfying relationship. The essence is simple. I say what is true for me; you listen, take it in, mull it over, and then respond with what is true for you. I, in turn, listen to you, take it in, and tell you my response. We continually go back and forth, weaving a bond between us. Listening, responding, listening, responding. Intimacy is created when we respond in a way that shows the other person we understand. From this, from our shared truths, our relationship takes form. It is woven from who we are. Our meetings have a freshness of spirit, reflecting our individual aliveness to the moment.

As our truths change, the form of our relationship may change. We may get closer, we may drift apart. We may redefine our involvement. We may go from being friends to lovers, from being colleagues to friends, or we may go our separate ways. And if we decide not to see each other, we can keep in our hearts whatever we learned from each other and part with good wishes. As Ken Keyes says, we don't need to throw each other out of our hearts just because we no longer want to be together. Paradoxically, if we've been true and honest in a relationship, parting is not experienced as devastation because we know we've given it our best. When we haven't been true we are plagued with "if only" thoughts, which keep us from moving on emotionally.

We are taught that "good" relationships last forever. This is simply not true. A relationship may be very significant to you for a period of time — a few moments or many years — and then the connection no longer bears fruit for one or both of the people involved. As you come to accept that friendships, partnerships, marriages, and work relationships change as a mirror of your own growth, you learn to "hold on tightly and let go lightly." Life is like a trip down a river in your own little boat. You may stop on the shore and stay with someone for a while. Hopefully, you enhance each other's lives or provide lessons for each other's growth. Sometimes a special person may join you for part of the ride. But when it's time for that person to go ashore, you always return to your own boat and your own course.

Some spiritual teachers suggest that as people evolve spiritually they naturally become celibate. I think it is important to distinguish between celibacy as an outgrowth of one's spirituality and celibacy as an attempt to create spirituality. A celibate Buddhist priest who was a former Catholic priest told me, "When I studied for the priesthood, celibacy was imposed on me from outside when I wasn't ready on the inside. So it had a reverse reaction when I left the priesthood. I had a lot of affairs. After years of spiritual growth I have chosen celibacy and it feels comfortable to me now." It seems to me that what many spiritual teachers are really saying is that one must give up lust, and using people sexually — what has come to be called sex addiction and codependency. I agree with this. I also agree that celibacy for periods of time can be very important, indeed crucial, to people who are recovering from sex addiction and codependency. I'm not convinced that enlightenment and celibacy necessarily go hand in hand, although it is certainly the path for some.

It's important to remember that the model from which all these teachers operate is grounded in patriarchy, which is based on inequality and sexually objectifies both women and men. Obviously, this kind of sex must be given up to create loving, harmonious relationships. We are only beginning to explore sexuality between truly equal people. We are only beginning to affirm that it isn't bad and dirty.

I have spoken repeatedly about the importance of learning to operate from an "us" perspective in order to have intimate relationships. The quality of our intimate relationships is reflected in our attitudes toward all people and all living things. Learning to operate from a nonadversarial, "us" stance brings us closer not only to our intimate others, but to our communities, our nation, and our world.

When a personal relationship is built on a spiritual foundation that includes equality, being sexual can be a deeply intimate, life-affirming experience. Intimate lovemaking can create a sparkling sense of wonder at the body's capacity for energy and intensity. It reaffirms a sense of bonding and closeness with a partner that expands our ability to love. It reminds us of our capacity for joy and excitement. Touching, caressing, and caring are extremely healing and nourishing actions. But addictive or codependent sex can bury the spirit and soul.

The spiritual teacher Ram Dass tells us that the purpose of a primary relationship is "going to God side by side." The strongest foundation for a primary relationship is self-knowledge and a commitment to following one's inner truths. The ideal relationship is one in which two people support and care for each other as they follow their separate callings.

CHAPTER 8

Appraisal:
Are You Wondering About Yourself?

THIS MAY well be the first chapter some of you read. Your immediate question might be, "Is this book about me or isn't it?" And a logical place to seek that answer is in a chapter called "Appraisal." However, for most women it is not that simple.

This is a book for all women, and no doubt all of you will recognize yourselves in some parts of this chapter. After reading the rest of the book you may find it useful to return to this chapter for a second look. You will have an in-depth understanding of sex addiction and codependency. And you will have given yourself the time to experience some of the material, and be more comfortable taking stock.

The chapter contains two methods for self-exploration. The first is a list of harmful consequences of sex addiction and codependency, including examples women gave in interviews and on the questionnaires. The second is a list of questions about specific types of behavior and feelings typical of women who identify themselves as sexually addicted or codependent. If you aren't sure of your answers, you may need to take time to let them surface. They are in you if you listen. The point of the appraisal isn't to find a concrete yes or no so much as to take a look at yourself and perhaps find answers to things that may trouble you.

You may be disappointed to know that there is no way to score your responses on a continuum from "Definitely an Addict/Codependent" to "Whew! Definitely Not!" Rather, you score yourself by monitoring your reactions to the questions and examples. The intensity of your response to a question is as important as the number of questions that apply to you. If you get angry, make excuses, or become anxious, it may be a signal that you've touched something.

HARMFUL CONSEQUENCES:
SEXUALLY ADDICTED WOMEN

More than anything else, the harmful consequences reported by SAA women underscore the devastation wrought by sex addiction. As you read the following, ask yourself if you have experienced any difficulties or harmful consequences in each category.

Work/Career   Sex addiction can affect women's ability to function at work on a daily basis and prevent many from seeking a career equal to their talents and education.

"At the height of a great romance, I was totally unable to concentrate at work and got terrible job evaluations."

"I got sexually involved with my boss, his wife found out, and I lost my job."

"Prostitution and selling drugs was my only career until now."

"What career? I don't even know what I want to do yet and I'm thirty-four years old."

Money/Finances   The saying "You do with your money what you do with your love" certainly holds true for many addicted women. Some indiscriminately throw their money away; others hoard it and dole out tiny bits to themselves and others, always fearing there will not be enough. Still others feel they have a right to expect someone else to pay for everything.

"I spent a ton of money on seductive clothes."

"I went bankrupt flying my new love up to visit me and spending money on her."

"I ran up a thousand-dollar bill in one month listening to pornography on the telephone."

"I tried to seduce wealthy men, knowing I could wheedle gifts, money, and trips out of them."

Relationships   Sexually addicted women do not develop safe, trusting relationships with people who can nurture them emotionally. There is always a one up, one down power inequality.

"I can attract partners who will do anything for me, but then I think they are fools for being such victims."

"Even in my monogamous relationship I knew I was using my partner for sex. I felt terrible about it, but unable to stop."

"I would have intercourse with men, but I wouldn't let them kiss me, and I would never hug them."

"I cheated on every one of my primary partners, slept with their friends, and sometimes their brothers."

"I left relationships saying they weren't sexual enough. I didn't have the skills to end relationships respectfully."

Parenting Women express regret over being irritable, irresponsible, or emotionally unavailable to their children while acting out their addiction.

"I risked losing custody of my children by having affairs during the last year of my marriage and during the dissolution."

"I left my son alone when he was too young because I just had to go out with a guy."

"I was afraid of losing my son because of the sexual stuff, so I turned off my sex addiction and turned to food."

Education The majority of the women say they did not develop their talents or skills because they did not believe in themselves, were too busy with their addiction, or were constantly lost in a fantasy world.

"Who has time or energy to develop the discipline required for school when they're busy obsessing? I didn't."

"Up until now I was never interested in my talents — not much anyway — because the right man would come along and take care of my needs."

Health The denial system used to blind oneself to sex addiction operates similarly in the physical realm. Women who are sick or hurting often fail to recognize or postpone taking care of physical problems. Many women never had the experience of being comfortable in their bodies — headaches, discomfort, and pain had been a reality since childhood.

"I think my hysterectomy is related to my abuse and my sex addiction. I hated everything about my sexuality and felt disgusted for sleeping with so many men."

"I didn't have a Pap smear for six years because I was so ashamed of my sexuality and afraid of pelvic exams."

"Did I have any connection to my body? Nope. I felt frazzled, ate funky, slept too little, slouched — hurt."

"I had two abortions because I never used birth control. I just thought it wouldn't happen to me."

Legal Women have far fewer legal consequences as a direct result of sex addiction than men do. They are rarely arrested for sexual crimes, except for prostitution. They are more likely to have legal problems related to the unmanageability aspects of sex addiction, particularly in the area of chemical dependency.

"I stole pornography when I couldn't afford to buy it."

"I didn't pay my bills and bill collectors were hounding me."

"I got a DWI [drinking while intoxicated] after returning from a drunken night with my lover."

"I got arrested several times for shoplifting."

Safety Women most frequently jeopardize their safety by putting themselves in dangerous situations. They may go to bars alone, walk in rough neighborhoods with strangers, go home with men they don't trust or know, and have sex in dangerous places.

"I was raped and beaten one night when I went home with a man I had just met in a bar."

"Working the streets is about the unsafest thing I can think of."

"I kept wanting more and more pain inflicted on me during S and M because I was feeling less and less."

Spirituality Once women have some recovery time behind them the issue of the effect of their addiction on their spirituality elicits strong responses.

"What spirituality? I was totally dead inside."

"I substituted men for God and used sex as a substitute for spirituality and sensation."

"I went to church every Sunday but never understood why I couldn't let any of it in."

"It was as if I saw the world through a plastic bubble. I would see flowers, but their beauty never touched me, I was so cut off from my emotions and my love."

HARMFUL CONSEQUENCES:
SEXUALLY CODEPENDENT WOMEN

Although the harmful consequences of sexual codependency may not be as blatant or dramatic as those of sex addiction, they are just as serious, and often more insidious.

Work/Career Many codependent women don't focus on work or career. Those who do have careers, particularly heterosexual women, may consider only stereotypical female work; others don't allow themselves to know what they want to do, or, if successful, aren't able to savor their work or take credit for their achievements.

"A career didn't matter. I wanted to be the perfect wife and mother."

"I spent ten years in a career that was not my preference — it was my parents' — and I tried to make it work."

"I allowed my partner to use and profit from my work and I didn't get recognition or profit. Even then, my work had to fit his schedule."

"I was always thinking about how to please the boss, how to look good, but never how to get ahead."

Money/Finances   Some codependent women give their hard-earned money to unreliable partners who show no evidence of being honest. When asked why, they may, in all innocence, provide a variety of reasons.

"When I was seventeen, I gave my boyfriend my inheritance so he could buy a car. He said he would pay me back later and I believed him. Of course he never did."

"I used to always give him money because I felt I could never deny him anything."

"My husband spent, I scrimped."

"I spent thousands of dollars on clothes and diet programs to keep my weight down and please my husband."

Relationships   The following observations are self-explanatory.

"When in a primary relationship I was constantly emotionally drained trying to keep his life together."

"While I actually needed more and more, I gave him more attention instead."

"I sought out his approval for everything. I didn't make decisions for myself."

"At a very low point I agreed to his having affairs because I felt guilty about his lack of satisfaction since I couldn't have orgasm."

"I would do anything to keep a relationship, no matter how bad it was."

Parenting   Often, codependent moms do all the right things but aren't present emotionally for their children. When push comes to shove, their relationship with the addict is primary, and some look the other way when their husbands abuse their children.

"I controlled or tried to control my children's behavior and appearance. They were frustrated and resented me for it. Also, they were afraid of me."

"My children grew up with an empty shell as a mother. They didn't learn or get much from the experience."

"I gave up custody of my kids to maintain my relationship with the sex addict. I lied and cheated on my kids and neglected them totally."

"I didn't do anything when my husband abused our children because I was so afraid. I still feel terribly guilty about that."

■

Education   Education suffers when the codependent's highest priority is someone else.

"I dropped out of college to get married and am still struggling to finish my degree."

"The only thing I developed was my fantasy life."

Health   Health problems besiege sexually codependent women because they use enormous amounts of energy trying to be "good" while denying their inner experience. Most codependent women lack energy, or else move from agitation to exhaustion.

"Now with the AIDS thing I worry about my health all the time. He's seen so many prostitutes and I'm afraid of what that might mean for me."

"My husband gave me VD four times from seeing prostitutes. Even when I knew he was seeing them, I didn't insist he wear a condom."

"I had chronic migraines and back and heart problems."

"I was chronically depressed and overweight."

"Insomnia."

"Anorexia."

"Bulimia."

Legal   Many codependent women find themselves with legal problems as a result of abdicating responsibility for their own actions, their own lives. Others cite illegal behavior.

"I still worry about the IRS coming after me because I signed all those tax forms he put in front of me, not knowing what he was reporting."

"I wrote bad checks to buy clothes and things I convinced myself I needed in order to keep the man I was dating."

"I had lots of minor traffic and parking violations because I was constantly so distracted."

"I had to bail my husband out of jail after he was arrested for soliciting a prostitute."

"While going through a divorce, I signed a release form allowing my husband access to my therapy records without ever reading it. I felt terrible when my therapist told me he broke in on a session, flashed the release form in her face, and demanded to see my records. My male lawyer had given it to him. I should have checked that out too. I got a divorce lawyer who stuck up more for my husband than for me."

Safety   Just as they avoid legal responsibility, many codependent women come to physical harm as a result of not looking out for themselves and not paying attention to their needs.

"Men have verbally and emotionally abused me and I didn't know how to protect myself."

"Even when my situation became physically abusive, I stayed because I really thought I could make him change."

"I have walked out in front of cars when I was in a daze and had minor car accidents, all while I was fixated thinking about the current man in my life."

"He pushed me down the stairs and broke my arm."

Spirituality "Men were my higher power. I didn't have a concept of my own spirituality."

"I stopped going to church because he'd rather 'work out' on Sundays."

"I went to church as part of the whole act, but it really didn't mean anything to me."

REPLIES TO GENERAL SEX ADDICTION QUESTIONS

Do you feel compelled to have frequent sex either with a partner or by masturbating?

"I would masturbate five or six times a day, sometimes in the bathroom at work."

"Having sex was the most important part of my life."

"I would promise myself to stop going to bars and picking up men, but I couldn't seem to stop."

Are you bewildered about your sexual behavior?

"I kept saying to myself, 'Why am I doing this? This isn't what I believe in, it isn't what I want.' "

"It was like something driving me and I had no control. I had no idea it was about sex addiction."

"I loved my partner dearly, yet I kept flirting with other women at work. It didn't make sense to me until I joined SAA."

Do your sexual fantasies or obsessions about romantic involvements interfere with your concentration or your abilities?

"I got a ticket for running a red light while I was fantasizing sex."

"I was constantly spilling coffee and breaking things while thinking about a lover."

"The fantasies were more real to me than the actual person I was with."

"I have probably spent more of my life in a fantasy world than in reality. I have accomplished very little."

■

Do you have a pattern of unsuccessful love relationships in spite of longing for a permanent relationship?

"I have had an overlapping series of relationships since I was a teenager. The longest one was five years, the shortest a few days. I dearly long for something that lasts and stays alive."

"I would stay high on constant sexual activity for six to eighteen months in a relationship. Then it would start to fade and the fighting would increase. Sometimes we'd get violent with each other. No matter how much I wanted to stay, within a month or two I was compelled to be off and running again."

"I wanted to love a man, but I scorned the men I seduced. I thought how stupid they were not to see that I was using them. Yet I longed for something different."

Do your sexual activities include the risk, threat, or reality of disease, pregnancy, coercion, or violence?

"I couldn't be sexual without smoking dope. One day I went to pick up a lid and found myself up against a wall with a knife at my neck."

"I knew I'd get VD if I slept with him, but I did it anyway."

"I've had five abortions."

Do you abuse or neglect yourself — cut, burn, scratch, lose valuable possessions, trash your belongings?

"When my lover left me, I smashed a lamp and trashed my apartment."

"When I had had a fight with this guy one night, and he got up and left, I banged my head on the wall. Another time I cut my arms with a razor blade."

"During a romantic high, I wouldn't eat, sleep, or go to work for days."

"I would tie myself up to masturbate, sometimes leaving marks on my body."

Have you engaged in sadomasochistic (S and M) relationships?

"When I couldn't get high from sex I started to do S and M."

"Violence became a high. It was all-consuming, running a good second to sex. In some ways it was better than sex because it was more intense."

"When I had to go to the hospital, I realized I could have been permanently injured from the cutting and the beatings."

Is your life full of chaos and drama?

"I would become lovers with friends, and friends of friends. There were ex-lovers at every gathering I went to. It was a big soap opera."

"I was always getting people mad at me by being late, missing appointments, and not getting my work done. Several times I told secrets about someone and really got blasted for it."

"I wouldn't pay the rent, the utilities, the phone. Some guy was always coming to shut down service for something."

"I moved four times in one year."

"I had five car accidents in two years."

"I took a year's leave of absence to complete a handbook. The day I packed to leave town I couldn't find my rough draft. I was always losing important papers — my birth certificate, my car registration. I felt possessed by some destructive force."

Has your sexual or romantic behavior ever made you feel hopeless or suicidal?

"For years I had constant fantasies of starving myself to death."

"Images of suicide gave me a comforting feeling of control. It was a way out of the pain, the last card."

"I didn't really want to die, but I was afraid this part inside would take over and I'd end up killing myself."

"Whenever I drove, I would imagine running off the road or crashing into cement viaducts."

"I've been hospitalized three times for depression."

"After ten years of therapy, treatment, and 'help,' I thought I was a hopeless case."

Do sex and romance usually involve alcohol, drugs, or compulsive eating or not eating?

"I never slept with a new partner without getting high on drugs."

"I would always lose weight at the beginning of a relationship."

"I would eat before sex and then afterwards I'd get up and eat again."

"I didn't eat. I lived on coffee and cigarettes. At the end of the relationship I just crashed."

Do you have trouble just being friends with men or women because you think about being sexual with them?

"My first thought when I meet someone is, "What would they be like in bed, and could I seduce them?"

"I can't imagine being platonic friends with a man."

"Nearly all my friends started out as sex partners."

"If I really like someone, the relationship doesn't feel real unless we have sex."

Do you usually feel remorse or shame after having a sexual encounter? Do you feel as if you need to get away after you've had sex?

"As soon as I've come, I want to turn over and go to sleep."

"I never make eye contact during addictive sex; I feel too ashamed."

"I never stay overnight with a partner. I don't want to face him in the morning."

"Before sex I feel a big rush, during sex I'm in another world, and afterwards there is an emptiness or I feel repulsed."

REPLIES TO GENERAL SEXUAL CODEPENDENCY QUESTIONS

Do you say yes to sex when you want to say no because of fear that your partner will reject or abandon you or be angry or violent?

"If you don't give them what they want they will go away."

"I never felt I had the right to say no."

"I used alcohol in order to be sexual when I really didn't feel like it."

"He always said he'd go and find it elsewhere if I didn't come across, and I knew from experience that he would."

"I was so excited that she liked me, I went to bed on the first date even though I knew I should wait a while."

Do you focus more attention on your partner's sexual wants than on your own?

"My wants? I hardly ever knew there was such a thing!"

"I accepted his view about sex, and about everything else, too!"

"I'm supersensitive to his every move, from the time he walks in the door at night until he goes to sleep. I'm always trying to figure out how to please him."

"At one point after he left me to be with another woman, I called him and said if he brought her home, I'd bring them apple pies in the bedroom, and rub their backs, just so he wouldn't leave me."

Do you refrain from telling your partner when you are dissatisfied sexually for fear of upsetting him or her?

"I just keep thinking, 'He's not really doing this,' but I never dared to say anything."

"He would be really hurt if I questioned his abilities as a lover."

"I just tried to change myself. I thought that if I accepted him sexually, he would change."

"I often found sex terrifying, but I kept the screams inside."

Do you fake sexual pleasure?

"The worse it got, the more I pretended."

"What sexual pleasure? I don't think he even notices me."

"I act like I want it when he comes on to me, but I feel dead and cold inside."

Do you fake orgasm?
   "For twenty-five years."
   "Yes, I only have orgasm when I masturbate."
   "I used to, but I don't bother anymore. He doesn't seem to care, as long as he comes."

Do you use sex to reward or punish your partner?
   "Yes. I get a secret feeling of power watching him blow up when I won't be sexual."
   "Sex is the best way to get him to buy me something."
   "After we've had a big blowout about him being with a prostitute or going to porn shops I don't let him touch me. I won't speak to him for days. Then he comes crawling back to me and I'll finally give in and have sex."

Do you make excuses (headache, stomachache, too tired, etc.) to avoid sex rather than directly say you don't want to be sexual?
   "I really did get headaches just thinking about having sex with him again."
   "When I was ill was the only time he would keep his hands off me. Even then it didn't always work. I developed some pretty bizarre symptoms."
   "I didn't know when I was being sick to stay away from him or when I was really sick."

Do you worry a great deal about what your partner is doing sexually (using pornography, engaging in prostitution, sleeping with other people)?
   One note of caution here: Some of the following statements reflect a natural response to an addicted partner giving off confusing signals or withdrawing. It's natural to be upset and want to validate your internal reality. It's natural to search the house for pornography if you know your partner is addicted to it and he starts acting strangely. It's natural to look for lipstick on the collar, to monitor the checking account for unexplained expenses, or count his condoms when he starts coming home late. These become codependent actions when you don't believe the messages you are picking up, fail to confront the behavior, silently suffer, don't get help for yourself, believe it's up to you to change the situation, and continue to be surprised after repeated incidents.
   "I'd have this constant knot in my stomach from worrying."
   "I used to search the house for his pornography, throw it away, then

act as if I didn't know what he was talking about when he asked about it."

"When she'd flirt with other women at a gathering, then deny it, I'd go drink until I passed out."

"I'd get mysterious phone calls from women and feel sick and crazy all day. I couldn't think of anything else for weeks but I never said a word."

Do you find yourself trying to rationalize your feeling that something is wrong in your relationship or that your partner is acting out?

"I'd keep saying to myself, 'Well, he's going to therapy,' or I'd think of the nice evening we had two weeks earlier."

"Even though my gut was churning, I'd say, 'Maybe she really is just having lunch with her for business purposes.'"

"I'd say to myself, 'If I just keep working my program and love him more, he'll change. All relationships go through hard times.'"

Do you say to yourself, "If I were better in bed, he or she wouldn't be sexually interested in others?"

"I believed if I was the 'total woman' the relationship would work."

"I read books, went for sex therapy, bought cute nighties, even some sexy lingerie. I thought his wandering was all my fault."

Do you withdraw emotionally or have your mind on other things while being sexual? Is it just something to get over with?

"I count the tiles in the ceiling and I usually don't get to finish the room."

"I feel totally distant emotionally, although I get a kind of masochistic high when he is pounding away. I imagine being a princess, doing my duty for my master, who is much older than me."

In order to please your partner, do you engage in activities that feel repulsive or uncomfortable to you?

"He brought home pornographic pictures and wanted me to pose like the women in them. I did, and I hated myself."

"We made sex movies together."

"I let him tie me up to be sexual."

"She wanted to do S and M and I went along with it."

"I let him pee on me."

"I let him come in my mouth and I gagged and hated it."

"He wanted me to be naked, kneel before him, and do oral sex with my hands tied behind my back. It was degrading."

Do you rationalize doing things you don't want to do?

"He told me I was a prude for not doing things his way. Eventually I started telling myself the same thing."

"I told myself we were just being liberal."

"She told me S and M would make us feel closer, so I said it was for our relationship."

Do you engage in sex even when it is physically painful?

"I had terrible vaginitis and it was excruciating to have intercourse, but I went along with it."

"If I didn't lubricate right away he'd just force his way in. It was awful, but I didn't say anything."

"I let him have anal sex repeatedly and it was very, very painful."

Do you live with chronic fear that your partner will leave you?

"Yes. And parts of me want him to leave, because I feel so powerless to get out."

"I am terrified of abandonment — as if I'll die if she leaves me. I know it's sick, but I feel so stuck."

Are you embarrassed to speak of your sexual behavior with another person or a professional counselor? (The answers refer to pre-recovery attitudes.)

"I couldn't imagine talking about this stuff with anyone. I was so ashamed."

"Sex was too personal to talk about."

"It's not something I've ever really discussed with anyone, even my best friend. I mean, we might talk about kissing and how men always want more, but we never go beyond that."

When someone is sexually attracted to you, does your self-esteem go up? Do you think it is a sign of love?

"Everything I was ever taught said that if a man is attracted to you, then you're important. And that's just what I felt."

"Absolutely. Is there any other way to feel important?"

Do you measure someone's love for you by flattery, presents, or how much money is spent on you?

"When I was dating my husband, he always took me to the best places and later he bought me the biggest engagement ring!"

"If a date spends a lot on me I figure he really likes me and wants to get serious."

"I was always telling my girlfriends about all the stuff he bought me."

"Is there any other way to know a man cares?"

In a new relationship do you say to yourself, "Once we are sexual that means we have a relationship"?

"Yep. It means I've 'landed' him."

"There's always this frantic feeling in the beginning of a relationship before we have sex, like we've got to have sex to make this real."

"I figure if I'm good enough in bed, he'll never leave, because all men really want is sex."

When you meet a prospective partner, do you have fantasies of living together? Being partners? Being married? Buying a house together? Taking him or her home to meet your parents? How glad you will be to tell your friends you have a lover or a mate? (Some women refer to this as the full-speed-ahead syndrome.)

"All of it — where the furniture will go in his apartment, what our children will look like."

"I start seeing us living together, taking trips, how we'll look at parties."

"I can just see my mother being pleased."

"I fantasize so much about the future, I don't ever notice if we have anything in common."

Have you suffered from chronic physical problems, including headaches, stomachaches, lethargy, tumors, or other physical symptoms?

"It's been one thing after another for twenty years."

"I felt like an old woman at thirty-five, I'd been sick and tired so much."

"I've had a knot in my stomach every day of our marriage. I have terrible digestive problems."

"Sometimes I have a knot in my throat that won't go away for days. Then I finally get a cold."

"My chest would just hurt all the time."

Have you suffered from depression or anxiety for long periods during your relationship?

"I'm always fighting depression. My husband says he doesn't want to hear about it."

"I'm one of the most uptight people I know. I'm always worrying about something, mostly my partner and my kids."

"I'm finally having a few days without anxiety. I never knew what it was like to feel peaceful until I got into recovery."

Do you sit around, not doing anything, waiting for him or her to phone?

"I'd turn down offers to go out with other people for fun just because he might call back."

"After a while, I start phoning him — I become a pest phoning all the time, I get so anxious to talk to him."

"My husband travels and calls me in the evening, so I never go anywhere after six P.M."

The following questions can relate to sex addiction, sexual codependency, and controlled addiction.

Do you sometimes wonder if you are "asexual" or have no sexual feelings?

"I feel clunky and numb from my waist to my thighs. I have no sense of that part of me."

"When my therapist asked me about my sexuality, I thought, what sexuality?"

"I felt nothing sexual for years. It's like part of me died."

"After I quit using alcohol, my sexuality died."

"It's a terrible feeling, as if I'm on the outside looking in. I think back to times when I used to be sexually active with a great yearning in my heart, but it seems almost impossible to think of being sexual."

Do you avoid sexual relationships altogether, or for long periods of time, because they are just too difficult or not worth the trouble?

"I tell myself I'm destined to be alone. It's not in the cards for me to have a sexual relationship. Something is wrong with me."

"Why bother? It's two weeks of pleasure — maybe two days — then another year of suffering."

"It's always such a mess when it's over that it's not worth it. It's like eating tacos."

Do you find it difficult, or even impossible, to ask to be held or hugged because you are afraid of sexual feelings?

"I could joke around with all the people in my office, but when it came to being alone with someone attractive, I would want to run away."

"I was terrified of being touched by someone I liked because it might stir up sexual feelings. I might have to do something sexual!"

"I have no idea of how to even talk with people."

Do you constantly tell yourself you could never have a positive sexual relationship?

"I can't imagine a really nice person wanting to be with me."

"I'm afraid if I lose interest in sex, they'll leave."

"I'm afraid people will feel devoured by my sexuality."

"I feel disgusted when I think about sex."

"I'm afraid of being sexually devoured by someone else."

■

Do you substitute obsessions or constant fantasies of unobtainable part-
ners for genuine intimate relationships?

"For twenty years I lived in a dream world of one day becoming lovers with a priest I met in France."

"I was obsessed with my swimming teacher at summer camp. I didn't make friends with any of the other girls."

"My therapist and I kept a sexual buzz going even though he said we would never be sexual. I never went out with anyone else the whole year."

Do you keep thinking, "Someday my prince or princess will come, and
everything will be different"?

"The only relief I had from the miserable way I was feeling was to fantasize a wonderful person who would make it all better."

"While I was in my addiction I had the belief that all I had to do was meet the right person and everything would be different. I had no idea my troubles were about my own fears."

"I became addicted to romantic novels and kept thinking something like that would happen to me."

Does masturbation bring feelings of repulsion, fear, or discomfort? Do
you avoid masturbation altogether?

"I want to scream when I touch my genitals."

"I never liked anyone touching me there and I didn't like it when I tried to masturbate."

"I have never masturbated."

PART II

OTHER PIECES OF
THE PUZZLE

CHAPTER 9

Anything to Fill Up This Emptiness:
One Addiction or Many?

Friend, please tell me what I can do about this world
I hold to, and keep spinning out!

I gave up sewn clothes, and wore a robe,
but I noticed one day the cloth was well woven.

So I bought some burlap, but I still
throw it elegantly over my left shoulder.

I pulled back my sexual longings,
and now I discover that I'm angry a lot.

I gave up rage, and now I notice
that I am greedy all day.

I worked hard at dissolving the greed,
and now I am proud of myself.

When the mind wants to break its link with the world
it still holds on to one thing.

Kabir says: Listen my friend,
there are very few that find the path!

— Kabir

THE AUTHOR of this poem was a fifteenth-century Indian mystic. I often read this work at the close of talks on multiple addictions, for Kabir clearly recognized the dance of the ego/addict, whose worth is determined by external sources rather than the inner spiritual light. Here is what Marlene, a forty-year-old woman recovering from sex addiction, wrote on her questionnaire about multiple addictions.

When I was a housewife and was bored, I would
go to the shopping center and spend hundreds of dollars on clothes.

169

After a sexual encounter with my neighbor, I would
go home and eat until I couldn't eat another bite, then take laxatives.

After I was with him,
all I could think about is how I want to eat.

After I've been on a diet, I'm so afraid of gaining weight
that I will remain on the diet until I am very thin.

Then I will start eating again
and gain until I'm fat.

Throughout all of this I'm an impeccable housekeeper
and I'm "driven" at work.

"No one needs to work that hard," my boss often tells me.

ADDICTION UPON ADDICTION

Can people have many addictions rather than just one? Are sex addiction
and codependency simply expressions of an addictive personality? Or do
separate addictions need to be understood and addressed as separate
entities? Do addictions form a hierarchy, with some addictions covering
others? My answer is yes to all questions. Yes, the essential source of all
addiction is a spiritual emptiness, a hunger for purpose and connectedness to life. Yes, we sometimes need to focus on one particular addiction
when it is operating in the forefront of our lives. Yes, addictions can exist
in layers, with some more deeply embedded than others.

Even when we address one particular addiction we need to keep in
mind that most addictions are interrelated to the functioning of the whole
system. Cutting off or spraying one branch of a sick tree does not necessarily get to the root problem. We need to identify our fundamental addictive behavior as well as address the internal source.

I have asked many women, "Do you believe other addictions are related to sex addiction?" Most agree that they are. In their words:

"Addictions are a way to fill an emptiness, another sign of feeling unloved."

"Because part of my sex addiction was to look good, I was compulsive
about my makeup. I couldn't go anywhere, not even to the store, without
it. I was also a chronic dieter, abused laxatives, and fasted to keep my
body thin."

"I'd start with one addiction and fall like Alice down the rabbit hole
into others. Too much coffee made me crave sugar. Too much sugar made
me compulsively hungry. Then I'd overeat and get depressed. Then I'd feel
anxious about getting my work done. Then my addict part would take
over and I'd say 'What the hell' and go out with some guy I didn't even
like just to have sex."

"All addictions are to avoid pain, but I believe sex addiction is the hardest to give up because it is the closest to being healthy. We are trying to find intimacy, at last, but we become addicted once more. I believe looking at this is the end of the addict's quest for recovery, because once this gets taken care of and understood, true clarity is possible."

This last sentiment was expressed by many women. Once they started to deal with sex addiction, other addictions became more manageable. For the moment I am sidestepping the notion that some addictions are more genetically based than others, particularly addictions to chemicals and food. If this seems to be a paradox, bear with me. I will cover it in the chapter on holistic recovery.

Some women have several addictions operating simultaneously, while others trade off addictions, giving up one only to get lost in another. For some the addictions are layered, from survival addictions down to core-level addictions. Sometimes two addictions are ritualized together, sex and alcohol (or drugs) being the most common, with sex and food running a close second.

Another prevalent combination is violence, drugs/alcohol, and sex. This usually has its roots in caregivers who were alcoholic, violent, sexually abusive, or unprotective. In some cases the only time a child received warmth was after being abused or after a family blowout. Thus violence and affection (sex) were paired. When addictions are ritualized, they tend to feed each other, intensifying the emptiness and, in turn, the tendency to be addictive. The more a woman hides from herself, the more she becomes lost in escapist behavior. It's as if she's on the wrong path altogether, so that the farther she proceeds on it the more lost she becomes. The whole system increasingly operates from a compulsive or addictive mode, so that nearly everything becomes addictive. Some escapes are "driven" in nature, such as work, exercise, buying things, religion, and staying busy; others are passive, such as watching TV, using chemicals, or sleeping.

The bottom line is often a life filled with compulsive, ritualistic behavior taken on to mask a growing time bomb of inner desperation. As one woman said, "Anything could become an addictive ritual. I used to roll cigarettes and get into a trance. I've been compulsive with alcohol, food, clothes, and, of course, sex. At one point, running was totally addictive. I'd run no matter what — shin splints, ice, sickness, you name it. If I missed a day, I felt terrible."

Addictiveness is a state of mind that permeates one's life. You are running frantically to keep one step ahead of the fearful feelings. I often think of an addicted person as someone scurrying through life to avoid getting drenched by a dark rain cloud that is in constant pursuit. To start recovery means to stop running, sit still, and get drenched in the rain.

MULTIPLE ADDICTION SCENARIOS

The Domino Theory

Addiction to sex and relationships is often at the center of other addictive behavior. Trying to *fit* one's illusion of oneself instead of simply *being* oneself takes a lot of work. The addictive inner force works like the domino theory.

Imagine a scene in Giovanni's, a posh restaurant with a view of a big city skyline. Setting: soft music, candlelight, flowers, linen tablecloths. There they are, Rhonda and Bob, two attractive, well-dressed people in their late twenties. From a distance these two look as though they belong in a romantic movie. Rhonda leans toward Bob, listening intently, her eyes aglow. Every detail of Rhonda's appearance spells perfection — smashing dress, perfectly manicured fingernails, meticulous makeup, snazzy clutch bag, subtly tinted stockings, designer shoes.

Now look behind the scene. What addictions are at work here? For starters, Bob is being codependent. Although he can't afford it, he's brought Rhonda to this restaurant to impress her. He has no idea how he'll pay his credit card bill for the dinner, especially since he recently got himself deeply into debt buying a trendy BMW to salvage his wounded ego after a girlfriend left him.

Codependency also underlies Bob's conversation. He's faking it when he talks about his great job. The truth is, he went into the retail lumber business with his wealthy dad because he didn't have the strength to follow his own yearning to go into architecture and defy his father's wishes. He was enticed by promises of wealth, but his father is making him learn the business from the bottom up, and he doesn't earn much money. Bob's sex addiction clicks in while he's talking to Rhonda. His palms sweat and his mind jumps to thoughts of seeing her with her clothes off.

He tries hard not to stare at her breasts, which show just a tiny bit, through her V-necked, otherwise innocent-looking, dress. At one point he realizes that he has wolfed down his steak — and can't even remember eating it. All he is left with is a bit of indigestion, which comes out in an embarrassing belch, along with the sudden realization that Rhonda is talking and he hasn't heard a word she's said for some time.

Across the table, Rhonda, who is recently divorced and has left her six-year-old son, Jimmy, home with a babysitter, feels dizzy; in an attempt to hide her nervousness she's had one too many drinks. That little shot of scotch she had before she left home was supposed to help her relax. While she struggles to look composed and not drop food in her lap or spill her wine, a voice in the back of her mind taunts her: "Stupid, you shouldn't have had that drink."

When she's not worrying about her appearance or alcohol consumption, Rhonda keeps slipping into a fantasy about being married to Bob and what their children would look like — she's tied the knot before dessert arrives. Next she wonders if she can stick to her promise to herself not to have sex with Bob until after at least five dates. She resolved to do this since she realized that men tend to leave her if she has sex with them right away. On the other hand, she thinks to herself, "God, he's spending a lot on dinner. Maybe he'll get mad if I won't have sex." Juxtaposed with that is the thought, "If we have sex then he'll love me and never leave me." These thoughts keep bleeping through her mind as she tries to be attentive to the conversation.

In the midst of all this, Rhonda has guilt pangs when she thinks of Jimmy. The image of his tear-streaked face floats through her mind and jabs at her heart. In the morning she broke her promise to take him to the zoo. She was so excited about her date with Bob that she just had to buy a new dress in the morning and have the afternoon to get ready. She lied to Jimmy about the zoo, saying it was closed. Later, she lashed out at him when he smudged her freshly applied nail polish. He only wanted to touch it to see if it was dry, he said, but Rhonda, in her anxiety to look perfect, lost her temper. Now she wishes she could take back those harsh words.

Rhonda is also worrying about her financial condition. When she bought the sexy dress she broke her promise not to charge any new clothes until she paid off more of her credit cards. She is up to her ears in debt, but she rationalized the purchase by saying today was a special exception, and the dress was on sale.

Are we having fun yet?

In reality, behind Bob's and Rhonda's facade is a pile of addictive behavior, anxiety, and discomfort. The sad thing is that neither of them is really having a good time or getting to know the other. Their images are having dinner together, not their genuine selves. And neither will be happy about the bills when they come, not to mention the emptiness both will feel when the evening and the sex are over and the grand illusion inevitably starts to fade.

What's missing from this picture? The truth.

Had Rhonda and Bob begun from an internal point of wanting to find out if they were a possible match for each other, rather than taking the externalized stance of winning the other's approval, they would have been able to be truthful with each other. Instead, both of them are taking a codependent stance, letting the response of the other control their self-esteem. Either could have initiated a discussion about who would pay for dinner. If Bob wanted to treat, Rhonda could have determined how much of a treat she felt comfortable accepting without feeling indebted to have sex in return. She could have suggested a more modest restaurant. If accepting a treat at any level left her feeling indebted, she could have insisted they go Dutch. If he had refused, she would have learned about his need to control — important information to have about a prospective partner.

Although it's perfectly natural to be a little nervous on a first date, Rhonda's mind-set — "Will *I* measure up? Am *I* good enough?" — put her psychologically on the sales block — Will he buy me? — and left her feeling powerless. This led her to take a drink in order to gain control. If she had thought to herself, "I wonder if *I'll* like him, I wonder if *we'll* hit it off," and "It's okay if we do and okay if we don't," she would have been in a position of power, thus reducing her anxiety. If she had thought of the date as a pleasant way to get acquainted, not a big deal, she wouldn't have felt the need to buy a new dress, could have kept her promise to her son, and wouldn't have incurred a bill she couldn't afford to pay. She probably wouldn't have lost her temper when Jimmy smudged her nail polish, since looking perfect would not be so critically important and she wouldn't have been so anxious about it.

We could go through the same routine with Bob, but I suspect you get the point by now. When we fake it and try to make the right impression rather than being ourselves, we get caught in a web of deceit that permeates everything.

There She Goes, Miss America

Claudia, an SAA member, is recovering from multiple addictions. Tall, graceful, and powerfully built, she is impressive to behold. She has a marvelous sense of style and is an accomplished singer and musician. She is also very intelligent and a committed feminist.

Claudia, like Gerri, had virtually no appropriate parenting. She endured physical, emotional, and sexual abuse and was out in the world on her own at seventeen. When I met her she was twenty-four and had been in SAA six months. She was studying speech communication and putting herself through school by playing in her own rock band.

Given her appearance and powerful energy, I was surprised to learn that Claudia had been a Miss "State" in the Miss America pageant. She had hoped to be the runner-up in the state competition in order to get enough money to go back to college. Much to her amazement, she won. So there she was, performing the duties of Miss State and preparing for the Miss America pageant — and wishing she wasn't.

Here's the nightmare beneath the image. To keep her weight down, Claudia became bulimic, alternating binge eating with self-induced vomiting. She used the official Miss State car to bring cocaine back from Florida to please her boyfriend, a drug dealer. On one run, she drove the competition car off the road at 110 miles per hour, with cocaine in the trunk. Much to her relief, the police did not search the car and let her go. Throughout all this, she abused alcohol and lived in constant fear of being discovered by pageant officials or the press. To complicate matters, she was becoming increasingly aware of a strong attraction to another woman.

Being Miss State was an exercise in codependency. As she was groomed, made over, and endlessly drilled on the *right,* not the *honest,* answers for the pageant judges, Claudia felt that she was being prepared for a high-pressure cattle auction. She was taught to be sweet, charming, and insipid: Never say anything with gusto and God forbid you should have a strong opinion on any controversial topic. Body and mind were molded with total disregard for the person inside.

Next time you watch a Miss America pageant you might ask yourself, How many of these young women suffer eating disorders? How many have surgically altered their appearance? What values have they sacrificed? How many souls are strangled in an attempt to create a body and a superficial facade to win a prize? A beauty queen is the archetype of a sexual codependent: the body is forged into an image for the sexual voyeurism of others.

Claudia did not place in the Miss America pageant. Afterward she became involved with a woman in a stormy, sometimes violent relationship. However, her journey changed dramatically a year later when she sought chemical dependency treatment.

The Miss America pageant is not qualitatively different from a Miss Wife or Miss Partner contest. Many women compete in this event daily, at great expense to their minds, bodies, and spirits. Like Rhonda, they focus on their body as a product; they measure their self-worth with a scoring system devised by male image makers. Their appearance determines their market value and leaves them to compete with one another to attain a blue chip rating that attracts the "best" men. Sadly, just as in the Miss America contest, the ratings are only about bodies, not souls.

What We Resist Persists: The "Holier Than Thou" Syndrome

Some of us are addicted to having no addictions, to being perfect, a nutty goal that our culture foists on us. Rather than learning to feel more centered, more loving, and more accepting of their humanness, we strive to have a perfect image or be perfectly enlightened — a misguided pursuit that actually renders us less human, and dreadfully serious. It's like trying to sing a song with all the words but none of the music. We need to realize that serenity is a journey and that the first step is to accept ourselves in the present, addictions and all. When we accept our addictiveness we accept our humanness and can start to heal.

Unfortunately, many psychotherapists, spiritual seekers, and clergy suffer from this affliction. They too often forget that the richest thing they can offer other people is the willingness to laugh and cry openly at their own foibles. When we try to rid ourselves of unwanted behavior, without seeking to understand the source of that behavior, it merely boomerangs on us. In other words, *what we resist persists*.

Laura illustrates this point. Lacking an outlet for her tremendous energy, creativity, and adventuresome spirit, she sometimes felt like a pressure cooker about to burst. For many years, the only way she knew to relieve the pressure was through an assortment of addictions.

I met Laura at a peace rally and immediately sensed a kindred spirit. I was attracted to her bright, clear energy and her sense of perspective. Humorously and gently she could lighten the sometimes heavy tone of the meetings to plan our civil disobedience action.

After one meeting we went to a restaurant, where she told me her story. Since early childhood Laura had been extraordinarily energetic and inquisitive. Of the four children in her family, Laura had screamed the loudest, asked the most questions, and had the most passionate spirit. She was always interested in other people and had her own ways of doing things. Laura's father was an active alcoholic and her parents were divorced when she was nine. Her mother weathered the divorce well, finishing college and finding a satisfying job. She was quite open with her children about the rough time they had been through.

At a very young age Laura was aware of a great longing for a nameless "something." She knew she enjoyed giving to others, but she needed something more than that, which she couldn't quite define. Not knowing how to satisfy her longing and feeling overwhelmed by her own energy, she started at age sixteen to be sexually involved with various men who were fascinating, charming, and usually abusive. Sex provided a channel for her energy, but being sexual with many men and being in abusive relationships conflicted sharply with her values concerning nonviolence and caring for others. She obscured the conflict through drug abuse. She went through chemical dependency treatment three times, the first when she was nineteen.

Over a period of years, in an attempt to fill her persistent longing and purge herself of what she experienced as an overwhelming sex drive and dependency on men, Laura went to several communes, worked on collective farms in various parts of the country, studied meditation, explored Buddhism, and participated in several psychotherapy groups. While she learned a lot, her sexual drive did not disappear, nor did her pull toward destructive relationships with men. "I usually found a man within the first day of arriving somewhere, anywhere," she told me. As a last resort, she went to India to work with Mother Teresa, hoping the experience would magically cure her sex drive.

I asked her if it worked and she laughed. "No. It was absolutely crazy. The day I arrived in Calcutta I met someone. I was this model of virtue in the daytime, working alongside the sisters helping the poor, and being my old self, out and about being sexual, at night. I lived a total double life. I always did." She laughed again. "I had this image that to be a good person I had to banish sex from my life. When I got home six months later I was at the end of my rope. I wanted to kill myself. I immediately got involved in another terribly abusive relationship. When, after a particularly bad fight, he left me battered and pushed my new car over a cliff, I realized I had to do something different. A light finally went on in my head and I realized something inside me had to change. No more trips. No more communes. I didn't know what it was, but I knew I would find it."

"What happened then?" I asked.

"*I suddenly realized that my passion was the greatest gift God had given me*. I didn't have to hate it. I didn't have to get rid of it. I knew I needed to stay away from sexual relationships with men for a while and that something in me was attracting abusive men and it would happen again unless something changed. In accepting my enormous passion for life and deciding to follow my own path, I came to accept that I'm not destined to have your regular kind of marriage and family. That's just not in the cards for me. I've been sad over that, but I feel a great sense of anticipation at what will come next.

"Right now I'd say I am at a turning point. I've been out of sexual relationships with men for three years, and stayed off alcohol and drugs for two years. I'm involved in coordinating a peace organization, but I'm almost through with that work. I'm halfway through writing a novel about my experiences and my sense is that writing will take me where I need to go. I don't have much sense of the future in terms of external events, but I feel excited about it. I feel pretty much secure within myself."

Laura paused for a few moments. Her ebullience diminished slightly. When she spoke again I felt a sense of sadness.

She said quietly, "I think I've been addicted to about everything one can be addicted to. I'm coming to see it was a way I denied my powerful energy, and this intense longing. I think I am finally accepting — although I don't admit it to many people because they take it as conceited — that I'm very bright, gifted, and destined to do something that will make a difference in the world. As I accept myself as a powerful woman, the sex drive lessens. Well, actually, as I accept myself and do what I feel called to do, my sex drive and need for men gets channeled into my work. I'll always be a very passionate person, but passion doesn't have to be expressed sexually. But" — she grinned — "there are still plenty of times when I think, 'If I don't meet someone to have sex with pretty soon, I'll go out on the street and find someone. I can't stand this one more week.'

But then, the urge is never strong enough anymore to get me to be sexual with someone I don't like.

"I am convinced that as I get more centered with my own power I won't keep attracting men who are powerful but abusive. I abused my power by not recognizing it, and I think that is related to attracting men with abusive power. I still hope that I will find a sexually powerful and loving relationship, but it is no longer the goal. The goal is to do what I am led to do and not flee from my true self."

I have heard many similar stories from women with powerful energy who attempted to harness it in stereotypical female roles, only to have it create internal havoc in the form of multiple addictions. All women are in a double bind with their power. We are told it is arrogant and unfeminine to acknowledge and express our God-given power, yet we destroy ourselves when we deny who we truly are.

CHEMICAL DEPENDENCY AND SEX ADDICTION

The use of alcohol and drugs with sex is pervasive for both sexually addicted and codependent women. In the vast majority of cases I have seen, sex addiction and codependency are the addictions underlying chemical addiction. This is evidenced by the great number of women who cannot maintain sobriety until they address their sex addiction and codependency issues. When I ask women to describe the role, if any, chemical use plays in their sex addiction, their answers reveal that the two often go hand in hand.

"It played a big part. Alcohol and drugs made me feel more desirable. I was also able to be more aggressive, especially sexually. I could come on strong with a drink."

"When I quit drinking I started acting out sexually."

"Before I did a trick I usually did some coke because I couldn't stand myself or what I was doing."

"Alcohol and drugs made it easier for me to act out in extreme ways and not care about the consequences. They made life feel even more surreal, dreamy."

"It was chemicals that helped me make out with a stranger on the dance floor while my lover was sitting not too far away. It didn't even occur to me that she'd be furious."

"I used wine to heighten the sense of romance and create false intimacy."

"I was always drunk when sexual and usually drunk before I began 'the hunt.'"

"I went through treatment four times but always got back to drinking when I got into sexual relationships. I always knew there was something else there I needed to look at, but I was scared of facing it. After the fourth time through treatment, I was ready. The 'monster' was sex addiction."

Alcohol and Sex Addiction

There seem to be two patterns of chemical use and sex addiction. First, some women use alcohol and drugs to repress their sexually addictive tendencies and to blot out the pain of a loveless existence. These are often married women who use alcohol and drugs to stay technically faithful to their partners and control their desire to act out sexually. They spend many hours in a romantic fantasy world, or read endless romantic novels, or focus on their house and children as a substitute.

The second and more common pattern is the use of alcohol and drugs as part of the sexual ritual, to numb feelings, gather courage for "the hunt," remove inhibitions, or heighten the romantic delusion. For many women, sex without drugs or alcohol is virtually unimaginable. Drugs provide intensity and courage. Nearly half the SAA women I interviewed had been through treatment for chemical dependency, and the vast majority believed that chemical use played a role in their sexually addictive behavior.

Anita typifies the cycle of sex and chemicals. She started using alcohol as a teenager to kill the pain of childhood abuse. In a perverse way the drugs and alcohol were a survival tool, getting her through the nightmare of her teenage years. Going through treatment and becoming sober ripped away her ability to submerge the agony of her childhood loneliness, shame, and desperation. But the treatment program did not address these issues, and she was left to white-knuckle her sobriety. Inevitably the stress of repressing her pain became overwhelming, and she reverted to behavior that brought temporary relief, namely, addictive sexual relationships. Once she headed for the bars or to a party to find a sexual partner it was only a matter of time before she started using chemicals again, both to gain courage to seduce men and to salve her wounded ego when they rejected her.

Some women engage in sexually addictive relationships despite being sober. However, most of them adopt other addictions, such as food, violence, work, and codependent relationships. Some become sexually dead, engage in other compulsive behavior, or become sick, anxious, or depressed. Although technically sober, they are not recovering at a spiritual level. The essential point is that for many women, treating chemical abuse without addressing underlying problems is a setup for failure, because chemically dependent women nearly always have other important issues to deal with.

It is common and understandable that women seek alcohol and drug treatment before they identify their sex addiction and codependency. It is often the most obvious addiction and one that gets in the way of seeing the others. It is crucial to address the drug addiction because change cannot occur when a person is constantly escaping with drugs and alcohol. It is important, however, that women be alerted to other possible addictions.

Despite the stories I have heard over the years, I am still amazed that those who manage addiction treatment programs persist in maintaining their tunnel vision. If treatment hasn't worked after three or four times around, why not consider that other problems may exist? For example, Margie had been through treatment fourteen times! At my meeting with other social service people involved in her case, everyone said amen to my recommendation that we assume chemical dependency was not the core problem and that we should try an alternative. The curious thing to me was why no one had thought of it sooner. If she had a slip and got drunk, they automatically sent her to chemical dependency treatment. Life is not always so black and white. Margie had to deal with childhood abuse and massive codependency with her family. Every slip followed an explosive visit with her family, who ruthlessly blocked all her attempts to be an autonomous woman.

This is why it is crucial to investigate core-level addictions and think holistically. When a core-level addiction is addressed, the secondary addiction may start to fade. But if the secondary addiction is treated in isolation, no deep healing occurs because you can't mend a wounded soul with a Band-Aid.

The path is different for everyone. Some will start by addressing food, chemical, or shopping addictions. Others will start with work on incest, abuse, and sexuality. It doesn't matter where you start as long as you keep an open mind and don't get locked into believing that there is only one solution.

Addictions and Shame

Women recovering from chemical dependency may feel intense shame when confronted with the idea of sex addiction. They either see it as one more thing wrong with them, or they compare themselves to the male stereotype of a sex addict. Women alcoholics long went unnoticed because they didn't fit male stereotypes: the falling-down, drunken bum; the violent, abusive, boisterous man; or the corporate executive with the three-martini lunch.

Confronted with the idea that sex addiction might underlie her problems, one woman responded, "Not something else wrong with me! Not something else I have to give up! *No! No! No!*" When I brought up sex addiction with one client, she lunged out of her chair and said angrily, "You just think I'm like those terrible men who abuse children and have sex with animals."

Renée, who once attended four twelve-step groups simultaneously, nearly screamed at me when I suggested that she consider an SAA group. "No. I won't go! I can't stand it! On Monday I'm a compulsive overeater, on Tuesday I'm an alcoholic, on Thursday I'm a codependent. I can't stand one more label, one more thing wrong with me. I won't go! *I won't say I'm a sex addict*." Her rebellion reflected a self-respecting desire not to be labeled as defective or continue focusing on what was wrong with her. After a pause I said, "You don't have to say you're an addict if you don't want to. You never have to use that word again for all I care. Just say you are Renée, and you are there to talk about your sexuality. You also don't need to attend so many groups. Pick what feels most important and have some fun the rest of the time." We'll return to Renée in the closing chapter.

CoSA Women and Chemical Dependency

Both SAA and CoSA women used alcohol and drugs to anesthetize themselves from the knowledge of their difficult or unhappy lives. They also used alcohol and drugs in conjunction with sex to deny their knowledge of the harm they were doing to themselves and others. The similarities between the two groups wane at this point.

While addicted women used chemicals for intensity and courage to act out the seduction role, codependent women frequently used alcohol to feel more "relaxed" about being sexual. One woman in a codependency group wrote, "I used alcohol and drugs when anything I encountered had anything to do with sex, to avoid the pain of the belief system that I could not define my own sexuality without encountering severe punishment." Her statement reflects the training many sexually codependent women have internalized, the belief that enjoying sex for oneself, not for men or procreation, is evil, shameful, dirty, sinful, or disgusting.

Codependent women have a double dilemma. Not only are they programmed not to enjoy sex, they must say yes to sex when their partners want it. No wonder so many of them use alcohol to deal with this painful situation. Between the lines, the frequent phrase "I use alcohol to relax" really means, "I use alcohol so I can stand being sexual." One woman said, "I used alcohol so I could fake sex." Another was even more graphic: "I was just a hole to stick it in, so I drank not to hate myself." The sad truth is that codependent women have rarely been sexual for themselves. They have been receptacles, or they use sex to reward or punish their partners.

For the most part their addicted partners used them as objects. The women simply did not think to protest, nor did they imagine that anything else was possible. Marsha, introduced in Chapter 3, spent nearly four years in individual and group therapy. In an early session with her husband, after a mountain of verbiage that went nowhere, she abruptly said to him, "Sex with you has felt like rape for twenty-five years." Terrified of retribution for her crime of honesty, she immediately curled up into a tiny ball in her chair, refusing to talk anymore. Finally, I asked if she wanted to go to a hospital for a few days. She responded with a slight nod of her head. She went directly from my office to a short-term depression unit, where I maintained contact with her. I suspect that going to the hospital was the only way she could permit herself to leave her husband.

Shortly after leaving the hospital, Marsha came to my office, still depressed and immersed in guilt for speaking the truth. I asked her if she had ever thought of saying anything to her husband about her feelings in all those years. She said, "No, it never occurred to me. I thought you had to do 'it' no matter what. That's what the Bible says. I grew up putting out for my father so he wouldn't beat me, so I just put out for my husband."

I wondered what it must have felt like for her to lie under a man night after night, tensing her body, shutting out her heart, strangling her God-given impulses in the interest of being a "good" wife. Was that the source of her continual back problems, pelvic and vaginal infections, tumors, and eventual hysterectomy? Was that related to her compulsive eating? Marsha had been so desperate about her weight that she had had her stomach stapled, only to regain the eighty pounds she had lost.

What a miracle of courage it had taken for her to spit out those words to her husband! Some kind of magical fire had ignited within her, allowing her finally to name her experience. Her discovery struck me as akin to a spiritual revelation, a wonderful discovery that she wanted to live. Later in the session I asked if she had ever heard the phrase "To thine own self be true" or considered a message of Christianity that love most surely begins with love of self. This religious idea struck a chord with her. Two affirmations became instrumental in her recovery: "God loves me when I take care of myself" and "God wants me to feel good." Eventually she stopped "putting out" for her husband, and almost immediately she stopped using alcohol and was less depressed.

Not all codependents' alcohol and drug use were directly related to sex. Women also stupefy themselves to keep their partners company, to be a gracious hostess, to fit in, to keep up appearances, to be outgoing — always for their partners, never for themselves; always to maintain a good image. They use alcohol to deny their buried rage, to be able to smile through, and hence to deny, their misery.

SEX AND FOOD: A COMPLICATED CONNECTION

This topic deserves a book of its own. Food, with its relationship to nurturance, to penetration of the body, to self-love, to escape from feelings, is an extremely complicated subject. It combines both physiological factors and some of our earliest psychological programming, lodged deep in our unconscious minds. For many people, food is the most reliable source of pleasure. You can't always count on sex or other people, but you can always count on chocolate. Food and body image are common concerns among a high percentage of women in the United States. Not surprisingly then, food, body size, sex addiction, and sexual codependency are inextricably linked for them. Some women shared their experiences:

"I starved myself in the midst of a codependent addictive relationship which was not going well. I lost fifteen pounds in two weeks over a man. I had the shakes, I couldn't get out of bed. My throat closed. I only drank coffee. I could see the bones in my back and it was horrible. I felt like a little girl, but it worked to kill the relationship pain. I could focus on the bodily pain."

"I remember dropping twenty-two pounds in college in three weeks when a guy left me. I wanted to turn myself inside out. It was like being little. I wanted to disappear."

"On the way home from work I would stop and eat a lot so I wouldn't feel anything if Art wanted to be sexual."

"I would not eat or sleep and lived on coffee. I became hypoglycemic. At the end of that time I just crashed and was diagnosed manic-depressive. There was a year when I could hardly get out of bed. I think my mood swings were because of my binge-and-starve eating and my sex addiction."

When we don't acknowledge what is true for us or believe we have the right to say no to sex, our psyche finds a way to do it for us. In a sense the truth is inescapable — there is no hiding from ourselves. Many women, unable to say no I don't want to be sexual, I'm hurting inside, I'm afraid, I'm sad, I need to change my life, use food as a language for their feelings.

As we have seen, a major feature of codependency is a lack of boundaries. The right to say "No, don't touch me," "No, don't kiss me," or "Yes, hug me, hold me, kiss me" is primary in developing sexual boundaries. When we say no to sex we find out if we are loved without being sexual. When we give a genuine yes to sex we find out if the other person is willing to meet us in a vulnerable, present way.

As infants we are utterly without boundaries. Food and touch come our way only at the mercy of our caregivers. If they are rigid, distant, manipulative, or intrusive, we are profoundly affected. If the nurturing one feeds or touches us with feelings of disgust or sexual shame, we may unconsciously associate all forms of nurturance with a fear of being invaded. When people force food on them, children can experience it as intensely as sexual intrusiveness or abuse. They fear that it will fill them up, explode them, tear them apart. I believe that many eating disorders mirror the essence of a child's primary bond with her or his caregiver. Many sexually addicted and codependent women have traits of or diagnosable cases of anorexia and bulimia.

Anorexic women shut out nurturance for fear that it will somehow poison them: "People being close to me makes me sick. Food makes me sick. The distance I keep from people and food makes me feel pure, safer, more powerful, in charge." The metaphor for bulimia is accepting nurturance and, finding it poisonous, casting it out.

I frequently use an image that takes women back to infancy to help raise awareness of their resistance to physical nurturance and food. After getting into a deep state of relaxation, the woman imagines that she is her own mother. I say, "I'm handing your new baby to you for the first time." I ask her to experience her reaction — not to change it, just feel it. Is it fear? Discomfort? Terror? We move along in time. "Now you are home with your infant. You're holding her. The baby is spitting up on your shoulder. She's having a bowel movement. Let's remove her diapers. Note your reaction." Some of the words the women use to describe their reactions include *uncomfortable, terrified, disgusted, repulsed, loathsome, hateful, violent*. When one woman recovering from anorexia role-played her mother holding her infant, her face suddenly contorted, and she spoke almost hissingly through clenched teeth, "Ooooo, you're poison, you're evil, you're dirty, get away from me, don't you ever touch me. I hate you. I hate you." She was connecting up with her mother's sexual shame.

By becoming anorexic a woman at once gains control in her family and brings them together. An anorexic's family often maintains a deceptive picture-perfect exterior when in fact every member of the family lives with a sense of emptiness they are ashamed to talk about. The anorexic child gives the rest of the family something to worry about, thereby distracting Mom and Dad from looking at their marriage, which is usually spiritually and sexually unsatisfying. Food becomes at once the anorexic's power and her emptiness, her means of control and her death.

Self-starvation may also be a child's unconscious defense against covert sexual energy, often from an immature or sexually addicted father who sexualizes his relationship with his daughter, flirting with her and treating her more like a girlfriend than a daughter. It may also be a reaction to a sexually or emotionally intrusive mother. Either way, the child literally shrinks from becoming a woman, and anorexia is both survival for the soul that craves love and a form of codependency, a sacrifice of self.

Like all addictions, food becomes a substitute for feelings one is afraid to express. One codependent woman said, "I used food and preparation of food instead of touching, to show affection. I put food out to show I cared and wanted to be cared about." Of course, when no one read the message and gave her the accolades she wanted, she was furious.

In another example, a woman's codependency to her husband led her to neglect her children physically and emotionally. "I used food to keep peace in the family when my husband drank, which usually got him to ranting and raving. I always bought candy bars for the kids and put Coke in the baby's bottle when she was fussy. I wanted to keep them happy so they wouldn't upset Bob. I felt awful when my baby's teeth had to be pulled." She, too, used food as an indirect boundary, instead of saying, "No, you can't treat me that way."

Another woman used food to express anger. "I would make all these delicious pies and desserts I knew my husband couldn't resist. I loved seeing him lose control and get fat. It served him right."

One supervisor of a treatment program in eating disorders said that 80 percent of the women at their intake interviews revealed that they were survivors of sexual abuse. From this one can guess that a high percentage of them also had problems with sex addiction and sexual codependency. Does the woman who shields herself with fifty pounds of excess weight do so because of sexual codependency — she's afraid to say no to sex — or is it an eating disorder? Or both? Which came first? And did fear of saying no stem from her being sexually abused as a child? As women work through their food issues, they open the door to recognizing their childhood abuse, sex addiction, and codependency. If the counselors ask the appropriate questions and help a woman find resources to help her continue healing, she has a greater likelihood of maintaining her food sobriety. If the eating disorders program fails to address other issues that arise, the woman may unconsciously protect herself from the cause of her pain by leaving the program and resuming her compulsive eating.

Switching from food addiction to romance addiction is classic. It is not uncommon for a woman who is doing well in an eating disorders program to fall in love, lose her appetite, and suddenly drop out of the program, going from total immersion in food to total immersion in a relationship. She is convinced that her eating problems have disappeared, but in fact she has merely switched addictions. Her compulsive eating is likely to return when the romance wears off.

Food and sex are used and misused for the same reasons, for they are experienced at a spiritual level in similar ways. Both are used in an attempt to satisfy a deep hunger. Consider the following statements in the context of your own life:

Food and sex can be a source of pleasure, fulfillment, and self-love.

Food and sex can be used compulsively as a substitute for nurturance and love or to assuage loneliness.

Food and sex can become obsessive.

Food and sexual energy are both sources of vital life-giving energy. We need food to live and we need to be comfortable with our sexual energy in order to feel truly alive within.

We can bribe, and act out anger toward others with food and sex.

The quality of food and sex affects our experience of it. As one woman said, "Junk food, junk love. With me, the two always seem to go together."

The setting in which we partake of food or sex affects our experience of it. A comfortable room, soft lighting, and plenty of time all make a difference.

Freely choosing to participate in eating or sex affects the experience. That is, did we consciously choose to have sex or food, was it pushed on us, or did we partake out of guilt?

Partaking of food and sex can leave you feeling shameful, desperate, empty, lonely, or sad.

Partaking of food and sex can leave you feeling content, filled up, and happy.

Food and sex can both be used in violent ways. Think of eating four thousand calories in less than three hours, the definition of a binge. Like rape, it overwhelms the system, is emotionally traumatic, leaves one with shame and self-loathing, and is physically damaging. While rape comes from an external source, binging comes from a source that *feels* external. Food becomes a substitute source of power — power to block out feelings, to fill oneself up, and to express rage. Women who binge and starve, binge and purge, or starve themselves have tremendous inner conflict about accepting their power as women and accepting and enjoying their female sexuality.

Think of the ways one can respond to being offered either sex or food. In my own case, I ate to please my mother. I was afraid of hurting her feelings — she had gone to so much trouble to make dinner — that I lost track of my internal fullness clock. Ask yourself if, when offered sex or food, you have the conscious control to say the following with ease:

· Yes, I'd love to.
· Yes, I'd love to, but not right now. Let's set a time.
· I'm not sure, I'd like to think about it. Let's wait and see.
· No, I don't feel like it now. Maybe some other time.
· No, never.

During the sexual act or while partaking of food, do you have the conscious ability to say the following with ease?

- That's enough now. I want to stop.
- Yes, more.
- No, thanks, I don't like that at all. I don't want to do that.
- A little more of that. I like it.
- A little less of that. I don't care for that so much.
- I think I made a mistake in getting started. I'd like to stop.

Part of a woman's deepest programming is the belief that she has no control over her consumption of food and participation in sex. This, in turn, leads to obsession, because we form obsessions with things we can't control. An obsession with food drains energy and distracts a woman from the deeper issues of her life.

Some women become incredibly codependent when it comes to food preparation. You'd think Moses came down off the mountain with a stone just for women that said, "Thou shalt prepare food for your mate, no exceptions." Many women make comments like, "It's so nice when my husband is away, I don't have to cook great big dinners every night. I can eat what I want and lose some weight." It's their codependency talking. They are overwhelmingly identified with their role of food preparer.

Emily spent a year in therapy gathering the courage to get a divorce. There was hardly a night in the thirty-two years of her marriage that she didn't have dinner on the table for her husband at 6:00 P.M. Whether she was sick or well, loved it or hated it, dinner was there. Even in the three-month interim between planning the divorce and his moving out, she did not allow herself one night off kitchen duty. She longed to go out with women friends instead of staring at him through the miserably tense dinner hour, but she couldn't bring herself to do it. She was programmed to believe that if there's a man in the house, you cook his dinner. We eventually used "gotta cook dinner for Don" as a metaphor for the way Emily avoided risks: "I can't show my feelings because someone might laugh"; "I can't take a trip because I'd have to use savings."

Most women have sudden changes in their eating patterns that follow the patterns of their addictive relationships. The most common is to lose weight at the beginning of a relationship, gain weight when the romance wears off, then lose weight again when the relationship crashes. The second most common scenario is for women to gain weight when the relationship ends.

It is important to remember that "not eating" can anesthetize feelings and give one a sense of power and a clear high feeling as surely as any drug. Not eating can also be as addictive in distancing oneself from feelings as compulsive eating.

The beginning of an addictive relationship is an incredible high. Not eating at the beginning of a relationship intensifies the high — two addictions at once. This combination increases the distance between the addictive self and the knowing self, thus greatly numbing one's knowledge of what is going on. When the high of the relationship wears off, one fills the reappearing empty place with food or denies feelings by not eating. Thus, preoccupation with food replaces romance.

One woman who lost a lot of weight at the end of a relationship said, "I was fascinated with the weight loss. Losing weight usually takes tremendous will power and work for me. Losing weight so fast was a real high. I loved feeling my clothes become suddenly loose and seeing the size of my body change so rapidly."

A woman who had recovered from anorexia and no longer experienced self-starvation as a high said, "I suddenly had the image that not eating was like self-cannibalism. In some terrible way I was devouring myself. I realized with a sudden sadness that I was doing it to myself — I was starving me. I never wanted to do it again."

The vicious cycle of addictions continues until we throw a monkey wrench into the system and change the patterns. We are jolted into awareness when we get to the source of our pain and recognize our feelings; only then can we satisfy our hungers in a positive, self-affirming way.

Tessie was an attractive woman of thirty-one who had been through a period of bulimia followed by bouts of compulsive eating. She had been the apple of her father's eye and vigorously maintained that she loved her father. She couldn't see that his jealousy of her boyfriends, his constant comments about her "sexy body," and his flirtatious touching were incestuous, an intrusion into her sexuality. When she got married she dutifully submitted whenever her husband initiated sex. He did not pressure her, but it never crossed her mind to say no. She did not derive much pleasure from sex. After a few months, she had difficulty lubricating and started having headaches.

Depression set in and she started group therapy. One day a woman in the group spoke of her own father, who screamed at her whenever she came home from a date. Tessie blurted out, "That's terrible!" Then she suddenly realized that her own story was the same. A wrenching insight, it left her with a sick feeling about her father.

A few days later she was in the bedroom, naked, when her husband suddenly walked in and went toward her to give her a hug. Something snapped. She saw him as her father. A voice burst out of her with the first scream of her adult life: "Don't touch me! Don't touch me! Stay away!" Phillip, a sensitive person, stopped in his tracks. "What's wrong? What can I do?" he asked. She stood there stunned for a moment. Her father's face slowly dissolved and she heard Phillip's kind voice repeating, "What's wrong? Can I do something for you?" Her husband's warmth and care melted something inside her and she started to cry. "Hold me," she said. Phillip picked up a towel, wrapped it around her, and took her in his arms. Tessie gave way to her tears as he held her for nearly an hour.

The next day, for the first time in her memory, Tessie had no compulsive desire for food. She described the feeling. "I felt both light and filled up." She laughed. "I was filled with light. It was as if my tears became food."

Not only had her tears fed her, but her screams had ignited her power, her sense of autonomy. For the first time, the compliant good girl said no with unrestrained passion. It was like a birth of the self, a moment of pure self-love, the sweetest food of all.

To hide from the truths about our lives, we immerse ourselves in a web of addictions. We are in a constant state of strife, split between our perceived reality and the buried reality. Because addiction is the psyche's way of seeking escape from buried feelings and easing the inner strife, the addictive agent can be most anything — alcohol, sex, cigarettes, religion, caffeine, TV, anger, depression, shopping, cleaning, eating, not eating, work, or an ever-changing combination of these.

We break through the addictive miasma by connecting with our truths and releasing our buried feelings and healing our tired bodies. Tessie had to suffer the pain of relinquishing her illusion about her wonderful relationship with her father. Her screams and her river of tears bridged the inner split and brought her into harmony with what, deep down, she knew to be true. Anger directed at the appropriate source is often the wakeup call, the monkey wrench that interrupts the addictive cycle. Anger at abuse and battering, anger at oppression and humiliation, is a way of saying, "I count, I deserve more than this, I am alive." When we connect with ourselves deeply, we calm the conflict that leads to addictive and compulsive behavior.

CHAPTER 10

Conflicting Values:
Sex, Addiction, Masochism, and Violence

IT'S AUGUST and I've just returned from a vacation in paradise — a cabin on a lake surrounded by mountains near my home town of Missoula, Montana. Since my return, I've been taking walks and sorting through drawers in an effort to avoid this chapter. I don't want to think about female violence and self-abuse. It's painful.

I'm also in a quandary about using the word *masochism,* which often comes up in the context of sexual codependency and addiction. Masochism has been proposed as a new diagnostic category. I shudder as I think of women having the masochistic personality diagnosis thrust upon them and absorbing it into their self-image. The belief that women are naturally masochistic and enjoy or are sexually aroused by pain has been used by men as a rationalization for abusing, humiliating, raping, and degrading them. Pornography is largely propaganda reinforcing this belief. In addition, current ads are permeated with images of women who appear to enjoy or be aroused by physical and sexual abuse. Attaching the word *masochism* to women makes it easy to discount women's suffering and oppression — she's just masochistic — rather than ask the reason why. Why do women's sexual fantasies often include being held down, overwhelmed, and even raped? I don't buy that some people are born masochistic, any more than I buy that others are born sadistic. I believe this is learned behavior. The paradox of childhood sexual abuse is that it conditions women unconsciously to pair sexual arousal with being controlled, manipulated, violated, and overwhelmed. Then the culture turns around and diagnoses such women as masochistic, which is a form of blaming the victim. Like codependency, what appears to be masochism is largely a trait of people with less power in a system, or people who have been abused.

According to the *American Heritage Dictionary,* masochism refers to deriving pleasure from "being subjected to abuse or physical pain." I challenge this definition. While it is indeed true that some women are sexually aroused by being subjected to abuse, degradation, or physical pain, I believe this differs from *deriving pleasure* from abuse. Moreover, these women's responses are usually a *result* of negative cultural conditioning and sexual abuse. I don't believe any baby desires to be hurt. I don't believe that deep down in her soul, any woman wants to be degraded and subjected to physical pain. Therefore I use the term *masochism* only to describe a role a woman sometimes plays. For the most part I will talk about how women wound themselves with the goal of being acceptable, to relieve shame, to fit in, to get attention, or as a learned response to sexual abuse.

There was a time when I would have said that there was no violence or self-abuse in my life. But when I look back at the big curlers that wrecked my adolescent sleep (in the interest of a beautiful page boy), the hours spent by the phone (waiting for *him* to call), and the years of foot and back pain I endured in my fashionable high heels, I'm struck by the fact that I was an active participant in my own pain. How did I stand in high heels for eight hours a day working in a gift store when I was nineteen? A few days ago I took an old pair out of a trunk and found I couldn't walk across the room in them.

I remember my adolescent fantasies of being injured or fatally ill so that someone would give me attention. One time when I felt lonely on a class hike in the fifth grade, I scratched my arm with a piece of sharp glass, cutting until it bled — the only acceptable way I knew to get tenderness and care. I remember my violent thoughts of wanting to light a match to the newspaper my husband put up between us. I remember drinking too much or eating too much to distract me from emotional pain.

What leads women to self-abuse? For me there was a direct connection to the negative messages I received about power: "You're too into the piano"; "You're too angry"; "You're too outspoken"; "You're too serious about your work"; and so on. These messages led me to hate myself. And the unspoken implication was, always, you're too powerful *for a man to love you*. I wasn't too powerful for me. I loved playing the piano. At twenty-two, I wanted to buy a Steinway grand piano with money I had saved from several years' summer jobs. When it was finally time to start shopping for one, my mother blurted out, "But what if you meet a man who doesn't want such a big piano?" My source of joy, my passion, my God-given talent was dismissed in one fell swoop as my mother played her cultural role of preparing me to be a "good" wife. No wonder I wanted to hurt myself.

The point of looking at self-abuse is to rip away our denial of ourselves as women. It forces us to admit that the culture hurts us. Men are acceptable because they are men; women have to work to be acceptable to men. We are not taught to be acceptable to ourselves.

THE MYTH OF WOMEN AND VIOLENCE

A myth exists in our culture that women are not violent. It is a myth that needs to be exploded in the interest of healing our wounds. It is a myth that leaves many women painfully alone, feeling ashamed about their secrets of self-abuse, abuse of others, and participation in violent or sadomasochistic sexual relationships.

Underlying female self-abuse is female oppression. Our basic female socialization includes learning to tolerate pain in an effort to please others, particularly men, and accepting self-punishing behavior as a given, not a choice. "I *have* to wear high heels to work"; "I *have* to be sexual when he wants." Women in China felt that they *had* to enhance their daughters' chances of finding a husband by binding and crippling their feet. Women in Africa believed (and some still do) that they *must* have their clitorises cut off or their vaginas sewn together to be acceptable to men. My mother felt she had to quell my inner fire to make me acceptable to a man. (By the way, I bought the piano anyway.)

We learn to sacrifice our minds, bodies, and spirits in order to fit into society and in the process we are trained to see ourselves as bodies, not souls. We are taught to take care of men's egos by playing stupid, acting afraid, and by accepting male definitions of female sexuality as passive and masochistic. The worst part is that many women have internalized such "norms" and do not see them as oppressive. They see them as truly natural for females. This is when oppression becomes complete.

Women are taught to turn their anger inward, which affects us deeply. It is a form of self-abandonment that can result in depression, chemical abuse, anxiety, and self-abuse. We absorb media images of ourselves as powerless. These images create an internal conflict with our knowledge of a power existing deep within us. We may suddenly erupt with anger, a violent act, or a cutting remark. When our usually good and caring selves lash out at someone, we may feel shocked and wonder, "Where did that come from?"

Female violence associated with sex is an incredible secret. We have great difficulty thinking of women cutting and abusing themselves, tying themselves up to masturbate, or being sadistic with men or other women. We cringe at the thought of mothers as sexual abusers. Psychologically we are conditioned to accept women as victims, but rarely as perpetrators, of abuse. We have shelters for battered women, but where are the treatment programs for violent and abusive women? Parents Anonymous exists for women who abuse children, but therapy groups are just being formed for female perpetrators of physical and sexual abuse. It is not surprising that female violence is at once common and a taboo. It doesn't fit our stereotype.

Atomic physics has shown that energy cannot be destroyed, it can only be transformed. By the same token, the violence done to a woman's mind, body, and spirit inevitably manifests itself in some way. All too often this violence is released through physical, verbal, or sexual violence toward herself or toward a less powerful group, namely children or other women.

While it is painful to reach deep within and touch our shadow side, accepting it as a part of us opens the way to healing. When we stop blocking this part of us we open up our true energy; otherwise these painful secrets stay locked inside of us and become a source of shame. They become an internal poison.

Self-abuse is learned. It is violence turned inward, often as a result of feeling shame. It is no more natural to female sexuality than it is for a baby to enjoy cutting herself. Masochism can be subtle or blatant, but what each of us considers normal depends in large part upon our own internalized set of beliefs. To get a closer look at yourself and ways you are or may have been self-abusive or neglectful, think about the following questions. Some of your responses may bring you back to adolescence. Ask yourself whom were you trying to please. Were you really acting for yourself, or for someone else? Whose rules, whose belief system, were you living by?

If we consider self-abuse as anything we do to abandon our body, mind, or spirit to please others, or fit in, then we can consider a wide spectrum of behavior on a continuum from self-neglect to abuse. Here are some categories for your exploration.

Time and Money Spent for Others   Have you wasted time, canceled activities, or felt anxious waiting for phone calls from him or her?

Have you spent on makeup and clothes time and money that you wish you'd spent for lessons, classes, or other pursuits?

Have you spent excessive amounts of money on another person to ensure that they stick around or to impress them?

Altering Your Appearance   Have you ever burned yourself with a curling iron? Had to cut electric hair curlers out of your hair? Had allergic reactions to makeup? Worn painfully tight or uncomfortable clothes or girdles?

Think about the time you've devoted to fixing the outside of your body rather than paying attention to your inside — exercising, meditating, learning skills, developing friendships, planning your future. Was it worth it?

Body Comfort Abandonment   Think of the foot aches, the sore legs, and backaches associated with uncomfortable shoes. Watch people walk.

Notice the difference between women striding heel to toe in comfortable shoes and those in high heels. Imagine how their feet and legs feel. Whom are they doing this for?

Physical Self-Abuse   Think of the times you have engaged in physical self-abuse: biting your nails, scratching a place until there is a permanent sore, picking pimples until you get scars. Do you have tattoos you wish you didn't have? Have you ever banged your head, hit yourself with objects, tied yourself up, pulled out hair, dug at your skin, scratched your arms, cut your arms, or burned yourself? Have you put yourself in situations where someone else is likely to abuse you? Do you associate any of these behaviors with sexual arousal?

Verbal Self-Abuse   How many times a day do you call yourself stupid, ugly, unworthy, unlovable, and so forth? Remember how it hurt when a parent or sibling said these things to you as a child. Are you aware now of doing it to yourself?

Think about your body. What parts do you regularly call ugly? Hair? Nose? Breasts? Butt? Thighs? Belly? Genitals? How much energy would you free up if you accepted your body just as it is? (You can accept your body without liking it all.) What about thinking of your body as simply a package for your spirit and soul, something to take good care of and nurture? Think how it feels when another person makes a derogatory comment about your body. Do you do the same thing to yourself?

Abandoning Self   How many times have you meant to say no to someone but couldn't get the word out? Think of the times you've been angry at someone, planned to say no, and ended up socializing with that person instead.

Eating   How much time do you spend obsessing about food or worrying about weight? Contrast that with time spent learning to eat nutritious foods that make you feel alive and healthy. What about exercise? Do you approach it as a way to feel good in your body, or in a desperate, self-hateful way to get rid of unwanted fat and pummel your body into submission?

Sexuality   Now think of all the things you have done sexually that didn't feel good to you. Have you said yes because you were afraid to say no? Have you ever had a sore vagina from letting a man penetrate you before you were ready? Have you sacrificed sexual pleasure because you were too afraid to ask for what you wanted? Have you taken part in any sort of sexual practice that didn't feel good? Did you let your partner tie you up, hit you, or be rougher than you wanted?

All these forms of self-abuse sap our God-given energy and distract us from bigger issues. We do not need to continue such behavior. We can make choices. Take a moment to imagine a world in which billboards and advertisements feature women of all different shapes, sizes, races, and ages, including women with body hair and with muscles. Don't forget to include physically disabled women. How would that feel?

When my friend Shirley turned fifty she said to herself, happily, "I'm fifty. I'll never wear uncomfortable shoes again. I wear pants with elastic waists, and my hair just does its thing. I don't care what anyone thinks anymore." Of course we don't have to turn fifty to make these choices. But age helps. So does feeling secure in one's career and friendships.

THE DYNAMICS OF SELF-ABUSE

At an unconscious level we are always seeking resolutions to childhood dilemmas. It is a paradox that we block the pain of childhood, thinking we are protecting ourselves, by recreating similar painful situations in our adult lives. On some level, we're looking for a second chance, to get what we missed the first time around. By attracting people similar to those in our families, we are given a chance to heal ourselves, to learn the lesson inherent to our childhood situations. A woman whose father was emotionally absent or rejected her marries a man who is emotionally unavailable, displacing her unconscious desire to change her father by changing her partner into the warm and loving father she yearned for. Outwardly, she may claim that she had a wonderful childhood and that she knows her father loved her. She just happened to choose a cold, troubled man — or a string of them.

A woman who was a scapegoat in her family repeatedly becomes a scapegoat in her workplace. A woman whose father beat her is unable to become sexually aroused without violent fantasies. As long as these women stay in similar dysfunctional situations as adults, painful childhood feelings remain in the unconscious, while the old scenarios are reenacted in present situations.

The family provides a child's basis for reality. I have heard many adults say, "I thought it was normal to beat kids," or "I thought it was normal for men to hit women." When you say to yourself "That's normal," you keep the pain and rage buried; childhood reality is never explored or questioned. But when you start having positive experiences of human interaction, you have a basis for comparison. After being in a friendly support group, you may start realizing the possibility of something better, something emotionally richer. You discover that differences can be tolerated; that anger can exist but doesn't have to be violent; that others care about your well-being; or that people need not be rejected when they make mistakes. You begin to think, "This feels good. I never knew life could be like this." The paradox is that when you experience love and acceptance, the old pain is released and you begin to grieve for your empty childhood. It is important to realize that the mind at this moment, wanting to avoid discomfort, may say, "This is painful; I'd better retreat." But it's only a trick of the ego to avoid change. This is what makes change a bittersweet experience. You feel relief and pain. "I feel cheated that my family wasn't this way. If I had been loved like this, I wouldn't have put up with so much abuse as an adult." "I'm angry to have accepted depression." "I feel sad that I've never let people love me before."

Confronting the reality of childhood means reconnecting with pain, anger, and shame. But until we begin to sense that there is a possibility for change, we look for addictive solutions. We say, "If I just find the 'right' partner everything will be okay," never realizing that we are attracted to abusive people because we are trying to heal old wounds. With new relationships we may repeatedly think, "This time it is different." And, on the surface, each new relationship may indeed have different characteristics. When we begin to look at the relationships in terms of intimacy levels, the differences disappear.

We shield ourselves from self-knowledge of our inner wounds with more denial: "Isn't this how it is for everyone? I know underneath they really loved me." We maintain the myth of a happy childhood, or at least the belief that it wasn't really *that* bad. If that doesn't work, we may even convince ourselves that we just made it all up. The internal havoc that results from this form of denial can be devastating. At its extreme it results in multiple personalities or feeling schizophrenic.

Most of us grew up with the unspoken injunction *"You must not be angry at your parents or see them as lacking in any way. You will always make excuses for their failings. You are bad to criticize your parents."* This explains why so many people have a nameless dread of leaving a painful relationship — leaving will give rise to the painful sense of abandonment and hurt associated with their parents' emotional or physical abandonment. So we suffer in empty, violent, or degrading relationships to avoid facing the truths of our lives and our heritage as women. For many women, chronic emotional starvation is preferable to self-examination and the feelings that go with it, particularly feelings of good old unladylike rage!

What does all this have to do with sex and violence? Self-abuse and passivity diminish our capacity to experience our passionate, powerful, female sexuality, the source of our creativity. Yet our minds, bodies, and spirits are cruelly invaded by the culture, conditioning us to pain, violence, and self-abuse. Consider a Maidenform brassiere ad, for example. A skinny, unblemished, sophisticated woman stands in the forefront wearing an open fur coat exposing a lacy bra and panties. She has a pouty, sexy look on her face. A male "hunk" lurks in the dusky background, eyes furtively fixed on her. A punching bag hangs to his right, his closed fist subtly pointing in that direction. Will buying this bra win you a handsome sadistic man? Are women supposed to be turned on by the implication of male domination, therefore buy the bra, and feel desirable wearing it? The sad thing is that these ads work. Many women are programmed to be stimulated by sexual fantasies involving masochism and passivity, and Madison Avenue is all too willing to play into these fantasies with ads that depict recurring themes of sex addiction and codependency. The images are all about arousal of the body but not the soul.

Why doesn't our culture associate sexual arousal with images of roses opening, dewdrops on orchids, sun bursting over the horizon, rapid flowing mountain streams, or surging ocean waves? Why is *My Secret Garden,* an early feminist book on women's sexual fantasies, filled with images of masochism, rape, and passivity? And why do we accept this as "normal"?

I believe that in the early days of this round of liberation, women were so glad to be opening up to their sexuality that they weren't ready to question what excited them. It was wonderful just to talk about sexuality and fantasies. But the time has come to question what turns us on — not to be judgmental, but simply to understand how our souls are poisoned by pairing violence and self-abuse with sex.

Advertisers have become adept at manipulating our conscious and unconscious minds. To say that we have been brainwashed may sound melodramatic, but the fact is that brainwashing is an intensive indoctrination aimed at getting people to replace their basic convictions and attitudes with a fixed and unquestioned set of beliefs. The techniques used in brainwashing systematically desensitize people, alienating them from their feelings and their internal connection with what is right and good. This is always done to meet the needs of the brainwasher. Pairing sex and violence serves the purposes of a consumer-oriented economic system — the brainwasher — which must constantly sell things. Lots of things. More than we need.

Images that pair merchandise with sexual arousal and fulfillment are everywhere. And images lie to us. To protect ourselves from the meaning of women-hating ads, we all engage in *psychic numbing,* a term originally used to describe our massive cultural denial to the threat of the nuclear holocaust, the most extreme form of self-abuse. To raise your consciousness about this, spend a day looking at billboards, magazine covers, and advertising, particularly in high-fashion magazines. Let yourself feel the themes of violence. What is your reaction? Disgust? Arousal? Do you feel pulled in? Then think of the personal lives of all the women in the ads. What might they have done to make the ad? Shave their pubic hair? Vomit daily to be skinny? Be sexual with the photographer? What was the process of making the ad? How did the woman feel as she was being "worked over" or "made over" to look the "right" way?

Advertisers are creating increasingly blatant sexual and violent images to get past the psychic numbing we use to protect ourselves from our inner knowledge of this insult to our souls. The violent nature of ads escalates, just as addiction does. Recently I went to one of Minnesota's finest department stores to buy a bathrobe. At the edge of the lingerie section, I was assaulted by a large TV screen showing a seductive video promoting bras. The headless, bottomless woman on the screen drew her hands tenderly over her shoulder, pulling down the bra strap and the right side of the bra until, *whoosh,* the picture cut away just before her nipple was exposed. The image was repeated over and over in different ways, teasing the viewer with an almost totally exposed breast. The lush, velvety voice-over described the beautiful fit of the bra. I felt both drawn to the video and deeply violated, assaulted by sexual images in a department store I had innocently entered to make a purchase.

It is a vicious cycle. Brainwash the mind to believe that things will make you happy; create ads that produce sexual arousal so that the turned-on feeling is associated with things.

Then watch the top spin. The more unnecessary things we have, the emptier we feel; the emptier we feel, the more we can be seduced by sexually stimulating ads that lead us to buy things, which in turn creates even more emptiness. We are the victims of a huge lie about what creates happiness.

VIOLENCE AND ADDICTION

If we remember that shame, stemming from dysfunctional core beliefs, is the foundation for addictive personalities, we can understand the role of violence in addiction. When people experience the emptiness underlying their negative core beliefs — I'm not lovable, life is hopeless — they feel shame and seek an escape. For some, an outburst or violent action provides an instant escape from feelings of shame. The cycle goes as follows: (1) precipitating event: feeling rejected, making a mistake, or feeling lonely; (2) a negative core belief touches consciousness: "I'll never be happy"; "I'm unlovable"; (3) shame overwhelms the system: "I'm so bad I should die"; "This pain is intolerable"; (4) the person seeks an escape from these deathlike feelings of shame. One form of distraction is through violence toward self or others. Violence can be turned outward by blaming, shaming, or physically harming and sexually using another person. Or it can be turned inward with a cut to the arm or a burn on the skin that provides a wake-up jolt or a distraction from the feeling of being swallowed up or "dying" from shame. Some women do this in a trance and hardly feel anything at all. Food, alcohol, and drugs can work the same way. You deflect the emptiness and underlying fear to something more manageable. A hangover or stomachache is preferable to feelings of despair and loneliness. It is important to remember that a positive intention underlies self-abuse. You simply do not know any other way to deal with or escape your terrifying feelings.

There is a paradox to self-violence in that you hurt yourself both to block out feelings and to achieve some sort of body sensation. The sensation feels good and reminds you that you are alive, even as you are trying to escape from life. In a shame-based person, the cycle escalates: "I feel rotten *when* someone says something cutting" becomes "I always wake up feeling rotten." Eventually no precipitating event is required; the self-hate is constant.

Addictive behavior keeps shame constantly recycling, and the shame increases the tendency toward violence. Many of the women interviewed engaged in some form of violence or self-abuse in their sexually addictive relationships. For some, violence became another addiction. "It took increasingly more and more violence to get 'high,' to become sexually aroused, or to feel anything at all."

Remember the addiction cycle? Eventually, harmful consequences jolt people out of denial, and the more intense and long-standing the addiction, the stronger the jolt must be. The woman who goes out at night to get a lid of dope and finds herself against a wall with a knife at her throat may well be jolted out of her addictive sleep into consciousness. The female victim in a sadomasochistic relationship who ends up in the hospital with lacerations that require stitches wakes up and asks, "What am I doing to myself?" The woman who attempts suicide to get attention comes to and suddenly realizes she could have died. Violence and pain are often part of the "bottoming out" process, that is, getting to the point where one is ready to do anything necessary to be released from the addiction nightmare.

Women speak of inflicting wounds on themselves or engaging in violent relationships for many reasons. Here are some of them:

Needing Pain to Feel Alive When we numb our feelings over a period of years, body sensations are also numbed. Women who have suppressed their feelings as a result of childhood abuse sometimes cut, burn, and hit themselves simply to have a sensation that affirms they are alive. "If I feel physical pain, at least I feel something."

Self-Abuse to Escape Feelings of Shame This often starts in childhood. Saying to a child, "You are worthless, stupid, clumsy, unlovable, defective," or communicating it nonverbally is like sticking a stiletto in the soul. A child who is made to feel bad about himself or herself instantly seeks an escape. I remember as a child wishing the earth would crack open and swallow me up so I could disappear. I didn't want to die, I just wanted to evaporate, to not be, to escape the feelings of being so terribly bad.

Shame creates a feeling of eternal loneliness and, at an unconscious level, a fear of death. When the stiletto of blame and shame hits the soul, children lose their connection with their source of life, their caregivers, and are left utterly alone. Because their lives depend on the caregivers, they experience a terrifying isolation and a fear of being swallowed up by their emptiness, a fear of dying. They think it is their fault and tell themselves, "There is something wrong with me. They hurt me because I'm unlovable." If the bond is not rapidly restored, a child seeks emotional escape to deny or redirect her pain. For most children it is preferable to focus on the pain of a banged head or a picked scab than to face the terrible void of being totally alone and helpless. Most adults do not consciously connect a fear of death with emotional or physical abandonment, but in my experience as a therapist I often find it lodged deeply in the unconscious.

One way to conceptualize this is to imagine a child as having an invisible umbilical cord connecting her with her parents. You can't see it but you know it is there. It is felt as a basic bond that reassures the child that she is lovable and worthwhile and that she will be protected and taken care of. When the bond is cut, terror strikes and the child adopts survival defenses.

For many, the pattern of self-abuse continues into adulthood as life becomes a frenetic dance to avoid the terror of being swallowed up in a bleak void. Marie revealed that twice she had left our therapy group to go to the bathroom to cut her arms. She eventually realized that her desire to do that came immediately upon feeling misunderstood by me or the group. When she felt that no one understood her, panic set in, as if her connection to life had been severed.

The cycle for her was "No one understands me; that means I am bad, I am worthless, I did it wrong; I'm all alone in the world; I will die; quick, go to the bathroom, claw my arms, see blood, feel pain, and know I am alive. This takes my mind off the fear of dying and being so alone and so bad." Simultaneously Marie was also punishing herself for being such a bad person, for being unloved.

I learned to notice immediately when Marie started to withdraw. I would ask, "Are you feeling misunderstood?" Just the question would reconnect us — we understood that she felt misunderstood — and her desperation would be allayed.

Others respond to shame by smashing their belongings, trashing their living space, breaking things, or tearing up letters. A person who has an object or article of clothing that was a gift from the rejecting person may break it, tear it, or throw it away in an attempt to "kill" the feelings, to get rid of the person who is the source of the hurt.

Violence to Create Intensity Women in recovery from sex addiction usually consider sadomasochism as addictive. One woman who engaged in prostitution was hired by men to beat them while they masturbated. She talked about the feeling of clicking over into another place, the addiction place, and just letting her rage fly. She said that even when the man was "through," she sometimes went on because it felt so good and was a tremendous release for her. She was describing an addictive high.

One woman who had fantasies of being tied, hurt, beaten, or tortured, became addicted to reading hard-core pornography describing the abuse of women. For many women violence in a relationship — playing the role of sadist or masochist — becomes a new addiction. The adrenaline rush, the anticipation, the secret world between two people, the furtiveness, and the feeling that no one knows give the relationship incredible intensity. Intensity is what the addicted one increasingly seeks to escape the dreaded inner abyss. As one woman described it, "It was such a high. It was all-consuming. I could forget everything. In some ways it was better than sex because it was more intense." The problem is that it often takes more and more violence to become aroused and eventually gets physically dangerous.

Sex as Part of the Battering Cycle Sex is often used as the glue to rebond a relationship after a battering episode. This is especially true in the early stages of battering relationships, while there is still a "honeymoon" period. After sex, denial sets in. Often the sexually addictive aspects of violent relationships are hidden from view, because the battering in the relationship is considered the "true" problem. In my experience, nearly all abusive men are sexually addicted and their partners sexually codependent. It is crucial that those who work with those in violent relationships explore the connection of violence to sex addiction and sexual codependency.

In *Men Who Hate Women and the Women Who Love Them* Susan Forward describes women who are sucked into abusive relationships through seduction and sex. All the men in her examples display the characteristics of sex addiction. The women, blinded by the sweet talk of seduction, are typical of those who identify themselves as sexually codependent. She correctly labels the men in her examples as misogynists, men who hate women, but doesn't note that men's hatred for women is nearly always sexualized. That is, they get high from sexually degrading a woman. The women who are drawn to them are usually sexually codependent.

Once the misogynist has his victim psychologically paralyzed and under his spell, sex fits into the battering cycle in the following way. After an episode of physical or verbal abuse, the denial lifts and the victim becomes "conscious" and says to herself, "This is terrible, I've got to get out of here." Then the perpetrator, fearing she might leave, lulls her back into her denial with seduction and sex, which she believes is proof of love. As the cycle escalates, the woman may be forced to have sex if she does not acquiesce willingly, and the violence becomes increasingly frequent.

One thing women need to learn is that excessive sweet talk, flowers, and phony promises are all means of seduction; they have nothing to do with love and everything to do with control and power. Codependent women typically listen to the words and don't observe behavior. When they become aware of the cycle, they can learn to observe that being sexual creates instant denial of the problem — even if they aren't yet ready to say no or to leave.

Violence When the Romance Wears Off　A number of women who become violent in relationships are able to trace the start of violence in their relationship to the time when the romantic high wore off. Sometimes the violence is associated with sex; in other cases it is sparked by any sort of power or control issue. Either way, it is part of the addictive process.

In many relationships sex is used to control pent-up anger. As long as the sexual romance continues, the anger is kept in check, but when the romance dies, violence flares up. Aggie's partner Jim came home late one evening and immediately wanted to have sex. Aggie stalled by saying, "I don't want to. I have a headache." Jim pressed her to be sexual anyhow, and when Aggie again said no by changing the subject, Jim started shaking her, hitting her, and screaming, "You bitch, you'd better show you love me." Jim, unable to have a sexual fix, became violent, an alternative fix. So long as Aggie was at Jim's beck and call the relationship appeared to be peaceful, but as soon as she asserted herself, violence erupted. Women in such volatile relationships often feel exhausted, for they abandon their own needs and expend enormous energy figuring out ways to keep the addicted one from getting angry or violent.

Verbal Self-Abuse　Verbal self-abuse often follows a definite cycle. As one woman described it, "I would constantly run a tape in my head. 'I'm bad, I'm no good, I've screwed up, I've made terrible mistakes, I'm not loved or lovable.' Then, memories of all the dumb things I have ever done in my life would shower down on me, plunging me into a vile sort of self-loathing. The self-hatred would persist until I bottomed out on the pain, which itself was a high. It was the internal equivalent of battering another person or being abused. At the bottom of the cycle I would think of suicide. 'This is it now. This is important.' Then after a while, the pain would lift."

Battering People with Logic and Arguments   Our legal system is based on logic and debate: someone wins and someone loses. It is a patriarchal form of problem solving, and the winner is often the best bullshitter. Have you ever felt sure that you were right and knew your mind, only to have someone try to convince you otherwise with "logic"? Battering by logic is carried out by the ego in the interest of winning, not in the interest of achieving clarity or even insight. It is a defense against intimacy. A person may batter with logic, acting cool and above it all, or get hot under the collar. Some of the lines most commonly used in the assault are "You shouldn't feel that way"; "How do you know that's true? You can't prove it"; "You can't always trust what you read"; "You can't believe what your friend Sue says." As a result you feel cornered and stupid as you stammer for words, not having your verbal evidence in order. No matter what you say, the logic batterer has a ready retort. He is right and you are wrong. You feel at once at a loss for words, shamed, and trapped into an argument you didn't want. If you say you don't want to argue, you're zapped with a stronger punch: "Oh, you never want to talk about anything. You're just running away."

The underlying dynamic is that the logic batterer is frustrated, ashamed, or upset, probably about something that has nothing to do with the victim. To release tension, the batterer overpowers someone with less verbal ability or confidence and gets them to explode.

Fathers often do this with children, especially daughters. Some mothers do it as well. While this kind of abuse is not overtly sexual, the child experiences an emotional penetration and is made to feel powerless. The logic batterer gets an emotional release by creating a scene that ends with the victim blowing up, crying, or running away and slamming doors. His or her anger is vicariously released by having the other person lose control.

The batterer may then feel guilty. He may go after a child to "talk" about what went on or to make an apology that the child *must* accept. The apology, offered because the adult wants to be relieved of guilt, feels even worse to the child, who may withdraw rather than accept the self-serving apology. If the child resists pressure to accept the apology, another blow may occur. In either case, the victim feels overpowered, invaded, and battered.

A variation on this theme occurs when someone delivers a monologue with no regard for whether or not the other person is interested or wants to be there. The child feels trapped while being "talked at" and freezes up or learns to lie to escape. Some of my clients who repeatedly experienced this intrusion actually developed traits of incest survivors. This same scenario is played out between adults, particularly in addictive relationships.

Violent Fantasies for Arousal　Women often use violent, abusive, or passive fantasies to get high, as a support for addictive sexual arousal, or as an escape from the pain and boredom of their lonely lives. It's important to remember that our fantasies are a form of energy, and are therefore alive at a psychic and psychological level. When we experience the mind, body, and spirit as one, the distinction between thoughts and actions disappears—what happens in the mind happens to the spirit. Thus, violent fantasies harm a woman spiritually. (This is to be distinguished from Catholic and fundamentalist teachings that thinking something, usually sexual, is as sinful as doing it. That sort of belief system makes people hate their minds and creates tremendous shame.)

If we have a fantasy or a thought, the idea is not to hate ourselves for it or even to cast it out as sinful or bad. Rather, the point is to become aware of what it means and how it affects us at a spiritual level. Does this fantasy feel light? Do I feel a happiness in my heart? Does it bring joy, a feeling of harmony? Or does it feel heavy or dense? Does it feel shameful, dirty, furtive? Do I wish I didn't need this sort of fantasy to become sexually aroused? How would I feel about sharing this fantasy with someone — would it feel okay, or would I feel ashamed? If unwanted fantasies come to mind, it is important to simply let them float through without grabbing hold of them or shaming ourselves.

Imagine for a moment the kinds of fantasies women might have in a world without rape or incest: where women are equal and validated as powerful, intelligent, and creative, where female sexuality is seen as beautiful, sacred, powerful, and life affirming. I don't believe we would associate passive masochistic fantasies with life-affirming sexuality.

I have worked with many women to replace passive violent or masochistic fantasies with beautiful, powerful images from nature, feelings of love, or simply images of a dazzling light radiating from an inner source. To help with the process I sometimes suggest a book with sensuously photographed orchids, some with dewdrops on the petals. The orchids provide a wonderful image women learn to pair with their genitals. For many, it is the first time that they have associated beautiful images with sexuality.

Suicide　I have talked with many women about suicide attempts and, more commonly, about persistent fantasies of suicide. We tend to separate thoughts of suicide from homicide, which we readily see as a terrible thing. But suicide is homicide of the self — an angry, desperate, hopeless act. For many addicted women suicide is reserved as a back-pocket option, a sure way out of pain. Most of those women don't really want to die, they want to kill the pain. Their addictive side mercilessly taunts the healthy side: "You're such a shit, you're no good, you deserve to die." Women suffering great emotional pain think of dying as a welcome relief from struggling through one more day.

Fantasies of suicide become a central part of addiction for many women, for knowing that one can commit suicide brings a feeling of control: "If I can't get what I want in life, if it is too terrible, then I can kill myself." Keeping suicide as an option, or using such fantasies to threaten a partner, is like an alcoholic keeping alcohol in the house "just in case." Part of recovery is to give up the suicide fantasies and threats and make a commitment to live, for better or worse. In essence, one has to close that back door, seal off the escape hatch, and get married to life with all its pain, paradox, and struggle.

We could take the above forms of violence and masochism and put them on a continuum from subtle to blatant. Many women — frequently survivors of abuse — would consider much of this behavior as normal for women; it would be a new idea to think of it as self-abusive or violent. Some women would see the more blatant behavior as definitely hurtful and necessary to change; others might see it as unpleasant or inconvenient, but not consider it important enough to change. Although most women would agree that literal violence is definitely harmful, they might still struggle internally to believe that they have the right to a life free from this sort of pain, whether it be inflicted by others or by themselves.

It is important that we understand these forms of violence on a continuum, with behavior differing in degree but not in motivation. It *all* harms our self-worth. The woman who cuts her arms with a razor is different only in degree from the woman who scratches herself until she has a permanent scar. The suffering of the woman who submits to dull, loveless sex without saying a word is different only in degree from that of the woman who stays in a relationship in which she is violently raped by her partner. Many women live in such a perpetual nightmare of pain and discomfort that they don't recognize pain and suffering. As they recover, self-abuse or violence they once considered acceptable is experienced as harmful and something to be avoided. This in itself is a painful discovery, for a woman must suddenly confront the fact that she was taught by a culture to accept suffering and pain as natural for her.

SUMMARY

Because violence and masochism are rooted in shame they are often commingled with sex addiction and sexual codependency. Shame is the hangover from an addictive high.

The seeds of violence and self-abuse are planted in childhood, and the wounds inflicted on a child often explode later in violence toward oneself or others. Women, so deeply conditioned to protect others, tend to turn their anger inward, directing their violence or abuse at themselves. Physical self-abuse is far more pervasive among women than we realize. Even in therapy groups, however, the subject seldom comes up without a nudge or an all-out shove. Unfortunately, self-abuse is often treated as an isolated condition by therapists. I believe it needs to be understood in the context of childhood abuse and addiction.

Talking about female violence toward others is culturally taboo, for we have been taught to be passive and compliant. The conditioning to ignore harm to ourselves pervades our sexuality to the point that we are often not even conscious of harming ourselves or of being harmed.

I want to make the connection between sexual violence in relationships and world peace because I believe they are directly related. As long as the model of sexual relationships between men and women is built on the assumption that males are violent aggressors and women are passive, masochistic vessels, we are assenting to inequality, and to victimization as a norm. By maintaining this dominant-subordinate model for any type of relationship, we are supporting oppression and violence. Until we question all we have been taught by our families and the culture, we may remain captive to these values. Only when we learn to see a soul every time we see a body, male or female, will we feel that stirring in our hearts that leads us to care for and respect all people. Only then will we move to a level of consciousness in which the thought of war or of violence toward others becomes totally unacceptable.

CHAPTER 11

We Are All More Alike Than Different:
Lesbianism, Heterosexuality, and Bisexuality

Homophobia, the irrational fear of homosexuality, hurts everyone. It is really a fear of sexuality itself, a fear of love, a fear of knowing all that we are, and, in the case of lesbian homophobia, a fear of female power.

I believe most people are born with the potential to have same-sex and opposite-sex attractions. However, homophobia creates an internal split, locking up a natural part of a person's psyche, sometimes to the point where the person is unaware that part exists. The culture, to promote heterosexuality, rejects, debases, and punishes same-sex attractions. As a result, women who are attracted to other women often experience shame and fear. They may think, "Something is wrong with me for having these feelings; I should stay away from women who stimulate those feelings in me; there must be something wrong with loving women, hugging women, or touching women; I'd better not get too close to *any* woman or it may bring up those feelings."

One way people control their own shameful feelings is by projecting them onto others. Instead of saying, "I hate, or am uncomfortable with, the part of *me* that is attracted to women," they say, "Lesbians are weird, unnatural, and disgusting." When we project in this way we are rejecting a part of ourselves. And self-rejection keeps us from the full power of our being and our sexuality. This in turn feeds into sex addiction and codependency.

The labels *lesbian* and *heterosexual* perpetuate the mistaken notion of two distinct types of women. Therefore, when I use the term "lesbian woman," it means a woman identified as a lesbian. When I use "heterosexual woman," it refers to a woman identified as a heterosexual. Referring to lesbian women may seem redundant, but it is done to reinforce the fact that lesbians are simply women. They are not some strange separate breed, as the culture so often portrays them. They are women from all classes, races, professions, and social strata. They have families, hopes, dreams, disappointments, ups, and downs. They live alone and as couples. They have wonderful sex, boring sex, and sometimes have difficulty being sexual at all. Like heterosexual women, they also have addictive sex and codependent sex.

The 1953 Kinsey Report estimated that from 3 to 10 percent of women live a lesbian lifestyle at some time. Lesbian lifestyle can be interpreted in different ways. For many it means living as part of a lesbian culture, whether single or with a primary partner. For others it means living in a primary sexual relationship with another woman. Twenty-eight percent of women recognize erotic responses to other females by the age of thirty, and by the age of forty, 19 percent have had some form of deliberate sexual contact with other females.

Think of it. Upward of twenty million women in the United States will at some time live a lesbian lifestyle; nearly forty million will have had deliberate sexual contact with other women; and close to sixty million women admit to recognizing erotic responses to other women. But whoever learned in school that this is normal, okay, or even wonderful? Instead of thinking, "It's fine to throw my arms around my girlfriend and hug her because I love her so much," women are left wondering, "Is it okay? What will she think?" or worse yet, "What's wrong with me?"

Is there anyplace — in the media, in churches, or in schools — where the culture communicates that same-sex attractions and fantasies are perfectly normal, whether a woman chooses to express them physically or not? The taboo, it appears, dictates that women remain silent on the subject. However, in the "How many women here . . ." part of sexuality workshops, same-sex questions always come up. "How many women here have been sexual with other women?" About one third of the hands go up. "How many women here have had fantasies of being sexual with other women?" Nearly every hand goes up. "How many women here are curious to try it but are afraid?" At least half the hands go up, accompanied by much blushing.

The Kinsey Report signified a tremendous break with traditional cultural views by documenting that few people are either totally heterosexual or homosexual. While most of us make a decision to identify with one or the other of these labels — an identification that may change over time — Kinsey suggests that most of us have some sexual attraction to both men and women. The majority of lesbian-identified women have been sexual with men, and one in six heterosexual women has been sexual with other women.

People at the extreme ends of the spectrum may have little inner conflict about their sexual preference. They don't feel they have a choice; they simply feel they were born lesbian or heterosexual. However, people who are somewhere between the two poles may experience inner discomfort or have doubts in the recesses of their mind. Or, after much inward exploration, a woman may arrive at the awareness that bisexuality most truly defines her inner world. She may choose to be in a heterosexual or lesbian relationship but she doesn't deny the other part of her.

Unfortunately, women who openly state that they are bisexual often get a lot of flak and are told, "You're just afraid to make a decision," or "It's an intermediate step to being a lesbian." But I think many people are genuinely bisexual. I suspect if it weren't for homophobia, most people would experience significant attractions to both sexes.

Some women say they choose a lesbian lifestyle because being with a woman partner helps them feel more integrated, equal, and whole. Sexual feeling plays only one part in this, and it doesn't necessarily mean that these women dislike sex with men. They simply prefer sharing their lives intimately with women. In any case, bisexual, lesbian, or heterosexual, every woman defines her own sexual preference.

Now to muddy the waters a bit. I think that something is missing in the Kinsey scale, because it pinpoints people at a given place — and people don't necessarily stay at any fixed place. I also believe that for many, the word *bisexuality* suggests someone who is ambivalent, sitting on a fence post, unsure of his or her sexuality.

In reflecting on my own sexual identity struggle, I realized I needed another term to make sense of what I felt. As an adolescent my first huge crush was on my female swimming teacher at summer camp. Following that, I had crushes on boys as well as other adolescent females. I wasn't ambivalent; I had strong feelings in both directions. To fit in, or because I didn't know I had an option, I identified solely as heterosexual until I was in my early thirties. But it never felt quite right; something was frozen. When my attractions for women emerged more strongly, emotionally and physically, I chose to be involved sexually with a woman. I was active in lesbian culture for nearly ten years. I loved it, but it didn't feel complete for me either. My inner experience again was that something wasn't quite right.

What I eventually came to know at a deeper level is that I am a sexual being open to emotional and sexual connections with either a man or a woman. I identify with both lesbian and heterosexual people. And my spiritual goal of unconditional love for all people remains constant. It doesn't mean that I act on my sexual feelings toward more than one person at a time — monogamy works best for me — but I no longer try to identify as one or the other. I'm simply Charlotte, child of the Universe and a sexual being. The word *bisexual*, as commonly understood, doesn't ring true for me because it suggests ambivalence. I don't feel confused. I feel that I've finally accepted the truth about myself and feel free to allow decisions about intimate partners flow from where my journey leads me.

HOMOPHOBIA AS FEAR OF SEXUALITY

I don't believe we can fully love other people if we don't love ourselves. When a heterosexual woman imagines two women making love, much of what comes to mind is a mirror of her feelings about her own sexuality. Part of fully loving ourselves as women is feeling comfortable with our sexuality, including the part that is attracted to other women. This can include sexual dreams and fantasies of being with other women.

If you want to explore your feelings in this regard, take a moment to let yourself imagine two women touching, hugging, stroking, making love. What happens inside you? What thoughts go through your mind? If you feel attracted to the image, does your rational mind create feelings of guilt? If you feel repulsed by some of your fantasy, for example, the image of touching a woman's genitals, is that a reflection of your feelings about your own genitals? What parts of yourself do you feel uncomfortable touching and looking at? Do feelings of tenderness, warmth, intimacy, power, passion, or sensitivity come to mind? If not, what do you think is the reason?

Homophobia or, more precisely, "lesbophobia" — the fear of female power and female sexuality — teaches women to fear the power of their sexuality. If we hate the thought of women fully loving each other, emotionally and sexually, what does that mean about loving ourselves emotionally and sexually? Being lesbian often leads to women taking a more active role in all phases of relationships — initiating conversation, touching, and sexual intimacy. This is counter to heterosexual female conditioning, which assigns women a more passive role. To play a passive, or covertly active, role in sexual relationships is to deny one's own power. Being an active participant sexually and emotionally in a relationship with another person is an empowering experience.

Homophobia results in many people having shame about their sexuality. If half of one's emotions are buried, so is half of one's potential for fully connected sexuality. If a woman fears being shamed or called a dyke for being a strong woman unreserved in her feelings for women, and a man is called a faggot for being tender and sensitive, everyone loses. Loving sexuality is an outgrowth of free-flowing emotions and self-acceptance.

The most powerful form of repression is to simply pretend something doesn't exist. In all the furor over Shere Hite's *Women and Love,* the hundred-page section on lesbians was not mentioned on any of the talk shows I saw or in the *Newsweek* cover article on her book. This is particularly noteworthy because the vast majority of heterosexual women Hite interviewed described sexual and emotional dissatisfaction with their male partners — the point the media leaped on — while the vast majority of lesbian women expressed emotional and sexual satisfaction with their partners — a point that was largely ignored.

The pervasive homophobia in our culture is also demonstrated by the total exclusion of lesbian women from mainstream history books, books on relationships, psychology books, and acknowledgment by lecturers, therapists, and political groups. Yet lesbian women have been political activists, suffragettes, homesteaders, authors, mothers, and businesswomen.

Imagine pretending that there are no Jews and Hispanics in the United States. Seems crazy: these two groups combined make up approximately 8.4 percent of the population, according to the 1985 Statistical Abstract, and represent a slightly lower percentage than that of lesbian women and gay men in the United States, which is estimated at 10 percent. That represents at least twelve million women. Refusing to acknowledge them is like pretending that the populations of New York City and Chicago don't exist!

That lesbian women, even if they are recognized, are understood only in terms of their sexual preference reflects the sexually addictive nature of our culture. In a patriarchy all women are classified as sexual objects in relation to men. A woman is either sexually available (single), sexually unavailable but possibly interested (married), unwilling to be sexual (frigid), or sexually indifferent and uninterested (lesbian). These categories don't tell us anything about a woman's identity apart from sex, or anything about how she personally experiences sex. Because the culture sexualizes its understanding of lesbian women, lesbians have to struggle not to do the same to themselves. Their sexual preference, which is just one part of them, is blown out of proportion in the face of an oppressive culture.

Consider the damage done by homophobia to both the lesbian and the people who view her negatively, in line with what happens when any negative label is applied to people. Take Margaret, for example. She is a teacher, loves bicycling, plays guitar, and is active in her church. People like her very much. But when Margaret discloses that her primary relationship is with a woman, she is labeled a lesbian.

People now relate to her as if she were branded with an *L*. Their homophobia obliterates their ability to care for her. She is seen not only as a body without a soul, but as merely a sexual body. Everyone loses, because the positive exchange of love that existed disappears. Margaret internalizes the fear of the others and begins to believe that she is bad for being lesbian. The cycle continues. She assumes some of the negative attributes, and people say, "She's just what we said she was." Everyone then feels increasingly separate.

Dismissing women's sexual love for each other as adolescent or immature is another attempt to discount the power of that love. It extends to denigrating passionate or loving adult female relationships whether or not they are sexual.

Carrie talked about a wonderful female friendship she had in college. "We were totally open with each other. We could snuggle up in bed, look at each other's bodies, talk about our bodies, laugh, cry, and share anything together."

"Did you ever wonder what people thought?" I asked.

"Well, we used to giggle and say to each other about our dormmates, 'What would they say if they saw us holding hands?' So we didn't in front of them, but we would have been perfectly comfortable doing so."

The friendship all but died when both of them married men. Carrie said, "Our love was acceptable when people saw us as two crazy girls, but when we became married women there was no place for that kind of love and care." In a sudden burst of energy Carrie said, "Oh, that makes me mad!" Tears came to her eyes. "I've missed her so much."

From a very early age lesbian women are shamed for their independence, strong-mindedness, and unwillingness to conform to stereotypical female behavior. "My mother was always trying to get me to wear little dresses and I hated them!" "I liked the dolls my mother kept giving me okay, but I wanted a cowboy outfit, too." "My sister got a lot more attention for having a date than I did for excelling in baseball." As a result lesbian women often go through adolescence feeling "different" and "wrong," which spills into their sexuality. As one woman said, "I would see other girls getting upset over guys, and I just couldn't get it. It was like they were from a different tribe or something. I kept thinking, 'Something must be wrong with me.' I didn't realize that they were feeling the same thing I was feeling for my girlfriend Jody."

Some adolescent lesbians are aware of their sexual attractions to other girls and date boys nonetheless. Some, however, follow their inclinations. Parents may react cruelly — "You are sick and you can never see Jane again" — and take their lesbian daughters to male psychiatrists to be "straightened out." More understanding parents may try to keep a dialogue going, but the message is clear: there is really only one acceptable choice — the heterosexual one. A daughter's open exploration of her sexuality can subconsciously threaten her parents' relationship if it has a poor foundation. "It's your fault she turned out that way. You shouldn't have bought her that baseball mitt!" Only parents who handle their own sexuality openly and honestly are able to accept their daughters' sexual choices.

Keeping secrets, feeling defective, not fitting in, knowing that your parents are uneasy about you at best and threatened by and afraid of you at worst create a fertile breeding ground for despair, loneliness, shame, and self-hatred. Young women whose developmental years are marked by this kind of pain are highly vulnerable to addictions. An adolescent who is attracted exclusively to females can become confused about her sexuality. After all, if *real* sexuality consists of being attracted to men, a young lesbian's sexual feelings are never validated — they have no name. And feelings that have no name turn into feelings of shame. The desire for acceptance as a sexual being, a sexual female, is unsupported, leaving the young lesbian alienated from herself, her feelings, and her female sexuality. Some adolescents deal with their lesbian shame by deciding that they are not really young women but boys in female bodies. This makes for even greater confusion: "What am I, and how do I act?"

However, lesbian women have a tremendous common ground, which makes equal relationships possible. They share similar bodies and hormone cycles. As women they have been trained to be nurturing and tender and to share feelings. What better foundation for creating warm, caring relationships.

With so much in common, women in lesbian relationships find that they also approach situations similarly. They tend to work together cooperatively — a value taught to them as little girls — whether on a household chore or a major project. Women who share feminist values put a great deal of energy into sorting out their roles, consciously trying to understand how they operate in the relationship and why.

I don't want to suggest that lesbian women, having internalized the programming of the culture, don't encounter difficulties with sex and with relationships. Their relationships are not always equal. There is usually a power difference between two people, but a great potential for equality exists by virtue of both being women.

STRAINS ON LESBIAN RELATIONSHIPS

The strains on lesbian women can also take their toll on their relationships. Feelings of being isolated, different, hated, and misunderstood lead to low self-esteem, which leads to addiction and codependency. Here are some ways this has been played out in lesbian relationships.

Playing roles. Many lesbians, especially twenty or thirty years ago, modeled their relationships on stereotypical heterosexual roles. Macho and feminine roles became known as "butch" and "femme," respectively, and a lesbian was supposed to choose one or the other. Playing a sexual role instead of being oneself leads to pain and confusion about sexuality.

Family rejection. Heterosexual relationships are sanctioned and supported by the culture. When people stray from their ethnic or religious background — a Jew marries a Catholic, a black a white — there may be a family uproar, but the couple seldom suffers the intense, long-lasting rejection many lesbian women do.

When Angie chose to be lesbian, her mother totally rejected her, refusing to speak to her for eight years. After a great deal of therapy, Angie decided to call her mother. Because she had heard that her mother, an alcoholic, was going to AA, Angie hoped she might have relented in her attitude toward her. But the first question her mother asked was, "Are you still *that* way?" Angie stammered, "Mom, what difference does it make? I just want to talk to you." End of conversation. Her mother said, "I won't talk to you," and hung up. What a loss for Angie, and what a loss for her mother. The sad truth that her homophobia was greater than her love for her daughter had devastating effects on Angie and her sexuality. Every time she made love to a woman, somewhere in her unconscious mind she knew that her mother had rejected her for this act. A terrible conflict resulted, once again pairing sex and shame.

Such complete rejections are rare. Far more common, after an original uproar or rejection period, is the deep-freeze treatment. Like the rest of the culture, parents may pretend the relationship doesn't exist. Many women describe writing long, heartfelt letters to their mothers, telling about their newfound identity, only to recieve a one-line response followed by two pages about the tomato patch, what the family had for dinner, and who was coming to visit next month. There's often a P.S.: "Don't tell your father, he wouldn't understand," which places a wedge between the lesbian woman and her father.

Even when a lesbian relationship has endured for a long time, parents may continue to ignore it. They might ask their daughter home for Christmas but not invite the partner with whom she lives. Imagine inviting a married daughter home for Thanksgiving and saying, "But don't bring your husband!"

Some parents do accept their children and their partners, but more often it is tolerance rather than genuine acceptance.

Keeping the relationship secret. Afraid of rejection or harassment, many lesbian women suppress their affection, care, and warmth for their partners in public and learn to lie about the very existence of the lover. Lunch conversations at work or at the tennis club rarely include comments like, "I met this really wonderful woman and I'm going to ask her out," or, "Mollie and I are having a hard time right now. I could sure use some support." This kind of secrecy and fear of being found out puts enormous strain on relationships. Saying, "Don't call me at work when you're upset, I'm so afraid someone will hear me," creates a painful rift. It may be difficult for partners who have hidden their feelings all day to shift gears and show their affection readily at home.

And, of course, if everyone believes you are sexually deviant, it is hard not to believe it yourself. After all, homophobia was indoctrinated in lesbian women as well as heterosexuals. The act of making love can be problematic for lesbians because it may summon up the pain of being excluded and dehumanized. As a result, some women find it easier to suppress their sexuality. This is particularly true of lesbian women who hide their identity, live in isolation, and do not have positive contact with other lesbians. If you cannot accept yourself, how can you accept others who are like you?

Isolation. In small towns and cities, with few openly lesbian women and no support networks, a woman may have to choose between one particular lover or no lover at all. She may well stick with her partner as a shelter from the homophobic storm, even if the relationship is dysfunctional, which can lead to massive codependency. People who stay together but do not face the conflicts in their relationship may bury the pain with alcohol, compulsive eating, and overwork.

In response to a hostile society, lesbian women may draw tight boundaries around themselves — an "us against the world" posture. As a result, lesbian couples risk wearing out their relationship by spending too much time together without replenishing it from outside sources and people. The fear of losing a partner, of being left alone in a homophobic culture, can make lesbians extremely cautious about letting anyone else penetrate the couple's boundaries. Thus, some couples tend to cling to their partners and are wary of anyone who might be a threat — particularly single lesbian women. As a result, couples spend their time chiefly with other couples, and single lesbian women often feel left out, just as they do in the heterosexual world.

Becoming enmeshed. Bonding is wonderful, and most women are conditioned to do it well. But it is easy for women to go beyond bonding and become enmeshed, to merge together and sacrifice their identity.

Because homophobia forces lesbian women to isolate themselves from the rest of the community, everyone in their group tends to know everyone else, and some become sexually involved with one another. Lesbian organizations frequently suffer from the strains of including former lovers, current lovers under stress, and women on the verge of becoming lovers.

Members of any minority group must bond together to survive, which forces people to deny their differences in order to avoid conflict. This in turn often creates buried tensions that surface indirectly or take their toll on individual members.

Recalling that underlying addictions are emptiness, shame, and isolation, we can see that lesbians are set up for addictive relationships. Two ever-present questions in the lesbian community are: "Why do so many relationships break up after two or three years?" and "Why do so few lesbian women remain single?" The answers lie partly in their conditions of isolation and lack of support, but I suspect that sex addiction and codependency are also major factors.

In comparison to the general population, a disproportionately high percentage of lesbian women in the Twin Cities join SAA groups and a disproportionately low percentage join CoSA. This makes sense because many lesbian women tend to reject the passive, codependent female role and take a more active stance in the world. However, this fact can have a negative side. They may deny their codependent needy side because it doesn't fit their self-image. As members of a brutally oppressed minority group, many lesbian women develop tough exteriors to ward off the pain of rejection by the culture. As women on their own and survivors in a homophobic culture, they become very strong.

When Kelly sought therapy, I realized that I had seen her as an organizer at various women's events, where she appeared to be the most competent, self-assured woman in the world. She explained that she cultivated that image as a defensive armor to hide the wounds underneath.

As she described it, "If I'm going to be one of *them*, then I'd better love it and never admit that there are any problems. Coming out — being a lesbian in my family, and in this culture — can be so hard sometimes that the best defense is to act like it's better! The only way to make the decision to be a lesbian was to say that women who haven't made that decision are dumb or oppressed. I'd put them down to retaliate for all the times I've been put down.

"The therapy group was the first place where I really learned about loving myself to the point that I didn't need to say those things about anybody. It was the first place that I got close to straight women. One of the things that was best for me was finding out how much alike we all were, and giving up my need to claim that lesbian relationships are better, when in fact I was in a really shitty one.

"Also, I think about similarities with women in the group — similar teenage histories, pain in our families, loneliness, and our struggle to get well. All these things made much stronger bonds than whether or not we were lesbians. Being straight or lesbian ceased to be the primary issue. Being in that group made me remember that being a feminist is about a really broad love for women and understanding all women's issues."

IN THERAPY: WORKING THROUGH HOMOPHOBIA

Because homophobia is so pervasive and has such a negative impact on sexuality, I include this section illustrating what happens when women in therapy groups confront it. I have learned that lesbian-heterosexual issues often have to be nudged to the surface because everyone is afraid to talk about them. If the group is withdrawn and the energy low, it is usually a sign that something important is not being said.

Marie, a lesbian woman who was a victim of covert incest, had been feeling unhappy in the group and was thinking of leaving. Athletic and good-looking, with a quick sense of humor, Marie was often the most insightful member of the group and the most willing to take risks. One day, in what appeared to be a sudden confrontation, she took on Marilyn, a very pretty, well-dressed, slender heterosexual woman.

While Marilyn was talking about her struggle to stop getting involved with abusive men, Marie interrupted and with uncharacteristic hostility said, "I'm feeling so impatient. I'm not at all tuned in to what you're saying. I can't stand the way you seem so naive about men sometimes. You never seem to get it. I don't like you very much."

A resounding silence followed as we dropped our jaws waiting for Marilyn's response. Marilyn, who six months earlier would have collapsed in shame, spoke back, albeit tearfully. "This is hard for me, I'm trying to learn, and I know I am dense about it."

"Well, it seems like you never get it," Marie continued, unrelenting.

"I get to take as long as I want," Marilyn responded weakly, expressing a newly learned retort.

"It sure is taking a long time!"

"You're really being a bitch," Marilyn shot back with renewed energy, much to everyone's surprise.

"But Marie," Katie, a heterosexual woman, broke in, "you don't get angry with me when I'm slow to get something. My God, I'm still struggling with a dumb job after two years."

Everyone sat, wide-eyed, watching Marie.

She replied with a smile, "That's because you're overweight, too." The group laughed.

"I scc," I said. "So you get to be slow if you're overweight, but if you're cute and trim you've got to be quick."

Marie grinned and replied in a cheeky way, "Yes."

"I wonder what this is really all about." I asked Marie and Marilyn how each thought the other one saw her.

"You just think I'm a fat, ugly dyke," Marie snapped, fighting back tears, her pain finally exposed.

"You just think I'm this stupid woman who can't say no to a man," Marilyn said, starting to cry.

We began to talk about envy. Marilyn envied Marie's spontaneity, insightfulness, and ability to get angry. She also envied Marie for not being addicted to men. Marie envied Marilyn's svelte body, her quiet demeanor, and the cultural acceptance she received as a heterosexual woman.

What each envied in the other was a part inside them longing to be acknowledged. Marilyn wanted more than anything to wake up her powerful side and stop being innocent and naive about men, and about the world, for that matter. Marie really wanted to go on a diet and lose some weight, but that was in conflict with her belief that women should accept their bodies and not fuss over diets and looks. She also feared rejection from the quieter Marilyn for being "too bold, too outspoken, too tough."

The group soon got into the act, pointing out how both were being tyrannized by external "rules" dictated by a homophobic culture. Marilyn could lift weights and express herself forthrightly and still be feminine, and Marie could express neediness and go on a diet if she wanted to and still be a lesbian in good standing.

On a deeper level, Marie's animosity toward Marilyn was related to her family. I asked Marie if Marilyn reminded her of anyone in her family.

She paused for a moment. "Oh, yes," she said, startled by the pain of recognition. "My sister." Her face dropped.

"Tell me about her," I said.

"She's cute and slim and married. And my parents have probably visited her ten times for every time they visit me." The anger on her face changed to a hurt that touched us all. Rejection by one's parents hits deep.

Marilyn, in looking at her family, realized that her parents didn't bring her up to be able to take care of herself. Anger was forbidden and men were gods. Unwittingly, her parents had set her up for a violent relationship that nearly killed her.

Finally, Marilyn and Marie found a common bond in their pain, anger toward their parents, and the negative effects of a homophobic culture. They didn't leave the session arm and arm, but after a few weeks they were able to joke with each other in a knowing way, like friends.

Homophobia had affected both Marie and Marilyn. Marie was rejected by her parents because of her power and strength; she was different from "normal" girls. Marilyn's power and strength were rejected by her parents (and herself) so she would fit the accepted female stereotype. They both ended up rejecting a major part of their humanness.

Homophobia also affected the energy level of the group. Buried fears led everyone to be careful, hold back feelings, and keep the conversation shallow. Once the issue was out in the open, however, the level of group participation rose dramatically. It was like lancing a festering wound to get the homophobic poison out of the system.

Some months later Marie spoke about a woman at work who was pressing for a much more involved friendship than Marie wanted. Marie felt powerless to say no to her. Marilyn, with a glint in her eye, said, "You sound as afraid of her as I was of Jim." Marie smiled. "Touché," she said.

"I can't believe I didn't see that when I was so angry at you for not saying no to Jim." They were both able to laugh. Eventually they came to respect each other deeply. When Marilyn offered to attend a Gay Pride march, Marie showed a softness we had seldom seen.

THE FREEDOM TO CHOOSE

Because homophobia affects all women by reinforcing a tremendous hatred of those who deviate from female norms, freely choosing one's sexual preference becomes extremely complicated. When powerful women, lesbian or heterosexual, challenge the patriarchial system or assert their rights, they are routinely squelched with such epithets as dyke, ballbreaker, cunt, witch, and bitch.

True freedom to choose means that one knows the choices and is allowed to make them without retribution. We can't make fully conscious choices when fear, anger, or any form of manipulation clouds the issues. It is important for both lesbian and heterosexual women to examine their decisions carefully, in order to understand the real issues behind them.

CHOOSING OUR SEXUAL PREFERENCE

"Coming out" is used to describe the process women go through in identifying as lesbian, accepting their preference, and telling other people. The process varies enormously, with some women recognizing their preference for women at a very early age while others are in their thirties or forties before they come out.

We don't think of women *choosing* to be heterosexual, because society promotes heterosexuality as the only legitimate form of sexual expression. It is important for heterosexuals to understand homophobia by examining their heterosexual conditioning. Once they are aware of that, heterosexual women must look inside themselves. Part of exploring the heterosexual "choice" means affirming whatever attractions — physical, emotional, and sexual — it has for women, and how they have blocked these attractions out or denied them in order to fit in.

Jane told the following story. "I remember when I first started in therapy and some women in the group had women lovers. It really threatened me. I remember later noticing that I thought that other women are really beautiful, and I thought, 'Oh, my God, *I can't think that way!* I'm supposed to be heterosexual, this is wrong.' Then I went through a year of questioning what I wanted. All of this homophobia came up like gangbusters. I was terrified. I thought I would rather hang myself than go through *that*. Self-acceptance would be so painful. I felt enough of an outcast in my family, and I thought, 'Oh, God, that would really finish it.'

"For a while during that period I lived in a community in Kentucky that was very open about these things. I opened myself up to the possibility, and during that time a couple of women wanted to have sexual relationships with me. I chose not to be sexual with either of them because it didn't feel quite right. Now, another year has gone by and I feel really clear that I want to be sexual with men. The difference now is that I feel much closer to women and I understand a lot more about my own homophobia. It was easy to sit there as a heterosexual and say, 'I'm not homophobic. It's fine with me how *you* are.' But when I thought of being there myself, having a woman as my sexual partner, it was a different thing."

SOME QUESTIONS TO ASK

It is enlightening to look back and try to determine how we make our choices. The following questions can help you explore the influences on your choices about sexuality and relationships with women.

1. Did you receive messages in your family that made females seem less important than males? If so, what were they? For example, was a clear distinction made between women's work and men's work? Was more attention paid to boys' or your brothers' activities? Were limitations put on girls for being athletic, outspoken, and exuberant but not on boys? Did your mother say things like, "I'm just a housewife"? Was there more excitement at the birth of a boy than a baby girl?

2. What limiting assumptions were made about your future as an adult? "*When* you date boys . . ."; "*When* you get married . . ."; "*When* you have children . . ."; "*When* you become a nurse . . ."

3. How were your relationships with other females regarded? Did you get a message such as, "It's okay to have close adolescent girlfriends, but that will pass when you grow up"? Did your parents ever convey negative messages about the intensity of your female friendships?

4. What messages, verbal or nonverbal, did you receive about females having physical contact with other females?

5. What messages did you receive about loving and spending time with other women once you dated males?

6. What messages did you receive about spending time with other males once you were married? Was there an implication that heterosexual relationships are solely sexual, that friendships outside the marriage pose a sexual threat?

7. If you don't quite remember the messages you received while growing up, can you recognize your current prejudices? Do you think that once

you're married you can't spend significant time with other women, or that other friendships have to fit in with your husband's schedule?

8. If you could set aside all your negative cultural programming, felt no pressure to live one way or another, what role would women play in your life now?

    a. Would you spend more time with them? How? Have dinner with a woman friend during the week? Go on trips or vacations with other women?

    b. Would you be more physical with them? Would you hug more often? Kiss each other? Walk hand in hand or arm in arm? When you visit would you snuggle up with each other or sleep together (nonsexually)?

    c. Would you want to be sexual with another woman? Just once to see what it's like? With a special friend you just love? Or would you explore having a primary sexual relationship with another woman?

Male readers can ask themselves the same questions with regard to men. What would your relationships with men be like if you had no fears of being called a sissy or gay? Go back to your childhood and think of all the messages you received, both spoken and unspoken, about feeling tenderness for other men, about feeling tenderness for anyone, including yourself. Were all the messages negative? What would happen to your ego if a woman in your life became sexual with another woman?

A male friend of mine told a story that illustrates men's fear of female indifference. He and his wife went to a "women's" concert where, in a lobby crowded with a mass of people — 90 percent of them women — he was overwhelmed by an empty feeling. Looking around, he realized that most of the women were probably lesbian. "No one was paying any attention to me. No energy was coming my way. It was as if nobody cared about me. I felt small. I wondered if this is how women feel in a man's world. I don't mind if women fight with me or even dislike me, at least they're still involved. But when they are *indifferent!* My ego was devastated. I felt so lonely. I wanted to get out of there and be in a place where people would notice me more."

LESBIANISM AND POWER

Heterosexual women are often unknowingly drawn to lesbian women because they are attracted by their power, and powerful people are compelling. They can tap a longing in us and wake up a buried part of ourselves. While power is not the sole domain of lesbian women (they can also be passive), lesbians in feminist political organizations are often at the forefront, taking the most risks and being the most outspoken.

What is your image of a lesbian woman? Even if such words as *deviant, wrong, weird,* or *tough* come to mind, do you also conjure up images of strength and independence, of powerful women who challenge the status quo? I contend that the culture's definition of lesbian women as sexually deviant actually has more to do with fear of female power than with sexuality. Men are threatened by women who reject or are indifferent to the male system. And heterosexual women may fear lesbians because they hold up a mirror to their own discomfort about their dependency on men and their own buried power.

In my experience, women who are trying to unlock their power feel pulled toward powerful women, while women who have not yet opened that door flee from them or put them down as unfeminine or abrasive. As evidence of the unconscious fear of strong women, I have observed that often in abusive families it is the strong-willed, nonconforming female child who is singled out as the scapegoat or the target of the most violent physical abuse.

Some strong women, especially public figures, adapt themselves to homophobic fears. I find it fascinating that many women athletes, for instance, walk a fine line between allowing their power full expression and making an all-out effort not to offend anyone. Two or three years ago I saw a calendar that showed world-class women tennis players in off-court attire often looking passive or, occasionally, seductive. Did they feel they had to reassure the world that they were "feminine"? Could they allow themselves to look powerful only on the tennis court? Or did men think up the idea to ease their fear of powerful women by getting them to look like "real" women instead of powerful and vibrant women?

Two great tennis players, Martina Navratilova and Chris Evert, represent opposite approaches in dealing with power. When she was not smacking a tennis ball with amazing control on the court, Chris Evert appeared to be the stereotypical nice woman. She seldom questioned a call, was extremely polite to everyone, and, until late in her career, even restrained her joy in winning a match. She would hold a trophy with a quiet, demure smile, as if she felt a little embarrassed. Martina, on the other hand, expressed her power on and off the court. At the end of a match she slapped hands with friends, hugged her coach, burst into tears (over wins or losses), and displayed her trophy victoriously, with a great grin on her face. She was public about her primary relationship with another woman. With disarming integrity, Martina dared to be herself, to cry, cheer, laugh, and make jokes, even with a few million people watching.

Whom did the public root for more? Chris Evert, of course. She epitomized the ideal double standard. Sweet and innocent in person and dynamite on the tennis court can easily be translated into sweet and passive by day and dynamite in bed at night. Men can fantasize about her and she doesn't threaten anyone. I don't know how many times I've heard women tennis friends say, "I like Chris Evert because she's so feminine." Not, "I like Chris Evert because she has tenacity, incredible concentration, and fabulous passing shots." Because she is so "feminine," her power is palatable.

Perhaps it is harder for many women to root for Martina because most women cannot root for themselves. They muffle their pleasure, their talents, their joy, their successes, and their dreams. It is still taboo for a woman to say she wants to be the best at something, to want a place in history.

Our society still has not connected power and success with femininity, gentleness, and sensitivity. How many people can conjure up the image of a female college president or a surgeon who is gentle, playful, and sexually passionate? How many people think of a successful businesswoman without imagining a sexless person in a corporate suit or a vixen who slept her way to the top? How many men can see a truly powerful, talented woman in action and relish her success without seeing her as someone to be tamed and conquered or fantasizing about being sexual with her?

Underlying the oppression of lesbians is an unspoken warning to all women to beware of the consequences of getting uppity and of not following the patriarchal rules of female passivity.

BRIDGING DIFFERENCES

If nearly one in ten women lives a lesbian lifestyle, there must be lesbians in most organizations, offices, schools, human service departments, and so on. Many people, whether they realize it or not, work with lesbian women. Unless underlying issues of homophobia are brought into the open, damaging tension persists.

People handle this tension in various ways. They may deny their differences by maintaining emotional distance, feeling the tension but saying nothing about it. Obviously, in a predominantly heterosexual group, the tension is felt primarily by the lesbian woman. But if all of us are to deeply understand ourselves as women, it is crucial that we work through our sexual differences, integrating and accepting our lesbian and heterosexual sides: our power and our vulnerability, our love for women and our love for men. The process is scary, exciting, emotionally intense, and immensely rewarding. It is the stuff of which intimacy is made.

CHAPTER 12

Men: Behind the Myths

*I just hope that your completed book will significantly
take into account that many men are people also, no
more and no less — just people . . . with hopes, dreams,
aspirations, and sometimes even a romantic dream that
they can sometime be fortunate enough to find someone
they love and respect, and who will love and respect
them back.*

— Mark Able

I LET this chapter evolve by asking men in recovery for their thoughts on
what was important to say. I interviewed men in an SAA group and
men who identify themselves as sexually codependent. Several men had
responded to my monograph "Women and Sex Addiction," which they
read in an attempt to understand their sexually addicted female partners.
I include observations from men who struggle with sexually addictive or
codependent tendencies. I hope that the somewhat impressionistic chapter that resulted will encourage men to reflect on their own sexuality and
that it will also increase understanding between men and women.

On a sunny November day in 1987, I was looking forward to organizing
my thoughts for this chapter before a late afternoon tennis match. I
opened a folder labeled "Men" and began to read a letter from Mark
Able. It was one of the first letters I had received from a man, and I was
deeply moved by it.

Dear Dr. Kasl,
A close friend gave me a copy of your [monograph] "Women and Sex Addiction." I have read it through several times, and each reading is both enlightening and quite painful. I encourage you to expand the thesis and case
history technique as much as possible and do the book you mention.

Mark went on to say that he was sexually codependent and had been in a devastating relationship with a sexually addicted woman who was unable to keep her promises to be monogamous. Their relationship ended abruptly after she slept with his best friend while he was on a business trip. The experience of losing both her and his best friend was shattering, and he went through a long struggle to regain his equilibrium. I was touched that he was able to acknowledge his pain and understand that she, an incest survivor, was struggling with something that wasn't about him. His writing flowed with eloquence and he offered to provide input for the book in any way he could.

Fondly recalling our several conversations, one over a long Sunday brunch, I called his work number to schedule an interview. A cheerful secretary told me that he no longer worked there, that he'd been gone about two months. When I asked for his new number, she paused, and I suddenly felt a silent scream in the back of my head.

"He died," she said.

I was stunned. "Do you know how he died?"

"Suicide," she said quietly.

After we finished our conversation, I sat in silence, my head feeling like a clear cold starry night. "Dead," I said to myself. "Dead."

I returned to the file and took out the poetry Mark had sent, which described the bliss and pain of his lost relationship. I began to read with great attention, as if I would find a way to see him again or an explanation of his death. It was beautiful poetry, full of passion, full of pain.

The one time we met in person, Mark had seemed eager to talk, and I was impressed by his willingness to show his vulnerability to me, a complete stranger. We talked for a couple of hours, and before we parted I promised this wiry, intense man with a wonderful grin that I would write about men's pain, too. I'm sorry it had to come this way.

When many people hear the term "male sex addict" they conjure up images of child abuse, rape, or indecent exposure. While these traits are part of some men's sex addiction, there is a far larger group of men who struggle with sexually addictive behavior who present a much less dramatic picture. They may be married or single; many are monogamous, hard-working men with humanitarian values. Yet they experience frustration or sadness about the addictive part of themselves that is preoccupied with sex and has not been able to have a healthy ongoing relationship.

When a man is unable to connect intimacy with sex, or to form a lasting intimate sexual bond, he may isolate himself or wall off his feelings, resulting in a life controlled by fear, emptiness, depression, and emotional dishonesty. He may distort the truth, flirt at work, make false promises to partners, or use pornography addictively. Or he may simply keep a huge part of his inner sexual fantasy world and feelings hidden from everyone around him, drifting around in a mild chronic depression, shutting out genuine intimacy. He may be aware, perhaps vaguely, that his sexual responses to others, and his sexual fantasies, are a distraction that doesn't really fit with his beliefs. But because the culture provides no framework, no words, no forum for talking about these concerns, this awareness stays at a semiconscious level, gnawing away inside.

He may appear perfectly normal to others, but he lives in a divided world of good boy, bad boy. What goes on within remains a shameful secret, often obscuring painful memories from childhood. If we envision sexual problems on a continuum, we might have, at one end, a man who is in prison for sexually abusing children, and on the other, a totally monogamous man whose sex addiction is completely in his head.

There are also sexually codependent men. While they differ from co-dependent women in sexual socialization and support in having a career, they nonetheless share with women a fear of abandonment, experience paralysis about expressing anger, or fail to protect themselves from abuse or exploitation by their partners.

MALE AND FEMALE ADDICTS

In our culture, women who have numerous sexual partners are considered promiscuous or loose and are conditioned to feel ashamed and sleazy about enjoying the full power of their sexuality. Men who have numerous sexual partners are considered macho; they can "love 'em and leave 'em" and never become vulnerable. Scoring — that dreadful euphemism some men use for sex — certainly does not connote emotional intimacy. Such a model of sexuality ignores men's tenderness and vulnerability. It prevents them from recognizing the damage they do to themselves with their addictive use of sex.

Males are arrested far more often for such behavior as peeping and indecent exposure than women, who are culturally encouraged to "expose" themselves with skimpy clothes and seductive behavior. A woman isn't arrested for undressing with the blinds up. Yet she is also using her body to get a reaction, to shock, or to "assert" herself. Women are less likely to be arrested for sexually abusing children because they do it less frequently, and legal definitions are culture bound, blind to the ways females sexually harm younger males. A sixteen-year-old boy thinks it's a sign of his manhood to be sexual with a twenty-seven-year-old woman, unaware that she is abusing her power.

A man is taught from childhood to go after what he wants, to achieve, to be a hero, because the more heroic he is, the easier his access to beautiful women. The media portray successful men as rich and cool, with desirable women on their arms. What the ads don't portray is the harm men may do to themselves and others to become heroes and the pain felt by the vast majority of men who do not live up to these models.

Every step of initiating sexual contact with a female — holding hands, kissing, petting — is charged with the fear of being rejected, of being considered a jerk. I have vivid images of my brothers as young men, struggling to gather courage to "call a girl" and the hurt looks they tried to hide when they were turned down. Because men are taught that their self-worth is connected to their sexual prowess, such rejection hits deep, and they learn to numb themselves out.

Because the culture considers many forms of sexually addictive behavior in men as normal, men rarely seek help. When they do, they may be told by therapists that they just have a high libido, or that visiting prostitutes or using pornography is normal male behavior. When a man says, "I think I've got a problem because I'm sleeping with too many women," his buddies rib him and say, "Hey, I wish I had that problem!"

In general, women's values are primarily concerned with relationships and the development of cooperative systems. Many addicted women are aware at some level throughout their acting-out period that they are violating their own deepest values. Most of them long to find a loving relationship. Sexually addicted men, however, are much less conscious that they are violating their values, for having numerous partners and emotionally disconnected sex are widely seen as the norm, as evidenced by the wide acceptance of *Playboy* and similar magazines.

In Western society men are taught to find their life's meaning and identity through work. They are encouraged to be independent, isolated, and goal oriented and to hide their vulnerability, which makes bonding with a woman difficult at best. This carries over into sex, which often becomes performance oriented or a means of control rather than a source of meaningful human contact.

If we look at homosexual men, we can see male sexual programming without the constraints of marriage. While some gay men have long-term committed relationships, it is not uncommon for many of them to have five hundred to a thousand partners, perhaps several in one night at a "bathhouse," where sex is routinely purveyed as a soulless, emotionless, genital-only event.

Lesbian women generally have fewer than eight partners and are far more likely to have long-term committed relationships.

CONFUSION AND BIAS

I feel a great deal of inner conflict when I think of men as the predominant class of people in power, in contrast to men as individuals. At a personal level, I have had special, warm-hearted, supportive, and caring relationships with men as brothers, friends, lovers, and colleagues.

On the other hand, over the past twelve years I have spent most of my working hours listening to women describe rape, incest, battering, and emotional abuse by men. I feel a fury at this male-controlled system that does so little to protect women and children.

Marilyn, a client whom I talked about in the previous chapter (pages 217–219), was nearly killed by her former husband. Within a year, he will be out of jail, where he received no treatment for his violence. She is planning to give up her career, her home, and her support system to move far away so she won't have to live in constant fear of assault. This shouldn't be her problem; it should somehow be put in his lap and in the lap of the culture.

To assuage my own inner conflict, I struggle to convince myself that we are truly all in this together. I try to listen to men, to understand their conditioning. I return to Gandhi's writings on *Ahimsa*, the love for all people. He writes in his autobiography, "It is quite proper to resist and attack a system, but to resist and attack its author is tantamount to resisting and attacking oneself. For we are all tarred with the same brush, and are children of one and the same Creator. . . . To slight a single human being is to . . . harm not only that being but with him the whole world."

Hearing men tell their stories, revealing their hurt and pain, has also helped. The more men open up and talk about their feelings, the more I am able to open to them. When the male perpetrator or the male addict tells his abuse story, including how he has used women, the word *perpetrator* slides from my mind and he becomes an abused soul struggling to heal his wounds.

I interviewed a group of SAA men who, among other things, spoke of ways they had used women, been oblivious to women's needs, and seen them as objects. They talked of anonymous sex, their immense need to control women, and their fears of being sexual with strong, independent women. They also described their tremendous struggles to see women as people, particularly when sexual feelings are involved. When I asked how many men they thought struggled with sex addiction issues, one man laughed and responded, "One hundred eight percent."

The morning after the interview, Geraldo Rivera moderated a segment on his program entitled "What Men Want Sexually from Women." I heard men talking warmly and sympathetically about wanting to please women sexually, about caring about how women feel. Several said they liked sexually assertive women. Several experts on the panel suggested that men are painted in a bad light in the recent proliferation of "relationship" books. "Am I living on two different planets?" I asked myself. What's true here?

It's all true. We are living in a confusing, changing time. Yes, men do use women's bodies; yes, men are terrified of surrendering control for genuine equality; and yes, men want to be intimate with women on a sexual and emotional level. This shift in values was brought home to me during a visit with a woman who had been a close friend of mine during the late 1960s and early 1970s. As we caught up on each other's lives, she told me about suggesting sex to a man she was dating. He had said it was too soon, that *he* wanted to wait until they knew each other better. "Can you imagine that!" she exclaimed as we both laughed at the tables being turned.

MALE SOCIALIZATION

While writing this chapter, I found myself observing men more carefully than ever. During the 1987 World Series, I became immersed in baseball. Even as I rooted for the Minnesota Twins, I made note of male bonding and touching. Lots of people were saying, "Oh, isn't it wonderful that men are hugging and patting each other." "But," I responded, "only when they win. If they don't win, then no hugs, no pats." After every game one team was embracing, while the other was slinking off to the locker room. Why don't men hug each other after they strike out or lose the game? Because males are taught to love themselves conditionally, on the basis of winning and achieving. Women, on the other hand, are taught to console and soothe. For the losing team members to hug and stroke one another would mean admitting to neediness, which is like admitting to dependency on others, and that, of course, is something our culture discourages in men.

Men's dependency on women may be buried, but it still operates as a controlling force in their lives. Men's violence toward women who leave them, for example, is an inappropriate response of a hurt little boy inside, terrified of his emptiness. Because he is not taught to experience his sadness, to reach out to a friend and cry his eyes out, he channels his pain and hurt into anger and beats up on the woman who abandoned him. Or if he doesn't get violent, his rage turns inward, contributing to ulcers, heart problems, or depression.

If the need to have power over others is directly proportional to the emptiness or powerlessness one feels within, many men must feel very empty. As the dominant partner in a relationship, a man doesn't feel sure that he is loved, because he never knows if a woman stays with him solely out of dependency or need for security and status. If a man felt lovable for who he was, why should he feel threatened by a wife going back to school, getting a job, or having close friends? Even when men *are* accepting, they are often afraid: "If she has money and work she likes, why would she stay with me?"

When I returned to school to work on a Ph.D. my husband said it was great. Yet I returned home every night to dirty dishes, complaints about there being no food prepared, and assorted hostile jabs related to nothing much. Months later he told me he had worried that I was having an affair with a professor I liked, an idea that had never crossed my mind. This example is not to shame him or any man; it is simply to acknowledge the deeply rooted fears of abandonment and preoccupation with sex that haunt many men.

If men would admit to their dependency, they could take the next step and ask for what they need. One of the most effective ways to release pain is simply to cry. "Blessed are they that mourn for they shall be comforted." Men seldom find this blessedness because they have internalized the belief that big boys don't cry. They are ashamed of sadness and want to get rid of it. Some may cry alone, getting relief but not comfort. But deep down men *do* want comfort and care. Unable to ask for it, they hold in their sadness and grief, thereby creating tremendous inner tension that often explodes in violence. The unconscious motivation runs something like, "You didn't give me what I wanted, so take that." This feeling is expressed at a personal level and at a national level. There are men who beat women and, at the international level, there are men waging war. In both spheres, the behavior is not that of people who feel good about themselves. Someone who feels loved and complete simply does not participate in violence, be it at home or in the public arena.

A FAREWELL TO MOTHER'S ARMS

In our culture the mother's role is to love and nurture a little boy, and the father's job is to teach him to be tough or, rather, to "be a man." This division of labor is a disaster for little boys who reject their feminine side and become dependent on women for gentleness and nurture. Here is one scenario.

A mother loves her baby boy. She holds him and cradles him as an infant. But, true to her conditioning, she begins to wean her son away from her nurture, to hand him over to his father and the man's world. I saw this process operate with my little brother. By the age of five he could have two forms of physical contact — either shaking hands or roughhousing with Dad. What a lousy tradeoff for Mom's hugs and warmth.

What happens in a little boy's mind? He feels rejected and pushed away from the softness and tenderness of his mother. And because Daddy doesn't show softness and tenderness, he concludes that it is wrong for boys to feel or express these emotions. So he shuts down his own capacity for softness and tenderness and buries his hunger to be nurtured deep within his unconscious. A rage develops at the loss. Meanwhile, the culture reinforces his notion of stoic manhood by impressing on him —

through books, media, and movies — that it is unmanly to cry, or to long for nurture and tenderness. (Mr. Rogers has not outweighed the rest of the culture.) And, of course, it is manly to work sixty hours a week and be financially responsible for a wife and family. The one comment most people in therapy make about their fathers is that they were never there. They were off working, being responsible.

For the most part, the psychological literature has blamed mothers for male rage, for Mother took away the nurture. This is unfair and inaccurate, for if fathers learned to take on a nurturing role with their sons, there would be no need to get angry at mothers.

Boys are angry at their fathers for not showing tenderness and care, but they are taught to vent much of this anger at women. Many sexually addicted men had distant, stoic, sharply critical, weak, or physically abusive fathers. One man's recollection is typical.

"I remember coming home from ice skating in the park in the wintertime, and the neighborhood bully had beaten me up, given me a black eye and a bloody nose. I came in the back door of the house and my older sister went running into the living room, where my father was reading the newspaper. He came out into the kitchen with his paper in one hand and turned on the light and looked at me. He lifted up my chin, then snapped his hand away in a very ungentle manner, and said, 'Ah, you'll live.' Then he turned around and walked away. And that was the sum total of nurturing that I got after being physically abused by a bigger, older kid. The only thing I got from my mother was 'Here's a washcloth.' "

Caught in an unconscious need to keep his own unquenched neediness at bay, the father was cold to his son. If he had been tender, his own grief at not having been nurtured as a boy might have risen to the surface.

Another man said, "My father was angry all the time. He was a well-respected community leader outside the home. But when he got home he turned into a goddamned demon and nothing was good enough. He beat me all the time. I took the brunt of a great deal of his anger. He used to say things like, 'Why are you so smart and act so dumb?' or 'You're a bad kid.' "

The boy's unconscious desire for nurturance and comfort does not go away. At some point he discovers that masturbation brings good feelings and an escape from hurt and pain. He may begin to masturbate secretly and in shame, feelings that contribute to his attitude toward sex. He may also get a sense of power looking at men's magazines and fantasizing being sexual with beautiful women. As he gets older he learns that the one way to have a physical connection with a woman is to have sex.

But this presents a dilemma. He still has an unconscious longing for his mother, mixed with a buried anger, which will surface if he becomes emotionally close to a woman. Better, then, not to get close. Furthermore, he has probably absorbed the message that women are inferior beings, which means that their sexuality is also inferior. At worst, women become chicks, lays, cunts, girls. At best, he chooses a woman who looks up to him and does not challenge him emotionally. Instead of associating sex with intimacy and nurturing feelings, he learns to detach and have orgasmic sex without intimacy, or to have sex with women he doesn't respect. When sex becomes dissociated from love, the genitals become dissociated from the spirit. No love given, no love received. This perpetuates the emptiness. The penis becomes a thing — a missile to raise, aim, and fire. The act may elicit momentary good feelings, but it is relegated to a separate, isolated compartment that has little connection with his emotional life.

(An aside: Helen Caldicott called her book on the arms race *Missile Envy*. The implication of her title is clear, and my interviews with men made it even clearer to me. There seems to me to be a chilling parallel between the ability of men to detach emotionally from their penises and their sexuality and to detach from the consequences of killing people. Dropping bombs and shooting people seemed like one step away from anonymous sex. Screw 'em and leave 'em. Shoot 'em and leave 'em.)

FEAR OF WOMEN AND CONTROL

Heterosexual men who use sex addictively have an underlying terror of their own neediness and an inability to engage with a woman in a reciprocal, loving way. Thus they fear women, particularly women they can't render into objects and therefore control. And remember, to a tiny boy all mothers are huge, powerful figures who have total control. As boys start school, they learn never to admit to their peers their need for feminine tenderness. As time goes on, they are socialized to translate the need for tenderness and intimacy to a need for sex with women they can control.

A double bind results because all the status, money, or charm in the world cannot force a woman to give her body lovingly and openly in the sexual act. Beautiful codependent women who are looking for men to take care of them are not apt to be comfortable with their sexuality, because they look to others for power. So men continue to be sexually attracted to women who fit their status image but are not likely to be satisfying sexual partners.

The penis is another control issue for males. Men repeatedly talked about their fear since childhood of having erections when they shouldn't and being unable to have them when they should. It seems paradoxical that the supposed symbol of male power and superiority, which women allegedly envy, is in truth a problematical part of the body that can be out of control and a source of great embarrassment.

THE VIRGIN AND WHORE DILEMMA

Feminist literature abounds with the ramifications of the virgin-whore dilemma for women, but men have to resolve this dilemma as well.

"I was raised to get as many notches on my belt as I could," said Daniel, who attended SAA. "Women are for sex. When I got married, it suddenly hit me: 'Oh, my God, *she's my wife!* I can't have sex with her. You're supposed to respect your wife.' So we've had a nearly sexless marriage for seven years."

Another man, David, recalled, "When I went to an English boarding school I found a totally schizophrenic atmosphere in that women were either absolutely idealized or treated like shit. I think the double message sets up a complex mechanism. When I was eighteen a friend of mine went out with a girl I had worshipped from afar. I never thought of touching her, or that she had anything so gross as 'tits' and a 'cunt.' My friend reported, 'Anne is so fantastic; she gave me a marvelous blow job.' I attacked him physically because I couldn't believe that this peaches-and-cream English sort of Lady Di playing tennis in the garden could actually suck a man's cock. And I nearly killed him."

Another man, Bill, described the liberal male dilemma. "I was brought up to respect women. I also got the message from my mother, even though she never voiced it, that men just want to screw women, that men were unreliable, insensitive, untrustworthy clods. I didn't want to be one of them, so I developed a dislike of men which carried over to myself and my sexuality. I stayed away from men, and considered bright, intelligent women desirable but unattainable, far above me as a jerk of a male. Other women didn't interest me. I was terrified to ask women out and didn't have sex until I was in my twenties."

Just as women are seen as either the virgin or the whore, at the extremes, men are seen as either tough macho types or nice guys. The addictive macho man buries his neediness and vulnerability beneath a tough exterior, while the nice guy strangles his anger. He may also be addictive, or he may be codependent to sexually addicted women who exploit or abuse him.

Histories of nice-guy codependents range from families that appear normal on the surface but exert enormous control over their children to families in which there is neglect, alcoholism, violence, and sexual abuse. The men grow up with a confusing combination of fear, respect, and anger toward women along with a profound desire for women's acceptance. They don't want to be like macho guys, but in assuming an opposite role, they deny their anger and feel ashamed of their internalized male sexual programming.

Because it violates their conscious values, these men try to suppress the side of themselves that objectifies women. Afraid to talk about their secret world of sexual fantasies and anger, they often feel profound inner shame, which only adds to their sense of isolation. Unwilling to risk disapproval by traditional men, they may turn to women for support. The sad thing is that they don't come to love themselves and their male sexuality, believing that their sexuality hurts women.

Nice-guy addicted men have a tremendous need for women's (read Mother's) approval, and like all caretakers, they build up anger inside. To control their anger, they often become drinkers or pot smokers who, although they seldom lose control, routinely take the edge off their awareness by drinking or smoking "a little," working too hard, or staying busy all the time.

Some men take on the burden of the culture's guilt for injustices toward women and become vulnerable to use or exploitation by women. They don't understand that, like women, they are entitled to dignity and respect and the right to protect themselves from criticism and badgering. Emotionally frozen, they say the politically "right" things — and are intensely lonely. They have difficulty developing intimacy because they hide so much of themselves beneath their liberal, "sensitive" exteriors.

An addicted woman may choose a nice guy as a partner because she can control him. She can take charge without concern that the man will complain when she loses interest in being sexual because he feels it's macho to pressure her. One such man told me that he hadn't been "allowed" to be sexual in six months. His wording suggested that, in his role of good boy, he didn't think he had the right to ask.

I told him that of course he didn't have the right to *insist* on sex, but that he could certainly ask that the two of them talk about it.

Some men mask their addiction with a nice-guy cover-up. Early in women's liberation and in the peace movement, I heard men joke that developing a liberal line worked even better than old macho methods for seducing a lot of women. One man advised another, "Be sensitive to women's issues and watch them come to you in droves."

Another cover-up is when a man goes to great lengths to please a woman sexually. He plays her like a fine violin, painstakingly doing whatever she likes. But he is attempting to gain control over her, to be special, better than all the rest, so that he can have access to being sexual whenever he wants.

FEMALE PERPETRATORS

Many men I interviewed emphasized the need to understand the impact of childhood sexual abuse and intrusiveness by women as well as by men. I believe that sexual abuse of boys, particularly by females, is far more widespread than any research has shown. The untold harm such abuse does to men has barely been explored, for we have not yet clearly defined the way males are damaged by childhood sexual abuse. Men may well spend up to three years in therapy or SAA before they can understand the impact on them of female sexual exploitation and abuse, which means that research that *has* been done in this area may be skewed.

Few people are willing to face this issue. Pointing the finger at men as the sexual abusers is safer for women, and it is safer for men to discount the profound power women have over them. Men don't want to admit that women, including their mothers, have the power to wound them sexually. Furthermore, to confront the knowledge that one's mother, the primary protector, was abusive is to profoundly challenge our cultural images of motherhood.

Professionals in the field of addiction have learned that when adults use children to fill an emotional void, the children suffer. Yet in a culture that does not empower women, it is little wonder that they often turn to their sons for the intimacy and meaning in life they so dearly long for.

Stories of mothers who had inappropriate, intrusive, or sexualized bonds with their sons recur again and again among sexually addicted men. Women harm boys sexually in both overt and covert ways. The harm is often insidious and deep because children place a special trust in mothers and are more open to them; the betrayal of that trust is extremely painful and can take a long time to recognize.

Aaron, in speaking of his therapy, said it was impossible for him to think his mother had done anything wrong, because, well, it's as American as apple pie to love your mother. "I first wouldn't have anything to do with it. I said in no uncertain terms that my therapist was barking up the wrong tree, that he was too involved in therapy to *really* understand. But now I don't think there is an addict who has not first been a victim. In every story I've heard, it started when they were young. It was almost always a parent, brother, sister, uncle, teacher, priest, or Boy Scout leader. And most of all there is mother-son incest. My mother was not exactly incestuous with me, but it was like incest because there were intrusions, no boundaries, just intrusiveness all the time."

David said, "When my therapist said to me, 'You don't have to love your mother,' I was completely taken aback, completely breathless. It was so obvious, but no one had ever said it. I said, 'But of course I do. I have to love her because she's my mother.' "

The unresolved feelings about mothers who use a son emotionally as a husband replacement profoundly affected these men and their ability to bond sexually with women, particularly strong, intelligent women who trigger unconscious or conscious memories of the overpowering intrusive mother.

Michael's mother was attractive, flirtatious, and preoccupied with men. She was more of a friend than a mother to her son. In particular she made Michael her confidant, telling him about her crushes and affairs and flirting with his high school and college friends. And from an early age she also used him as a husband substitute by relying on his advice for decisions she felt too insecure to make on her own.

Because his mother's primary self-definition was as a sexual creature seeking men, Michael unconsciously erected a barrier against her covert threat of incest. On the surface he idolized her as beautiful and charming and felt special because she shared so much with him. It was difficult for him to realize that she played a childlike dependent role with men and with him. Instinctively, he learned to control his desire for nurture and care, because her affection made him feel uncomfortable. He was deprived of being a little boy whose mom cared for him. As an adult Michael strongly defended his wonderful mother, rarely got angry, and always had to have control in his relationships with women. A woman had to be either younger, less intelligent, or less talented. She could excel at something, as long as he was able to maintain control in some major area.

For years he said that he just hadn't found the right woman. Meanwhile, he perfected the art of enticement, giving a woman just enough attention to keep her in tow and becoming more attentive only when she threatened to leave. When she responded to the starvation diet by pushing for more, he could say, "Oh, these women get so needy and so dependent. She wants to trap me. I don't want someone like that. I want someone stronger." Echos of an overwhelmed little boy.

So Michael fled from women who were truly his equal, for they would kindle his buried rage at his mother. They also challenged his profound loyalty to his mother, a tie that would have to be broken before he could have an intimate relationship with a woman.

Many SAA men describe covert incest by their mothers, echoing women's themes in regard to men. Having had up to seven years of recovery and considerable psychotherapy, these men could recognize that they had transferred their relationships with their mothers into their adult relationships with women. They had not come by these insights easily. In answer to the request "Tell me about your relationship to your mother," men made the following statements:

"At the age of six I pushed my mother away. I didn't let her get up and make my breakfast. I learned how to make my own. I didn't want her smothering me with questions and so-called love. She was very inappropriate, wearing a lot of see-through nighties and parading in front of the picture window in panties and bra. I remember one time when I was eight, my mother came so close to me wearing a see-through nightie that I punched her breast because I just felt she was getting *too close* and it scared the heck out of me."

"My mom would pout if I didn't say hi in the proper tone of voice or talk with her or kiss her. It was like she was my lover. And what's ironic is that's exactly how I ended up treating my daughter. If she didn't say hi to me, I would pout and feel that she didn't love me."

"My mother was like a helpless baby sitter to me. She was not inappropriate sexually, but she did a tremendous amount of shaming. I got a tremendous amount of power from controlling my mother's emotions at an early age. She'd say 'Nobody's ever done this, nobody has ever made me cry.' She played the role of victim, putting me in the role of abuser. What I did not understand is that my mother put me in the terrifying position of having power over her, the ability to destroy her, which got translated to my mind to 'I am a destructive person. I hurt women.' " From my perspective there were sexual overtones to this relationship because the mother put her son in a peer situation as her male partner. The male peer of the mother is supposed to be the father. Transferring that role to the son suggests a sexual relationship in the unconscious mind, even though it is never acted out.

David continued the discussion. "The mother is, after all, the person who first touches your body and wakes your erogenous zones. In my case, there's no doubt that my mother took me as her lover. I felt that into the middle of my life. In fact my wife said, 'My God, your mother always wants to kiss you on the lips.' It was just the most blatant invasion of boundaries. It is terrifying for a child to be sexualized and, at the same time, utterly powerless. Such childhood abuse, I think, is the basis of a lot of sexual acting-out in men. We think of incest as that miserable father who is always after his daughters, but let's not forget there are different ways of abusing a person."

Aaron spoke again. "When I was very young I would lock the bathroom door when I took a bath and I remember hearing the doorknob rattle. I knew that it was my mother on the other side wanting to come in. No word was ever said, that's how I knew it was my mother. If it was my brother or sister they'd say, 'How long are you gonna be in there?' I'd feel sick inside when I heard that door rattle and knew she was there."

"I remember, especially after taking a bath when I was eleven and twelve, coming into puberty, my mother would insist on coming in and sit on the stool holding a towel and look at my penis. I have that terrible memory of her staring at my penis, and she would say, 'Oh, darling, what lovely broad shoulders you have.' Actually I was a rather skinny kid. Now, if a woman comes really close to me I occasionally click into that image of my mother and get really scared. So intimacy becomes fouled with this feeling of danger."

EFFECTS ON INTIMACY

How do men who have been sexually invaded or abused control the terror of being overwhelmed that engulfs them when a woman gets close? I approach the subject with the question "What is your first reaction to strong, intelligent women?" One man's immediate response was to jump off the couch as if to leave the room. Everyone laughed in recognition.

"I'd say basically there's something not right with that woman," said another. "I'd guess that she probably was a lesbian. I'd feel a strong fear that said stay away from this person, she's dangerous. Before I got into recovery I had a tough time with homosexuals of either sex. I couldn't accept their presence, much less understand them. Before recovery I wouldn't have been able to acknowledge that I have a dilemma about this."

"My reaction to a strong, bright woman is that she is unattainable, and I would desire her from a distance. I would not pursue her at all, but I would masturbate thinking of her."

"I am strongly attracted to women like that, especially intellectually, but they must be younger than I am. I guess there's an undertone of exhilaration, but I have to be able to control them because I'm older, in the role of a teacher."

"If you had added the word *attractive* as well as strong and intelligent it would bother me. I feel safe with somebody with that description you gave. But as soon as you add attractive, I get the feeling that she is unattainable."

Men deal with their fear of being engulfed by women by either staying away from strong, bright women altogether or by mentally neutering them — in effect, making them buddies. The men I interviewed acknowledged the pain of this split: much as they want equality, they feel bound by conditioning that tells them they can't have it. If they do enter relationships with women who are genuine equals, many have difficulty being sexual. Although they want to be close, they are also hindered by buried feelings about the incestuous or intrusive mother.

Although issues surrounding their mothers were of primary importance to most men, some told stories of sexual exploitation by female baby sitters and older women. In these cases the men spoke of their difficulty recognizing that they had been sexually used. They had been conditioned to believe that all sex that feels good is okay, and that males are always in charge.

By the same token, since they grew up believing in male authority, they did not recognize it as abuse when they were sexually exploited by older men. If a priest, rabbi, teacher, or Boy Scout leader masturbated them and it felt good, what was the big deal? Lots of big deal! Even though it felt good physically, the shame of the secrecy and the intuitive feeling that they were being used penetrated their psyches. They felt responsible, as if they had caused it. "If I didn't want it," they would think, "I would have said no." Wrong again. Boys have the same confusion that female abuse victims do. If they are exploited or manipulated into being sexual by a trusted person with more power, they think it is their fault.

Many men have a difficult time understanding that more sex is not necessarily better. When I told a couple at a party about writing this book, the man, like so many others, said, "You mean women addicted to sex? Hey, I want to meet one of those." His female partner, also a therapist, tried to explain to him, to no avail, that he wouldn't like it, honest.

Because they need to maintain control, sexually addicted men are sometimes afraid of sexually addicted women. As a man in recovery said, "After an AA meeting an older woman said, 'I'm going to seduce you tonight.' I always thought I would jump at a chance like that. It scared me so much I walked right to my car and drove home." The epilogue to this story, however, is that the following day he called the woman, went to her house, and had sex. This gave him the illusion that he was in control and put the notch on *his* belt.

Asked what cultural factors they feel have been most damaging to them, men responded as follows:

"For me, it's been the constant and continuous objectification of women sexually, especially in magazines, starting with *Playboy*. I discovered that literature could be erotic. Then it was everywhere. That really fueled the fire — I couldn't get away from it."

"Would you ban books?" one of the other men asked.

"I'd sure ban pornography if I had my way. All I can say is it's been very destructive and harmful for me. It's been one of the primary reasons I've had a difficult time looking at women as people. I am tremendously sad about that."

Another man concurred and then went on, "But even before *Playboy,* the tamest TV show could trigger my addiction. Remember the *Mickey Mouse Club,* that all-American show? To me it objectified Annette Funicello because of her body. She was kind of comely, she was always kind of on the make, and Spin and Marty were always after her."

Everyone in the group laughed in recognition.

"Oh, yeah, I remember Spin and Marty."

"And there were jokes about her anatomy, not on that show but on others, like Johnny Carson."

A man who had been devoted to Captain Marvel, Superman, Captain Midnight, Tom Mix, and the like remembered thinking to himself, "How can I ever be like them? I'm just a little boy." He also had been confused by the admonition, "Big boys don't cry." "When I was little and someone said that to me, I always thought, 'How am I supposed to be a big boy when I'm just a little boy?' It was as if it was demeaning to be little. You were supposed to act big even when you weren't. I got the message that the important thing was to grow up, have a big penis, and be bigger than women."

I felt enormous respect and warmth for the openness of these men as they talked about the pain and frustration surrounding the socialization they'd been saddled with. It was even better to see how they had dug in and struggled to change.

RECOVERY

Recovery is hard for men. Since they grow up believing that they are the dominant group, it is a difficult leap for them to understand that what they have learned is not the ultimate truth. They are also used to being in control. When they enter a men's support or recovery group, the domain of feelings and vulnerability is foreign to them. Their immediate impulse is to debate, to discuss, and to set concrete goals for recovery.

Arnie, a successful businessman who has been in a recovery group for seven years, laughed when he told me about his first SAA meeting. When he found out that there were twelve steps to recovery, he figured he could do one step a week and be done. It is extremely difficult for most men to realize that they have to surrender their rational mind to an unknown process to find their spiritual side. They can't control recovery by reading a book, doing an assignment, or following a simple list of don'ts.

Men usually start by defining sexual sobriety as a list of don'ts that pertain to their particular form of sex addiction: don't have sex, stay away from pornography and bookstores, no prostitutes, no flirting, no masturbation, no peeping, no exposing, and no extended fantasies. It is fine to use such a list as a starting place, but *not* doing things is only a beginning to recovery.

It may take years to realize that recovery is a holistic process. You can't be obsessive in one area without that obsession affecting all areas of your life. The men in the group revealed that it had taken them a long time to understand that recovery is also about loving yourself. Sex addiction recovery groups encourage "progress not perfection," and each man is responsible for setting his own boundaries around expressions of his sexuality. Given their male programming, it is not surprising that many men start by setting rigid rules for themselves, then feel ashamed when they can't live up to their expectations.

When men question their right to have sex, use pornography, and flirt with women when and how they want, they also call into question essential definitions of manhood. Arnie said, "I always believed I had a right to sex in a relationship. That's what it's all about. Sex is how I understand everything is okay. For me it was the major affirmation of being a man and of being loved."

When I asked him to describe his recovery, he answered, "The major issue was to connect intimacy with sexuality. It's taken me seven years to get to the place where it feels bad to my spirit to have sex without feeling emotionally connected. At age forty-eight I'm in the first relationship in which I respect the woman enough to take care of her needs. Before it was — I got what I needed, and if she wanted more, well hell, tough luck. The greatest reward for me is to live free from a web of lies, deceit, and dishonesty. It's just great, free! I can actually feel joy and love and express it."

Another man underscored the struggle of recovery. "In nine months in SAA maybe I've hit two hours when I really felt spiritual." He turned to the man on his right. "It was when you, Aaron, helped me through a real tough time about a gambling slip. I just felt that God was with me. I felt so good. I didn't obsess and preoccupy myself with women. I didn't see them as objects, I just saw people."

Another man spoke of letting go of his need to lay blame. "I was going through life as a victim. I always had to have somebody or something to blame. There always had to be a reason outside myself for my discontent. Over all, what I'm doing now is healthy and respectful to myself. It's so different to pay attention to myself, to feel that I deserve things. There is this belief that I'm doing the right thing and that things are going to be okay. Before recovery when I felt trapped I had to act crazy in order to break out of my shell."

Many men suppress their childhood pain and rage with alcohol, drugs, and sex. They may also bury it in anxiety and periodic or chronic depression. Many men report drinking or acting out sexually during therapy for depression, anxiety, mood swings, or career problems. As a result, they have never explored the roots of their sex addiction and codependency. In many cases anxiety and depression abated significantly once such issues were addressed.

FROM MEN TO MEN

When asked what advice they would like to give other men, the men in the group included the following.

"I hope they'll get over 'being men.' "

"Banish forever the statement 'Big boys don't cry.' "

"Realize that sexual abuse hurts men too."

"Learn to share feelings and talk honestly with other men."

"Learn that a man doesn't need a woman to be whole."

"Cherish differences between men and women."

"I hope both sexes will learn to honestly express their feelings to each other. I'm just learning to do that now in the men's group, after three years. It's something I've never had before in a relationship. I get to be honest and be accepted no matter what I've done and what I've said."

"I wish men and women would realize that most men are, by and large, emotionally crippled or retarded."

The following points sum up what men have told me and what I have seen prove helpful to men in therapy.

1. It's all right to cry. (You may have to say this five hundred times a day for a few months or a year to convince yourself, but eventually it will sink in.) Crying is a wonderful release of energy that helps open your heart. And remember, when the love comes in, the tears come out. Be thankful for tears; you've paid your dues for them.

2. You don't have to perform sexually. The purpose of sex is to have an intimate, pleasurable experience and an erection and orgasm if they come. One man wrote that it was terrifying to have his wife initiate sex because he would panic and think, "Oh my God, what am I going to do, what if I *can't?*" It is really, really all right if you can't. The goal is not orgasm. Your manhood is not riding on your sexual performance. Your ability to share, talk, and show emotion is far more important.

3. Tell your partner when you are afraid, uncomfortable, or uneasy. If you don't you will put up a wall and withdraw. Your partner will feel it. If she or he asks, "What's the matter?" try to express your feelings. If you don't exactly know, you can say, "I'm not sure, but something is bothering me." Eventually you will be able to pinpoint your feelings more accurately. If you have no idea what it's like to express them, you have a lot of male company. But there are no excuses for not learning.

4. Don't expect that experiencing feelings will come easily. It may feel like risking death, ripping open your chest, or falling into a great abyss. These sensations are really about the death of the ego, which dictates that a man must not have feelings.

5. You have the right to say no to sex. Many sexually addicted or codependent men think it unmanly to refuse to be sexual or, like female codependents, that they don't get to say no. The whole point is to be true to your heart, and say both yes and no.

6. Work to detach your ego from your sexuality. Your worth as a human being has no connection to your ability to charm, seduce, and be sexual with a partner. Healthy sex is not about winning, overpowering, or scoring.

7. Recovery can feel like a trip to a foreign country. Persevere. It may take years or even a lifetime. All the men I know who have made it to the other shore say it is well worth it. Only with recovery can you trust that someone loves you for yourself, not as a status object or someone to take care of him or her.

8. To have a balanced relationship, don't act all-knowing and wise. Don't try to impress women by spending large amounts of money on them. You are likely to attract dependent women who want a caretaker (read father) and provider, not a partner. Self-assured, independent women are often more sympathetic to your uneasiness or fears and more aware of cultural roles.

9. It is okay to admit making mistakes. It may feel like risking excommunication from the planet the first time you own up to a mistake and say you are sorry. However, you will nearly always feel better. Most people have an amazing capacity to forgive when someone genuinely makes amends.

10. You can't do it alone. You can only white-knuckle it alone. It is important to bond with men in a group and learn to express feelings and to give and receive nurture and support from them. This will relieve you of your dependency on women and help you expand your own image of what it means to be a man.

11. Learn that what you think, feel, and believe is cultural and family programming. It is not etched in stone. You have a spirit and soul totally separate from your indoctrinated beliefs.

12. There is hope. Men who have been out of control, compulsively or addictively attached to pornography, women, children, exposure, violence, sleaze, obsessive fantasies, and the like have embarked on the road to recovery.

13. Be gentle. Even if you slip and slide, you can still recover so long as you commit yourself and stay on the path, no matter what. You are not your addiction and you are not a bad person for having an addiction. It is just a pain and a drag.

14. Surrender to the little boy within. Get to know him. You will have so much more energy when you stop fending off feelings of insecurity, neediness, and dependency and share them instead. It is okay to cry in someone's arms — isn't that what a part of you has craved since childhood? It is also okay to say "I'm confused. I don't know the answer. This is over my head. I'm afraid." You were told to cut out the feminine part of yourself because the culture says it's second class to be female. Have your feelings and confusion. You won't dissolve as a man. If someone calls you a sissy or gay, big deal. Pray for him. It's his problem; don't take it on.

15. Learn to understand that sexual arousal can become a cover for

other feelings. Many men said that if they were hurt or angry, they would immediately have a sexual fantasy and get sexually aroused. If you do get aroused, do not shame yourself. Sexual energy is life energy. Simply breathe into the pelvic region and draw the energy up into your heart area and imagine your heart opening up.

16. You don't need to know what recovery is about to begin. Just say, "I will do what it takes to feel whole. I am willing. I commit myself to recovery."

Others have done it. You can too.

EVERYONE CAN WIN

Men and women have everything to gain by giving up their polarized images of what it means to be a man or a woman. If men could learn to love themselves unconditionally and expose their vulnerability to each other, they would feel more comfortable when women take on an equal role in personal relationships and in the power structure. They would no longer be jealous of women bonding with each other or earning equal money, for it would no longer be perceived as a threat or loss of nurture. Men are often ashamed of their dependency on women for nurture and warmth. One solution is for men to learn to nurture and care for themselves and other men. *I believe that men control women to the extent that they are unable to realize their own capacity for nurture and emotional vulnerability.* I believe control always stems from feelings of powerlessness and fear. Men's fear that women will withdraw love and nurture is a mirror of their own inability to love and nurture themselves.

Historically, people in power don't give up their control or dominant position without a struggle. The paradox is that the more one seeks power over others, the greater the wound to the soul and the greater the internal split. The exploitive part is constantly trying to obliterate the spiritual part, which knows it is wrong to exploit others. The result is a nonstop inner battle in which the tender, empathic, loving parts of men are sacrificed. The current solution to the dilemma? Addictive sex. Addictive everything. Use sex as an illusory way to get touch and care and love and to feel powerful. Of course it doesn't work because sex is not care and love. Sex is not power. Sex is only sex.

As men give up trying to control women and participate instead in creating a system where women have equality, they will also gain access to their own capacity for caring, emotional vulnerability, and love. This is the wellspring from which intimate, loving friendships and sexual relationships grow.

One of the most difficult lessons
            I have had to learn
                      is the necessity of letting go of a
  person I deeply love
                without letting go
                      of love itself.

  I am still learning that and it still hurts
The hardest thing for me to do
                          still
          is to commit myself for myself
          to emotions and feelings
          I know are there
              and to realize
              that just because I have them
      there is no guarantee
              I will be loved back
              or that someone will be there for me
              the way I wish
     That hurts
     but I cannot run away from truth forever.
                        — Mark Able

CHAPTER 13

How Did I Get This Way?
Culture, Family, and the Grace of God

THERE IS an exquisite interconnection between culture, family, and inborn individual traits that relate to sex addiction, sexual codependency, and recovery. I remember feeling frustrated being taught in sociology courses that everything is about "the system," while individual differences were discounted. Then, in psychology classes, it seemed inane to try to understand individuals in isolation from the broad cultural context of their lives. When I studied family therapy, I was struck with the tenacity of the belief that all behavior could be understood in terms of the family, almost always presented as Mom, Dad, and two or three children. What about race, class, ethnic background, and gender? And what about the class and gender of the person developing the theories? White men, who create most theories, see the role of families differently from many women.

Culture provides the setting for the family, and the family provides the setting for the individual. Knowing this, and taking into account such factors as race, class, ethnic background, and sexual preference, we can make numerous predictions about human behavior. These are important and help us structure our thinking, but they are only predictions of tendencies. My fascination lies with people who don't fit the mold because I learn so much from them. When I think about some of my clients and friends and observe their relentless struggles to get well in the face of tremendous obstacles, I stand in awe of their will and bow to the mystery of life. The more I observe people, the more I am convinced that a "grace of God" factor contributes to individual differences beyond anything we can ever measure "scientifically." Some people do almost anything to heal, to be whole. Their curiosity, willingness to risk, passion for life, and burning desire to grow lead them to push through fear, pain, and terror to find contentment and happiness. Others, with seemingly similar backgrounds, back off when the road gets tough. Some people stumble over something that changes their path. A seemingly random event in their life lights their fire or causes them to change major beliefs about themselves and their lives. Some seem born with it. As tiny children they seem to reach for the stars. No matter what we start with, every one of us can open the door to recovery. It is simply a matter of saying, "I choose life above all else. I am willing to go to any lengths to be my true self. And I am willing to let go of anything that blocks my path."

HOW DID I GET THIS WAY? CULTURAL FACTORS

Sex addiction and codependency in women may be the most painful addiction to confront because it makes women conscious of the neglect, sexual abuse, and childhood injuries they have sustained in a patriarchal system in which they are viewed as the "second sex." It is important to understand that I am referring to patriarchy as a system, and not pointing a finger at individual men. In fact, the patriarchal system is extremely damaging to men, too, as confining to their souls and sexuality as it is to women's.

For men and women to confront sexual practices in patriarchy is to confront our whole political system and the ingrained belief that men and women are unequal classes of people. Anything that is unequal at a systems level eventually makes its way to the personal level and, hence, into sexual relationships.

The story of Kathi Vanderharr, a white female high school student in the Twin Cities area, poignantly brings home the internalization of unequal standards between men and women. In July 1987, the *Minneapolis Star and Tribune* reported that fifteen-year-old Kathi had been sexually assaulted by three boys she knew, all members of the high school hockey team. Much to the dismay of Kathi and her parents, neither the boys' parents nor the members of the high school hockey association pressed the boys to take responsibility. After being charged with the assault, they even tried to have a court date changed so they wouldn't miss a hockey game. According to the *Tribune,* in the months after the assault Kathi was deserted by a number of her friends; while she was being labeled a slut, two of her assailants became hockey heroes. "While their exploits on the ice drew ovations, an ever-growing circle of admiring friends, and glowing newspaper headlines, her hallway locker drew the scrawled invective 'Kill the bitch, she took our friends to court.' "

When Kathi pressed charges against the boys, her family was pressured by officers of the Youth Hockey Association not to do so; after all, boys will be boys. "Parents of the boys came to the Vanderharrs, not to apologize for their sons' behavior, but rather to gain sympathy, saying, 'Look at him. Do you really think he could do anything like that to your daughter?' "

The reminders stayed with Kathi. She was faced with articles in the school paper quoting the hockey coach speaking positively about the "hungry" and "aggressive" styles of two of her assailants. "The vice principal rebuffed Kathi when she came to his office upset about the messages scrawled on her locker." Finally, at the age of eighteen, Kathi killed herself.

This tragedy is the product of a hierarchical system that regards some people as being more human or more valuable than others. Kathi wasn't executed directly, but her death is rooted in a culture that does not consider a female as valuable as white male athletes. She was not given equal protection or equal respect at many levels of the system.

Who is blamed for sexual assault and who controls sexuality depends in large part on the position each person is assigned in the cultural hierarchy. White upper-class men are highest in the pecking order and we move down from there through race, class, gender, sexual preference, and ethnic background. At the low end are women of color, especially those with children, who are poor, single, and on welfare. Status at any level drops further for lesbians, the physically handicapped, and the psychologically impaired. One's rank can be raised through money, status, fame, or recognition as a hero of some sort, often through athletics. Within any group men are always higher than women. These roles have a profound impact on sexual relationships, and their very existence promotes sex abuse. One way men increase their status is to sexually use or abuse someone lower in the pecking order and get away with it. Kathi Vanderharr's assailants were male and known athletes, which puts them two steps up. So it follows that they were protected and she was blamed. If, however, Kathi had been assaulted by poor black males in the South in the 1950s, the blacks might well have been lynched.

Patriarchy is a system of social organization in which descent and succession are traced through the male line and the family and culture are ruled by men. To understand our sexual conditioning, we need to understand how patriarchy defines males as dominants and females as subordinates. In *Toward a New Psychology of Women,* Jean Baker Miller gives a brilliant analysis of these dynamics.

> Once a group is defined as inferior, the superiors tend to label it as defective or substandard in various ways. . . .
> It follows that subordinates are described in terms of, and encouraged to develop, personal psychological characteristics that are pleasing to the dominant group . . . submissiveness, passivity, docility, dependency, lack of initiative, inability to act, to decide, to think, and the like . . . qualities more characteristic of children. . . . If subordinates adopt these characteristics they are considered well-adjusted. . . .

It is perhaps unnecessary to add that the dominant group usually holds all of the open power and authority and determines the ways in which power may be acceptably used.

If you read those lines thinking in terms of women's sexuality, you will have a fairly accurate description of women's sexual programming. Women should be sexually pleasing to men by being passive, docile, childlike, and dependent, and relinquishing power and control over their sexuality. In other words, if women are sexually codependent, the culture considers them well adjusted. Yet paradoxically, many such women are massively depressed — and rely on the male medical system to treat their depression.

The sexual liberation movement of the 1960s and 1970s has not *essentially* changed the hierarchical model. This can easily be observed in the treatment of lesbian women, especially lesbian feminist women. Because they openly reject the passive role assigned to women and the role of wife, they are shunned by a culture that refuses to acknowledge their existence. It was all right for women to be sexually liberal so long as they were liberal with men.

For any dominant group to maintain its position, it must control the subordinate group by diminishing its power. Women's power is in their capacity to create life. Therefore, to maintain control in patriarchy, men attempt to control women's sexuality, reproduction, and, of course, their minds, lest women question male superiority and right to define the role of a woman's body and sexuality in the scheme of things.

The self-hatred many women feel for their bodies and their sexuality is internalized oppression. That is, when women lose track of the source of their oppression and believe their feelings of self-hatred are "true," they are cooperating with patriarchy and seeing themselves as bodies, not souls. For years women were told that premenstrual discomfort was all in their heads, and that it is natural to deliver babies while lying on their backs, defying gravity.

This left women feeling crazy: they had one set of words in their heads and a contradictory experience in their bodies. It is not surprising that much of the feminist movement has centered on women defining sexuality and reproduction on their own terms.

Oppression is complete when the subordinate group buys into the dominant group's values. Some examples include:

Men treat women as sexual objects. Women treat themselves as sexual objects.

Men are obsessed with women's bodies. Women are obsessed with their own bodies.

Men believe that they have to have sex. Women are taught to believe that men have to have sex.

Men are ambivalent about women's bodies. They consider them beautiful; they also abuse, beat, and violate them. Women are ambivalent about their bodies; they work to make them beautiful and also hurt and violate them.

Men believe that women should wear high heels and skirts in corporate places (even at 40 degrees below zero in Minnesota). Women feel that they *have* to wear high heels and skirts in corporate places (even at 40 degrees below zero in Minnesota).

Men hate women for the power of their sexuality, because they can't control it. Women hate or are afraid of their sexuality and its power, and they believe that it is not theirs to control.

A particularly blatant example of male definition of female sexuality that caused untold pain for women was Freud's concept of vaginal orgasm. In his *Three Essays on the Theory of Sexuality,* Freud promulgated the notion that girls have orgasm through stimulation of the clitoris (clitoral orgasm), and shift to vaginal orgasm when they become mature women, the implication being that they can then attain orgasm as a result of male penetration. If a woman didn't have orgasm through penetration she was considered "vaginally frigid." So for decades male psychiatrists and sex experts told women who didn't have orgasm through penetration that they were immature and unaccepting of their womanhood.

For decades no one challenged Freud's lack of evidence to prove his point. Even more extraordinary, but typical of subordinate groups, is that women bought the myth, in spite of the fact that any woman who has ever used a tampon knows that there is virtually no sensation in the vagina. Finally, in the 1960s, Masters and Johnson, in their study of human sexual response, dispelled the myth of vaginal orgasm, saying that there is only one type of female orgasm. They also dispelled the notion of female frigidity by helping countless women learn to have orgasm through stimulation that feels good to them. Betty Dodson's statement in *Selflove and Orgasm* put the subject of frigidity in perspective for many women: "Frigid is a man's word for a woman who cannot have an orgasm in the missionary position in a few minutes with only the kind of stimulation that is good for him."

It makes perfect sense that women talked a great deal about sexual experience in the early days of 1960s feminism. The new openness about sexuality led women to speak out on rape, abortion, and childhood sexual abuse. And what has happened since women started to take a stand? Family planning clinics have been bombed, anti-abortion groups have grown enormously, and rape, battering, sexual abuse of children, media images of violence against women, and pornography have all increased. The use of pornography and its increasing violence is well documented. There is conflicting thought on the rise in wife and child abuse, for some people believe that the change is in the reporting and not the frequency. In a discussion I heard on a talk show, it was reported that one study of high school girls in a metropolitan area found that 25 percent had been physically abused by a male in a relationship.

We are horrified and sometimes righteous when we read about torture, hostage taking, and the denial of basic human rights in other countries. Yet our own cultural conditioning blinds us to the continual abuse of women taking place in our own lives and all around us. Tacit guerrilla warfare is aimed at women in the area of body safety, sexuality, and reproduction.

How do oppressed people gain power? They rebel from their area of greatest strength — for women, that is their sexuality and ability to create life, which they learn to use for reward and punishment.

When sex is used for power, it becomes addictive. When it is used for barter, it is codependent. The codependent says, in effect, "You can use me for sex if you provide me with a home, money, security, and the status of being married." The addicted woman, on the other hand, uses her sexuality in angry rebellion: "You hurt me, you used me, you wounded me, and now I'm going to get back at you. I'll show you. I'll bring you down to my level. I can make you hurt. I can feel powerful by turning you on, leaving you, and seeing you suffer. If you want to be sexual with me, it has to be on my terms!" She shows her anger, while the codependent woman hides hers, whispering her discontent to other women behind closed doors, lest she offend her man and lose her security.

When asked what cultural influences played a role in their becoming sexually addicted, women say:

"The emphasis on sex — that you're nobody without it, and you do anything to get it."

"Learning that sex is bad or that sex has nothing to do with internal feelings of love, care, and respect."

"The existence of pornography and prostitution."

"Religious teachings that women are temptresses."

"The idea that it is hip to sleep around, to be kinky."

As might be expected, codependent women's responses to the same question contain only a slightly different interpretation.

"You're nothing without a man."

"Divorce means failure."

"Sex is this big mysterious thing."

"Bodies are shameful."

"Women are sexual objects to be used and abused."

"Men are terribly fragile and you have to be careful not to upset them."

"You make a relationship work by keeping silent."

WHO'S THE EXPERT?

In traditional circles the patriarchal system still defines women's sexuality to a large extent. The very notion of sex experts suggests that sex is to be viewed as a compartmentalized subject, separate from the rest of life. Unfortunately we tend to associate academia and advanced degrees with expertise, when in fact the academic focus is heavily skewed to the rational mind and away from subjective experience and spirituality. Typically, "experts" take it on themselves to define the experience of others. Thus sex has often become a subject for research rather than integrated into a spiritual realm related to mind, body, and spirit. Women who become sex experts in academia may also adopt male ways of thinking and perpetuate the patriarchal oppression of women.

In an extraordinary meeting of Minnesota Women Psychologists, a panel of women spoke on treatment for rape, incest, and sexual violence. The three women who worked in the trenches — rape crisis centers or private practitioners dealing with incest — spoke with warmth, presence, and power about their work. Following them, a woman from a university explained, in a thin monotone, the various categories they used for rape and incest, ranging from "nonviolent rape and incest" to "violent rape and incest." A resounding hush fell over the room as we looked at one another in disbelief. Finally one woman broke the silence by asking with polite amazement, "Excuse me, but did you say *nonviolent* rape?" The woman answered with scientific detachment, "Yes."

Someone asked her to describe a nonviolent rape.

Nonplussed, the university woman proceeded to explain the criteria. Essentially, if the victim didn't have a knife stuck in her throat, the rape wasn't violent. I felt sad for that woman. Rape of any sort is violence to the mind, body, and spirit operating as one. If rape feels violent to a woman, it is by definition violent. The university woman departed in a huff, saying she had never seen so many "overemotional" women. From my perspective, she was trying to fit into academia by parroting male modes of thinking.

We also mistakenly compartmentalize sex when we view it as separate from love, honesty, and human relations. Have a sexual problem? Find a sexual answer. That's exactly what sexually addicted and codependent people do. They want therapists to "fix their sex lives" or, more graphically, their genital lives, without looking at the big picture — their self-esteem, their relationships, and their ability to love. What's the solution for those who are uptight about sex? Some treatment programs prescribe movies of explicit sex as a way of desensitizing people. That's what the codependent woman does: she desensitizes her body so she can have sex whether she wants to or not. The addict does likewise, desensitizing herself to her fears and needs for genuine intimacy so she can separate sex from her emotions. That's exactly what people do with pornography.

Many women who consult male experts are codependent, for part of being codependent is wanting a man to do it for you. And a man who sets himself up as a male expert on female sexuality is apt to be operating with a lot of ego, because a man simply cannot understand female sexuality at an experiential level, just as a woman cannot understand male sexuality at an experiential level. Even if he has the best of intentions, he has swallowed the values of a system repressive to females and is likely to convey them to women.

Another problem that arises when we call people experts is that we abdicate our own role of expert. If we think Mr. X is an expert, we credit him with knowing more than we do. The fact is, each of us is our own best expert. Rather than looking for someone else to supply the answers, each person must look inside and ask, "What is my experience? What is true for me?" Then we must follow the wisdom that flows from that inquiry. Of course, this doesn't preclude consulting trained people for sexual concerns. The point is to let one's own mind, body, and spirit be the judge of what's best.

WHAT SHE CALLS RAPE, HE CALLS SEX

Male and female definitions of sex are sometimes separated by a chasm as wide as the Grand Canyon. In some cases, what a man calls normal sex — the slam-bam-thank-you-ma'am approach — a woman sees as doing her duty. At the greatest width of the chasm we find that what a woman calls rape, a man calls sex.

The story of Jessica Hahn in the November and December 1987 issues of *Playboy* illustrates the discrepancy. Sadly, it also illustrates how her search for love and power led her instead to exploitation and abuse. Hahn is a classic example of a woman who moves from the role of victim to that of codependent, then, to gain power through her sexuality, shifts to a role typical of sexually addicted women.

Jessica Hahn was a lonely, vulnerable fourteen-year-old when she became involved in fundamentalist religion. Socialized in this culture, she was faithful to her training. Rather than seek her own personal power, she attached herself to "powerful" men. She started by baby-sitting for their children, and when she was older, worked as their secretary, waiting on them and doing anything they asked, virtually without question. "If they told me to jump off a balcony I would have done it."

Jessica wanted love and personal power. Of TV evangelist Jim Bakker she said, "I was obsessed with this man. How was he able to do all of this? I wanted something like that in life, where I could reach that many people or do something that good. . . . I always wanted to be in on something. I hated being on the outside looking in. . . . I always felt maybe there was something missing." What could more clearly express her longing?

Jessica was eventually raped by the men she adored and served. Well, she called it rape; they called it sex.

This would not be an unusual story except that after seven years of suffering in silence she decided to reveal that her heroes, Jim Bakker and his colleague John Wesley Fletcher, had abducted and brutally raped her when she was twenty-one. They told her she was "ministering to them," that "when you help the shepherd, you're helping the sheep."

Extreme? I wish it were. But I have listened to too many stories and talked with too many women who work at rape crisis centers to call Jessica Hahn's story unusual. I continue to be puzzled by the assertion that rape is not about sex, it's about violence. It depends on whose perspective we're considering. Rape is often the perpetrator's idea of sex. It is not unusual for a rapist to ask a woman, "Did you like it?" following an assault. Nearly all X-rated videos deal with sex paired with violence and degradation. From a woman's perspective, rape is about *sexual* violence and has a profound affect on sexuality.

We make many assumptions about "natural" sexual responses without examining our separately socialized roles of women and men. Julius Fast, in *Sexual Chemistry,* talks about what stimulates a sexual charge between men and women. His observations are certainly accurate in our culture, but I question his assertion that they are all innate. Why does a man have to feel that he has overpowered or won the woman in order to feel turned on? Why is a woman turned on by being taken?

As part of the subordinate group, women must be conditioned from the earliest possible age to believe that they choose and enjoy their subservient role. In the sexual arena, we are not taught to acknowledge openly that we want sex; instead we learn that men need to be the initiators, the ones in charge.

This causes women to be indirect and coy about what they want and puts men in the unenviable position of having to sneak up on women, with the possibility of rejection every step of the way. It also creates some of the confusion in men's minds about when no means no. A woman feels furious when she tells a man no and he persists in trying to be sexual. But when I asked a group of men about this they claimed genuine confusion, at least some of the time. Nice girls are *always* supposed to say no before they say yes, and that had been their experience. Some former "nice girls" I interviewed gave the same reply. Of course you say no at first; a man would think you were dirty if you didn't.

The dominant group is taught to believe that the subordinate group is innately deficient, sexual organs and all. In the late sixties I was among a group of people having dinner together who had just come from a protest in support of a fair housing ordinance. One of the men referred to the woman he was with as "cunt." I remember the instant nausea I felt, not just at his words, but at the fact that everyone, including myself, just sat there despite having just marched in support of the human dignity and rights of blacks. What blind spots we have.

At its most brutal extreme, Jessica Hahn's story exemplifies the clash between men and women in defining sex. Immediately after the rape, Jessica Hahn saw Jim Bakker and John Fletcher on national TV, smiling at the audience and saying that God had really ministered to them that day. Jessica, meanwhile, was held hostage (she had no money and didn't know where she was) in the hotel bedroom, wishing that they would either leave her alone or that she could die. Her back was bleeding from being scratched, her body was aching all over from the trauma of the assault. When John Fletcher returned, he told her that by "ministering to Bakker," she had saved the PTL. That's giving a lot of importance and power to sex/rape.

When asked why she had waited seven years to reveal the rape, Hahn replied, "I kept thinking this had to be God's will — maybe I really did help Bakker. I started to feel crazy. Don't forget these were two men I looked up to. They were the top, the ultimate to me. They could do no wrong." She kept remembering the phrase "Touch not God's anointed." It never occurred to her that she was one of God's anointed whom they should not have touched. Jessica was a well-conditioned woman. She believed their words instead of her pain. And, like so many abuse survivors, she suffered alone, speaking out only when her depression and crazy feelings felt life threatening.

Jessica's acceptance of her stereotypical role as a woman, coupled with her longing for self-esteem and love, blinded her to the exploitation of her situation. Behind her reluctance to credit her definition of rape rather than theirs was the constant nagging suspicion that it was somehow her fault. When she found her anger, she also started to believe herself and trust her reality rather than theirs. At this point she began using her sex in both a controlling and angry way, just as the addicted one does.

The next part of her story illustrates how women's move from victim to the "sex as power" arena still results in exploitation. *Playboy* had been willing to pay Jessica Hahn nearly a million dollars for an interview *without* nude photos. She was the one who wanted the photos showing her nude from the waist up. She called it taking control. "For the first time in my life, someone took the time to ask, 'Jessica, what do you want?' No one had ever done that before, certainly not the church." The article was entitled "Jessica on Her Own Terms." The subhead declared, "No longer a victim, Jessica Hahn emerges in a glamorous portfolio of photographs."

Choice is indeed a form of power. But by posing for the pictures, Jessica was gaining power in the sexual realm as a body, not a soul. Instead of being exploited, the sexually addicted woman controls the exploitation. Anger rings through Hahn's story. "If you're going to check me out . . . in a bathing suit, you may as well stop with the pretending and take a good look. . . . My terms, you know. You want to look? I'll *show* you." Her oppression was in the sexual arena, and she fought back in the sexual arena. As Ellen Goodman wrote in an editorial, "Here is a woman who found no way out of being a victim; so she became the manager of her own victimization. She is damaged enough to believe that being in charge of her exploitation is the same as being free of it."

Hahn was seduced to think that *Playboy* cared about her just as many women are seduced by pimps and charming men. She did not comprehend that it wasn't a clear "choice" and evidently couldn't see that *Playboy* is part of the system that implicitly supports the evangelists' definition of sex. Women in prostitution, who put up with abuse, use similar rationalizations: "I am making a choice, so I am not being exploited." The exploitation is then complete.

CAPITALISM AND SEXUALITY

Such basic aspects of capitalism as free enterprise, consumerism, competition, imperialism, individualism, and militarism have some essential parallels with addiction and codependency. Some of the concepts that go hand in hand are dualistic thinking, encouraging people to crave possessions and status, to believe that bigger is better, and using external measures for self-worth and self-gratification at the expense of others.

Capitalism started with the idea of free enterprise and competition. People made their goods, presented them to consumers, who based their decision to buy on their real need for the items and the quality of the products as they saw them. The products stood on their own, and early advertising was essentially a means of informing the public. Products were presented with messages about usefulness, quality, and durability. A blue jeans ad in an old Sears, Roebuck catalogue, for example, simply showed blue jeans in good, better, and best qualities. Then advertisers discovered that products sell better when the ads play to our insecurity about our desirability, sexuality, and lovableness. Over time, advertising shifted from extolling the quality of a product to associating its use with the consumer's sex appeal. Show a cute teenager sticking her butt out in tight blue jeans, with an attractive guy looking at her, add a classy label, and you can triple the price of the jeans.

Sexually stimulating ads are designed so that consumers will associate the high of sexual arousal with the product. From mechanical tools to perfume, a disturbing sexual quality permeates most advertising today. Sometimes the images are blatantly erotic, sometimes subliminally so.

Along with greater violence toward women and implications of female masochism, advertisers are reaching for an increasingly younger market. Rock videos are sexually stimulating, portraying a kind of continuous foreplay that keeps teenagers aroused for long periods of time without eventual release. Hence, they come to associate entertainment and feeling good with sexual arousal. These videos also portray objectified sexual images, completely separate from anything even resembling genuine intimacy or mutuality. While both males and females are treated as sex objects, the men are repeatedly cast in sadistic or domineering roles, with women as passive recipients.

Pornography is at the end of the continuum — eliminate the product and sell sexual stimulation. When competitors observe the success of this policy, they up the pornographic content of their advertising, and the downward spiral is complete.

Prostitution is another form of sex as free enterprise. Men can buy time on a woman's body, and women in prostitution learn to allow their minds to go blank as their bodies are used. The notion of buying sex and rape go hand in hand, because if sex is for sale, well, why not steal it? Rape a woman and you don't have to pay. As long as sex is a commodity in any way, we will have rape.

The media have become terrifically adept at playing to our insecurities about how we look and feel sexually. Bodies are easy targerts. Unsightly hair? Fat tummy? Rough skin? Cellulite? Does your smell offend him on "those" days? Has the spark gone out of your love life? Once you're convinced that underarm and leg hair are unsightly, and that your love life *should* be a constant high, you can be convinced to buy hair removal cream, diet aids, clothes, makeup, and books on better sex.

The media hand us a false model of life, one that does not involve acceptance of loneliness, hurt, anger, old age, or troubled days. Feeling blue? Lift your spirits with a makeover. The problem is that the makeover is for the body and has nothing to do with the soul. Indeed, most of the articles in women's magazines, by implication, suggest that women should focus on the externals: the right body, the right interior design, the right recipe, the right wardrobe. Women's magazines are a good example of how women have so internalized their oppression that they maintain the status quo and oppress each other. And they are effective. I leaf through them at checkout counters and have bought my share.

They usually leave me feeling the pull to be thinner, have a flatter stomach, a more coordinated wardrobe, a more elegant hairdo — to whip up a gourmet feast for dinner. And I hate thinking these things, because I don't believe in them. Yet they are in me. I've been seduced, too. Body hatred makes us uneasy sexually, and all too much of what we confront in the media plays right into our shame, so that we learn to pair sexuality with our body appearance, not with our glow, our passion, our courage, and our wonderful capacity to love.

We have difficulty imagining women being sexual after fifty, or that we can be sexually alive and lovable even though our bodies do not conform to some inane, nonexistent model. Fashion models built more like adolescent boys than mature women serve to further devalue women's bodies. The message, again, is to hate your body, particularly those parts associated with its reproductive capacity — breasts, abdomen, hips, and thighs — and to buy, buy, buy, to fix, fix, fix.

The extent to which we swallow this message is directly related to sex addiction and codependency. If we experience our bodies as objects, we will have sex separate from our souls: stay detached, turn the lights out, look away, roll over, then go to sleep. The body will experience sex without the energy, playfulness, tenderness, connectedness, and joy that make sex an expression of genuine love and care for another human being.

HOW DID I GET THIS WAY? FAMILIES

Families are microcosms of the culture: the best and worst of it filter into our families, ultimately affecting each person. A well-functioning cultural system responds to the changing needs of the family: unfortunately, in a culture whose people are assigned varying levels of worth, those lower in the hierarchy have to fight harder for less change than those of higher status. Consequently, the culture is slower to respond to the needs of women and children than of white men. While families have a powerful impact on individuals, and can mitigate negative cultural influences, the complex interplay of family and culture makes it difficult to discern the line between family and cultural influences.

One responsibility of the family is to pass on to its children its cultural values. Unfortunately, this includes internalized values of oppression as well as life-affirming, positive ones. The parents of Kathi Vanderharr's assailants implicitly taught their sons that sexual violation of females is acceptable behavior, perpetuating the sexual double standard. Kathi's parents communicated values of female respect by taking legal action, thus encouraging Kathi to know that she was not to blame for the assault. But the attitudes of school personnel, other students, and the hockey support group underscored the cultural standards.

Kathi's suicide was not the failure of her parents, who alone could not possibly be powerful enough to overcome the culture's value system. That's why, in considering the role of families, we must never lose sight of our cultural context. Some elements in this sad story show a shift from twenty years ago, when Kathi might have kept the incident a secret, her parents might not have believed her or spoken out, and the newspaper might not have given it sympathetic front-page coverage, albeit after her death.

When we examine the care our culture provides for the least advantaged people, we come to understand its bottom-line policies and attitudes. The feminization of poverty, the lack of health care for children and poor women, the lack of maternity leave, and unequal pay are all indicative of the culture's attitudes toward women. Considering the plight of millions of impoverished women in this country, and the inadequate support for battered women's shelters and rape crisis centers, it is not surprising that SAA and CoSA women reel off a litany of painful stories of abuse and neglect. These are not isolated or unusual accounts. Studies by Alfred Kinsey and David Finkelhor indicate that from 19 percent to 25 percent of women suffer the scars of childhood sex abuse. Many more struggle with the fallout from neglect, abandonment, and poverty. Twenty-five percent of children live in families beneath the poverty line. Acts of abuse and neglect do not occur in a vacuum.

Negative values toward women can be passed down in a multitude of ways. One of the most powerful messages my mother gave me about letting my talent and passion flow was when she gladly made a beautiful prom dress for my sister to wear at her first dance, yet I had to plead for weeks to convince her to alter some hand-me-downs into a long dress for my first solo piano recital when I was fourteen.

BOUNDARIES

Understanding boundaries is an important step toward understanding culture, family, intimate relationships, and self-esteem. Incest, battering, abuse, and negative messages about one's sex and sexuality are all forms of boundary intrusions on the body, mind, and spirit.

Boundaries must be defined in every relationship. This is true between countries, between individuals, and within our inner psychic system. Boundaries define what belongs to you, what belongs to me, and what belongs to our relationship. Appropriate boundaries vary according to the power assigned to individual roles. The boundaries of a teacher-student relationship are different from those of a friendship between peers. The teacher, by virtue of his or her power over the student, has more power in the relationship. *The one with more power in a relationship always has the most responsibility to maintain appropriate boundaries.* The paradox within our system of inequality is that the people highest in the pecking order, usually men, presume the right to invade, rather than respect, a less powerful person's boundaries. Sexual harassment is a typical example. Subordinate people, usually women, are trained to believe that they are to blame when someone violates their boundaries. If they recognize the intrusion, there is a taboo against speaking out about it.

Think of a boundary as a fence that surrounds all that belongs to you — your right to succeed, to fail, to control how you are touched, your feelings, your opinions, and to bear the consequences of your behavior, both the successes and the failures. Essentially, we are talking about your right to run your own life. No one has a right to enter this domain without your permission: not parents, friends, lovers, clergy, or medical professionals.

The internal signal that someone is violating a boundary is a rush of anger. Hey, you stepped on my foot; you shoved ahead of me; you manipulated me to be sexual after I said no; you raped me. Because women are conditioned to repress their anger, they don't learn to recognize boundary intrusions and to see red flags indicating danger. This keeps them in a victim role.

Marilyn, who was mentioned in Chapter 11, sought counseling after her former husband assaulted and nearly killed her. She was terrified of ever going out with a man again, fearing that she would be drawn to the same kind of person. In the first weeks of therapy she maintained, "I had no idea he would become violent. I was totally surprised." But as she reviewed the relationship over a period of time she came to realize that there had been many prior boundary intrusions. From early on, he didn't want her to see her friends; he got jealous when she talked with men; he used to tell her what to wear; he got angry at her when he was frustrated with anything; and when he wanted sex he wouldn't take no for an answer. He was constantly overstepping his bounds. What was most difficult for Marilyn to see and accept was that his charm and sweet talk were also boundary intrusions. He was smoothly seducing the vulnerable, hungry, unloved child within her to believe that someone loved her at last. Once she was "in love" he had the power to use her as he liked. Another tip-off to danger was his keeping *his* boundaries completely impenetrable, never showing his fears, weaknesses, or emotional vulnerability.

Over a long period, as Marilyn learned to recognize boundary intrusions and let herself feel angry about them, she realized that she had the power to choose not to be victimized again.

Boundaries between parents and children are not easy to define because the role of the parent is to protect and teach in a way that is not appropriate between adult peers. The appropriateness of a behavior is determined by the parent's motivation as well as by the behavior itself. In addition, appropriate boundaries change throughout a child's development. While it is necessary to dress children at age one, they may start having choices about clothing at age two and three, and be allowed a wide range of choices and primary control of dressing by age four or five.

While there is certainly a large gray area in defining boundaries, there are also clear intrusions that are damaging to children. Parents and caregivers have a responsibility not to invade their children's boundaries. Moreover, parents need to teach children appropriate boundaries, particularly in the sexual realm.

It is perfectly normal for children to have erotic feelings toward their parents. Children may flirt with parents and try to kiss or hug them sexually, imitating what they have seen on TV or between the parents. *It is the parents' responsibility to place a boundary around a child's sexual energy.* A mother or father can gently tell a child that such kissing is not appropriate between parents and children, that they express love in different ways. The parent can give examples of loving behavior such as rocking the child in her arms, reading, or sharing other activities. Parents can show their love by listening carefully, by talking, and through nurturing touch. It is crucial that parents convey that sex is only one of many ways to express love, and that it is reserved for adulthood, with a special peer partner. They also help the child accept sexual feelings as natural.

Sexually addicted and codependent women were rarely taught these messages as children. On the contrary, their boundaries were more often flagrantly violated by parents who used their children for their own needs, either sexually or emotionally or both. As a result, one common characteristic of sexually addicted or codependent women is a lack of boundaries. These women enter adulthood with little sense of when they are being invaded or of when they are intruding on someone else's domain or entering dangerous territory. They do not understand the differences between being helpful and butting in. They cannot differentiate between being loved, being used, and being seduced. For many, love equals a sexually symbiotic relationship or just plain sex.

Their childhood stories reveal endless intrusions into their bodies, minds, and spirits. Incest, sexual abuse, physical abuse, and overpossessiveness are the obvious boundary violations, but there are many others that are just as harmful, although perhaps less overt. Some examples:

- Hugging a child to assuage the parent's loneliness, while making the child think the affection is for her or him.
- Telling children whom and when to kiss and hug. "Come on now, give me a kiss"; "Are you going to kiss Uncle John? Good girl."
- A parent acting hurt when a child doesn't want to kiss or hug. This creates enormous guilt in the child, who unconsciously gathers that the parent's self-esteem is tied to the child's display of love.

- Not teaching children that they have a right to say no to touch from anyone, including caregivers.
- Objectifying a child by showing embarrassing photographs of him or her to others in the child's presence. This is particularly mortifying to an older child.
- Great concern and obsession with a child's body, diet, physical development, and appearance.
- Excessive interest in bowel movements, urination, hygiene, menstrual periods.
- Commenting on body development in front of a child. "I think Jeanne is going to be full breasted, don't you?"
- Frequent enemas given inappropriately or by a parent who becomes sexually aroused in giving them.
- Inappropriately controlling what a child wears to please others. "Now you have to wear the pink dress to Grandma's. It's her favorite."
- Squeezing pimples. Women talked about parents, usually mothers, seeming to be obsessed with a daughter's face and having a compulsive need to do something to it. "I just wanted to scream at her to leave my face alone."
- Forcing diets or repeatedly commenting on fatness or thinness.
- Blocking moves toward autonomy and separateness with constant admonitions to be careful. "You might drown"; "You might get run over"; "You don't want to go play with them." By using guilt a caregiver may tie a child to him or her, narcissistically using the child to fill his or her emptiness. Of course children must be taught to be careful, but too many parents block their children from age-appropriate ventures and from developing an inner identity in the interest of possessing and controlling them.
- Forcing children to talk about their feelings. It is an intrusion to coerce a child into participating in frequent "heart-to-heart" talks to fulfill a parent's need for intimacy.
- Flirting with a child or with the child's friends.
- Using a child as a best friend.
- Having a child sleep with a parent after a spouse has gone away. The child ends up feeling like a replacement for the partner, which has sexual connotations and causes confusion about the child's role.
- Sudden withdrawal from daughters when they reach adolescence. This is extremely common, especially with fathers who can relate to a daughter as genderless until she develops a woman's body. Uneasy about his own sexual feelings for her and unable to deal with his discomfort or shame, a father may withdraw from her. The child experiences his behavior as a profound rejection of her womanhood. She may then play out her longing for a loving father in sexual relationships with other men.

Parents must also set appropriate boundaries around their own sexuality. When they don't, a covert incestuous dynamic occurs. Marie came from such a family and had the characteristics of an incest survivor. Moreover, she felt disturbed about this because nothing explicitly sexual had taken place. In fact, she had been deeply affected by her parents' sexual behavior.

Marie's realization of the covert incest began when she dreamed that she was in bed, saw a man's genitals, and felt curious about them. Marie hated her dream. She was a lesbian, after all, so why was she dreaming about a man? She somehow knew it was about her father.

As Marie described how her parents had kissed and touched each other sexually in front of her, she started to feel embarrassed and angry. Her father's jokes were always about sex, and he constantly evaluated the sex appeal of the bodies of all the women around him. "Everything was about sex in our house. Touch, magazines, jokes, everything." He sexualized his daughters with comments such as, "Boy, you're going to drive guys crazy when you get older." When he wasn't flirting with his wife, the two were fighting. The message Marie picked up was that you either fight or have sex.

In therapy Marie remembered her nameless fear as a child whenever she thought of her father touching or hugging her. The unpleasant feeling she described was his sexual energy penetrating her. She came to understand that to protect herself from the ominous, threatening feelings, she shut down her feelings toward him and toward her own sexuality. Touch was dangerous, Daddy was dangerous. She was left with an overwhelming anger and fear of men. Underneath this was a profound grief at having had to give up her dad to protect herself from his emotional/psychological sexual penetration.

Much as she hated to admit it, there was still a little girl inside Marie who longed to be close to her father. But whenever she thought of caring about him, she unconsciously thought of being sexually violated. Once the old longing resurfaced, she was able to feel her loss at not having a caring father.

In contrast to Marie, Jane became her daddy's darling daughter. As an adult she had difficulty being sexually relaxed, having orgasm, or bonding with a man. Unconsciously, she felt she was being disloyal to her father. While she engaged in numerous sexual relationships, she was imbued with the basic creed of the sexual codependent: if you want a man to love you, let him be sexual with you. Her ambivalence toward her father was played out again and again with other men. She longed for them to be close, but when they became sexual, she wanted to scream at them, to hurt them, to get away, as she had unconsciously wanted to do with her father. Following a common progression for the codependent, she was eventually unable to control her rage, which she began to vent at her male partners with sideways digs below the belt as well as all-out blasts at them. She felt powerless over her behavior until she realized that her father was the real target of her anger. Even then, it was a long time before she was able to resist the urge to abuse men verbally rather than be appropriately angry at her father.

No matter whether the child attempts to block or accept a parent's sexual energy, she has been sexually victimized. Marie did not socialize with many men as an adult. She became an ardent feminist. Even so, when she was sexually harassed at her job, it was extremely difficult for her to realize that it wasn't her fault because the harassment so closely resembled her father's behavior. Jane was easily exploited by men. She played the sweet innocent role, took control in relationships, and was inwardly seething with anger. Both ended up with the buried belief that their sexuality was shameful, powerful, and dangerous, that if they let it loose, something terrible might happen.

Psychological boundary intrusions are more subtle and difficult to grasp, but equally important to understand. They affect children in a way that often makes them think they are crazy. The parents appear to be doing something for a child's good, but in reality they are doing it for themselves because their identity and self-worth depend on their child. Imagine that each of us has an internal self-esteem thermometer that measures how we feel about ourselves. Then imagine that it is attached by an invisible cord between a parent and a child. If a parent's self-esteem drops when a child gets a low grade, doesn't make the soccer team, or doesn't have a date, the child has been violated by having been made responsible for the parent's self-esteem.

A child has to be granted the right to succeed and fail without its affecting the self-esteem of his or her parents. Parents must understand that they are also intruding when their self-esteem rises as a result of a child's success. It's one thing to feel good about a child's accomplishment; to celebrate with them and be glad for them. It's quite another thing to base one's self-worth on the success of the child. The more the parents are symbiotically tied to the child, the more likely the child is to have an extreme reaction. They may either surrender to the dictates of the parents or strongly rebel. They lose a sense of self either way.

Many people, particularly addicted people, have difficulty drawing a mental line between their self-worth and their labels. To return to the thermometer, imagine that you have a self-esteem thermometer attached to other thermometers inside you that record money, status, the success of your children, awards, sex, looks, weight, age, and career or job. Imagine that your self-esteem reading fluctuates, rising with increased status, money, success, and so forth, and falling when you lose money, status, friends, or somehow fall on your face. In other words, your self-esteem is determined by outside forces, most of which you can't control. The result is a loss of self-control and a sense of powerlessness, for you feel that you are a victim of fate or a failure when outer circumstances are difficult. Now imagine that your self-esteem thermometer is attached only to the internal knowledge that you are a sacred human being, lovable and worthy of respect because you are alive. Imagine this knowledge as a radiant, warm glow at the center of your being. Whether you win or lose, feel happy or sad, your self-esteem remains constant; it is not determined by the external events of life.

Many boundary intrusions belie an attempt to control what one can't control, namely, another human being. Many people feel that they disappointed their parents by not living up to the parents' ideal of the "right" child. They were asked to do what was humanly impossible, to become someone they were not, or to be responsible for another's happiness. Listening to them, I think of how many parents plant a mysterious seed in the ground, not knowing what will grow there. It may produce a beautiful daisy, but the parents who want a rose, keep yelling at the daisy to be a rose and never notice the beauty of the daisy. After being shouted at to be a rose, the daisy eventually wilts.

THE UNHOLY ALLIANCE

Many women who become sexually addicted or codependent grew up in two-parent households in which the spouses were distant from each other, or with a single parent who did not have strong peer relationships. As children, they were often a parent's primary source of intimacy. In both two-parent and single-parent families, it is important for the parents to have primary peer relationships that mitigate the intensity of the relationship and keep the children from feeling emotionally responsible for the parents.

In a healthy system, the parents are both autonomous and closely aligned with each other, and even when they spend time alone with a child, they maintain a parent role and do not undercut the authority of the other.

In dysfunctional systems, many parents discuss their sex lives with their children, thereby burdening them with adult problems and depriving them of their right to childhood. Children hate hearing a father say such things as, "Your mother is cold to me, she doesn't satisfy me." Sometimes this is used as a rationalization for incest, but even when it isn't the child is violated. This sort of thing happens in all possible combinations. Father is aligned with the daughter or Mother co-opts the son to her side, or one child is placed directly in the middle as a pawn between the parents.

Another variation on this theme, which my cotherapist Sigurd Hoppe calls an "unholy alliance," occurs when a parent is obviously more "alive" to a child than to a spouse. There is no spark or loving energy between the father and mother, but a parent always lights up when a particular child comes into the room. As a result, the child is made to feel at once special and afraid, and ultimately responsible for the parent's happiness. Assigning a child the role of intimate other or best friend to a parent is to set that child up to fail. There is no way a child can fill the emptiness of an unhappy parent. Essentially, when the overall intimacy level between a parent and a child exceeds the intimacy level between the parents or caregivers, a boundary violation occurs.

The boundary between the family and the rest of the world is very important. In abusive and dysfunctional families, there is often a rigid boundary that isolates family members from other people. Isolated families are out of touch with external input and resources that might allow them to recognize the pain and suffering they consider to be normal.

In upper-middle-class and upper-class families the isolation may be emotional rather than literal. They may have parties, entertain, and look good, but inwardly everyone is suffering alone, without any sense of how to truly connect with others.

While not all sexually abused women become sexually addicted or co-dependent, most of those who do have experienced some traumatic losses in their lives. They may have lost the love of their parents and the right to be a child because they had dysfunctional caregivers. They may have walked on eggshells trying not to rock the boat in families where violence, mental illness, or suicide were ever-present threats. Many lived under the shadow of family secrets — arrests, drug abuse, children born out of wedlock, past marriages — that cast a cloud of shame over the family. Many exhibit symptoms of post-traumatic stress syndrome, as described in the *Diagnostic and Statistical Manual of Mental Disorders*.

Such a diagnosis is usually reserved for war veterans who have been in active combat and have suffered "a traumatic event that is generally outside the range of usual human experience." These symptoms include reexperiencing the traumatic event, blocking of responsiveness to, or reduced involvement with the external world. "A person may complain of feeling detached or estranged from other people . . . and has lost or had a marked decrease in the ability to feel emotions of any type, especially those associated with intimacy, tenderness, and sexuality. . . . Survivors often describe painful guilt feelings . . . about the things they had to do in order to survive. Activities or situations that may arouse recollections of the traumatic event are often avoided."

Gerri's and Claudia's homes resembled combat zones; but even women with no history of overt incest or physical violence can develop the symptoms to a marked degree. Psychological abuse is violence at a spiritual level, and the resulting pain can be crippling. By thinking of violence only in physical terms, we perpetuate the duality of bodies as separate from souls. The truth is, you can't hurt one without hurting the other.

While some families tend toward either neglect or abuse, many combine both. Neglectful parents don't set rules, limits, curfews, or notice children's drinking, depression, or mood swings. Some may go through the motions of appropriate parenting — reading stories at bedtime, family vacations — without being emotionally present. Others seem oblivious on all levels and do not attend to children's physical needs, deny the seriousness of accidents and physical problems, do not attend school functions, or do not applaud their children's accomplishments. In general, neglect is likely to produce children with low self-esteem and highly developed coping skills. Severe neglect may result in an inability to bond, severe depression, and anxiety.

Women from symbiotic families feel they are committing a crime against their parents when they strive to become whole and healthy. They are unable to "leave home" physically or emotionally. Parents contribute to their uneasiness with dramatic tirades — "How can you do this to your mother?" — or by getting physically sick or depressed, or threatening to die. Some use more subtle techniques to instill guilt or devious ploys to imply that they are acting for the child's own good. One of my clients said that she simply couldn't get a divorce until after her mother died for fear of displeasing her. This cost her more than twenty-eight years in an unhappy marriage. These loyalty ties are as intense as those of Siamese twins joined at the heart. Each fears death or retribution if they separate.

On the surface, the families of sexually addicted and codependent women may appear strikingly different. But whether families are tight, rigid, and covertly incestuous, or characterized by outright violence and abuse, they are all missing certain ingredients: safety, be it physical or psychological, warmth, tenderness, and appropriate boundaries between parents and children. It is a parent's responsibility to help a child accept a full range of human emotions, to accept that we all win and lose, to accept that we all have imperfections. Above all, a truly loving parent encourages and allows a child to be truly herself or himself.

When I ask women what nonverbal messages they feel contributed to their becoming sexually addicted, they point to boundaryless or intrusive relationships and lack of intimacy, care, joy, safety, respect, and understanding.

Many SAA and CoSA women say that one or both of their parents or stepparents were sexually addicted or sexually codependent. The father was most apt to be described as sexually addicted, although quite a few suspected that their mothers had similar traits.

If there was ever a case for sex education, it was made by the women telling about the sexual messages they received in their homes. Messages were usually negative or nonexistent. Many women have satisfying long-term sexual relationships with little or fairly clinical sex education. However, they did not get the blatantly negative messages that sexually addicted and codependent women receive from their families.

It is important to remember that *not* talking about sex is a powerful message in itself. Children often interpret it to mean that sex is so big, so powerful, and so frightening that you can't even talk about it. One woman said, "Whenever I asked a question about sex, my mother would be silent and shake her head." Silence is often translated to mean "Sex is dirty, secretive, exciting, and extremely important." "Don't talk about it" is a relatively mild negative signal. For the majority of addicted women, sex was associated with being bad, horrible, dirty, abnormal, or a whore.

In other cases women said:

"Mother didn't answer questions about masturbation. She'd say, 'Don't get in a close situation with a man. If he has an erection he won't be able to control himself.' "

"My mother gave me a Catholic-approved book called *The Wonder of Life* to teach me about sex. It had two diagrams which explained how sex was for marriage. I used it to masturbate and felt guilty."

"I learned that sex is sexual abuse. I saw my father 'rape' my mother. He tore off all her clothes and wouldn't give them back while they were fighting. Sex means giving up something and losing something. My parents' sexual violence led to incest with my brothers."

"Mom said not to rub my seat (masturbate) but did not shame or stop me."

"I was told, 'Be cute and a pleaser and you can get or have anyone you want. Sex is beautiful between married people.' "

One woman described the source of her sexual codependency, which summed up many women's responses. "Being emotionally neglected, feeling low self-worth; I knew I would be cared for if I was 'good' and took care of the home. In my marriage I just added sex to the list of things I needed to do to be loved; I had to second-guess everyone to keep them from becoming violent. My body wasn't my own, and I couldn't have needs, wants, or say no. I developed a lot of shame as a woman, seeing how abusive and hurtful my father was to my mother, and how she took it. That was my model for being a woman: to be abused and powerless."

PORNOGRAPHY IN THE HOME

Children who are exposed to pornography get a distorted lesson in how to be sexual. Girls who see their usually distant, dull fathers intently reading pornography sneak a peek to find out what Dad is so excited about. If he reads it in private the children usually find it anyway and associate the sexual images with something sneaky and exciting. When a father watches sexually explicit movies with his daughter, he covertly draws her into his sexual realm. The child may become sexually excited herself, adding to her confusion.

Renée told of sneaking looks at her parents' pornography after seeing them read it. By the age of five, desperate for love and attention, she would strip and dance in front of her brother and his friends, mimicking what she had seen in a magazine. Because she had no other sex education or models of loving relationships, pornography became the primary model for her sexual development. The violation was doubly wounding because along with the pain of having been used, she assumed the responsibility for her "willingness" to perform. While there had never been any overt incest, Renée had many symptoms of an incest survivor. Over the years she struggled with bulimia, alcoholism, sex addiction, and sexual codependency. We'll return to Renée in the final chapter.

Joan's father was a military officer who sadistically beat his daughters when they came home from dates, calling them sluts and whores. He kept pornography on the nightstand by his bed. When he was out, Joan and her sister would sneak in and read it. Soon it became a compulsion and before long Joan was buying pornography herself and masturbating to it. Later in life she was involved in sadomasochistic relationships modeled after the pornography.

It takes a huge denial system to argue that the models we set for children don't affect them. If parents speak Chinese at home the children will speak Chinese. We expect children to learn what they read in their schoolbooks. Why, then, are we surprised when they act out the sexual messages in pornographic books, magazines, and videos?

I have seen children as young as five in therapy because they already have a negative sexual understanding of themselves. Many have been in trouble at school because of inappropriate sexual behavior. One little boy whose father read pornography had been labeled "the kisser" by age five. He had no friends. By giving children inappropriate models of sex we set them up to be sexually victimized and to become sexual perpetrators.

PSYCHIC MESSAGES

Children pick up on the sexual energy in the home. On two occasions in my experience fathers have described sexual fantasies of their daughters that their daughters reported dreaming. Sometimes a woman with the symptoms of an abuse survivor starts having "memories" of incest that, while it may not have occurred physically, did take place at a psychic, spiritual level; the father's obsessive sexual fantasies made their way into the daughter's psyche through her dreams and fantasies. This is not to say that a woman who starts to have dreams or memories did not experience overt abuse. Often the dreams signal that memories of abuse are starting to surface.

As parents, we would like to believe that what goes on in our heads, in our private world, does not affect children. The fact is, children are often two steps ahead of us because their ability to tap in at a psychic level has not been diminished by our linear, logical, rational world. Children naturally absorb messages intuitively, and we are constantly teaching them by what we say, do, think, and have in the home.

EARLY MEMORIES

Women who become sexually addicted or codependent recall that as children they received the impression that sex was mighty important. Sex permeated their play, their sibling relationships, and their thoughts. As one woman said, "I remember thinking to myself as a young child, 'Is *everything* about sex?' "

Many women can remember when sexually addictive behavior started to play a part in their lives, usually in fantasies, dreams, and drawings:

"It started at twelve years old. I never touched myself, but every night I would lie in bed and put myself to sleep fantasizing about women rubbing me in a sexual way. I remember that feeling of wanting to get to bed, turn on those fantasies, and have all the pain in my life fade away. It was my secret world, one of pleasure for me. There was a clear sense of crossing a line."

"I drew a sadistic picture of a little boy being spanked by his mother while he had an erection."

"I used to draw violent pictures. As soon as I was able to, I would draw Dracula-type figures and voluptuous women with babies. . . . I always felt a kind of sexual energy. I would draw their breasts and I would feel sexual. I don't know how that would all fit together. I had a tremendous amount of hatred for the baby. I always had these triangles, a little person, two adults. And . . . that usually involved a knife — somebody was always getting stabbed, usually the child. And there was a real sexual feeling attached to it."

These memories all suggest the presence of inappropriate or violent sexual energy in the home. What was missing in most of these households was the nitty-gritty of everyday life. Emotionally ossified parents did not reveal their inner struggles, failing to impart to their children the concept that life involves confusion, disappointment, joy, and normal ups and downs. When caregivers do not provide a model for conflict and struggle, children regard their thoughts as being wrong or bad, which they further translate to "I am bad." One of the greatest things we can teach our children is that we, too, have confusion and turmoil. I remember an occasion when I couldn't make up my mind whether to give my daughter permission to do something, and she kept pressing me for an answer. When it finally occurred to me to tell her why I was torn, she was fascinated by my reply that while I thought it would be nice for her to go to a movie with her friend on Saturday night, I was feeling ill, I wanted to get to bed early, and I didn't feel comfortable with her taking a bus that late at night. Instead of my throwing up the impenetrable boundary of just plain no, we could talk about options. Thus she didn't think I was trying to prevent her from having a good time, and we were able to work out a solution. After that, when I couldn't make up my mind, she would ask, "Is it like the movie time? Tell me the two sides."

I also hold dear to my heart one glistening memory of a moment when my father revealed his own inner struggle. "Every day I say to myself I'm not going to fight with Charlotte," he said, "and then there I am fighting with you. I don't want to. I don't know how to stop myself. I feel so bad." So he felt powerless, too! I was touched and relieved.

Every child longs for a human bond and for a sense of belonging. Through a process of trial and error, children attempt to fit in with their particular family. In a functional family, they learn cooperation, care, and respect. In a dysfunctional one, their lessons and choices have to do with survival. Like oppressed people, children in dysfunctional families are so busy trying to "dance" in the world of their parents, their oppressors, that they don't have the opportunity to look inside and get to know themselves. When their appeals for love and efforts to be noticed repeatedly fail, they retreat into a secret world to forget, for a moment, the terror and lack of love that permeates their lives. Children may find solace in fantasies, sex play, masturbation, food, being cute, or other behavior that brings release from the harsh realities of life. This is how addictions take root.

As children we identify with our parents. We grow under their influence, we absorb their values and behavior, and they become part of us. If their behavior and beliefs are noxious and frightening, we may try to reject them. But in the absence of other models and influences, chaos and confusion may take the place of healthy, positive identification. Ruth remembered thinking early on, "I hate these people. I don't want to be anything like them." But this repudiation left her with the question, "What should I be like?" Her teenage years were rampant with destructive sexual experiences.

If our childhood memories are by and large pleasant, we store them away, ready to be pulled out and relished to ease the pangs of a loss or a rejection or simply a hard day. If we were loved and cared for, we can draw upon that reservoir of love in difficult times. In our hearts we know that we are lovable, and our self-esteem is built upon that solid foundation. If, however, childhood was permeated with neglect or abuse, we erect a boundary around those painful memories to shut them out. We may exhaust ourselves keeping them locked up, but anything is preferable to the raw pain of rejection or victimization. Most of us have had an unpleasant event spring the lock on our hated memory box, when every hurt ever suffered, every stupid word ever uttered, comes crashing down around us, overwhelming us with shame. Abuse survivors go to nearly any length to avoid this devastating experience because they have so few positive memories with which to balance them.

Childhood is a vulnerable, crucial time. Children have no defenses against the pain their families inflict on them. The events of the first few years have a profound, lasting impact on a child's ability to trust and to function successfully as an adult. We know when we plant a field of corn that we must do certain things to allow it to grow. Yet our culture doesn't seem to make that connection with children. We think we can starve them emotionally, physically, and spiritually, and still expect them to grow to their full potential. The cost of child care is paltry in comparison with the cost of group homes, treatment programs, mental wards, and prisons. At a spiritual level, the cost to us as a society is even greater. How do we shut out the knowledge that while we eat dinner and sleep in warm beds, others are starving or homeless or suffering abuse and neglect? As members of this culture, we become like the perpetrators or addicted ones who anesthetize themselves to the harm they do to others. Unless we are part of the solution, we lose a part of ourselves. In an abusive family, children struggle to survive. In a spiritually bereft culture, we struggle to keep our spirits alive.

HOW DID I GET THIS WAY? THE GRACE OF GOD

One of my most vivid childhood memories is of being three years old and standing, late one afternoon, in the living room of our new house, watching my family playing their parts: my father, with his feet up, reading the paper after work; my mother cooking diner; my sister practicing the piano. It was all predictable, on schedule. I stood there motionless, as if looking in from outside. Then the thought struck me, "Is this all there is? When I grow up, is this what it will be like?" Even then I was overwhelmed with a longing for something more. Then another thought entered my head: "My life won't be like this." And it hasn't been. I believe my childhood epiphany had nothing to do with my family or the culture. I believe I had touched an inborn truth about myself.

Beyond our cultural and family programming, there is a special part of each one of us, a unique blueprint of our own potential. Some call it karma, others don't try to explain it, but I believe it is a mystery beyond comprehension, simply the grace of God.

I don't know why I was so excited at the age of five to find out there were stars beyond the stars and that everything went on forever. One day when my mother and I were together in the kitchen, I brought up the subject of all the worlds in the world and ventured the question, "If it all goes on forever, then is there a world just like ours? Do you think there is another little girl just like me somewhere talking to a mother just like you?" My mother laughed and said, "Well, there's probably another little girl as silly as you." Ouch.

I don't know why I was so drawn to the globe of the world that sat like a sacred object on a table in our living room, or why I loved to ask my father questions. Are people made different in different countries? How many different languages do people speak? Is there more water than land? Which is the biggest country?

Adults said I was cute to be asking such big questions, but rarely in my childhood did anyone understand how important my questions felt to me. At about the same time, I became concerned about the reality of Santa Claus. I gathered my data in little bits from my parents, who were unaware of my motives. "Mom, does every house in the world have a chimney?" I knew Aunt Myrl's didn't. "How many houses in Alexandria?" "How many cities in Virginia?" "How long is the night?" "Does he go to everyone in the world?" At last I felt certain that there simply could not be a Santa Claus.

Thrilled at the brilliance of my discovery, I shared it with Tina, a younger girl who lived across the street. Instead of being grateful, she ran crying to her mother, who called my mother to tell her what "Charlotte had said to Tina." With great discomfort and obvious irritation my mother asked where I ever got such an idea. Her reaction hurt terribly and left me feeling alone and ashamed. Tina seldom played with me again and her parents always viewed me with suspicion. As a result I feared sharing my passion and curiosity with others. In spite of feeling that my essence had been attacked, another part of me was proud of myself, absolutely convinced that I was right and the adults were stupid.

A yearning for truth lies deep within all people. It is the core of our spirituality, the source of personal power, the home we return to as we seek a spiritual path.

As I listen to clients' family histories I wonder, "Why did this one out of six children maintain the fight, a will to survive while the other five did not? Why does one child hang on to her soul by continuing to defy her parents even though it means continued cruel beatings while a sister collapses and loses her sanity?" When I ponder such things I again surrender to the essential mystery of life.

While there are plausible explanations for most behavior, and we can make some predictions about them, we simply cannot account for all individual differences. A psychoanalyst might theorize that I became so interested in the world and other cultures because we had a globe and my father dignified my questions with sincere answers. But Columbus didn't have a globe. And my sister couldn't have cared less. She was far more interested in drawing, which she did beautifully, while I scrawled.

Why does one sister from a family end up married in the suburbs while her sister ends up in prostitution? Why do many women who participate in sadistic sexual relationships have histories of ritualistic sadistic beatings as children, while others with similar backgrounds do not become involved in such behavior? I don't think we'll ever know.

A great and passionate yearning is common among many women who struggle with numerous addictions. When I ask about an early sense of longing or of feeling different, there is often immediate recognition. Laura, who worked with Mother Teresa, immediately understood. "Oh," she said, "the longing was so intense. I yearned for something wonderful, for something different from what I saw. That's what drove me to different communes, to different religions, to work with Mother Teresa, and finally to accept that I'm not destined for a typical marriage, home, and family. I think acting out my addictions was part of the search. It taught me about my shadow side."

Another woman said, "I remember pondering about life as a young child, especially as dusk settled in the woods. I would think to myself that there *had* to be something more soaring, vast, and adventurous than this neighborhood, this string of houses, and what Mom does every day. Once I found out that God was the most important thing . . . I wanted to work with God. I was a Catholic girl, so that meant being a nun. I wanted to be a nun, until someone told me that nuns couldn't go swimming or take baths. So then I wanted to be a missionary."

Jeanne instantly recognized my questions as well. "I felt bigger than life sometimes. I didn't know what to do with all the energy I felt. I know that a lot of it came from being abused and beaten, but there was this place inside of me, a place of joy, a world of beauty that gave me hope. It was like a gift to me to keep going."

When we deny our power and our passion, it becomes an undirected force within us creating enormous pressure that seeks an outlet. When we as women self-reject for feeling bright, strong, and aware, it is all too easy to use food, drugs, relationships, sex, whatever, as a momentary distraction to relieve the pressure.

My own inner conflicts, my passion, and my longing for that vast, soaring place have led me on many false paths — to abuse alcohol, experiment with drugs, have a number of addictive love affairs, be depressed, be anxious, eat too much or too little, work too hard, and sleep too much. The same passion has also led me to practice the piano diligently, run, practice yoga, climb Mount Kenya, adopt a child as a single parent, engage in civil disobedience, change careers at age thirty-five, learn to play tennis after I turned forty, and write this book. Most of all, it has kept me searching for my own truths.

It is important to acknowledge the profound impact that culture and family have on each one of us. But there is more. When we accept the mystery inherent in our individual differences, we free ourselves to go beyond the concrete facts of life, the analytical, the measurable, and the mundane, and to recognize a spiritual realm where all things are possible.

PART III

RECOVERY:
THE JOURNEY HOME

CHAPTER 14

I Surrender:
The Process of Recovery

A SIGN in my waiting room says, "You have come here to find what you already have." People seek therapy saying that they want to change. What they usually mean is "There is something wrong with me that makes me bad. I want to get rid of it so I'll be good." They approach therapy as though they were taking a beat-up car to a repair shop. Get those dents out of the fenders, a quick paint job, and it will be fine. New clients also tend to think, "When I'm fixed I won't have all these sloppy emotions, life will be easy, and I'll be able to handle any situation with ease." If this is your notion of recovery, you're in for a surprise.

Recovery is a journey to the core of your being. It means turning inward and embracing all that you are, the light side and the shadow side, and being guided by the wisdom that resonates from the center of your being. It may mean casting out beliefs you learned in school, in church, or at home. It means being true to yourself, even when it may create havoc, get you fired, or end a relationship. It also means learning that falling into your addictions or making mistakes is inevitable, but that they can bring valuable lessons for your growth.

LEARNING FROM ADDICTION

Addictions can be used as a way to grow if we look below the surface of the addictive impulses. A journey into my own codependency and addictiveness that helped me forgive my mother for rejecting me most of my life is an illustration. At the age of forty-two, about to receive my Ph.D., I asked my mother to attend my graduation. Wanting more than anything in the world to have her say, "Good for you," I offered to pay her fare to Ohio and put her up. My mother stalled and kept hedging. At the last minute she said no, saying she had to stay with my dad, who had Alzheimer's disease. When I arrived back in Minnesota I was greeted by a cheery letter from her. Mom wrote that she had just visited my younger brother and was leaving soon for California to visit my older brother and his family. No mention of the graduation. Ouch again.

Three months later, after my father had to be placed in a nursing home, I planned to visit my mother for a week. I hadn't seen her in nearly a year. I knew she was exhausted from caring for my father, and I wanted to care for her. Four days before I was to leave my younger brother telephoned to tell me that my mother had died of a heart attack. I was overwhelmed with grief and rage. I knew her death had nothing to do with me, but her dying just before I got to see her felt like the final rejection. How dare she! I couldn't get it out of my head.

Five years later, I no longer felt acute pain, but I hadn't totally let go either. Whenever I thought of her I still felt hurt. I prayed to the Universe to help me get over it. Enter the lesson in the form of Sam, a charming but emotionally unavailable man. After a few dates with him I was totally hooked. In an attempt to extricate myself from the relationship, I wrote a list of reasons why I should not see him — he smokes, drinks, has no conscious spiritual path, is depressed, anxious, self-absorbed, has a rocky history with women, and shows little empathy. He whooshed into my life with tremendous sexual energy on the first date and then disappeared for ten days. Unfortunately, my resolve not to see him repeatedly crumbled in the face of my addictive side, which most definitely wanted to be with him.

I didn't speak up for myself when we were together. I let him smoke in my no-smoking house. (My friend Shirley, a smoker, ribbed me good-naturedly. "Oh, different rules for different people, eh?") I would decide that there would be no sexual stuff between us and then my hormones would take over when he got seductive. When I was able to stop myself it was only because I *knew* better.

Yet I maintain that I have a lot of recovery and am in pretty good shape. Here's why. Throughout our saga, I could acknowledge my dependent and addictive behavior and not berate myself for it. Part of me could stand outside the drama and smile as I watched myself caught in the struggle. I could tell when my addictive side had the upper hand and when my true self was in control. When I got lost I'd call a friend. I continued to ask, "How do I return to my spiritually centered side? What is the lesson to be learned from this?"

Fortunately, my body was aligned with my healthy side: my back needed adjustment after a night when I had been more sexually involved than I truly wanted to be. I groaned and smiled when my chiropractor asked casually, "Any idea what caused this?" I remembered the exact *moment*. As she worked on my back I said to myself, "Charlotte, have you got the message yet?"

At the same time, I began to realize that my obsession with Sam was not about him but about my mother. Like Sam, she was charismatic, talented, funny, seductive, and loved by many. She would also pull me close to her emotionally and then abandon me. Yet I adored her and constantly sought her approval, which was rarely forthcoming. I knew that my attraction to Sam had reawakened the part of me that still felt terribly wounded by my mother, that still yearned for her to say, "You're doing good. I'm proud of you." I realized that I wanted Sam to be impressed with me. (I hated the thought, but the kid in me still wanted a proud mom.)

I arranged for a session with my old therapist and began to write down my dreams. To calm the obsession, I swam laps, repeating the affirmation "I will do what is loving to myself." Because I didn't say what I wanted to when I was with him, I wrote Sam a letter. I poured out my thoughts, and asked for a response. For several days I repeated the following affirmations hundreds of times: "I am willing to learn the lesson in all this"; "I am willing to feel whatever I need to feel."

Then, on an impulse, I began to write about my mother. While none of the content was new, the feelings were. The knowledge of her shaming, degrading sexual remarks hit deep, causing a raging nausea and disgust to explode inside me. Despite how awful I felt at first, I also felt relief — at last, I was cleansing the old wound that was keeping me from choosing a good partner.

Over the next few days, I ran, did Reiki healing on myself, shared what I had written with a close friend, sat in a whirlpool and imagined that the water was washing away the bad feeling I had received from my mother.

Then something almost magical happened. Again drawn to write about my mother, typing as fast as I could, censoring nothing, I got inside my mother's skin. I was she. I could identify with her hardships — her fear as a nine-year-old, alone, bravely riding a train from Missoula, Montana, to Fargo, North Dakota, to care for her widowed uncle and his three-year-old daughter; her buried feelings as she helped her widowed mother struggle to bring up seven children. I could see her at the age of eleven starting to take violin lessons — while her older brothers went to work after school to help earn the money for their talented little sister. I saw the beautiful young concertmaster of her college orchestra who got married and relegated her violin playing to something to do after the dishes were done and the children in bed. Suddenly I broke through to a profound feeling of compassion for the lonely, frightened, sexually uneducated woman who hid behind her charm, talent, and charisma. I had known in my head, but could finally accept fully that she wasn't purposely mean to me. She simply couldn't get past her own pain.

Soon after this, as I drove home from a therapy session, the words *I forgive you* bubbled up from deep inside me. Tears streamed down my cheeks as I said, "I forgive you." I understood. "I forgive you for not making me a new dress for my piano recital. I forgive you for not coming to my graduation." Seeing me receive my degree would have been too painful a reminder of the unlived part of her own life, and perhaps kindled the fear that I would no longer love or need her.

At long last I was freed from being a rejected daughter and I could be a grown-up woman instead. I could remember with joy the many happy, lighthearted times we had together and a lovely long dress she made for me just for fun when I was nine.

After that, my obsession for Sam faded rapidly. I think the lessons I finally learned were, don't try to get blood out of a rock, and if people reject your power and passion, it is because they reject their own. It sounds simple, but it is so hard to believe.

Sam, with all his admirable qualities, could not provide the flowing, honest relationship I wanted because it simply was not in him to give. And neither he nor anyone else could supply the approval and praise I had wanted from my mother. Neither one of us was bad or wrong. I simply accepted our relationship as a lesson.

I would wager that nearly all addictive sexual relationships are mirrors of unresolved relationships with parents or primary caregivers. Obsessive relationships can provide a key to unresolved childhood longings. When we become like needy children with others — Am I pleasing them? Will they want me? — we mistake them for the parents we didn't have. At an even deeper level, we mistake them for God, the energy of light and unconditional love.

Recovery is not about becoming perfect; you are perfectly human right this minute. It is not about being happy all the time; indeed, the journey can be gut-wrenching. Recovery won't remove all the ups and downs of life or keep you from putting your foot in your mouth on occasion. So why try? Because the process of self-discovery will help you stay centered in your power, accept your humanness, and develop a sense of humor. It will help you stay calm in the midst of a storm, and open your heart to love. Once you've experienced the warmth and safety of knowing that your body and soul are truly connected, going back to an addictive way of life ceases to be an option. You know too much. The rest is all a sham.

In recovery you learn that while you may be powerless over your impulses, you do have power over your choices about them. You can want to be sexual, yet choose not to be. You can feel intensely attracted to someone, yet realize they are probably not good for you.

Part of the recovery process is learning to be gentle; to accept yourself — obsessions, mistakes, imperfections, addictions, and all; to stop shaming yourself or being ashamed of your shame; to dance lightly with your goblins; to see that the dramas of your life are simply dramas about your programming, not your essential worth; to seek help when you slip into the addictive morass; and to open yourself to the lessons the Universe places in your lap every day of your life.

Recovery also involves learning skills for living and surviving. You can learn to pull yourself back on center when you are falling off. You can learn to use obsessions about others as an opening to learning about yourself. You can learn that recovery is not so much about "fixing" yourself as about stripping away the negative conditioning that gets in the way of your being the vital, sacred person you have always been. Eventually, you can realize that while you may occasionally visit your addictive places, you will never have to live there again. And that is worth anything.

UNDERSTANDING ENERGY

Before listing the steps of recovery, I would like to discuss energy. Everything is easier when we understand it because it helps us perceive events and situations from a gut, intuitive level rather than an intellectual level. I imagine it on a continuum from density to light. Take a look at this density to light image and store it in your mind for energy readings.

FROM DENSITY TO LIGHT

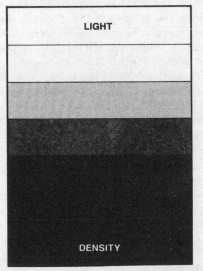

LIGHT

DENSITY

Most of us understand energy better than we realize. We use the word *light*hearted to describe a happy or joyful feeling, and when we talk about someone sending "bad vibes" we mean they are projecting *dense* energy. One key to this is that we feel heavy or tired around them. When we see the *light* at the end of the tunnel, we know that we will get through a hard time and feel good again, or that we will find a solution to a difficult problem. We might tell someone who is getting too preachy to *lighten* up.

People with dense energy are powerful transmitters of that energy. When two people get dense with each other density is squared, a situation most parents with teenage children have faced. The child zaps the parent, the parent gives a little sermon, and two minutes later everyone feels lousy. Have you ever thought, "I shouldn't bring up this topic with X because it will lead us nowhere, it will be like sinking into a quagmire." That's because the conversation is not about the truth. The truth spoken from a loving place always lightens up a conversation. Conversations lacking awareness or with hidden agendas and manipulation create density.

A "light" person in a dense organization often starts to feel pulled down. Conversely, in a therapy group with a lot of light energy, new members begin to recover and find hope more easily. When you say that someone brings out the best in you, you mean that that person's light energy is strong and pulls your light energy to the surface, making you feel good.

Children use the words *yuck* or *icky* to describe touch that is uncomfortable. They intuitively know when a person's touch is an expression of genuine caring (light energy) or for that person's sexual or emotional gratification (dense energy). Couples who bicker about "anything" are usually at a dense communication level. So are people who silently withhold the truth from each other. They are not honest about feelings of hurt, anger, or their need to be held and told they are loved. We may say to someone, "Don't be dense," when they see only what's on the surface and don't get the hidden message, the subtleties, or the joke.

Most of us have experienced feeling "lighter" after weathering a conflict, having a good cry, or telling a big secret. That's because we have broken up and released dense energy from the body. Think of trying to learn a new concept and being unable to grasp it. You feel dense and in a fog. When you get it, bing! It's like a light going on. You feel clear and delighted. Have you ever been crabby and snarly to someone who stayed calm and friendly? Because the person didn't snarl back, you started to feel nice again, and grateful that she didn't get caught up in your mood. By staying steady in light energy, this person helped pull you back to your own light side. You can tell by listening to people who is emitting dense energy — being judgmental or rude — and who is giving off light energy — listening, accepting, and keeping a sense of humor.

Light energy has the capacity to transform addiction and shame into power and love. When we pull light energy into body, mind, and spirit, we inevitably break up dense energy, just as enough heat inevitably pops a kernel of corn.

The essence of recovery can be summed up simply. *Go toward whatever feels light, and avoid whatever feels dense. Light energy is fire energy, the source of transformation. All that is light feeds the spiritual healthy side, and whatever is dense feeds the addictive side.*

In recovery one repeatedly moves from dense places to light ones. You may clear up one area of your life so it feels light, then tackle another dense area and lighten it. You might first work on making a relationship feel lighter, then work on making a job situation feel lighter. In the process you will begin to organize and simplify your daily life better. You will find that the more light you create in one area of your life, the more will spill over into every other area. When you succeed at anything that challenges you, when you push through your fears and do something difficult, you send an important message to your addict side. You tell it that your healthy fighting side is in charge.

Basing decisions on energy readings simplifies life and does away with much analyzing and gnashing of teeth. Learning the process speeds recovery immeasurably. For example, Katie, a therapy group member, was trying to make a decision. After consulting a financial adviser she concluded that she could maintain her current lifestyle and be in debt for ten years, or move to a one-room apartment for two years and be out of debt. There were plenty of rational arguments for either side. I suggested she take a deep breath and repeat "I'm going to stay where I am and be in debt for ten years" a few times and take an energy reading. How dense — heavy, depressed, lethargic — did she feel on a scale of one to ten? Then I suggested she say, "I'm going to move to a one-room apartment and get out of debt," and take a similar energy reading. As she voiced this option, Katie broke out in a big grin and said, "What a relief that would be after all these years." She gave the first alternative a 3.0 energy reading and the second a 7.5. Members of the group laughed because their energy reads coincided with hers. At that point, not surprisingly, her ego acted up and Katie said, "But what will my friends think of me, a fifty-year-old woman, living in one room?"

After making a decision, all the negative thoughts that keep you from doing what feels right jump into your mind. Don't try to stop them, but don't take them seriously. Think of them as static interfering with a radio station that is broadcasting the truth. They are old programming.

Addictive energy is heavy. Therefore, recovery from addictions involves changing dense energy into light energy. To hide addictions people lie, act sneaky, and minimize or shut down their feelings, their minds, and their hearts. This generates dense energy within them and for the people around them. We talk about addictive family systems because everyone, not just the addicted person, is pulled down.

In recovery you work on mind, body, and spirit to change addictive energy into light energy. In the mind one can learn to change dense or negative thoughts such as "I'm stupid, worthless, and hopeless, and nobody cares" to light ones: "If I work hard enough I can get out of this mess. There are people who care. I *am* lovable." You don't have to become a Pollyanna, you just say what is true. You can also use your mind to choose to avoid situations that lead to addictive behavior.

Think of people who make you feel light, hopeful, and loving about yourself. If you don't know people like that, it is important to find some. If something painful happens to you, whom could you call on for understanding and cheer? And who might make the situation worse? From your answers you start learning who are the friends of your spirit and who are the friends of your addiction. Put a list of friends you can call by the phone, because when you slip into your addictive place you may forget who those light-generating people are.

One interesting aspect of recovery is that the more time you spend in "light" places, the more intolerable "dense" situations become. A job that was once bearable eventually feels unbearable. Staying with an abusive person for security becomes intolerable. Just to stick it out doesn't work anymore; you come to realize you can make choices and that there are alternatives.

Other decisions will arise as you learn to evaluate whether it is worth expending your light energy on people or situations that resist change. To parallel the saying "Don't cast pearls before swine," don't put your energy where it doesn't do any good. Codependent people, in particular, have a huge struggle to change this pattern because they feel drawn toward people more dense than they are, in order to feel superior and have someone to "fix." They tend to become angry at or run from people who are more in charge of their lives.

Feeling light within your body has little to do with weight; it means being respectful toward your body, thinking kindly of it, feeding yourself gently, and exercising. You learn to pay attention to its physical signals because they help you know what is true.

Creating light energy around your sexuality means accepting sexual feelings as good and normal, asserting that you have a choice in expressing those feelings, and learning to accept the body for what it is, a sacred home for the soul. It is not a sexual object to be used for an addictive high or as a means to control someone.

Another way of creating light energy in the body is to carry it upright and learn to flow with it. The way you move, sit, stand, and walk, and your tone of voice, all affect your sense of power. When people whine they usually stand with caved-in chest and speak from the neck up with little effect. If a client is whining, I might ask her to stand up, put her hands on her hips, place her feet apart, open her chest, think of her collarbones stretching out, and breathe deeply. In that posture, it is virtually impossible for her to whine or feel powerless, especially if she stomps her feet a few times and makes loud sounds from her gut.

Massage, yoga, karate, and rolfing are just a few of the ways to help people work to lighten the body and release dense energy. Painful feelings that were buried in childhood can be locked in the body at a physical level, dormant for years. When you release the blocks in your body, memories and painful feelings may come to the surface. It can be uncomfortable or frightening for a moment, but if you experience the feelings fully and let them go, you will feel lighter.

Living in a light-centered place means grasping the concept that you are a child of God or the Universe, sacred because you are alive. You are part of a greater whole that includes all living things. At the spiritual level, light energy increases with inner honesty and honest relationships. The lives of addicted or codependent people are contaminated by a myriad of little lies used to cover up the inner pain and fear. If you have sex when you are angry, this is dishonest. If you have sex to hide from feelings of failure, that is dishonest. Such lies as "I feel fine" or "I don't need anyone" create density, and one of the biggest lies is not talking about what is going on inside. Being honest does not come easily to women who have never stopped to think about what they feel and believe. They are not always consciously dishonest; they are simply out of touch with their honesty.

WHAT IS, IS, THE TRUTH IS . . .

We create light when we accept the truth of the moment and let it guide our lives. To draw your truths to awareness you can breathe deeply and say repeatedly, "What is, is," or "The truth is . . ." and let the answers come. "I'm lonely; I'm angry; that person is not good for me; I'm afraid; I don't want to be sexual right now; I do know what I need to do." There is no need to feel ashamed when you make such nonjudgmental statements. *The more you live by the truth, the more freely the energy will flow in your body.* If you are in a dense spot, feeling down, depressed, scared, clear out your mind, write down everything in your head — all of it, no censorship. Speak with a friend. Say exactly what hurt you, what you are afraid of, whom you are angry at, and how long you've been feeling down. Talk with somebody who supports your light side. When we lighten up, solutions often pop into our minds.

THE STEPS TO RECOVERY

The recovery process varies and each individual has to find her or his own way. Even so, growth embodies some essential steps. Our linear ways of thinking and writing, in making lists, for example, don't reflect the process accurately. The steps, like a mandala, have component parts that we address with different levels of commitment and depth. We return to each of the steps again and again, sometimes approaching them from a new angle.

Most people have to shore up their commitment to the journey repeatedly. I may be totally willing to do whatever I must to stay on my path one day, and succumb to caffeine, chocolate, or being a couch potato the next. That's okay, too. The earth must lie fallow sometimes. The important thing is to stay away from judgments and stand strong in your willingness to return to the path come what may, again and again and again.

The steps to recovery are the reverse of those in Figure 4.1 (page 45), where we moved from victimization to core beliefs to addictions. See Figure 14.1 (page 290). In the journey away from addiction to your spirit, you acknowledge your problem, examine the operational beliefs you adopted in your search for love and power, and start to become aware of your core beliefs. Then you connect with the victimization by family or the culture that inculcated these beliefs. These steps can take years and coincide with learning skills for living. Then, with hard work, you gradually replace the dysfunctional core beliefs with a set of true beliefs that lead to inner peace, healthy connections with other people, and a centered healthy sexuality. Sound easy? Lists appear to make it so, but it is not.

Here are the major steps from the model, interspersed with others that are part of the process.

1. Surrender: admit that you have a problem.
2. Realize that you can't recover alone. Ask for help.
3. Be willing to do whatever it takes to recover.
4. Challenge your operational beliefs.
5. Identify your addicted and healthy sides.
6. Challenge the ways you reduce anxiety.
7. Use the addiction to grow.
8. Establish your definition of sexual sobriety.
9. Accept slips and recognize red flags.
10. Stay awake, stay aware.
11. Dive into your core beliefs and heal the inner child.

12. Learn new beliefs.
13. Acknowledge your spirituality.
14. Have a love affair with life.

Surrender   The first step of recovery is saying, "I have a problem that is out of control. I'm powerless over it. It's messing up my life." In AA, the term *bottoming out* is traditionally used to describe the moment of truth, usually a devastating experience, that catapults the addicted one out of denial long enough to get her into a recovery group. The bottoming-out experiences for women who join SAA and CoSA vary considerably. For Gerri it was her twelfth case of VD and thoughts of suicide. Anita was easily persuaded. She bottomed out when she was sentenced to a workhouse and alcoholism treatment. She knew she had a life-threatening problem, and when AA didn't provide relief, she was open to other avenues.

Many women join SAA or CoSA as part of a search that started with other events that changed their lives. A CoSA woman said, "I went to my twenty-fifth high school reunion and saw a lot of losers. Then I thought, 'I'm a loser too. I'm in an awful marriage, I never finished college, and I hate my life.' At that moment I decided to go back to school. That was the beginning of giving up codependency. I started to focus on myself."

One woman said, "I realized that lying and dishonesty were at the core of everything in my life, that part of me was psychopathic. I went for therapy." Another confessed, "I was sitting, half drunk, on the couch in my fancy home and a thought clicked into my mind: 'I was a happy person once. Life wasn't always like this. I've got to do something.' "

Several women mentioned that books or women's studies courses opened them up to the journey. No one knows why something suddenly triggers the journey, but some women are jolted by a memory or have an awakening that just seems to happen. Perhaps it is the grace of God.

As a therapist I have suggested SAA and CoSA to many women, whose responses vary widely. Some accept the idea immediately, while others struggle against it for a long time. Others are defensive. Sometimes I have no idea what is going on in a woman's mind. When I suggested SAA to Kelly, she acted as if I was off my rocker. Several years later she told me, "The first time I came to see you, you asked me if I had heard of SAA. I laughed. I thought it was a joke. But deep inside I knew that my days were numbered."

Angie was absolutely resistant to the idea of SAA when she first came for therapy, even though several of her friends were in the program. No way! Since she continued to make progress in her growth, I didn't press the issue. Then, nearly two years later, she casually announced to the group that she had scheduled a twelfth-step call for SAA on the following Saturday. I grinned, musing at the wonder of it all. I remembered the

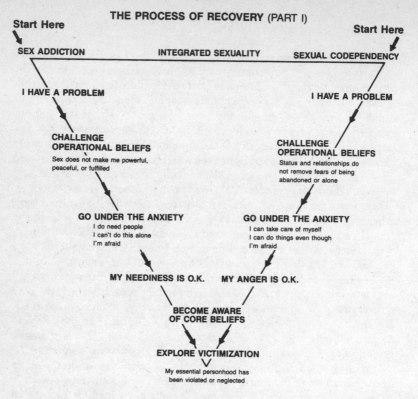

Figure 14.1.

THE PROCESS OF RECOVERY (PART I)

Start Here

SEX ADDICTION   INTEGRATED SEXUALITY   SEXUAL CODEPENDENCY

Start Here

I HAVE A PROBLEM

I HAVE A PROBLEM

CHALLENGE
OPERATIONAL BELIEFS
Sex does not make me powerful,
peaceful, or fulfilled

CHALLENGE
OPERATIONAL BELIEFS
Status and relationships do
not remove fears of being
abandoned or alone

GO UNDER THE ANXIETY
I do need people
I can't do this alone
I'm afraid

GO UNDER THE ANXIETY
I can take care of myself
I can do things even though
I'm afraid

MY NEEDINESS IS O.K.   MY ANGER IS O.K.

BECOME AWARE
OF CORE BELIEFS

EXPLORE VICTIMIZATION
My essential personhood has
been violated or neglected

immense wall she had thrown up two years earlier. She smiled knowingly and said, "It's time. I'm ready."

Other women are not at all resistant, at least at the beginning. Their lives are in turmoil and learning about sex addiction and codependency is like finding a missing diagnosis for their troubled lives.

On the other hand, it's necessary to give some women a strong nudge. When the addiction is overwhelming and the client is making no progress, it is like trying to do therapy with a practicing alcoholic — it just doesn't work. In these cases more dramatic action is necessary.

Jackie, a lesbian who participated in one of my earliest interviews, described the kick her therapist had given her at just the right moment. "It was a year's progression for me. A man friend and I used to joke that we were sex addicts. 'We need a fix right now.' We joked, but we knew there was something wrong. He had told me about Al-Anon. Then he

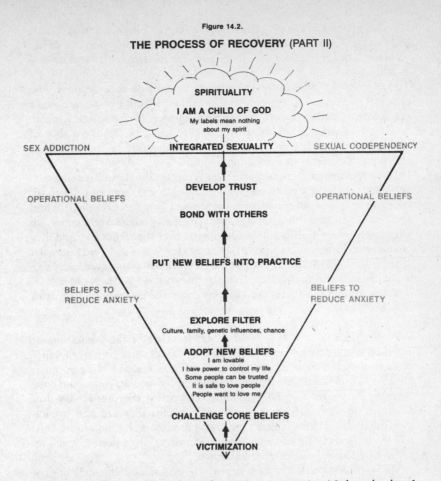

Figure 14.2.

THE PROCESS OF RECOVERY (PART II)

SPIRITUALITY

I AM A CHILD OF GOD
My labels mean nothing
about my spirit

SEX ADDICTION   **INTEGRATED SEXUALITY**   SEXUAL CODEPENDENCY

OPERATIONAL BELIEFS   OPERATIONAL BELIEFS

DEVELOP TRUST

BOND WITH OTHERS

PUT NEW BELIEFS INTO PRACTICE

BELIEFS TO   BELIEFS TO
REDUCE ANXIETY   REDUCE ANXIETY

EXPLORE FILTER
Culture, family, genetic influences, chance

ADOPT NEW BELIEFS
I am lovable
I have power to control my life
Some people can be trusted
It is safe to love people
People want to love me

CHALLENGE CORE BELIEFS

VICTIMIZATION

went to SAA and told me about that. 'How interesting,' I thought, but I didn't do much about it.

"I started discussing sex with my therapist. She said, 'Sex seems like a big issue. We can't deal with it all here.'

" 'Why are you making it such a big deal? It's not what I want to talk about,' I responded. Then I started telling myself, 'I should talk to someone from SAA.' For three months I said that, but I knew I wasn't quite ready. I wasn't willing to give up that crisis stuff yet. Finally my therapist said, 'Either you get yourself into an SAA meeting or you're out of therapy.'

" 'It's time,' I thought, laughing to myself. 'Now I get it.' "

Many women go through a period of bargaining with their addicted side. As one woman put it, "After I broke a contract not to be sexual, I knew there was a problem but I could only let it in a little at a time." Gerri had to slug it out with her addict side all the way. She'd hop out of her addictive side for a little while, then retreat to the familiarity and control of addiction.

Even after the decision to recover has been made at some level, you may still need a jolt to get you to take action. It could be a rejection, a car accident, getting abused by a sexual partner, losing sobriety, or an onslaught of anxiety attacks. Harmful consequences are like a shot of energy to the healthy side. The part of you that wants to live gets scared and says, "I'd better do something."

The important point is to persevere. Women talk about breaking two appointments for a twelfth-step call and finally making it on the third. Some don't feel comfortable with the women they meet on the call and arrange for a second one. Others "forget" the appointment a couple of times before their healthy side predominates over the addict part and they "remember." Some women go to meetings a few times and quit, then start again several months later. The point is, if you keep trying, eventually you will gather the strength to stay. None of the women I know found it easy, but they all hung in there and came to enjoy the increasing rewards of recovery.

Realize That You Can't Recover Alone   One of the addict's most common statements is "I can do it alone" or "I will work on it by myself." Addiction cannot be overcome alone. Addiction means having an inner force you are powerless to control. If you could control it, you would have done so. People try to cope by themselves because they are ashamed of admitting to an addiction. They think it means they are bad or that something about them is defective. The paradox is that admitting to it relieves the shame. By not admitting to it and staying isolated, you only perpetuate shame, the food of addiction.

Many professionals do not appear to understand the meaning of powerlessness in the context of addiction. Dr. Ruth, the delightful TV dispenser of advice about sex, tried to help a woman whose man was mean to her, forced sex on her, and was completely insensitive to her. The caller said she knew she should stay away, she had tried many times, but she kept going back and being sexual, even when she didn't want to be. What could she do? Dr. Ruth, in her friendly way, said the obvious. "Well, you must say no to him." But what Dr. Ruth didn't seem to understand is that a sexually codependent woman feels *powerless* to "say no to him." The words freeze inside and the body feels paralyzed. She can be destroying her life and still not find the voice to say no. That's why you need a group of peers to support your healthy side.

People who try to do it alone sometimes stop one addiction, but they usually switch to another one because they haven't healed internally.

Twelve-step groups are effective for many women recovering from sex addiction and codependency because they provide an unshaming group of peers who struggle with the same problem. The members commit to being available by phone whenever possible. They become a reliable source of support. Recalling her early sessions in SAA, Gerri said, "A little bit of me would pop out and no one went away. They just kept listening, understanding, and caring. It was so amazing. So I'd share a little more and a little more. Slowly I stopped feeling so rotten inside."

Anita said she phoned people once or twice every day at the beginning of recovery to keep herself from acting out. It's like "dial a loving message," "dial for support," or "dial light energy." Making genuine connections with other people foils the addict part.

Be Willing to Do Whatever It Takes to Recover Many people want to get better. But *wanting* recovery is not the same as being *willing* to do whatever it takes. Continued use of the word *want* is a red flag that the person has not yet committed herself to do the work: I *want* to stop going out with sexually abusive partners. I *want* a loving relationship. I *want* this pain to go away. It's easy to make these statements. They don't threaten the addicted side. And they don't lead to action.

Now think of these statements: I'm *willing* to share my pain with another person. I'm *willing* to reach out for support when I'm lonely. I'm *willing* to say affirmations twenty minutes a day. I'm *willing* to stop using sex compulsively. These statements have energy and commitment. You can increase the energy by saying, "I *will* go to SAA. I *will* learn to stop my addictive sexual behavior." People who continually say "I want" believe that recovery will take place magically with no effort on their part.

One way to test your willingness is to breathe deeply, close your eyes, and say, "I am willing to do whatever it takes to be well" (or "be whole" — use any phrase that has meaning for you). You need to draw the words into your body, not just have them pass through your head. You can think of swallowing the words and having them fill you up. After you say one of these phrases a few times you will probably hear another voice protesting: "But not give up sex. Not change jobs. Not give up seeing Randy. Not work less. Not eat healthy food. Not quit drinking. Not be in a twelve-step group." That's the addict part feeling stunned by the willingness statements and mobilizing to con you into thinking you couldn't possibly give up those things.

Many people feel a ripping fear when they say, "I am willing to do whatever it takes." Some are tense and whisper the words; others feel the fear before they even utter a word. One woman said, "I'm scared to even say it." That's because they can sense that the tyrant addict is going to have a fit when they do.

The addict part may get extremely defensive: "You're making a big deal out of nothing. Why are you listening to that stupid therapist? I'm too busy for a group." The addict will also want to make bargains, and that's natural. It's important to simply listen to them and keep telling yourself that genuine recovery precludes bargains. As the process unfolds you have to give up bargains, a cover-up for fear, in order to live in harmony with your knowledge of what is loving and respectful for yourself.

Most of us spend time stuck between knowing that something is addictive and being unwilling to give it up. If we don't accept that the *knowing* hasn't caught up with the *doing,* we will make rationalizations every time we give in to the addiction. Have you ever been with a person who makes twenty excuses for ordering a hot fudge sundae? — "It's good to treat yourself sometimes; I don't usually eat sugar," and so on. Listening, you think, "Just eat the damned thing if you want it, but spare me the excuses. I'm not your mother." They are voicing an ongoing conflict and perhaps hoping that you'll encourage them by saying, "Sure, go ahead." If you are going to do something addictive it's better to simply acknowledge it. "This isn't a good idea, but I'm going to do it anyhow."

When we accept the statement "I am willing to do whatever it takes to be well," it may feel like a spiritual awakening, a light going on. Gerri described her moment of realization: "I heard it in my head. 'I'm willing to give it all up. All of it.' It was like a bolt of lightning, a knowledge I could be free, and I knew it would be worth it." She laughed. "It didn't stay for long, but once I had that feeling, I had hope."

You don't have to "give it all up" at once. In fact, falsely giving up things before you are ready creates greater disharmony within. Faking where you are at is the greatest block to recovery. You need to create a balance between firmly nudging yourself to keep moving and not expecting too much at once. Even so, each new step requires a certain leap of faith. There will be uncomfortable feelings of withdrawal as the ego-addict dies at the hand of a growing spiritual side. That is inescapable. The most important thing is to put yourself in a state of willingness.

Challenge Your Operational Beliefs   Your operational beliefs — I feel powerful when I seduce someone; I am secure if I have a partner; sex makes me feel good — have probably come to feel like the truth. But they are not the truth. They are what keep you on an addictive path. To challenge your operational beliefs you must start observing yourself and using your adult rational mind to evaluate your behaviors and their harmful consequences. Remember to look at the big picture. You may feel good when you are sexual, but what about the rest of your life? Do you have peace of mind? Are you following your personal dreams? Is your life manageable or is it chaotic?

Identify Your Addict and Healthy Sides   Barbara, a woman struggling with a powerful sex addiction, said in a therapy group early in her recovery, "I am just dying to go out and get laid." I told her I was glad she was so honest. Then I asked, "Which side wants to get laid, the addicted part or the healthy part?" After much consideration and thinking of the consequences, she decided it was her addicted part. I asked what her healthy part had to say. "I'll probably feel awful afterwards, and then I'll obsess more, and I might overeat. I guess I really don't want to do this."

It is important not to confuse addictive impulses with innate feelings. The old advice to go with your feelings should be adjusted to go with your loving, self-respecting side; go with what you know to be true for your healthy, spiritual self. The addict side can trigger powerful feelings or self-destructive impulses. But if you think them through you will know the difference because harmful consequences follow addictive behavior.

Understanding the addictive part and the healthy part means separating the addict part from the self. Instead of "*I* want to get laid," you can say, "*My addicted side* wants to get laid," thereby making the distinction between your addiction and the core of your being. When Barbara was overwhelmed by her desire to "get laid" she thought of herself as a terrible, self-destructive person. It felt awfully serious. Once she could say, "This addicted part of me wants to get laid, what else is new?" she was no longer lost in her shame. She had more energy to summon her healthy part to take action and support healthy behavior.

I try to help people lighten up about their addictions. When they say they hate being addicts, I write them a prescription for the week: "Rx 100 × /day: 'I am not my addiction.' " They can add to it any or all of the following: Say to yourself, "My addiction is a part of my programming. It came from being hurt as a child. It's a drag but I can learn to live with it." The most important part of recovery is to accept yourself exactly as you are at any given moment. Sometimes the phrase "I am as God created me" helps bring one back to oneself.

Challenge the Ways You Reduce Anxiety   As we have seen, the victimized child reduces her anxiety by adopting certain beliefs. The addicted one tends to say, "I don't need anyone, I can do it alone," while the codependent one says, "I'll find someone to take me away from all this." One of the most terrifying things for an addicted person to accept is "I do need people. I'm lonely and I crave affection." Addiction thrives in isolation and separateness. Anxiety is like a veil over your feelings. Survivors learn to reduce anxiety by numbing out and disassociating from themselves and others. To get through this step you must plunge into the anxiety and the feelings you are avoiding. It gets easier with time.

You also let people know that you care about them and need them. You have to convince the little kid inside you that it is safe to care about people, that not everyone in the world will let you down. Every time you choose reliable and trustworthy people and note that they do hang in there with you, you gather evidence that helps you develop trust.

The codependent woman who says "I'll find someone to take me away from all this" needs to gather data to show her scared kid that she can indeed take care of herself. She *can* pay the rent, buy a car, balance a checkbook, call friends, earn money and learn to ask for help when she is stuck. In fact, she probably does most of those things already. Instead of operating from the little kid who needs a mom or dad, she has to become the mom to herself: "I understand that you're scared, but I'm grown up; I'll take care of you and protect you."

Use the Addiction to Grow   By learning to track back to just before you had an addictive urge you can acquire deeper knowledge about yourself. An addictive impulse can be a way to flee from a painful current event or from an old memory that is surfacing. When I asked Barbara what was happening just before she had the addictive urge to "get laid," she recalled that a man at work had made a sexually derogatory remark to her. It had triggered feelings reminiscent of those she experienced when her father exposed himself to her or made sexually derogatory remarks. When you are suddenly feeling drawn toward your addictive side, instead of focusing on the addiction it is often more productive to go underneath and ask, "What was happening before? What am I feeling? What am I needing?" Or even, "What is troublesome in my life that I'm not dealing with?"

Establish Your Definition of Sexual Sobriety   Definitions of sexual sobriety or abstinence can be subtle, take a long time to formulate, and undergo dramatic changes as one recovers. I prefer *sexual sobriety* to *abstinence* because people associate the latter with not being sexual. I was once quoted as saying I believed in sexual abstinence for sexually addicted people. Not quite! I had said that I believed people had to abstain from *addictive* sex so they could learn to have loving sex, and that *might* include a period of celibacy.

For most women sobriety starts with a list of don'ts, which varies from woman to woman. They might say they must give up compulsive masturbation, visiting bars, pornography, seductive clothing, sex out of anger or need. Some women, after starting SAA or CoSA, dispose of clothing and makeup they associate with their addictive side. Others get rid of music, magazines, or pictures that trigger their sexually addictive feelings.

To start, it is important to set clear and safe limits around the addictive behavior. The first thing one does for an open wound is stop the bleeding. Setting limits on the addictive part is comparable to a parent's fencing in the play area of a rambunctious two-year-old because the child isn't wise enough to stay out of the street. Setting limits is a way of honoring the destructive power of the addiction. It is not, as many people think, being unnecessarily rigid. People need strict limits in the beginning. The addictive side will try anything to regain power over you. You can put a gate in the fence at a later date. As sobriety becomes more secure you can be less rigid.

Defining sexual sobriety involves understanding the motivation underlying a sexual behavior. What is addictive for one woman might not be for another. Anita told of having to avoid certain AA meetings because the men acted seductively toward her and she was unable to set limits. She also had to discard the vibrator she associated with compulsive masturbation and the phone numbers of addictive friends who were willing sexual partners.

Jane related that part of her recovery process was to buy a vibrator to help her be orgasmic. Because she did not experience orgasm with her partner and felt she was incapable of it, she withdrew from sex and was angry at him. The vibrator helped validate her normality in being capable of orgasm. Paradoxically, it took her focus off attaining orgasm and helped her relax and enjoy being sexual.

For some women early sobriety means the excruciating task of extricating themselves from a destructive relationship. Claudia, Miss State, said, "A lot of my early sobriety was trying to stay away from a woman in a frantic attempt to remain celibate. We had had a relationship for a year and would break up and get together over and over, mainly for sex. When we did spend time together, I would try to be healthy about it instead of checking out emotionally and being there only physically."

This underscores an important point. In most cases it is unrealistic to expect someone to terminate a destructive relationship instantly. Leaving can be a goal, but the point is to start being honest about the relationship and staying emotionally present with the person. Honesty forces the dishonesty of a relationship to the surface. Honesty scares the partner when the relationship is based on dishonesty or a covert struggle for power. "I am unhappy in this relationship. I am planning to spend more time with friends. I want us to have therapy." Speaking honestly about dissatisfaction and pain in the relationship challenges the partner to grow.

If you are working to convince yourself to get out of a harmful relationship, keep a daily log of how many hours you spend feeling upset, afraid, preoccupied, worried, or plotting how to change your partner. What is the cost to your life, your work, your energy, your integrity? You might go through the twenty questions of SAA, or CoSA, or review the appraisal chapter. How many of your hours together are satisfying and nurturing? One woman had a flash of awareness when she read her three-year-old journal. "I was saying the exact same things then as I am now: 'It's better now. He's really trying to change. He's got a lot of potential.' I couldn't believe it. Nothing has really changed; we just have a good day now and then."

Your definition of sexual sobriety will change with time. It is based on an inner recognition of when the addictive line has been crossed. "If I was having a hard day at work and knew I had to talk to the boss, but slipped off into sexual fantasy instead, I knew it was addictive." "When I was feeling afraid my lover would leave and started wanting to seduce her, I knew it was addictive." "When I started thinking about those seductive clothes in the closet, I knew a time would come when I would wear them for the wrong reason." The definition involves determining when sexual behavior or fantasies have crossed a line, which you will learn to recognize.

As you progress in recovery, definitions of sexual sobriety become increasingly subtle. "I started realizing how I talked to people. It wasn't the manner that was seductive, but it was setting people up by saying what my idea of the perfect lover would be, manipulating them to behave in those ways . . . and then consider them fools for doing it."

The next aspect of sexual sobriety is the list of do's. Renée said, "My definition of sobriety has changed. It's the opposite now. Once I surrendered to what I couldn't do, I could turn my attention to what I can do and be aware of what I want and need."

Here are some of the do's women describe: "Follow my intuition in making decisions. . . . Say honestly what I need and want. Go to meetings, stay connected with friends and feelings"; "Allow my creativity expression."

Anne said, "Be gentle with myself. If I got nothing else out of going to SAA that's it. That's a goal I have for myself because I tend to be very judgmental. Now I allow myself to do things that I would have been afraid to try, simple things like going to a different restaurant; being a lot more playful with myself and with my son; not being so rigid; learning to just see how things go and not always having to make plans; just in general being more low key."

"My do's include monitoring how emotionally honest I am with myself and people in my life," said Kelly. "I ask myself, 'How open is my heart?' and if it's not, 'Why?' In the process of recovery I decided that being in a relationship that wasn't sexual for three years was not okay with me. I gave myself permission to be sexual and told myself it could be different from when I was young and fucked a lot of strange men in really dangerous ways. I said to myself that I had learned something in the past few years. It was okay to try again, knowing I'd make mistakes but I could just stay conscious. Sobriety is not just about this behavior and that behavior."

Makeup rituals are a huge part of sex addiction and codependency for many women. Again, sobriety involved determining the underlying motivation: Was it addictive or not?

Jeanne spoke about her need to know what was happening inside her in relationship to using makeup. "The fine line is to really stay in tune and decide if I'm using it as a mask or as a way to define my features. If I'm needy my tendency is to do full makeup, and that's a mask, so it's addictive. If I'm not needy I can do full makeup and feel connected."

"As a lesbian this is a big issue for me, too," Claudia said. "I know when I dated men, and even to a certain extent now, there are definitely two sides to me. I feel a subtle shift in my personality. When I was drinking or went to a bar I always had on makeup. I sometimes don't wear makeup now, but there are times when it makes me feel attractive and it feels okay."

Kelly added, "I feel that if you really loved yourself as a woman you wouldn't *need* makeup. It could be something colorful and bright that is fun and creative, but I wouldn't ever feel I *have* to wear it to be acceptable. I hate the pressure to wear it."

Jane said, "All that time, money, and energy. And all those people making millions of dollars on makeup. Men don't think they have to wear makeup, and I think they look great." Everyone laughed in agreement.

Anne said, "Last night when I went out with some friends I got dressed up and put on makeup and thought, 'I really hate this. I wish I didn't have to do it.' Then I said to myself, 'I will not wear makeup more than five days a week, God damn it. That's it! I do it for work and I do it to make a living. Other than that it's totally optional.' "

Renée laughed. "In the beginning of my recovery I thought I had to be pure and not wear *any* makeup. I also got rid of lots of clothes. Most of what I wore for a couple of years varied from medium gray to brown and made me look super plain. That was in the rigid rules days. Now I can make choices, and it simply isn't a big deal anymore. I hardly think about it. If I want to wear a little makeup I just do. I'm also having fun with clothes again, but it's coming from a very different place. Now I think, 'I really like that outfit, it's pretty.' Before I would have thought about how it would turn some guy on or make me look like a sex kitten." Renée's comment again underscores the point that recovery means being able to say "What do I want to do? What is true to me?"

Sobriety eventually becomes a synonym for a loving, self-respecting life that includes a healthful diet, exercise, quiet times, and most of all staying connected to your feelings. Renée summed it up with, "What it's been for me is having love in my life in all different ways. When I cook myself good meals, take bubble baths, get a massage, go for walks with friends, then sex is also the most fun, and it has the least amount of inappropriate attention given to it."

Accept Slips and Recognize Red Flags   A slip means acting out your addiction. Traditionally in AA circles, people recovering from alcoholism used a simple measure of sobriety: the number of days free of alcohol or drugs. It's not so easy with sex addiction and codependency. It might take a year or more to define sobriety, the definition will keep changing, and slips are inevitable. Many people, on having a slip from chemical sobriety, feel depressed, get discouraged, and think they have failed. Those who are only a month away from getting a medallion marking their first year of sobriety have to start counting all over again. Medallions can be wonderful, but for some they put too much emphasis on the addictive agent and the calendar and not enough on the quality of recovery. It is far more important with any addiction to use slips as red flags, wake-up alarms that you are not paying attention to yourself.

We don't plan to slip, but, like any mistake in life, it's the way we handle it that counts. If a slip is kept secret, the inner shame increases and leads to a web of deceit and denial. As recovery progresses you learn to pick up signs that you are heading for your addictions.

Amy had to have several painful experiences before she learned to notice red flags. She was trying to stay out of relationships with men for a while and needed some time to develop a sense of self. During a therapy session, she mentioned in passing that she had met a man named Mike at work. She went right on talking, and when I brought her back to the subject, she immediately said she wasn't planning to go out with him. *Red flag number one: denying that the addict part is playing with fire.*

She had made that comment for a purpose—to bait me to take responsibility for her. If we protest strongly that we won't do something, it means a part of us wants to do that very thing. I said, "Amy, why are you assuring me you won't date Mike? You don't come to therapy and say, 'I won't fall down the stairs today.'" She laughed. I continued, "That's because you have no desire to fall down the stairs and it isn't an issue."

It would be more honest for Amy to say "I'm feeling attracted to a man named Mike who I know is bad news for me, and I'm scared I'll give in and go out with him." Then she could ask for help to stay in her healthy side. Also, note that Amy said she wasn't "*planning* to go out with Mike." It is a slippery phrase, kind of mushy, a sign that the boundaries around the addiction are weakening. Saying "not planning to" is not the same as saying "I won't." If she were being honest with herself she would say, "I must definitely watch my step."

Amy didn't mention Mike for three weeks and she became more distant from her emotions. *Red flag numbers two and three: not talking about the addictive impulses and avoiding feelings in general.* When I asked how often she was seeing Mike, she got slippery again. When I continued to press her for a straight answer she became testy. Why was I making such a big deal of this guy? *Red flag number four: becoming defensive when pressed to talk about addictive signals.* Yes, she was having lunch with him. Yes, she was talking to him on the phone. But no, she wasn't going to be sexual. She knew that was a bad idea. *Red flag number five: denying the power of the addiction.*

I pressed her further: How much was she thinking about him, and what were her fantasies? She was thinking about him "a lot." Fantasies of sex and marriage had indeed crossed her mind. *Red flag numbers six and seven: obsessing and excessive fantasizing about the future.*

No one can say exactly when the slip occurred, but it was well in motion long before she actually had sex with Mike, which of course she did. As had happened in the past, the situation eventually got messy at work and she lost her job.

She was then quite able to be emotional in therapy. "It isn't fair. How could he do this to me? Women always get the shaft." Eventually her desire to avoid such dramas helped her set strong limits against becoming close friends or dating anyone at work, and to face her dependency. She was finally willing to go to CoSA.

You might draw up a list of red flags and put them in an obvious place. Better yet, give them to a friend who will agree to read them to you if she observes that you are slipping. Once you start to slip, you are likely to deny the truth of the red flags and need support to stay awake.

Stay Awake, Stay Aware When it is clear to me that a client is definitely going to act out sexually, I do not use my energy trying to stop her. She needs to learn to stop herself. I do ask that she stay conscious while engaging in her addiction and come back and talk about it. I say to her, "Be aware of what you were feeling or not feeling beforehand: What kind of day did you have? Be aware of your body and your connection to the other person when you are being sexual. Can you look your partner in the eyes after being sexual? Check your feelings about yourself and your partner after being sexual." A woman will often be furious with me at the next therapy session. "I just hate you. You're always there in my mind, saying, 'Be aware of what's going on.'" Being conscious destroys the addictive high.

Dive into Your Core Beliefs and Heal the Inner Child Many people can say, "I know I have this addiction. I need to work on it." They can look at their operational beliefs and say, "Yeah, having sex that way was not good for me." They can try a little patch-up Band-Aid therapy. But genuine recovery necessitates going back to the core beliefs and reexperiencing the events that set them in place. Buried feelings from painful childhood events form a dense shroud around the soul. If you are unaware of your negative core beliefs, you are probably unconsciously setting up situations that reenact childhood traumas to "prove" that your core beliefs are true.

People who are unconsciously trying to prove that other people are rotten, untrustworthy, and uncaring are blind to the kindness and love that comes their way. If they stay connected and don't run away they are apt to feel angry at people who hang in with them. "How dare you treat me as if I'm lovable? I'm meant to be abandoned and unloved. Abandon me. Throw me away." If no one does it for them, they often get furious at the person or abandon themselves through self-violence, failing, and literally running away. The horror of having negative core beliefs lodged in the unconscious is that they are like inner bondage, controlling and sometimes ruining our lives.

Delving into core beliefs will help you put the puzzle of your life together and relieve the shame. "Oh, that's how I learned to act this way." "The abuse taught me to hate myself. I'm not a bad person and I'm not to blame." One woman who had been hospitalized as paranoid schizophrenic said after a year of therapy, "I'm not crazy. I was treated shitty as a child and now I treat myself shitty." This was a tremendously important connection for her to make. Profound childhood abuse, not "mental illness" that came out of the blue, was at the root of her problems. Those who are not loved as children don't learn how to love themselves as adults.

Diving into the wreck, going back to the pain that lies beneath the core beliefs, is the most excruciating part of the process. Reexperiencing the horror of childhood beatings, sexual assault, incest, neglect, abandonment, insensitivity, parents' incessant bickering or battling takes a strong will and a lot of determination. I believe it is best done in a therapy group of people with similar pasts and a therapist who understands addiction and abusive family systems and is not afraid of strong feelings, particularly rage and anger.

One of the most agonizing feelings is to reconnect with the terror of being trapped, alone, and powerless in the face of someone assaulting or exploiting you. I have learned to recognize a bone-chilling scream as what I call the incest scream, which comes when a woman connects with the childhood terror of being overpowered and abused.

Once you understand the source of your wounds you can start jarring loose the core beliefs under the addictive behavior, and your life will begin to make sense. "No wonder I was so afraid of people," women say, or "No wonder I wouldn't let anyone love me." Some women recall a time when they made a pact with themselves: "I'll never love anyone again, it hurts too much," or "I'll never let them see me cry."

Part of recovery for many women includes feeling their grief about the "healthy" people they ran away from. When a woman is trapped in an unloving family, she needs to deny the reality of the abuse in order to survive. Later, if someone acts lovingly toward her the old pain comes to the surface. Therefore, abuse survivors are caught in the trap of craving love yet fleeing from it until they embark on the journey to recovery.

Learn New Beliefs   Once the negative core beliefs have been exposed and challenged as false, you need to adopt positive, life-affirming beliefs. "I am unlovable" becomes "I can love and be loved, I am a sacred child of the Universe." Feelings of hopelessness are counteracted by the new belief "I have the power to change my life." "I am defective" slowly changes to "I get to make mistakes and be loved." Some of this will happen through osmosis from being in a twelve-step group or therapy. When we experience understanding and care and aren't abandoned, when we share our secrets, a new belief system emerges. People accept us for what we are. We are lovable even though formerly abused.

To speed the process, I suggest affirmations; they are a bit like prayers. By saying them repeatedly you pull light energy into the thoughts and transform them into reality, thereby crowding out the dense energy that feeds the addiction. It takes *many* affirmations to counteract a lifetime's worth of negative core beliefs. I'll tell you how affirmations have most recently worked for me, because it is a kind of microcosm of recovery.

When I was stuck trying to get a sample chapter written for this book I went to the Ken Keyes Center for a week-long workshop. Ken Keyes worked with me at length until we arrived at an affirmation that felt right: "I get to love myself by writing this book." I knew it was right because I cried the moment I said it. I asked him how often I should say it. In an offhanded way, he responded, "Oh, about a thousand times a day for three months would probably do it." So I jogged daily, carrying a tally counter that gave a nice kinesthetic click to each affirmation. It took about twenty-five minutes to say a thousand affirmations.

In the beginning it was easy to say them during my run. That's because my addict/ego thought it was invincible. Here is the image I had in my head: As the "I can do it" side got stronger, the ego/addict side became a little alarmed. After a couple of weeks I felt exhausted just before my running time. I started misplacing my counter, having anxiety attacks when I wanted to get out of the house, and became easily distracted from what I wanted to do. This kind of resistance usually occurs when the two sides are nearly equal. When I finally got out, my mind would wander and I'd suddenly realize I'd run a block or two without saying the affirmations. That was evidence that the affirmations were taking hold. My addictive side was getting scared and mounting a counterattack.

It was immensely important to understand that the anxiety, resistance, and forgetting were just the sneaky little addict part trying to get me to give up. This kind of reaction is not a cue to stop. If anything, it is a time to

escalate the work and develop strategies to sneak around the addict side.

At this point, in recovery or in changing a belief, it feels as though a war is going on inside. Over and over again, I see people quit just as they are about to make a breakthrough. They quit to relieve the anxiety and inner struggle. Those who get well learn to push through these times. People in therapy may say, "I heard this voice in me saying I should kill myself. I know I won't, but it sure was a surprise because I've been doing so much better." That voice is a last-ditch effort of the addict part, which feels its power being stripped away.

To help myself through this time I bought an extra counter for when I misplaced the other one and began to lay out my running clothes at night. To convince my ego that I was in charge, I would say a thousand and five affirmations instead of the thousand. For a while, getting out to run felt like pushing through a huge force, as if I'd have to dance around the addict part and then make a run for the door to escape its clutches. Everyone can be creative and find something that works.

Eventually the resistance starts to fade; the affirmative finally overcomes the dominant addict/ego side.

When my psyche accepted the new belief, a warm glow filled me up, and my body felt extremely light, as if it was running on its own while I looked on. At that moment I knew for certain that this book would get written and, indeed, everything started falling into place. After that the morning anxiety attacks lessened, I could concentrate on the affirmation, and I stopped misplacing my counter. I kept up my daily practice because I knew that the negative part would start creeping back if I quit.

This example may seem inconsequential to someone who is trying to give up chemicals or an addictive relationship. Yet for most people it works best to start with one small thing in life and get control over it. Start with the possible, not the hardest thing. But go for something. Anything!

Affirmations can also flush out negative core beliefs. If you say, "I have the power to change my life," a core belief will reply "No you don't" or "You're a jerk" or "Give up." These are echoes of the messages you grew up hearing from your parents or the culture. Listen to the arguments, but only to one before repeating the affirmation.

Affirmations challenge dependent loyalty ties to the dysfunctional family. When you affirm your right to be well, you may feel as if you are killing your family, will be killed by them, or both. In fact, it's the family's belief system that will die. The fear is, "If I don't act in accordance with my parents' beliefs, they will abandon me." Remember, it is disloyal to a sick family to get well. You risk excommunication. One well person provides a painful contrast to less healthy family members. When someone acknowledges an addiction and names the family dysfunction, the family feels threatened and mounts a counterattack: "You're not really alcoholic. You don't have a sex problem. We were a happy family before you started therapy." Siblings may say, "It's not nice to talk about our parents that way; they did the best they could." The goal of dysfunctional families is to bring the errant recovering person back in line so that they can continue their denial.

But affirmations will work *if you repeat them long enough and put energy into them. Light always breaks up density.* Some people say they've tried it but it doesn't work. I'll ask how many times they've said them. "Oh, ten times for a few days." Katie, by contrast, lifted a severe thirty-year depression by taking a walk every day saying the affirmation "I have the power to change my life." Nothing else had worked.

It takes self-discipline to recover. Unfortunately, for many people the word *discipline* conjures up anything from images of physical abuse to laborious boring tasks to drudgery. It becomes easier when you realize that recovery is for yourself, the goal being your own happiness, productivity, peace of mind, and joy. It is not to get a good grade, to please anyone, or to look good. While you will have to nudge yourself and be firm about doing light things for your body, mind, and spirit, remember that one affirmation a day is better than none, ten minutes of stretching in the morning is better than two, and a walk around the block is better than a walk to the garbage can. You will meet resistance along the way, but keep pushing. It gets easier, guaranteed.

Acknowledge Your Spirituality   The very fact that you are reading this book means that you are on a spiritual search. Something special inside you brought you to seek recovery and make the effort to learn more about yourself.

Some women start therapy with a partner, thinking that a few sessions will solve their sexual difficulties — and instead they open a Pandora's box. Somewhere along the way a light goes on for them, and they hunger for something warmer, richer, sweeter, more intimate and spontaneous in life. It is often the same passionate hunger that first fueled an addiction and led the person on a mistaken search. Once they validate the hunger and realize there is a way to satisfy it, they can rechannel their marvelous energy into their journey toward recovery. From the moment we say, "I have an addiction, I'm going to do something about it," we start releasing our inner light, the light of truth, the holy source within us. We start the homeward journey.

As you recover you dwell in a spiritual place more and more of the time. Spirituality is the antithesis of addiction, which is essentially a spiritual breakdown, a journey away from the truth. When you are spiritually centered, you are grounded in and accepting of the truth. You see, you are awake, you feel alive yet calm. When you are entangled in addiction you become increasingly caught up in delusion, denial, and separateness. As the addictive cycle progresses, your spiritual connection disintegrates with it.

Spirituality carries with it a feeling of fullness, richness, and hope. When you are in contact with your spirituality you feel connected to the positive life-force energy in and around you. You experience a sense of wonder at the power and beauty of the universe. You can revel in the humor of life's paradoxes and contradictions as you follow your calling in life.

When you are spiritually grounded, you can win and lose with grace. You are willing to know the truth about yourself and others without judgment or blame. Spirituality can be equated with being awake and conscious, addiction with being asleep, spiritually unconscious, ignorant, and out of control. Your feelings of inner goodness are not defined by achievement, but by striving to be all you can be. You are committed to growth, joy, and service. Balance and harmony permeate your existence. When in need you ask for comfort from others; when you are full of life you find joy in giving. You accept your talents as gifts from the Universe, and while you enjoy and nourish them, you are aware they are not of your making. By the same token, your weaknesses are not seen in a negative light, but rather as a given part of you. You know that part of life's dance is that we all win some and lose some. We all make mistakes.

When you are spiritually centered you feel a sense of control from within. You can connect with your higher power — God, Goddess, Creator, Great Spirit — to assuage loneliness, to help you through difficult times, and to find joy. You know that God can be manifested through other people, situations, and nature. You remain open to the many messages life hands you. You see troublesome events not as good or bad, but as lessons that, while painful, can lead to your growth. You embrace your feelings without shame, weeping in sorrow, feeling angry when violated, and delighting in the spirit within you throughout each day. You don't fight yourself; you accept where you are in your growth.

You have a profound reverence for life and strive to live in accordance with your beliefs. You know that while no one is special, everyone is special. We are all part of a bigger picture.

Have a Love Affair with Life Do you have a passion for doing something that belongs to you alone? The love affair you are seeking is about living with awe and wonder, having faith in the Universe, and having something so wonderful to do that it's worth going through all the trouble of recovery to get there. Remember a time when you felt really good. The idea of recovery is to feel the essence of that high by being in love with life.

I always encourage women in recovery to find something they love to do — painting, writing, sports, music, yoga, meditation — and do it. It doesn't matter how advanced or talented you are at it. What matters is that it brings a challenge, ignites your energy, helps you stretch yourself, and satisfies your inner hunger. If you love something enough, you become willing to give up some of your addictions to have it.

My passions for tennis and running create my desire to be mentally alert and energetic and keep me from eating brownies and using caffeine, which sap my energy. I gave up caffeine not to be virtuous but because I wanted the tennis game more. My desire to prevent athletic injuries led me to yoga, which was like torture in the beginning. The fact that it stretched and strengthened my muscles and ended my injuries was what dragged me out to class on chilly winter nights, not a love for yoga. But slowly the vibrant feeling that filled my body as a result of the class became the reason for going and I no longer had to drag myself there. Eventually yoga became a part of my life. Start with the easiest step. You don't have to have a noble reason.

Once you develop a passion for doing something, you move beyond it and start to feel wonder about simply breathing air and watching birds fly. Kelly talked about doing two-second meditations throughout the day. "Stopping on the way to the car to notice a dewdrop on a leaf. Stopping to wiggle your fingers and marvel at how they all work. Stopping to notice the miracle of a new bud forming on a plant in the house." The people who have joy in life are those who find wonder in daily little things from spider webs to whistling to hearing a beautiful song to seeing a seed sprout.

Savoring the wonder of life also leaves you with a sense of humor and honesty about yourself. Oprah Winfrey led an audience to a good laugh when she said, "I believe all things come round. And when people who've hurt me get theirs, I want to be there to watch." She spoke with gusto — no phony holier-than-thou stuff for her — and that's precisely why people love her so much. She's honest and doesn't act above it all.

Warm relationships and deeply fulfilling sexual experiences flow from a person who feels enthusiastic about life and is on a path to fulfillment. I believe a beloved partner or friend is a gift from the Universe. Sometimes when we are receptive, no one appears. At other times people enter our lives when we are looking the other way. We all have within us the power to be a lover or a friend. When we have that replete feeling, we find that the greatest joy is in loving others.

If we seem to have strayed from the topic of sex, it is because sex addiction and codependency are spiritual problems. The sexually addicted one substitutes sex for spirituality, and so the first step in recovery is to take the focus off sex and to begin to rediscover the sacred self, the source of one's love and power.

CHAPTER 15

Wellness:
Body, Mind, and Spirit

To RECOVER from addiction, an affliction of mind, body, and spirit, we need to heal at all levels. Unfortunately, for the most part our institutions of education, health care, and religion do not make the link between these aspects of our beings. We often refer to people who seriously approach body, mind, and spirit as one as "new age people." They are often viewed with suspicion by leaders of traditional institutions.

We are in the process of a major shift in our attitudes toward health, from a pathology approach — waiting until symptoms occur — to a wellness approach, which is about prevention and feeling good in body, mind, and spirit.

In terms of training our minds, our educational system focuses on teaching us to read, memorize facts, and solve mathematical problems. It seldom teaches us to overcome negative thinking, use our minds to create organizations for the common good, or learn to work cooperatively with others. To integrate mind with body and spirit, we need to learn that our thoughts create and direct energy into the body and spirit. For example, if you call yourself stupid fifty times a day, your body, mood, and ability to concentrate and be creative are negatively affected. If you create positive thoughts that affirm yourself and support the belief that change is possible, you have more energy and are open to possibilities that come your way.

At the psychological level, few people are taught that the mind, to a great degree, controls emotions. Our attitudes and core beliefs create our responses. For example, if you believe people are basically mean, you will be suspicious of others and assume they dislike or want to hurt you. When you emanate this kind of energy, people may feel your negativity and pull away from you, just as you suspected they would. If you believe that people want to love you, you will tend to attract people and situations that fulfill these beliefs.

In the traditional medical model, people are considered to be well unless they have explicit symptoms. Wellness is more than an absence of symptoms. It is being alert, having abundant energy, and feeling happy. Traditional Western medicine does not teach us to be aware of the effect food and drink has on our bodies, a wisdom possessed by indigenous peoples and healers through time. Most people are unaware that their concentration, ability to solve problems, and emotional stability are affected by everything they ingest in the body.

Our education system fails to help children develop their bodies in a way that maximizes use of the mind. Learning, in general, is strongly linked to the development of the body and the free flow of energy. In the Soviet Union I observed a kindergarten and a primary school where great emphasis was placed on developing physical coordination through eurhythmics and exercise, as well as art, music, dance, crafts, and shop. Knowledge of other cultures and a sense of oneness with all peoples was also emphasized and reinforced with world images and signs saying things like "Peace begins with you and me." The children appeared to be extremely relaxed. The extraordinary skills they demonstrated in art, music, and dance at a very early age reflected, I believe, the integration of body, mind, and spirit in their educational program.

It is important to separate religious institutions from what we call spirituality, for the two do not necessarily go hand in hand. Our religious institutions have taught us rituals, prayers, and belief systems, often without teaching a profound love for self and people of all faiths. They dwell on a system of rigid beliefs rather than teaching us to search within for the source of our spirituality or to explore other belief systems and adopt from them what is meaningful for us. Such a narrow perspective blocks our ability to love ourselves and others.

Spirituality is at our core. We are troubled spiritually when we create dualities such as good-bad and right-wrong, or when we exploit others or do not resist exploitation ourselves. When we are spiritually out of balance or not striving to get on center, there is usually a breakdown at a psychological/mental level, of which fear is a basic component. We fear knowing ourselves because we feel shame and guilt, and we fear others' knowing us because they might see our shame and guilt. Our thoughts are permeated with judgments, our minds may rattle with incessant rationalizations, analysis, paranoia, or grandiosity. We have difficulty listening or concentrating. We become obsessive in a variety of ways. We are afraid to tell others what we feel or think. Some people become sad, depressed, anxious, and afraid. Others control their fear by righteously trying to control other people. Some people may develop insomnia, others may sleep more and more.

Wellness is intrinsically linked to our physical, psychological, and spiritual well-being. Another way to understand the concept of the body as a holistic system is to think in terms of physical, spiritual, and psychological boundaries. Our external physical boundary is our skin, which is violated when we are hit, touched against our will, or sexually assaulted. The space around us, our invisible boundary, is also invaded when someone gets too close without our verbal or nonverbal permission.

Our internal physical boundary is our immune system, which guards us against viruses and disease. Our spiritual boundary, which is harder to define, is invaded when someone desecrates our sense of being sacred and worthwhile by telling us how to feel, think, be, and look. We violate our own spiritual boundary when we think that our achievements, failures, status, or personal attributes make us better or worse than anyone else.

If one system is invaded all systems are affected. A physical ailment affects us mentally, just as emotional stress affects us physically. Think of someone out of control screaming at you. Even though you aren't physically touched, all boundaries reverberate with the assault. Your body responds by discharging adrenaline, your muscles contract, you tense your shoulders or tighten your jaw. You may get a stomachache or headache if you hold back your anger or hurt. You slouch in shame or tense your shoulders in preparation for a fight. The belief that you are bad and unlovable invades your mind. Such negative thoughts affect your spirit as they travel from your mind to your heart. "I'd better not love people because they hurt me so much." Cutting off your capacity to love and be loved strains the immune system. Being self-centered and greedy is hard on the heart. Studies show that the immune system is affected by trauma and abuse. It is not surprising that immunologists are finding that, along with survivors, oppressed minorities have weaker immune systems than those of more advantaged people.

When your physical resiliency is down, so is your psychological resiliency. When you are feeling sick, unkind comments may sting very sharply because you are more vulnerable than when you are well. You may become irritated or cry more easily. The flip side is also true. When you are psychologically down, anxious, or afraid, your immune system weakens, leaving you more vulnerable to illness. According to Dr. Bernie Siegel, author of *Love, Medicine & Miracles* (a book I'd recommend to anyone seeking more light energy), your immune system may be depressed for up to a year after the death of a loved one. Imagine what happens to the immune system after years of living in a violent household, being sexually abused, or frantically acting out addictions. After a talk I gave on this subject, a woman medical student said, "I just realized that I developed all kinds of allergies right after I was raped."

If we do not attempt to resolve problems at a spiritual and psychological level, eventually the physical level tends to break down. I suspect that if therapists took physical and psychological histories in combination, we would find tremendous parallels in the breakdowns of the psychological and immune systems. This can result in many form of physical difficulty — skin problems, thinning hair, tumors, colds, bronchitis, low energy, allergies.

This is not to say people are to blame for their illnesses. Abused children are set up for increased physical difficulties. Much sickness is a symptom of the culture. The prevalence of heart disease and cancer in the United States is partially attributable to an unhealthy ecological system that includes pollution, radioactive wastes and insecticides we ingest with our food, in addition to overwork, pressure, loneliness, and alienation. While I believe that as people grow spiritually, they experience better physical health, it is important not to equate physical health with spirituality. It's a terrible setup for people to be ashamed of being sick. Illness or symptoms of fatigue can be signals to slow down and look inside.

I urge people to focus on physical well-being as well as their psychological and spiritual healing process. I have seen depression lift, anxiety diminish, energy expand, and their general state improve immeasurably when women begin to respect their food allergies, improve the quality of their diet, get some form of regular exercise, and simply have fun. You can best wage the battle of psychological and spiritual recovery when your body feels good.

A TALE OF TWO CITIES

The Twin Cities, Minneapolis and St. Paul, Minnesota, provide an interesting model of holistic recovery. While they are plagued by crime like other American cities, there is also a remarkable atmosphere that values social consciousness, cooperation, community commitment, and recovery from addiction. Minnesota has been called the Land of Ten Thousand Treatment Programs and Co-op Heaven, for its many food, child care, apartment, and medical cooperatives. Minnesota has more cooperatively owned businesses than any other state. St. Paul was the site of the first battered women's shelter in the nation. Minnesota passed the first indoor clean-air act in the country. On the average, Minnesotans give more voluntary contributions for education, welfare, human services, and the arts than citizens in any other state. Its Fortune 500 companies rank between third and fourth in the country in returning money to the community. And Minnesota has one of the largest peace activist networks in the country. I may sound like the Chamber of Commerce, but I find it exciting to be part of this community.

People in other parts of the country are amazed to hear me speak of our resources and the immense support network among professionals working with incest, sexual violence, and addiction. Professionals often talk about the Twin Cities as a mecca for recovery from addiction and childhood abuse. Along with traditional models of treatment, Blacks, Afro-Americans, Native Americans, and feminists have set up programs for recovery that are sensitive to minority needs. People come from all over the country to attend addiction treatment programs, including the first one on sex addiction. Many end up staying because the atmosphere is so conducive to recovery. Once they tap into the recovery network, they can't imagine returning to a place without this kind of community support and consciousness.

Minnesota's attitudes about health care and community involvement can be attributed in part to the Scandinavian socialist background of many residents who value social welfare and cooperation. It is also related to the growing commitment to recovery from addiction, as evidenced by the number of twelve-step recovery groups. The Twin Cities have one of the highest per capita number of twelve-step recovery programs in the country, and by far the largest number addressing sex addiction and sexual codependency.

The twelve-step model of recovery embodies a wisdom that, when followed, leads to profound human growth. Some of the aspects stressed are owning up to one's addictions and understanding the harm they cause oneself, taking responsibility for oneself without blaming others, learning to make amends for mistakes, developing a sense of a higher power, or a power greater than oneself, and making a commitment to reach out to help others in need. These groups support people working together to create peace of mind and spiritual growth. Ideally, they also provide a model of community in which all people are seen as equal and supported to pursue their recovery no matter how many times they fail. One woman broke down crying as she recounted the patience and understanding shown her by Alcoholics Anonymous members through her eight years of major slips in abstinence.

The traits fostered by twelve-step groups are good for individuals, and good for communities, too. This is not to say that the groups are perfect, or that people haven't had negative experiences in them. I agree with those who believe that the wording of the steps is too focused on a male, external God, and sometimes have a righteous ring. But when one cuts through the words to the wisdom of the steps and experiences the supportive care of other members, a twelve-step group can be a wonderful medium for healing.

When we follow our hearts and instincts, we will be led wherever we need to go. A similar progression has taken place in the evolution of addiction treatment programs. We started by working with alcoholism, which led us to a series of steps that brought treatment for incest, abuse, and finally sex addiction and codependency. The first modern treatment programs for alcoholism, based on the twelve steps, started in Minnesota. When women got involved, they found that alcoholism in women was often the result of childhood sexual abuse and neglect. Because traditional treatment programs resisted adopting a broader view of alcoholism or addressing "women's" issues, women formed treatment programs of their own. Alcoholism was no longer seen as an isolated disease, but in relation to childhood abuse, race, gender, affectional preference, and privilege. We also began to see how alcoholism is related to diet, nutrition, body chemistry, and genetic disposition.

Light energy feeds light energy. I believe that the evolution of general health care and addiction consciousness in the Twin Cities has had a major impact on the health of these cities and their sense of community. Anita once said, "My God, what if I hadn't lived here? What if I hadn't found SAA? I might be dead now."

This feeling of community was brought home in 1987 when the Minnesota Twins baseball team returned from Detroit after winning the American League pennant. More than fifty thousand men, women, and children were gathered in and around the Metrodome to greet them. Even more extraordinary than this spontaneous congregation was the fact that there was virtually no sense of danger. Although no guards or ushers were to be seen, there was no crowding in the stadium; people weren't pushing one another to get a seat. There was an incredible sense of pride and excitement, but not craziness. We waited a couple of hours for the team to arrive; when they did, the members entered the Metrodome with their wives and children. It occurred to me that this event was a perfect metaphor for recovery: it was fun, exciting, joyful, and no one was hurt.

Throughout the series, no one took individual credit for the Twins' surprise season. The team members refused to be made individual heroes, claiming that their success was the result of the whole team's pulling together, helped along the wonderful energy of the fans. On the night the Twins won the World Series in Minneapolis, I was downtown for the celebration. Again, tens of thousands of people were celebrating in the streets and there was virtually no feeling of danger. There were many children, hugs and "high fives," balloons, joy, and fun. More than a sense of winning, there was a sense of pride, of being part of something larger than any one of us, a part of a miracle. The feeling that permeated Minneapolis that night was truly that of a love affair with life, emanating from a community committed to human values.

SEX AFTER SEX ADDICTION

What do the Minnesota Twins and baseball have to do with healthy sexuality? It's the attitude that is relevant. The celebration after the final game was an explosion of excitement. No one person was the star — we were all in it together. It was a tremendous high, a release from a buildup that had been going on for weeks. It was also a banquet of feelings, and in that regard a sensuous experience with tears of happiness, feelings of gratitude, euphoria, and a sense of camaraderie. Strangers were hugging, laughing, breaking down the usual boundaries of separateness.

Making love, as opposed to having sex, is also a banquet of feelings, a sensuous experience that can trigger tears, happiness, gratitude, and a sense of well-being. Making love is two people together, creating oneness, giving pleasure to each other and accepting pleasure for themselves. It can be playful, light, fun, and exciting. Lovemaking is an extension of an attraction that goes beyond looks or status; it occurs between two people when each is attuned to the soul of the other. Sex out of fear, duty, boredom, anger, sadness, or neediness is no longer making love, it is having sex, either by exploiting another or being sexually exploited.

"Having sex" is a physiological experience involving stages of arousal, tension building, orgasm (for some women), and resolution. If the woman does not experience orgasm, the resolution phase may be extended and include feelings of restlessness or discomfort.

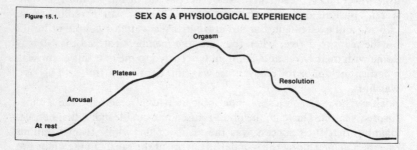

Figure 15.1.   **SEX AS A PHYSIOLOGICAL EXPERIENCE**

Orgasm

Plateau

Resolution

Arousal

At rest

This physiological response does not always happen by choice, nor is it necessarily related to emotional intimacy or care for one's partner. Thus, this response can happen during addictive sex or even rape.

Sex that involves the body but not the soul can be harmful at two levels. First, a person usually does not find what she is seeking and is left spiritually hungry, which leads to more addictive behavior. Second, when sex is genital to genital, not heart to heart, sexual energy is built up in the genital and pelvic area. Think of it as a balloon being blown up in the genital region. With orgasm, the balloon pops and the energy is released downward, leaving a vacuum to be filled by energy from the rest of the body. This creates an energy drain. But where love is involved and two people open their hearts to each other, the sexual energy is free to rise through the body, opening the heart more fully.

Following this explanation, a woman in a sexuality workshop once pressed me to be clearer about the difference between genital sex and spiritually connected sex. As I groped for an answer I thought to tell her about a friend of mine who had been hell-bent on losing weight. This woman forced herself to run because she loathed her body. Her only goal was to get rid of the hated pounds. Not surprisingly, she found running totally joyless and was left feeling empty. We then talked about how different that was from running while noticing the trees, hearing the birds sing, relishing the sunshine, and feeling good about just being alive and strong, along with wanting to lose weight.

Returning to the sexual response diagram, we added a second line, in lavender, for the spiritual connection (see Figure 15.2). Throughout the rest of the workshop, we talked about adding a lavender line to anything you do.

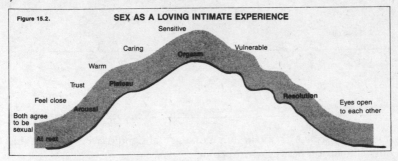

Figure 15.2.

SEX AS A LOVING INTIMATE EXPERIENCE

The words women used to describe the spiritual aspect, the lavender line of sex, included fun, comfort, trust, relaxation, energy, talk, sensitivity, accepting sweat and smells, eye contact, lubrication, taking time, overall warmth, vulnerability, willingness, childlike curiosity, and care for each other.

The basic question you can ask yourself if you are trying to become more spiritually attuned is, What is my motivation? Is it sex for care and love, to create wonderful energy between two people, or is it sex for the ego — to score, feel important, or hide from feelings? Is masturbation a way to feel alive or a compulsive act?

It's fine to love having sex, as long as you are only sexual when it feels true to your wisest self, just as it is fine to want to win or take on a big challenge if you don't do it solely for external accolades. When someone asked Billie Jean King why she kept playing tennis after she was no longer ranked number one, she said, "Because I love playing tennis." When you do something for the sheer joy of it and give it your best, you may lose the game but you won't feel like a loser. If your ego is attached to it and you think winning says something about you as a person, you may be arrogant when you win and hate yourself when you lose.

This philosophy also applies to sexual relationships. Having or not having sex with a loving partner on a given day is only a teeny part of the cosmic picture. But if you are being sexual with a partner, do it with your heart. Make love, get involved, open the senses, and revel in the joy of communion with another soul. If it's wonderful, enjoy it; when it's over, let it go. Winning a tennis match or making love from a spiritually alive place is a momentary high, a wonderful feeling, to be followed by the next step of life. Don't be surprised, as you find greater joy in life, that the desire for sex may lessen for the addicted one and increase for the codependent who has rarely liked sex.

In addictive sex, the partners are often at great emotional distance from each other, connecting only during the act of sex. It looks like this.

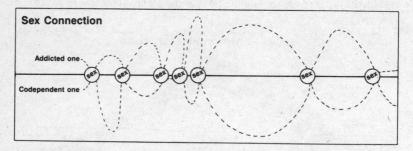

Sex Connection

Addicted one

Codependent one

It is easy to see why sex takes on monumental significance when it is the only connection between two people.

In loving relationships an affection connection permeates the bond between two people. It involves being committed, trustworthy, and honest in the relationship. Love between two people is expressed not only during sex, but all through the day, by thought, word, and deed. It includes affectionate touching, learning to resolve conflict respectfully, expressing appreciation, making eye contact, being friendly, sharing feelings, and being playful. It also includes being bonded in a variety of ways.

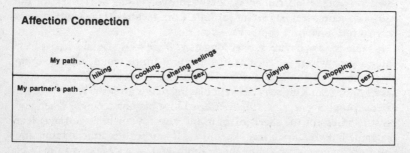

Affection Connection

My path

My partner's path

hiking   cooking   sharing feelings   sex   playing   shopping   sex

As you can see, this sort of relationship does not have the wild ups and downs of an addictive sexual relationship. This can be very hard for recovering people to accept because their energy was fueled by the drama and chaos of addictive relationships. *Affectionate sex flows from an affectionate relationship.* It sounds so simple. Yet when people have difficulty feeling close sexually, they think it is a sexual problem. While on rare occasions such problems may have a physical cause or component, for the most part the feelings missing in sex are exactly those that are missing in the relationship itself, or within the individuals. No affection out of bed, none in bed. In loving sex, neither partner avoids eye contact when it's over. The affection connection continues. Few people are truly at this place all the time; the important thing is to understand that feeling connected is the goal. Becoming sexually open and present with a partner is a process that happens over time. There may be times when an emotional hangover is the first signal that sex wasn't coming from a loving place. If you pay attention to your dreams, fantasies, and your mood and energy level following sex, and listen to your deepest self, you will know whether you are having sex for sensation only or as an expression of loving someone. The trouble for many people is that they don't want to know their motivation for being sexual, because they don't want to give up the power and physical sensations.

Masturbation is simply another aspect of sexuality. You can have a genital-only experience in a few minutes, or you can do it lovingly, feeling the energy flow through your body. You could make a date with yourself for an hour or two to take a bubble bath, light candles, play beautiful music, and take a long time to massage and explore your body. It creates a wonderful feeling of intimacy with yourself. It is fine to reach orgasm or simply to massage yourself. The only goal is to create a more loving connection with your body, the home of your spirit. Some people use masturbation as a way to open up energy. As you are aroused, you breathe the energy into your heart and up through your head and stop before orgasm to expand the energy in your body.

Most of us have periods when we are without a sexual partner. This doesn't mean that we have to stop making love to ourselves or stop celebrating life. Sex is just one part of life, with an ebb and flow unique to each individual. The harmony you feel with your sexuality is related to the aliveness and peacefulness of your inner spirit.

MODIFICATION OF TRAITS

As you move toward integrated sexuality, you do not have to cast out all previous behavior; you can adapt and modify it instead. The addict can incorporate modified traits of the codependent, and vice versa. An addicted woman would do well to learn about empathy from a codependent, and the codependent one could learn something about standing up for herself from the addicted one.

Integrating Addict and Codependent Traits

Addict Behavior	Integrated	Codependent Behavior
Concern only for self when being sexual ➡	Concern for self *and* partner	⬅ Concern only for partner's sexual pleasure
Superdramatic about events in life ➡	Talks honestly about self *and* listens to others	⬅ Minimizes events and accomplishments
Goes after what she wants, ignoring cost to self and others ➡	Pursues goals for self with concern for others and welfare of community	⬅ Abandons developing self for fear of threatening others
Has a right to sex anytime ➡	Enjoys making love sexually with consenting intimate partner when both people *want* to	⬅ Must be sexual at partner's request, i.e., sex is a duty
Impresses partner with sexual performance ➡	Sex is an active and spontaneous expression of love and passion	⬅ Can't wait until sex is over
Has relationship to have sex ➡	Sex is an outgrowth of a caring intimate relationship	⬅ Has sex to have relationship
Winning is all important ➡	I do my best and winning is fun	⬅ It's not nice to win

If, for the moment, we consider codependent behavior as basic programming for women and addict behavior as basic programming for men, this chart has further implications. If men and women would learn from each other, adapting and modifying their extreme traits to more integrated functional ones, the rift between them would narrow greatly and we would have one standard for an integrated human being.

Men and women could be angry and sad, needy and powerful, acquiescent and assertive, passionate and gentle. And, of course, they would no longer appear so incredibly different from each other. Certainly we would see less hostility between the sexes because we disdain in the other what we do not accept in ourselves. The addict disdains the needy codependent, and the codependent disdains the blustery addict. The addict thinks the codependent is a prude, and the codependent thinks the addict is sexcrazed. But when the codependent learns that she has a right to sexual pleasure and stops allowing herself to be a sexual vessel for someone else's use, and when the addict stops demanding sex as his or her right, we will find greater common ground between us and, as a result, sexual exploitation, and the mind-set it creates, will disappear.

Carrying this one step further, as men and women stop seeing each other as objects to use and be used, exploitive thinking itself will start to vanish. *Our sexual relationships provide microcosms of the relationships that exist between all groups of people.* I believe that peace and equality between the sexes is intimately linked to peace on this planet. We will not have exploitive thinking on any level if we promote unconditional love for all people. There is no better incentive for healing and recovery!

CHAPTER 16

Rx for the Culture

I HOPE one day to be out of the field of therapy for lack of clients. Such a development is unlikely in my lifetime because cultures change slowly. I believe the great proliferation of therapists is largely a response to an addictive culture that has lost sight of its spirituality and that group and individual therapy is getting to the problem too late. I am interested in prevention.

In an enlightened world in which there is reverence for all life, rape, incest, childhood abuse, battering, hunger, exploitation, and dire poverty will cease to exist. As a result, there probably won't be much chemical abuse, sex addiction, codependency, depression, or anxiety requiring professional help. My guess is that 95 percent of the people I see would never have needed an hour of therapy had they been loved and cared for as children. Instead of spending years of gut-wrenching time in therapy, they would be out living their own lives, having fun, and working for the good of humankind. Ongoing emotional support would come from friends and family and members of their spiritual community.

In an enlightened world, individuals would accept the natural feelings that accompany life and death, pain and trouble, with no need to flee from them in shame or reach for a bottle, or a body. Instead of psychologists and psychiatrists, we would have teachers, mentors, and guides, who could lead rituals honoring life transitions — adulthood, marriage, childbirth, divorce, changing jobs, middle age, and old age. We would honor all aspects of life and not glorify some segments while deriding others.

A journalist who interviewed me for an article on psychotherapy said, "I think just about everyone I know could use therapy. What do you think?" I responded that while I understood what she meant — many people are certainly hurting and need someone to talk to — I believe that what we truly need is an increased ability to love and care for one another. Instead of more therapy, we need more community. To heal from addiction in an addictive society is a little like an alcoholic trying to recover in a bar. To heal from sex addiction in a culture that routinely sees bodies without seeing souls is just as difficult.

Recovery from any addiction is about empowerment of the self. It requires holistic thinking and community programs that work in concert with each other. Many of our human services institutions are not geared toward individual empowerment; they are set up to maintain the status quo. Thus the individual recovering from addiction often feels like a warrior against much of our social system. I have watched clients struggling to deal with welfare and insurance companies while trying to sustain the dignity and self-respect that are the foundation for any holistic recovery. It is an arduous battle.

We have talked about individual solutions, and indeed the transformation of the planet starts with individual transformation and growth. But in the long run, it is immensely unecological in terms of human energy and spirit to neglect and abuse children and then try to fix them. Why not prevent the damage, so people can have lives of joy and service rather than battling for years to gain their equilibrium and sense of self, and even then live with the scars remaining from childhood abuse.

The ideas in my prescription for the culture are not new, and many are being discussed and acted on. As you read my list you may say, "Oh, you dreamer you." That's exactly what I am, a dreamer, and I hope you will dream with me. I believe and I pray we will see many positive changes in the coming decade.

THE PROBLEM: INSTITUTIONS OPERATING WITHOUT LOVE

As of 1989 the United States doesn't rate very high in the human services department. In fact, since the beginning of the Reagan administration, we have seen a deterioration of many human services and human rights programs. Twenty-five percent of our children live in poverty; an estimated one to three million people are homeless; affirmative action has regressed considerably; and health care and school lunch programs have been dramatically cut back. But in response to the government's blatant neglect of human needs, people are organizing at a grassroots level and fighting back. The plight of the homeless and poor is finally gaining recognition and starting to shake more advantaged people out of their complacency, challenging them to become personally involved rather than turning their heads. Most important, the victimized groups are mobilizing their power and speaking out. Action and healing have started from within.

To understand sex addiction and codependency we inevitably return to childhood abuse. Therefore my list of recommendations starts with suggestions for the care of children. How we care for children and others who cannot care for themselves is a strong reflection of the spiritual climate of our country. It tells us a lot about how we value life.

THE SOLUTIONS FOR SPIRITUAL RECOVERY OF OUR CULTURE

1. *Make infant and child care a priority.*

If we believe that life is sacred, we must care for those who cannot care for themselves. This includes medical, physical, and emotional care for all people along with day care for children, and maternity leave for mothers with guarantees that they can return to their jobs. People who provide child care should receive salaries commensurate with this important responsibility. The benefits could include professional training and substantial pay for foster care of children. (The low pay scale for child care in this country is a sad reflection of the attitude our culture has toward children.)

Children grow up to be adults. That seems like an obvious statement, but when it comes to caring for children we act as if it isn't true. We can't ignore the needs of infants and tiny children and expect them to become healthy adults. We don't expect flowers to grow healthy and tall without good soil, water, and sunlight. It's unreasonable to expect children to grow into productive adults without love, physical care, attention, and respect.

We also need to care for the caretakers. A woman or man who is stretched beyond his or her capacity to cope, through poverty, discrimination, lack of medical or psychological care, will have difficulty being a nurturing parent.

The big empty place that leads to addiction usually starts forming at birth. As previously noted, early bonding and the development of trust are crucial to the development of an integrated personality, as opposed to an addictive one. These crucial developmental stages have occurred by the age of three, and even with a good start in life, subsequent abuse and neglect can break the bonds of human trust and leave a person trying to fill his or her inner hunger with various addictions. Child care must be considered a cultural concern, not a women's problem. Children are our greatest "crop," the next generation, the ones we will entrust to take care of the planet.

2. *Prevention rather than crisis orientation.*

Until things are crashing down around them, addicts deny that they have a problem. They live from crisis to crisis. Our addictive culture operates the same way. Instead of funding preventive measures, we wait until there is a crisis before taking action. Instead of responding to cues of trouble we wait until the alarm is sounded. I have heard countless other professionals venting their frustrations at having reported suspected child abuse only to be told that nothing can be done if there is no physical evidence to prove it. Many children have died or been severely damaged as a result. There has to be a more cooperative, less combative approach.

All the arguments against funding social programs and national medical care and prevention focus on the high cost. But the fact is, prevention is cost-effective in nearly every case. It is far cheaper to pay for child care and support of families than for shelters, group homes, prisons, or treatment for chemical abuse and other addictions. Unfortunately, we are mired in a system afraid to empower people to control their own lives.

For example: I am often caught in the crossfire between clients and insurance companies. In filling out insurance forms for reimbursement, I must respond to nosy and intrusive requests for information. I attempt to present my clients as sick enough to "deserve" reimbursement yet not put on the record anything that could be used against them. Worse than that, I sometimes get caught in a ridiculous charade in trying to refer to other agencies clients who require more intensive help than I can provide. But what is good for the client — usually the least expensive alternative — and what insurance companies are willing to pay for are often at odds.

When Carol started dealing with her childhood abuse her seven-year sobriety from alcohol seemed threatened. Believing she was on the brink of a relapse, she called me for help. We set up a plan to get through the night, but she was still feeling suicidal and wanting to drink the following morning. After considerable thought, she decided that an evening out-patient program would keep her going and allow her to keep working, which was very important to her. It sounded like the perfect solution — until she called a representative from her insurance company. The agent said that Carol had to be currently drinking before the company would pay for treatment. Carol and I discussed the alternatives with some amusement: she could stand outside the door of the treatment program, take one sip of wine, and immediately walk in the door and say she was drinking; she could become an inpatient in a hospital ward (which the insurance company *would* pay for and which would cost more for four days than three months of outpatient treatment), taking herself away from her job and not addressing the real problem; or she could go to the treatment program and "say" she had been drinking, which I call a holy lie, for she had relapsed in spirit if not in body.

This might have been amusing if Carol hadn't been truly desperate. Making a phone call when you are on the brink of relapse takes tremendous energy. Dealing with an insurance company that virtually tells you that you have to go on a binge in order to get help is insane. The process was tremendously frustrating for this woman. Showing the wisdom to know she needed help, willing to walk in the door before suffering the devastation of a relapse, she was forced to engage in either a lie or a ridiculous antic to get help in a dignified way. In every case the solutions that truly addressed Carol's need and maintained her dignity were cheaper than the ones that didn't. Sadly, Carol did relapse and her insurance carrier eventually paid for inpatient treatment.

Most insurance policies allow for several months of inpatient psychiatric care, which can add up to $20,000 or more. However, many insurance companies grant only about $700 a year for outpatient psychotherapy, which is far cheaper and can be a powerful preventive measure. On a bad day I can't help but think that these agencies are designed to provide maximum harassment and minimum support. Nearly all people on welfare are constantly having salt rubbed in the wound of their poverty by the very system that is supposed to help them.

Healers, therapists, and doctors need to work together. Each discipline may have a piece of the answer, but individual journeys follow many paths. No one can be in charge of another person's recovery. Healers should be guides, not rulers. The core of recovery is empowering each individual to take responsibility for his or her own life and well-being.

I believe that if people were given support to follow their instincts, with one person to help them form a plan, their recovery would usually be quicker, cheaper, and more empowering. I look forward to a day when experiments in holistic practice will convince insurance companies to reimburse people for natural, holistic, and preventive measures. It is difficult to convince people that systems in which everyone wins can be created, because our minds are so deeply infiltrated with win-lose, right-wrong thinking.

3. *Entrust treatment policies to on-line staff, not corporate executives.*
Despite advances, most treatment programs are still run by men who use male models of treatment. Men and women have significantly different approaches to learning. One is not better or worse. The main problem is that it simply doesn't work very well for women to be taught with a model designed for men.

In the last few years corporations have noticed that treating addictions has become big business. (In Minnesota health care is the number one industry.) As a result, many corporations are now taking over treatment programs. Programs for sex addiction and codependency are in the embryonic stages, but the same trend is true for them. Judging by results in the Twin Cities area, corporate takeovers do not always work well in the area of human services. Too often traditional corporate thinkers try to impose a rigid formula of treatment without consulting on-line therapists. Corporate beings don't appear to understand that the humanness, strength, power, love, and experience of a counselor who has client contact makes all the difference in a treatment program.

Corporations think "logically" — "We could hire someone cheaper." And they often do. So in the classy offices with well-paid PR men and loads of administrators, increasingly we find inexperienced, poorly paid, overworked counselors attempting to do one of the most difficult jobs on earth. Along with shortening lengths of treatment programs, hiring less talented and less skilled people prevents clients from getting the help professionals know how to administer. Nearly everyone who works in such a system agrees that handling the stress of the work can be done; it's fighting with administrators who don't listen or understand that causes burnout. Such policies are not cost-effective, particularly in sex offender programs in which short-term treatment often results in increased recidivism of child abuse and rape. But corporations, operating on an addictive model — more money quicker — will have to see some terribly harmful consequences and be strongly confronted before they realize the damage they are doing.

I believe this trend will be challenged, and more professionals will start their own programs. As with insurance companies, corporations could make a reasonable amount of money and deliver first-class human services if they consulted with human service professionals and gave heartfelt consideration to people's needs.

Providing excellent recovery services is the most powerful form of public relations. In an excellent treatment program that relied on very little PR and had a long waiting list, the director had firsthand knowledge of addiction and recovery and was down to earth and accessible. The agency was a pioneer in recognizing that alcoholism was related to other problems. As early as 1980, I was among several women who provided in-service training on the recognition of incest, childhood sexual abuse, and later on issues of affectional preference, sex addiction, and sexual codependency. I was happy to do the work gratis or for a minimal fee, because it was fun to go there and people were eager to learn. To my knowledge it was the first traditional treatment program in the Twin Cities to focus on healthful nutrition. The agency's treatment programs were carried out by people with heart who networked with professionals in the community out of an interest in providing good care. Word-of-mouth praise from satisfied clients increased the number of applicants for treatment.

When a corporation took over everything changed. The focus shifted to PR and money. Several women on the staff called me to voice their frustration and ask if there was anything I could do to help. When I was called in to consult on how to raise the falling census, it was as if we were talking on different wavelengths. Those in charge wanted a corporate answer, something for the PR people to do, and I was suggesting ways the program could be more responsive to staff input and address the needs of the clients and community. The treatment program eventually closed — death by corporation.

4. *Assure maternity leave policies.*

I cannot repeat often enough that the most difficult damage to repair is that which results from the lack of infant bonding with a caregiver during the first two years of life, particularly in the crucial first six months. In tracing the lives of sexually addicted and codependent women we almost always get back to a lack of good early bonding and appropriate care. A physically present, but emotionally absent, parent cannot create this all-important bond.

I believe that working women and men should have the option to stay home with a newborn child for at least one year, to create that bond without losing their jobs. The parents should have a choice of arrangements. Women and men could work half time for a while so that both could share equally in child care, or child care could be offered at work so mothers could visit their children throughout the day. Some solutions are more practical than others, but we must apply all our ingenuity to create support systems for young mothers, poor mothers, or overwhelmed mothers to facilitate healthy development in their children. Ours is the only Western country besides South Africa that does not guarantee maternity leave. In the Soviet Union women receive full pay for six months' leave and partial pay for up to a year and a half. Their jobs are guaranteed for up to two years, and all children are guaranteed medical care, not to mention child care at a nominal charge.

5. *Encourage men to bond with infants.*

We need to adopt the attitude that children are the responsibility of all men and women, not just parents. They are the children of our society. When men learn to love and bond deeply with infants and children, they gain a whole new perspective on care and love. Since men are in positions of greater political power in this country their voices should be raised to help create a system that prevents childhood abuse, poverty, and neglect.

6. *Teach children cooperation at home, in schools, and in churches.*

Competitiveness breeds a you-against-me attitude that creates separateness and isolation, the food of addiction. Cooperation breeds a sense that we are all interdependent on one another, we all matter, and each of us has a role to play in the bigger picture. It teaches us that everyone can win. Studies show that in corporations, in industry, and in schools, working cooperatively is more efficient, in both financial and emotional terms, than working competitively. An ideal grade school curriculum would be designed to set up learning tasks in a way that builds self-esteem in children. This could be done through regular physical exercise, learning to express feelings appropriately, learning how to use affirmations, having children talk about their lives, and helping them learn to solve problems and carry out tasks cooperatively.

7. Teach children in school about touch and sex abuse prevention.

People who oppose this, as well as sex education, always argue that parents should teach these lessons to their children. But parents may not know how to impart this information, or don't even think about it. This stance also denies our communal responsibility for children and the effect on them of cultural media.

What is nice touch? What is "icky" touch? I have yet to meet a child who can't tell the difference. Children have to be taught that they have the right to say no to any touch that feels uncomfortable, and to report anyone they feel is touching them inappropriately to an adult in their lives who takes them seriously. And all adults, particularly those in the helping professions, need to learn to listen, to believe children, and to protect them. Preventing childhood sexual abuse is the bottom line for preventing sex addiction and codependency.

8. Train human service professionals to recognize symptoms of childhood abuse and neglect so that they can identify children in need of help.

It is important that all those who work with children understand both the blatant and subtle symptoms of childhood abuse. They must be able to make informed decisions on children's behalf. The juvenile justice system needs to operate in the best interest of the child by promoting cooperation among parents, children, teachers, social workers, clergy, and judges. Untold damage has been done to children in an adversarial juvenile justive system that is set up much like an adult system.

9. Teach parenting skills to children.

Teach students about developmental stages so they will have realistic expectations of children and skills for communicating with children. Let children experience working with younger children throughout their school years, perhaps by having older children tutor younger ones. Provide opportunities for male and female teenagers alike to work in child-care centers and with infants.

10. Keep pornography out of the home.

Pornography has caused lasting damage to many children and has contributed to the sexual abuse of others. Parents cannot "hide" X-rated movies from children, who will inevitably find them. The fact they are kept secret makes them all the more important, enticing, and desirable.

Pornography is highly addictive. Men and women are becoming willing to discuss the subject. On one talk show two women told how their sons died as a result of using an autoerotic sex technique they learned from an article in a popular men's magazine: holding a rope around the neck like a noose, tightening it while masturbating; the lack of oxygen intensifies the sexual high. Unfortunately, one side effect is death. Both died with the article in their hands.

Listening to pornographic messages, Dial-A-Porn, is rapidly gaining popularity. Like other forms of pornography, it is highly addictive, yet it is easily accessible to anyone with a telephone. Many parents feel overwhelmed in their efforts to teach values to their children. Parents used to have more control over their homes. Increasingly, though, homes are being invaded by X-rated TV shows, including rock videos, Dial-A-Porn, and a barrage of seductive advertising that parents have little power to control without taking drastic measures.

In a recent case, two sets of parents sued a Dial-A-Porn company when a teenage boy, after listening to hours of Dial-A-Porn, sexually abused a little girl. Wisely, the girl's parents were able to recognize that the problem was not just the boy. He, too, was a victim. At one point the company proposed that parents be charged for the privilege of excluding Dial-A-Porn from their phone service, which amounts to extortion. Again, what is lacking is a broad social perspective that takes into account the good of all as opposed to the addictive needs of a few. In a culture that cares for and protects all its people we must sometimes forgo individual desires and business for the highest profit.

The paradox is that when children act out inappropriately, civil libertarians, their sympathizers, and purveyors of pornographic media respond by claiming that children should be taught better values at home and that their parents should keep them from using the phone. One father quipped, "You put the Dial-A-Porn into the house without our permission, then blame us. What are we supposed to do, chain our children to the bedpost, the way they do in the pornography?"

Children deserve protection.

11. Broaden the notion of sex education.

I believe sex education in the schools should include an exploration of values in human relations and talks on masturbation. Children can be taught that sexuality is most alive and fulfilling when the people involved feel good about their bodies and their lives. They can also be taught not to deny or be ashamed of sexual feelings and how to handle those feelings appropriately, through sports, dance, aerobics, yoga, and other creative activities.

12. Teach all girls to plan for a self-supporting career.

Teaching girls that when they grow up they will find a man to take care of them is to put them on the road to sexual codependency. A woman who is dependent on a man is likely to feel that she has to be sexual. If she doesn't find a man to support her as planned, she may be in for a rude shock about the cost of living. Poverty and lack of self-esteem are a perfect setup for a woman to become engaged in prostitution or become a victim of the exploitive sex industry. Suggesting to a young girl that she will grow up and have a career is a way to communicate respect and value for her. It's important that staying home to raise children be a choice, and not be done by default.

13. *Stop the use of women and men as sex objects in advertising.*
   Portray women in the media in a variety of shapes, sizes, and ages. Use the media to reinforce loving images of men and women and children. A great example is the American Express commercial that portrays a corporate man rushing to get somewhere. It's storming, his plane has been canceled, and the only available seat on another is in first class. Whipping out his American Express card, he says. "I'll take it." He arrives at his destination, rushes to a building, and slips into his seat in an auditorium. "Where is *she?*" he asks his wife. "She's the second potted plant from the left," his wife replies, pointing to a little girl grinning from the stage in a school play. Now there's a wonderful use of the media, a commercial with a soul. It's one of the few I watch without flicking the channel.

THE DAWNING OF A NEW AGE

We are moving into a new age, the age of Aquarius. Many believe it is an age of enlightenment, in which we will learn to see the soul in every body and look with wonder on the miracle of every human life. Wisdom and healing powers once considered the domain of a chosen few will become common knowledge, available to all.
   We are learning that each of us has a great influence on our own emotional and physical health. We are learning to think of the body as a holistic system. And we are beginning to transfer this knowledge to all communities and nations on the planet, seeing them as part of a vast, interdependent system. In 1978 the Twin Cities supported four programs for peace and justice; in 1988 there are over one hundred. How remarkable it was on New Year's Eve day in 1986, 1987, and 1988, when hundreds of thousands of people, organized by the Peace Is Possible Now movement, gathered at zero Greenwich time all over the globe to visualize world peace in a synchronized effort to raise human consciousness. Native American spirituality, which regards all living things as interconnected and sacred, is being resurrected from the ashes of a culture that

was brought to its knees by a holocaust rarely mentioned in history books. The native American's relationship to the earth as our mother is also being embraced by many white people seeking a more satisfying and holistic spirituality and to heal the planet.

Commitment to social issues on the part of professionals is growing by leaps and bounds. I used to feel that my life was incredibly compartmentalized: I had peace-activist friends, psychologist friends, holistic healing friends, feminist friends, neighbors, and tennis friends. I talked about peace with peace activists, holistic healing with new age healers, but rarely mixed these topics with my psychologist friends or tennis buddies. Now there is an organization called Psychologists for Social Responsibility; therapists are having workshops on spirituality; my Quaker meeting sponsored a forum on addiction; and some of my tennis friends are interested in hypnosis and the use of affirmations to improve their game.

Clearly, we are entering a transformational period. Perhaps the planet is in the process of bottoming out from an addictive mode of exploitation and victimization. We are realizing that these things don't work. Perhaps the onslaught of pollution, AIDS, homelessness, child abuse, and other social crises have conspired to wake us to the fact that we must either destroy our civilization or learn to love and care for one another.

CHAPTER 17

Codependent Sobriety:
"Know the Truth and the Truth Shall Set You Free"

> *Power, in my way, is the understanding of the spirit of*
> *medicine energy that flows through all beings. . . . Power*
> *is strength and the ability to see yourself through your*
> *own eyes and not through the eyes of another. It is being*
> *able to place a circle of power at your own feet and not*
> *take power from someone else's circle.* True power is
> love. *(Emphasis added)*
>
> Agnes Whistling Elk in
> Lynn V. Andrews, *Flight of the Seventh Moon*

WHENEVER I am asked to speak on women, sex, and addiction,
people want to hear accounts of sexually addicted women, the
Looking for Mr. Goodbar stories. These stories sell; they hold an
audience. When I bring up the subject of codependency, interest wanes.
Sex addiction is more exciting and dramatic, but you can't separate the
two. Nearly all sexually addicted women also struggle with aspects of
codependency. Jayel, who has been warring with her codependency in
one of my therapy groups for nearly two years, prompted me to write this
chapter. When I said at the close of a therapy session that I was going to
take a week off to write, she asked, "Are you going to include that list
about codependent sobriety you talk about?"

"I haven't decided," I said.

"Well, I think you should," she said strongly. "I know it's helped me
a lot. Besides," she said, starting to laugh, "I'm sick of the addicts' getting
all the attention."

That convinced me.

AN ELUSIVE SUBJECT

Sobriety for a sexually codependent woman is difficult to define because codependency is often about what a woman is *not* doing in order to be an acceptable female. She is not speaking up for herself. She is not alive to her sexuality. She is not focusing on her needs. She is not creating goals for herself. She is not saying no when she needs to.

A codependent woman lacks a sense of self, which leads her to control others, whom she mistakes for herself. "If my husband is important, then I am important. If my children fail, then I fail. I'm responsible for everyone." Codependent sobriety is a process of creating an internal identity by learning to listen to signals coming from deep within you. When a woman understands fully who she is and accepts that knowledge, her need to control others automatically diminishes.

Many codependent women are reluctant to explore their emotions, terrified of the rage that lies beneath their excessive caretaking. They don't want to acknowledge what they know — that they are hurt, that they are being taken advantage of, that they have abandoned their dreams, that they are capable of thinking for themselves.

Most women will need to follow the guidance outlined here time and time again. It is important to adopt the mind-set that recovery is for *you.* There is no schedule, no such thing as doing it perfectly. There is just making a deep, heartfelt commitment to recovery. You are not doing it to please your therapist, to impress a friend, to get back at someone, to fix a relationship, or to be a good person. You are doing it because *you* want to feel more alive.

GUIDELINES FOR CODEPENDENT SOBRIETY

1. *Be willing to know what you know.*

Or, be willing to feel whatever is inside you; or, be willing to know whatever is true for you. One woman used the phrase "I am willing to do what it takes to find my soul." Remember I suggested in Chapter 14 that the addict say, "I am willing to do whatever it takes to get well." Often the addicted one has to give up destructive behavior. While that is also true for the codependent woman, the key to recovery is going within yourself and finding a self. That is why the first step involves the willingness to go inside, the willingness to be an autonomous person, a woman unto yourself. In essence you are saying, "Yes, I will give birth to myself."

Women who try to look within before they put themselves in a state of willingness end up repeating endless circular arguments against it. "But I can't, Jack might not like it." "I'm selfish to spend so much time on myself." All the recovery groups and therapy in the world will be useless if a woman really doesn't truly want to know what she knows and let that knowledge guide her life.

2. *Learn to listen inside.*

Once you are determined to find out who you really are, you can proceed to the next step, listening. There are many approaches to listening. My favorite is to start by taking a quiet time to be aware of your breathing, your insides, and how you feel. Follow your breath as it goes deep inside and then releases. Imagine a balloon filling your abdomen and diaphragm. Put your hand on your solar plexis or your abdomen and feel the motion as you breathe deeply. Many codependent women breathe in a tight, shallow way, which is part of holding themselves and their power back. They literally pull in their solar plexis and gut — the energy centers where anger and power reside—so they won't do anything to upset anyone. As codependent women recover, their voices usually become fuller and deeper because they speak from deeper inside themselves, unblocking their energy.

When you wake up in the morning, before you have a chance to put on your defenses, tune in to your breathing for a few minutes and imagine a radiant light around and within you. Say whatever reminds you that you are a miracle of life, a child of the Universe. If you are seeking a solution to a particular situation, put the problem in your mind and ask for a solution to come. Say to yourself, "I am willing to find the solution that is true to me." Then pay attention to your breathing again. Just feel the breath going deeper and deeper down inside. You may want to think to yourself, "The answer is within me. It will come." You may experience fear and resistance as you do this; keep telling yourself that you want to know what you know because in the long run it will help you feel better.

Conscious deep breathing will take you to your Knowing center, the God within you. After you feel quiet and tuned in, ask yourself one of the following questions, either in general or in response to a question you have seeded in your mind. It is best to pick one question and stick with it for a while. Your codependent side will probably resist this work, saying such things as: "This is stupid. I've done it for ten minutes and nothing has happened. I quit." "This therapist is weird, telling me to breathe. Why doesn't she just tell me the answers?" "I don't see why I have to stick to one question. If I do them all, I could get this done sooner."

Ignore the rattling of your mind and gently ask yourself:

What do I feel?

What do I think?

What do I really want? (Not for someone else to be different! Not for someone else to love you. But what do *you* want to be?)

What is true for me?

What is my opinion?

Breathe, stay quiet, and let the answers and feelings come to the surface. Usually the minute you reach a decision, a ton of arguments will come to your mind. "That would be too hard. I'd have to give up something. I'm afraid." Let them float through your mind. Don't grab on to them. To counteract these arguments, say firmly to yourself, "There is always a way."

Trust that this process will work even though you don't feel immediate results. It is simply a matter of time. I once spent several months seeking inner guidance regarding a family situation before I woke up knowing the right thing to do. Persevere. Do it daily until it becomes a habit. Codependent women often say, "I have no idea of what I want or feel." My response is always, "Take time and listen." You won't find your inner truth while analyzing, talking, or trying to figure out other people. A class in meditation or yoga can be a wonderful tool to help you connect to your own center.

3. *Ask no advice.*

Codependent women keep themselves feeling "little" and others — usually men and so-called experts — "big" by asking advice. They play innocent and not too bright. Every time you are inclined to ask advice, look within and say, "I know the answer." If nothing comes, take a walk and say nonstop for twenty minutes, "I know what is true for me. I can find the answer for myself." Part of sobriety is learning to live with ambiguity, paradox, and unanswered questions. You can't force an answer to come. It will come in its own time.

4. *Think no advice, give no advice.*

Because the self-esteem of a codependent woman is tied up with other people, her mind is constantly humming with plans to change others to fit her script. Resist the temptation to tell or hint to other people what's best for them. Interrupt yourself every time you start to think about how you'd like someone else to change and ask, "What do I need to do for me?" or "What do I want them to do that I really need to do for myself?" Often the way you want them to change is a mirror of what you really want for yourself but think you don't deserve.

For a week stop yourself every time you start to give advice, make "helpful" suggestions to others, or ask leading questions. Or every time you give advice write in a notebook how you were feeling. When I suggested to one woman that she give or take no advice for a week she laughed and said, "I won't have much to say." And she was right. It was difficult at first but she persevered. A few weeks later she said she was learning a lot about herself by being quiet. For the codependent woman, giving and receiving advice prevents intimacy because it places one person in a role of superiority or inferiority. (I'm not saying that giving and receiving advice can't be useful in some situations. I appreciate my friends setting me straight if I'm getting in a rocky place. It is different, however, for the codependent, who uses advice as a way of life.)

5. *Don't make "fix it" statements.*

Codependents often attempt to smooth things over when people are upset. They quash other people's anger and expressions of strong feelings because they are afraid of their own. Let people be upset. When I have just pulled a muscle or broken a favorite dish or received bad news, I want to be upset for a few minutes. When someone nervously rushes in, saying, "Oh, it's not important, everything will be all right, calm down," I feel angrier. What I want to hear is, "Oh, that's a bummer. You're upset." In other words, I want to be understood and accepted just as I am. I don't want to be changed or fixed. There's nothing wrong with being upset for a moment.

The same is true when people are sad. The codependent tries to hush others' sadness in order to quell her own inner sadness. Her typical response is "It's all right. Don't be sad." Again, she is not truly responding to the other person, who may be feeling release through having a good cry and just wants to be held or acknowledged. You don't have to do much when someone is hurting. You can just say, "Oh, you hurt, you're sad," and comfort or hold the person. If this is difficult for you, practice imagining someone being sad. Take a deep breath and say, "She's just being sad. It's natural to be sad sometimes."

6. *Let yourself have a good gripe session.*

Stomp around and complain about everything you don't like in your life. Soft-spoken Katie continually minimized her problems. At one point she quietly said to the group that she had had a bad day. I said, "Tell us about it. Let it rip."

She responded, "But I don't want to be a baby and whine."

"What's wrong with being a baby?" I asked. "We all feel like babies sometimes. How about trying five minutes of whining and complaining and see how it feels?" She did, and it was really not whining at all. Her voice got increasingly powerful as she sounded off about some difficult situations. When she was done, she broke into a big grin and said, bemused, "This feels good."

Spouting off sometimes is an affirmation of yourself, your life, and what's going on inside. It gets the energy flowing. I enjoyed the speaker who opened a Women in Psychology workshop by saying, "This talk is on physical fitness. The first important thing women should do is have more fits."

The second thing is to let someone see your anger. Codependent people are always telling you about the feelings they had yesterday. One way to bond with people is to be real with them. Don't call a friend in the afternoon and calmly say, "I was upset this morning because I lost my job." Call in the morning when the bad news arrives and let your anger and pain show. One time when I received such an after-the-fact call, I asked the person, "Why didn't you call me this morning when you were upset?" Her response belied her shame of strong feelings. "I wanted to get myself together before I talked with anyone." It is difficult to empathize and give support to someone who is cool and all together.

7. *Stop telling stories that could be titled "What He (She) Did to Me."*
This keeps you in a victim role. Women often tell lengthy stories about what others did to them in an attempt to have friends reinforce their sense of powerlessness. They often tell the story with great surprise even if the person has done the same thing a thousand times. The unspoken goal is to have a friend say, "Yes, he sure is a jerk. Poor you, it's really terrible what you go through." Blaming others creates dense energy and is one of the greatest blocks to recovery. Instead of, "Did you hear what Charlie did to me?" learn to take responsibility for your feelings. "I am angry at Charlie for seeing a prostitute again, and I need some help figuring out what I'm going to do." This statement places you in an active role that leads to change. Simply repeating your charges against your partner will get you nowhere.

You also need to stop listening to your friends tell stories of what their partners did to them. This can be difficult because women are taught to be good listeners. When you encourage your friends' constant victim stories you create a victim bond between you which is dense energy for both of you. Codependent women think they have to listen to other people's complaints because it would be rude to interrupt. One rule of thumb is to give support when a friend is looking for a solution or taking action, but to set a limit on the telltale stories after the first or second round. You can say to a friend who does nothing but complain, "I'm willing to support you if you work to find solutions, but I'm not willing to hear you repeatedly say how bad it is."

In *Daughters of Copperwoman*, Anne Cameron describes American Indian women's circles, which are comparable to modern women's support groups. These women had a wonderful way of setting gentle but clear limits when one of their members was stuck in her problem and not doing anything to find a solution.

> A woman would come to the circle as often as she needed, but the circle wasn't there to encourage a woman to only talk about her problems. . . .
> It was expected that besides just talking . . . you'd do something about it. The first three times you came with the same story, the women would listen and try to help. But if you showed up a fourth time, and it was the same old

tired thing, the others in the circle would just get up and move and re-form the circle somewhere else. They didn't say the problem wasn't important, they just said, by movin', that it was YOUR problem and it was time *you* did somethin' about it, you'd taken up all the time in other people's lives as was goin' to be given to you, and t'was time to stop talkin' and DO somethin'.

8. *Stop giving reasons for everything you do.*

Stop using the word *because,* except to say "because I feel like it." Codependents tend to feel they have to justify themselves and build a case for what they think or do. You need to learn to say "I want to go to that movie." Period. Not, "I want to see that movie, because it would be good for me" (or "because I read an excellent review," or "because Judy said it was really great"). You don't have to bring in an army of reasons to support your stand. If you want to go, just say so. You've got the right.

Learn to get to the essence of what you want to say. Codependents get lost in detail because they have a difficult time sorting out the essence of a situation. This makes it difficult for your listener to hear what you are saying, and you can get confused yourself. For many women such behavior stems from growing up in a family where no one listened. Thus long-winded explanations sometimes have the desperate quality of a child trying to be heard but not believing she will be.

Codependent women often talk from their guts for a second and then jump outside themselves and explain or comment on what they've just said or how they said it. A strong statement is immediately diluted by remarks like, "Oh gee, now I'm afraid of . . . or the reason I said this is . . ." I call this the Greek chorus syndrome. The chorus stands just offstage and comments on what is taking place. It can be tedious in conversation. When women do this in therapy groups, people start tuning out. They long for a period to the sentence, for the speakers to take a breath and simply say what is true for them. It takes a lot of work to sort through all the extraneous information the codependent woman uses to justify her feelings and actions.

Here is an example of the long version of a codependent explanation. See if you can identify the Greek chorus parts.

"I called my mother. You see, it was the day before her birthday and I thought she might be feeling lonely. I called about three-thirty because she sometimes naps. I asked about her birthday plans. I haven't called her in a long time because I'm trying to be more independent from her. When she answered I asked her about the plans for her birthday. She said my brother thinks we should all go out to lunch. That's because he has a restaurant and he hoped we would all go there so he wouldn't have to be away from work too long. My sister wants to go to her house in the evening so she can have her children there. I finally said to my mother,

'Well, I would rather have dinner than lunch. That's because I have a meeting at work at one-thirty and I would have to rush to get back and the traffic can be bad at that time.' So then my mother said I should call my brother and work it out with him. I said, 'Why didn't she figure it out? It's her birthday.' "

This is the kind of dialogue codependents replay in their heads. The excess baggage keeps them from getting to the point and to their feelings. It has the effect of pushing away people, who don't want to spend the effort to sift through the verbiage.

Leaving out the excess explanations, which often start with "because," we could reduce the above to a much more straightforward statement: "I called my mother to ask about her birthday plans. My brother wants to go out to lunch and my sister wants to have dinner. When I said I'd prefer dinner, my mother suggested I call my brother and work it out with him. I thought my mother should just say what she wants."

Distilling it even further, leaving out all irrelevant content and adding feelings, gets to the essence: "I called my mother about her birthday. Our family can't seem to agree on plans because different members of the family want it at different places at different times. I'm feeling confused and upset about what to do."

This kind of statement has power and will hold listeners. The original version will put them to sleep.

9. *Stop making excuses for others or rationalizing situations.*

This behavior can take different forms. Here is a typical scene in a therapy group.

Jane says, "I'm so unhappy with how my friend is acting toward me. She isn't calling, and I'm very upset."

Lana responds, "Well, maybe your friend is having a hard time. I'm sure she really cares about you." Instead of responding to Jane's feelings, Lana tries to make excuses for the friend. This kind of response conveys a superior attitude and creates distance from Jane.

Jane's energy drops and she responds listlessly, "Yeah, I guess."

The group works to help her say instead, "That's not a helpful response. I want you to understand I'm feeling upset. I need help finding a solution."

Codependents tend to interrupt other people — and themselves — just as they are about to find solutions or move into their feelings. If you have the urge to change the subject when someone is upset or sad, stop and ask yourself, "Am I on track with that person, or am I just afraid of feelings and conflict? Am I turning the focus to me or keeping it on the one who's upset?" It is a gift to people to be with them right where they are at.

Codependent women often relate how their partners abused them and then give a litany of excuses for the partner. Listeners are drawn in to be sympathetic, and then their sympathy is discounted. The conversation usually goes like this:

CHRISTIE: My husband was screaming at me again. Et cetera.
JANE: Oh, that sounds really awful.
CHRISTIE: Yeah, and you know what else he did. Et cetera.
JANE: That must be hard. Did you say anything to him?
CHRISTIE: Well, it's really not so bad. You know he has a hard time at work.

The codependent rationalizes for two — herself and her partner. The sober approach would be to state her gut-level response to her partner's behavior. Instead of making excuses for her partner, Christie needs to learn to say "I don't like it when Jack gets so short-tempered and yells at me. I'm going to start walking out of the room when he does that."

10. *Take your emotional temperature after visiting various people in your life.*

After you spend time with someone take a density-to-light reading. On a scale of one to ten, density to light, how do you feel before and after? Become aware of what brings light feelings into your life and what brings dense feelings. Write them down and keep a journal. This can be with statements such as, I feel _____ when I spend time with _____. Or I feel _____ when I _____. List the lightness score along with the feeling.

11. *Learn when to talk and when not to talk.*

People who have had a lot of therapy or been through treatment often think they should discuss everything with their partners. I believe there are times to talk about something and times to be quiet. One way to determine this is to stop and ask yourself, "If I say X, is it likely to lead to a blowout or a heavy conversation where we'll both feel worse as a result?" Talking endlessly about "the relationship" can be a defense, a way of not taking responsibility to go inside yourself and discover your true feelings. Part of achieving harmony in a relationship is knowing when to talk and when not to. In general, when people get clear for themselves and speak the truth, most conversations are quite brief.

As I arrived for dinner at the home of a Quaker couple who had just had an argument, Leah greeted me at the door asking for a hug and said, "Jim and I just had a terrible fight. We're kind of upset." She smiled and went on, "I don't want to upset you, we'll get over it, but things are kind of tense for the moment." She gave me a brief explanation of what had happened, then asked how my life was going.

I went into the kitchen with her. When Jim came in, he said, in his charming, boyish way, "Did Leah tell you we just had a terrible fight? I came in from working on the roof and got real angry." They didn't offer much more, and it didn't feel right to ask questions. I was impressed by the way they simply let me know what was going on without making it a tragedy. No massive explanations, no shame, no hiding the conflict, no blame, no rationalizations.

We proceeded to have dinner. Afterward, Leah suggested that we sit together in silence, as people do in a Quaker meeting so they can listen within. About ten minutes into the silence, Jim said, "I was having a hard time fixing the roof, and I was feeling really bad that I didn't get the scholarship I applied for. I took my anger out on you, Leah." After five more minutes of silence, Leah said, "I was upset that it took you so long to finally get to fixing the roof and wishing you had started sooner. I hadn't let you know that. Instead of saying, 'I'm glad you're getting to it,' I put you down." After another five minutes, we reached for one another's hands and gave the familiar squeeze signifying the end of the silence at a meeting. Leah and Jim got up and hugged each other, then they both hugged me. The air was completely cleared.

I have suggested this process to many people. Most fights start with one little thing, then each person hauls out the whole artillery of old grievances and World War III begins. Sitting in silence and reaching for one's inner truths saves time and hurt feelings.

12. *Don't give gifts you can't afford.*

Codependent women are in the habit of doing things for people out of guilt, or to control them by making them feel indebted. There are some fine lines to draw here. For example, let's say you are trying to build a support system. You start by calling a new woman acquaintance to have tea and take a walk. If you do this in a spirit of exploration and hope that you will make a friend, that's fine. If, however, you say to yourself, "I called her four times; she should call me back; she's not being fair," your calling her the third time was a gift you couldn't afford. Before you make a move, ask yourself *inside*, "Can I give this time, money, energy, present, free and clear, with no strings attached, and no demands of reciprocity?" If the answer is yes, go ahead. If you start thinking of what the recipient will owe you, stop. The gift would be more like a bribe, and you will be better off not giving it. If you do want to have an exchange with someone, suggest it openly. "How about I cook dinner on Wednesday and you cook on Saturday?" Or ask directly why that person isn't calling you.

13. *Change the question "Will they like me?" to "Will I like them?"*

Most codependents walk into a party or gathering trembling and thinking, "Will anyone like me? Do I look all right?" This puts a person in a victim role. Instead, ask yourself, "Whom would I like to talk to here?" The reality about gatherings is that sometimes you meet people you click with and sometimes you don't, and it's really no big deal.

14. *Learn to keep your energy inside.*

Codependent women may feel their energy spill out of them when another person walks into the room or spends an evening with them. I call it an acute codependency attack. I remember sitting with a friend, watching a tennis match, when suddenly my mind was jumping with worries about her liking me. "Am I talking too much? Does she really like me? Does she really want to be here with me?" Totally focused on her, I felt terribly anxious. Some people clam up when this happens, others tend to babble. I took some deep breaths and tried to imagine all my feelings and energy going back in my body. I imagined golden light around me holding them in. For good measure I imagined a Plexiglas wall between us. I focused on my breathing and said to myself, "She will like me or she won't. It's no big deal one way or another. All I can do is be myself." In a few minutes I felt more relaxed, and my self-esteem was no longer tied to her liking me.

15. *Pay attention to behavior, not words.*

Codependent women are easily seduced by words. But talk is cheap; behavior is the true measure of a person. Addicted individuals, to whom codependents are attracted, know just the right words to make you think you are cared about. They come on strong, want to be sexual immediately, are jealous of your friends, shower you with gifts, present themselves as being "all together," and have sudden, inexplicable mood changes. Watch out for these red flags. I urge recovering codependent women to make a red-flag list entitled "Ways I Get Seduced." Scan past relationships and try to remember the fleeting thoughts of danger you submerged, the warning signs you ignored. Include your internal responses. Did you start feeling young or acting cutesie around the person? Were you afraid to speak the truth? Did you turn to mush or violate your values to please the person? Use this list for future reference and as a reminder when you find yourself slipping.

16. *Learn to walk through fear.*

Codependent women say they can't do something hard because they are afraid. Who isn't? Ask yourself what the fear is really about. Remember, too, that you can do things even though you are afraid.

Many codependent women find that fear of asserting themselves harks back to childhood fears of abandonment and abuse. It is important to say "That was then, this is now. I am not a powerless child. I can make choices. My parents abandoned me, but that doesn't mean everyone else will. My parents betrayed me, but I don't have to betray myself." Paralyzing fear usually stems from handing our self-esteem over to other people or thinking a situation is do-or-die.

It is a paradox that codependent women aren't afraid to live with abusive partners, yet they experience terrible fear in opening their own checking accounts or stating their opinions. We all feel fear. Sometimes it is a signal to be careful. If you are treading close to another's addiction, he or she may well blow up when you raise the subject.

17. *Accept that being human is messy.*

Most codependent women want everything to be clean, clear, and under control. No sloppy feelings, no getting upset. A woman in a therapy group was postponing getting a divorce. When a member asked her why she was waiting, she said, "I want to have everything worked out so it will go easily. I want to get rid of all this rage first." The group laughed. That's like saying you can prepare for your beloved's death so you won't feel sad. Divorce is messy; people have big feelings, and that's okay. The group urged the woman to accept her rage for a week. Whenever she was tempted to say "I should get over this anger," she said instead, "I accept myself feeling angry. In fact, I'm angry about _____."

18. *Stomachaches usually signify anger.*

If you are talking about someone or an event and your stomach suddenly hurts, it is usually anger churning up. The impulse is usually to double up. Do just the opposite. Stand erect and breathe into the feelings. Stomp and swing your arms. Sometimes I ask, "Who are you sick of? Who do you want to throw up on?" Imagine moving the energy up from your stomach into your throat and out into words. Sometimes it helps to put your hand on your stomach and imagine breathing the feelings up.

19. *Protect yourself.*

When codependent women are being harmed or attacked they tend to want to analyze the situation rather than take cover. To illustrate the point, I often ask clients, "If you are standing under a window and someone starts to dump garbage on top of your head, what do you do?" There is often a long pause. Many women reply tentatively, "Ask them to stop?" instead of the appropriate response, which is, "You get out of the way. You move." Who cares *why* when you're getting covered with garbage.

Codependent women find it difficult to protect themselves when it might upset their partners, particularly when the partner is threatening or dangerous. They need to learn a balance between showing respect and concern for others and showing respect and concern for themselves.

Dorothy came to group therapy saying she was ready to tell her husband she wanted a divorce. They had separated for several months and she knew that the marriage was beyond repair. She said she was going to tell her husband on the following Tuesday when he would be at her home taking care of their child. She also planned to set up a therapy session for the next day because she was afraid of his reaction.

Members of the group asked what she meant by "afraid." Dorothy said he could get emotionally violent, he might not leave, he might keep pressing her for reasons. Because he had displayed evidence of his rage in the past, the women expressed concern for her and suggested that for protection that night she have a friend or neighbor drop in or call at ten o'clock. Then someone asked, "Why are you telling him face to face if you are so afraid of him?"

"I feel I owe him that," Dorothy said.

"What about you?" someone else asked. "What do you owe yourself?"

"That's right," she said. "I'm thinking only of his feelings and not about mine."

I commented that it was goodhearted of her to consider him, and it is often respectful to discuss important matters face to face, but when there is a risk of danger, the need to protect oneself takes priority. "Just think only of yourself for a moment. What would be the most comfortable way for you to tell him?" I asked.

Dorothy's body visibly relaxed, as if someone had given her permission not to jump into a bramble bush. "What would I like?" she said, pausing to think. "I'd like to phone him and hang up if he starts getting abusive."

"Well, you get to do that," I said.

Dorothy grinned. The group cheered.

I had the feeling that a gong had gone off in her head and she could now carry out her difficult task in a way that was simple and protective of herself.

20. *Become powerful rather than being righteous and superior to others.*

The codependent high is being righteous and judging others as wrong, stupid, or jerks. It is tough to give up because this superior stance brings a feeling of power. Women may put down others to hide their shame about being dishonest, dependent, or jealous. Women may feel ashamed of staying with a partner they don't respect for the security he or she provides. If a woman feels ashamed of her power, and fears rejection for being strong, she may be hostile to women who are successful, powerful, or independent. When you feel righteous, jealous, or want to prove someone else wrong, ask yourself, "What's really true? Am I jealous? Am I afraid I could never be on my own?" To confront these truths and give up being righteous is to get to the core of codependency.

REGARDING SEXUALITY

1. *Stop faking orgasm.*

I know many women who have faked orgasm with their husbands for years and years. To lie is to wound your own soul and the relationship. Actually, it is not much of a relationship if you feel the need to lie. You don't have to make a grand announcement that you've never had an orgasm, although you may feel the need to do so. You could just stop faking it and say during sex, "I haven't come yet. Would you do this a while longer?" You have to find your own approach to the situation. You might want to have a joint therapy session and talk about it there, along with your whole relationship. Whatever you do, think it out until you arrive at the approach that clearly feels best for you.

2. Stop faking enjoyment of sex in general.

Everything in the guidelines above applies. You can change the process gradually by suggesting little things when you are sexual. Or you can say you have been thinking about your sexual relationship. You can say you'd like to take more time, do massage first, or have more eye contact during sex. You might tell your partner you have not always been honest about your response and want to work together on it. Your partner may take your words as an attack on his or her ego and sexual performance. But hang in there. No one ever said the path was easy. You can't keep faking it if you want peace of mind.

3. Stop being sexual when you don't want to be.

Having sex when you don't want to is to a sexual codependent what taking a drink is to an alcoholic. Tell yourself over and over, "I don't have to be sexual if I don't feel like it. My body is mine." You have to be able to say no before you can say yes and mean it. Many codependent women have said, "I don't care if I'm ever sexual again" or "I just put up with having sex so we can get to the good part, the hugging and cuddling." You don't have to pay for hugging and cuddling with sex. It is a violation of your body and spirit. Again, saying, "No, not now" or "No, later" or "No, but I'll tell you when I feel like it" may be terrifying. Some common rationalizations to continue the deceit are: "But he'll get mad"; "It will hurt his feelings"; "He'll feel threatened"; "She won't like it." Note who is being left out. What about *your* feelings, *your* soul?

Honesty is the food of a caring relationship and self-esteem. Faking one of the most intimate aspects of a bond with another person poisons the relationship. You are likely to feel resentment. When a woman says, "He never gave me any pleasure," I ask if she has ever said anything to him. The response is usually no. Women fear that if they ask, their partner won't respond or take them seriously. This may be hard to face, but remember, recovery means a willingness to know what is true and to face up to it, come what may. There is nothing to lose by bringing this up. Your partner may have the reactions you fear, but may instead be glad that you opened the door to talk. In either case, nothing is worse than living in the middle of a lie.

4. *Ask your partner to talk about your sexual relationship.*

Take time to think over how you feel about your sexual life with your partner, then sit down and talk! You may first want to talk to friends or women in a support group. Start telling the truth about how you feel. Are you dissatisfied? Do you feel he or she is insensitive to you? Are you having sex because you are afraid he or she will be mad at you if you don't? Do you have sex out of duty? Do you feel your sex life is lifeless? Start talking. Keep talking. If you are afraid to talk alone with your partner, ask him or her to accompany you to a counselor. You may want to go alone a few times to get the issues clear for yourself, although thinking that everything must be totally clear is another codependent trap. It's fine just to say you are confused about your sex life, that you don't know quite what you feel, but you know you are dissatisfied.

5. *Make love to your body.*

Do self-massage, masturbate, get involved in some form of exercise, aerobics, or yoga. Take an hour to enjoy a bubble bath to music, and get to know your body. Pleasure yourself all over. How can you tell another person what you like sexually if you don't know yourself? Masturbation will help develop your sensuality and sexuality so it will be too precious to trade or give away.

CODEPENDENT SOBRIETY IN RELATIONSHIPS

1. *Let relationships find their own level.*

Codependent women typically put much more energy into relationships than their friends or partners do, which leaves them exhausted, irritated, and feeling ripped off. And because they usually repress the anger that comes from giving much more than they get, they get depressed.

Sometimes a woman is so excited about finding a friend that she initiates nine out of their ten get-togethers. If you tend to do this, one rule of thumb is to let the relationship find its own level by not putting out more energy than you receive: don't call more than you are called; don't spend more money on friends than they do on you; don't listen to them more than they listen to you; if you initiate one event, wait for your friend to initiate the next. It may be weeks or months, or not at all, but you will find the true energy level of the relationship. Not all your friendships will work out, but the relationships you form will be equal, honest, and satisfying. You won't have to wonder if your friends really care and feel angry because you are doing too much.

I know this "keeping score" approach may sound petty, and it is not necessary in a healthy reciprocal relationship. But a codependent woman needs this kind of mechanism to get past her tendency to give too much and not know who her true friends are.

2. *Anything besides yes means no.*

Addicted people are masters at keeping relationships vague. They want relationships with the least emotional cost — that's why they choose codependent partners. They lead their partners to believe they are involved without making a commitment. They never quite say yes, but sustain the relationship with muddy maybes. A codependent tends to grab at the 5 percent of the addict's behavior that indicates he or she cares, and ignore the 95 percent that demonstrates indifference.

As a result you feel a churning in your gut wondering if the addict means what he is saying. A typical addict trait is to allude to a future time together, then rescind the offer when he becomes afraid. He may even deny having made the offer. When Charlie says, "We really should take a vacation this summer" and you don't believe him, voice your uneasiness. "I don't quite trust what you are saying, you sound rather vague. Do you really mean it?" If he says, "Sure," press for a time and place. As a codependent, pay careful attention to the energy of the response. Does he say, "Absolutely. I've talked to my supervisor at work and I can leave by three P.M. on Friday" — a high-energy response — or "Well, I have a lot of work to do. I don't know exactly when we can leave; they might have a meeting Saturday morning, but I *want* to go." If he starts to back off or tells you not to be pushy, it was a bogus offer. Forget it and plan your own vacation. Don't sit around waiting. Remember, when the addict says, "I want to," it is often an expression of avoidance. Commitment phrases are "Yes, I will," "Let's set a date," "I'll start making arrangements." Anything muddy or low-energy means no. So don't set yourself up by expecting the addict to come through.

People who want to keep you on the hook will let you think they are saying yes without really saying yes. Codependents are afraid to press for a clear answer because they subconsciously know the answer and don't want to hear it. They would have to face the truth, possibly have a fight, and hear that the addict is not committed or truly involved. It sometimes helps to remember that if you give up an unsatisfying relationship or friendship, you will have more energy to find one that feels better.

3. *Define relationships.*

After an initial getting-acquainted process, or if a relationship is murky and you are getting the runaround, press to define the relationship. Addicts sidestep this issue and want to keep things foggy. It is important to define for yourself what you want. If you ask your partner to define the relationship first, you put yourself in a victim role. You become powerful and raise self-esteem by taking the lead.

Once you have leveled with yourself about what you really want — I suggest you write it down — ask your partner to define the relationship. What is his or her commitment? Is the relationship monogamous? Is he or she willing to consider living together, to get married? What is the level of involvement? Getting together once a week? More? Less? Does he or she have a significant other or an on-again, off-again relationship lurking in the background?

You don't have to define a relationship all at once, but it is important to define it over time. Addicts flee from clear definition and commitment. If the person is not interested in the kind of relationship you want, don't try to get him or her to want it your way, unless, of course, you want a lot of grief, depression, and frustration.

ERRONEOUS ASSUMPTIONS

Codependent women make numerous erroneous assumptions that are part of the operational beliefs that promote codependency.

Erroneous: Feeling guilty for saying no means you made a mistake.

True: Guilt is a withdrawal symptom of codependency; you will inevitably feel guilty for saying no and setting limits.

People tell me that this is one of the most important things they learn in therapy. When a codependent woman says, "No, I won't come to your birthday party"; "No, I won't drive you to the airport"; "No, I don't have time to talk now"; "No, I don't want you to call more than once a week," she feels incredibly guilty. After all, women were made to give, give, give, and guilt is a withdrawal symptom. One must simply live through it for a while. *No* is a beautiful word for codependents.

Many women think that because they feel guilty for saying no or expressing anger, they must have done the wrong thing. Withdrawal from codependency, refusing to play the caretaker's role, may be the most painful type of withdrawal I have ever witnessed. When a woman sets limits and boundaries, she often feels selfish, bad, mean, unlovable, and disloyal because she was raised to believe she was these things if she didn't sacrifice her needs for others'. She fears loss of love or abandonment simply for being a whole, self-respecting human being.

Saying no is the prerequisite for learning to say yes. If you say, "No, I don't want to be sexual now," you can discover your own longing for a caring physical bond. After asserting yourself you will probably feel a sense of relief, along with the guilt, for a couple of days. Call friends, go to the movies, stay busy, and accept the guilt as part of the journey toward recovery. You'll live through it. Another survival tactic is to flip the guilt into resentment. "I feel guilty for not calling my mother every day" becomes "I am resentful of my mother for expecting me to be her best friend and take care of her all the time." Eventually you'll want to get past the resentments, but in the beginning they help you feel your anger, which helps you keep boundaries.

Erroneous: The truth hurts people.

True: The truth heals.

Nearly every time a woman asks her parents to come in for therapy to clear the air about childhood events, a codependent sister or brother will write her and say she is being cruel, unkind, and selfish to want to hurt their parents. Such people interpret talking honestly and having feelings as hurting others. In truth, if it is motivated by a desire to let go of the past, talking has a high potential for clearing the air and resolving old misunderstandings and hurts. Elisabeth Kübler-Ross, in her writings on death and dying, stresses that resolving unfinished business, old conflicts, and hurts allows people to die in peace and eases the grieving process for the survivors. It would be nice if we didn't have to wait until people are on their deathbeds to have the courage to talk about our anger, our hurt, and our love.

Erroneous: Stirring up feelings is dangerous.

True: Feelings are natural and can help you feel alive.

Codependent people have learned that feelings are dangerous. In their original families, feelings were usually either buried or out of control, leaving them with the belief that anger equals violence, and sadness equals unending depression. Thus, having feelings equals shame. They think that if they get upset or someone is mad at them, they are bad. This results in victim responses to feedback or suggestion such as, "You are picking on me"; "You don't like me"; "I must have done something wrong," all of which block useful dialogue.

Learning to work through conflict depends on learning to hear other people express their feelings without interpreting them to mean that something about you is bad or wrong. Feelings need not imply blame or shame; they are just expressions of how people see things. When you start getting upset by someone's remarks, say to yourself, "Whatever anyone says means nothing about me! I can simply listen and try to understand."

Feelings don't kill and they don't injure people if shared appropriately. It is one thing to hurl feelings around at anyone who happens to walk by, and another to attach feelings to specific events and say in a nonblaming way, "I felt hurt when you _____" or "I felt angry when you _____." Anger is not the same as rage or wrath, which usually means dumping pent-up hostility on someone who doesn't deserve it. Anger is an important emotion for codependents to identify. It can signal that you have been violated.

Family therapy sessions in which battering, incest, neglect, and abuse are discussed need to be approached in the spirit of love and concern for all involved. This can pave the way for inner resolutions and often improved relationships and understanding. Family members may discover that some wounds stem from misunderstandings: "Oh, I thought you hated me." "No, I was just afraid." Resolution does not always lead to reconciliation, however. Sometimes people feel continued involvement with their families is harmful, but at least they know they've spoken the truth and leave the session feeling clearer about their family situation. This helps them move on and let go. There are times, of course, when even talking to a family member is futile and could be dangerous, though this is by far the exception rather than the rule.

Erroneous: "But I *have* to see my family. I owe them something."

True: You have a *choice* about seeing your family. Respecting them doesn't mean you have to allow yourself to be hurt by them.

Codependent women are often terribly tied to their families. While I believe that you owe your parents respect, you also owe yourself respect. If you want to recover, you need to protect yourself from an abusive family. When a codependent woman visits her abusive family before she has the strength to handle the situation, she comes back upset, depressed, doubting her reality, and feeling guilty. It can take her weeks to recover.

As you recover from codependency, you may be able to spend a little clearly defined time with family members without trying to change them. In the meantime, if you visit your parents or other family members, pay attention to how you feel when you are with them. Also, be aware of your agenda to change them. Are you still thinking you might at last have a wonderful, close time with them, even though that hasn't ever happened before? What do you really feel when you talk with them?

When people are about to visit a dysfunctional family, I suggest they do four things. The first is to say to themselves in advance, "The truth is, my father/mother/brother will probably put me down, shame me, ask nosy questions, ask, 'Have you got a husband yet?' whatever. That's the way they are. My mother is being my mother. She is running off her programming. My father is being my father. He is running off his programming. I can totally expect them to _____." This keeps you from hoping for the happy family scene that won't happen. And, when you react by blowing up or getting wimpy, don't forget to say "I am being myself, I am running off my programming."

Second, I advise people to go as observers, to watch the whole scene like a soap opera. One woman jokingly called this "Put your money in the slot and watch the show." Be aware of how everyone, including yourself, interacts. Do they change the subject, talk about others, make shaming statements? How do you act with them, and how do you feel around them? Do you start trying to convince them to change their politics? Do you get whiny, pleasing, rageful?

My third piece of advice is to take along phone numbers of recovering friends or make arrangements to visit or stay with other friends if worse comes to worst.

Fourth, I suggest attending a local Al-Anon or Adult Children of Alcoholics (ACOA) or other twelve-step meeting if necessary. If you are losing control or getting depressed, the kindness of like-minded people committed to recovery will help validate your reality — you're not crazy — and help you relax and be less reactive to the situation.

If a person keeps going home and comes back to therapy with "what my mother did to me" stories, my response is usually, "Are you surprised? If you had a hundred bucks to bet on your family's being suddenly loving and kind, what would you bet? It's good to seek love, but how about going to a well that has water in it?" Those who get angry at me for saying these things still believe their families will change and are not quite ready to give up hoping for the happy family scene. But once you accept the fact that your family will not change, you are free to form relationships with all the other people in the world. If your primary emotional bond is to a parent, you will have difficulty forming a primary peer relationship.

Erroneous: Being called a bitch is bad.

True: People may call you a bitch when you start to take care of yourself instead of devoting your energy to them.

When women become powerful, they step outside their assigned cultural role, and society may attempt to put them back in that role by accusing them of being pushy, selfish, self-centered, a dyke, or bitchy. So if someone calls you a bitch when you start asserting yourself, say thank you.

■

Erroneous: The expert knows what's best.

True: You're the expert. Don't take any suggestions, including these, too seriously.

If some of them fit, take them as guidelines, not as rigid rules. Remember that you are the expert on your life. No one can tell you what's true for you. Different situations require different solutions. Codependent women can go through life looking for the all-knowing one, and many predatory, addicted people are more than willing to play the part. Wouldn't we all like to find the all-wise and all-knowing teacher who could give us the answers? How easy that would be, but also, how dull. If we enter situations with a sense of excitement and interest rather than with fear or preconceived notions of how everything should be, we learn and grow. If we go into situations with a script for how everyone should act, we don't see the gifts we are given because we are so busy keeping score and being hurt and angry when people don't say the lines we've written for them. If you have an agenda, let it be known. "I want you to tell me how wonderful I look tonight and listen to me tell about my recent success."

While preparing to write this book, seeking to gain the confidence that I could do it, I repeatedly dreamed that I was about to be in a play but no one would give me a script. I felt tremendous panic. My need for control — a script — betrayed my lack of faith in the process of learning as we go. I wanted promises. As I surrendered to faith, a belief that the wisdom would come and I would be guided in my endeavor, my dreams changed. I stopped feeling panic. More and more I dreamed that I was walking in a beautiful forest with a pretty black-haired woman who signified my higher power. In one dream, when we got hungry, a kiosk appeared, serving chicken soup with a bright orange carrot in it. After that I knew that whatever I needed would come.

Codependency involves a tremendous need to control external events and people because one feels so little control from within. Codependent women have to take the inward journey to the chaos and fear inside them, knowing that if they persevere the process will surely take them to their love and power. When you first let loose your anger, it may come out messy. We don't do things perfectly the first time. Remember Emily, who loyally cooked dinner for her husband long after they had decided to divorce. She stuck with therapy for three years. Sometimes she'd hold in her anger, other times she'd jab people with it. Once she told the group of an event that had just taken place.

"I bumped into the woman who had fired me from my job last year. I walked up to her straight on and said, 'I need to say something to you.' The woman looked real scared but I went right on. 'When you fired me, you lied to me and I don't like to be lied to.' The other woman made a lot of excuses about being new in management, but I just said again, 'You lied to me and I didn't like it. You knew they had to let staff go and you made me look like I'd done something wrong. But I hadn't. You lied and I didn't like it.' The woman then said, 'I'm sorry, I was wrong.' "

Emily's demeanor and her words were in concert — strong, powerful, but not abusive. The group cheered for her. Emily grinned from ear to ear and said, "It felt good. It felt really good."

CHAPTER 18

On the Path of Recovery:
Where Are They Now?

I HAVE always loved "where are they now" stories — the governor becomes a cab driver; the former juvenile delinquent works for social reform. For this chapter I re-interviewed many of the women I have mentioned.

Since our first meetings, over three years ago, I have been in touch regularly with Anita and Gerri. Anita and I talk on the phone every now and then, and Gerri has become a particularly special person in my life. Recently I spent an evening with Anita, Claudia (Miss State), and Kelly at a surprise birthday party for Gerri I organized at the restaurant where she had her twelfth-step call. I arranged for Gerri to arrive first and have the other women "happen" to drop by, so we wouldn't overwhelm her. We sat at a beautiful old oak table, in a room filled with plants and nostalgic signs. As the group formed, we became engrossed in catching up on one another's lives. There was a sense of excitement in just being together.

Later, Kelly produced a small carrot cake with a few candles. With tears in her eyes, Gerri said, "This is so special. I've never had a birthday party with cake and candles and girlfriends. Just having a good time with girlfriends," she repeated quietly, and started to cry.

"Really? The first time?" I asked in amazement. My heart ached. I, too, felt close to tears as I reached over and put my arm around her. It had felt like such a tiny thing, to invite these women to supper and to have a little cake in a modest restaurant. I continue to marvel at Gerri's survival.

The stories that follow highlight a number of themes of recovery that ran through many of the questionnaires and interviews. Repeatedly women voiced their gratitude at gaining control over their chaotic lives and learning to form deeper bonds with others. Many were still in SAA or other twelve-step groups. Others were not. For the women who had become involved in new sexual relationships, the answer to the question "Is sex different?" always brought a similar reply. There would be a burst of energy, a laugh, as in "Are you kidding?" and a struggle to find words to describe the new experience — "totally different," "incredible," yet "not the most important thing."

There were some interesting sidelights with other addictions, notably in the area of weight. Three of the women who had had chronic weight problems lost weight with little effort as they grew more at home with their sexuality and relationships. But I don't want to give away the surprises. Here are their stories.

ANITA: JUST A NORMAL BIKE RIDE IN THE PARK

Whenever I see a man and a woman taking a bike ride together on a sunny day — and I often do on the bike path that runs near my house — I think of Anita. I remember the summer day she called and said with great excitement, "I had a normal date, just a regular bike ride with a guy. I noticed the trees and the sky and the water in the creek. No big thing. We didn't get into talking about sex. I didn't flirt. I didn't think about if we'd get married. We just biked, had coffee, talked about light stuff, and he went home afterwards." While this may be a totally unremarkable experience for many people, for Anita a pleasant bike ride with a man signified a trip from a nightmare of addiction into what had once been the distant never-never land of "normal."

The word *normal* comes up often in conversation with recovering women. As one said, "I never knew what 'normal' was, but I think this is it. I'm just here doing this thing I've seen other people doing. I'm not outside looking in. I'm not different. I'm normal."

If you can imagine always living in a blur, in a bubble that is constantly churning with chaos, then suddenly being released into a calm, pleasant garden with friendly people on a warm sunny day, you will understand what *normal* has meant to many of these women. Abuse survivors often have fantasies of sudden escape, glory, or fame — being taken away from "all this" by rich and loving people or by instant success. Anita, like other women in SAA and CoSA, was finding that place, but it didn't happen suddenly, and it wasn't full of glitter and glory. It was a simple bike ride, a chat, and a cup of coffee with a friend.

Anita has been a wonderful contributor to this book. She came to three group interviews lasting as long as four hours each. When I'd ask her to come to an interview she'd say, "Maybe that would be good for me, but I don't know if I'd have much to say." Then a day or so after the interview she'd call to say, "I'm really having a lot of feelings that came up," and we'd talk for a while. Anita walked through her fear again and again. It was never easy for her. But she did it.

When Anita arrived for her final interview, she told me that we had to finish by three o'clock because she was going to meet her mother to go to a department store sale. I asked about her relationship with her mother.

"It's different," she said with a grin. Anita has a way of talking and then breaking into a slightly self-conscious "Am I doing okay?" smile. Less often than previously, she ends statements with, "You know what I mean?" There is still a small remnant of that child without a language for life, checking to see if she is making sense.

"How is it different with your mother?" I asked.

"Before, if we went shopping together, I'd be thinking, 'If she loves me she'll buy me something.' Now I go more for myself, just to spend a little time with my mother. Of course" — the grin again — "if she wants to buy me something, that's fine, I'll accept it. But, you know what I mean, she doesn't have to. I have enough money of my own."

Sometimes in groups I play with the idea that you do with your money what you do with your love. There are the hoarders and those who throw it away indiscriminately. There are people who con others for it or perform for it. In Anita's family, money and love had been synonymous. To recover Anita had to get past a double bind. If she remained a victim, her parents would give her money/love. If she became financially independent, what would they give her? What would be left of the relationship? In the end, she got past the problem: when Anita said, "I have enough money of my own," she was also saying, "I have enough love of my own. I'm no longer dependent on them."

Since our first interview, and after many attempts, Anita finally ended an addictive relationship with a man. "Leaving Matt was the best thing I've ever done. I started growing after that. After I let go of him I started to feel the grief about my father. I could see how much the two of them were alike."

She then spent a year without dating, and continued attending SAA, AA, and a therapy group for incest survivors. During that time she had a therapy session with her father. She had called me the day before, so scared I felt as though the phone cord was vibrating with her fear.

The next day, Anita called back to say she had done it. She had talked to her father about his pornography and its effect on her. She wasn't sure he understood or felt the impact of what she said, but she had spoken her piece (peace). "I told him, since his first love was pornography and I wanted his love, I acted seductive just like his porn objects."

"Wow! You said that!" I was impressed at Anita's succinct way of putting it all together.

If we can assume for a moment that Anita's dad was addicted to pornography, it makes sense that she was afraid to bring up the subject to him. It's frightening to push on someone's addiction. I still have a sense of dread when I do it with clients. Which of the addicts' defenses will be hurled at me? Will they blow up? Will they shame me? Will they storm out of the room? How will they counterattack? Not everyone does, but it's always a risk. To confront the addiction of someone close to you, as Anita did, is immensely more frightening. It feels as if you are attacking that person's identity and risking the whole relationship. Anita feared that he would discount what she said and never want to see her again. But she was ready to face the possibility.

Her father didn't blow up, but he acted as if he didn't get it either. In response to her talking about the way his pornography had made her feel, he either changed the subject or slipped away. Even so, it was a victory for Anita. She stood up like a grown-up woman and said what was true for her. Her father didn't die, and she didn't either. Afterward, she was able to visit her parents' home, maintaining much more sense of identity and personal power than before. Even though her father appeared not to understand what she had said, something changed. He seemed to notice her more as a person. She refers to the therapy session as a turning point.

"It was like I gave up my little-girl relationship to my dad and with Matt all at once. After that, the fear of being alone, on my own without a man, just faded away. That was when I gave myself permission to succeed."

"Tell me about that."

"Well, as you know, I've bought a little townhouse, I'm working as a freelance typesetter and earning more money. But most of all I feel like there's no way I'm going to stay with a loser or sell myself short over the long haul. I recently started getting seduced by a man who bought me a lot of presents. When I started to feel like he was buying me and I was supposed to pay him back with sex, a part in me said, 'No way.' This voice just went off inside saying, 'You don't need this.' It was so wonderful. It has been a total battle inside me for so long, to feel that I deserve anything, and there it was, this voice going off inside my head saying, 'You deserve better than that.' "

KELLY: STRONG BUT NOT SO TOUGH

Kelly is the woman who appeared so competent when she entered therapy and ultimately let go of her tough role as a lesbian. She spent over three years in one of my weekly survivor therapy groups. When she started, her most pressing goal was to stop being violent in her relationship with her female partner. That opened the Pandora's box to numerous other issues, many surrounding sexuality.

Kelly comes from a well-to-do, professional upper-middle-class, extremely violent family. She was severely beaten throughout her childhood by a tyrannical father and left unprotected by a chronically ill mother. She knew from early adolescence that her father had a sexual relationship with a woman he called his "friend." From ages fifteen to nineteen, Kelly went through a period of indiscriminate sexual acting-out with many men. She used a lot of alcohol during that time and put herself in dangerous situations. She had moved out on her own at age seventeen and supported herself through all the turmoil.

Early in her twenties she identified herself as a lesbian, although she had somehow known much sooner. She was in one brief relationship with a woman before starting her six-year partnership with Madge, a relationship that broke up while she was in the therapy group. When the initial sexual romance wore off with Madge, the relationship turned violent, with Kelly being verbally or physically abusive. They were not sexual during the last three years of the relationship. Kelly was able to stop being violent as she came to realize that her terror whenever her partner withdrew was related to childhood abandonment. For a period of time she worked with affirmations. "I can stand it if Madge withdraws. I won't die if Madge withdraws. I can call a friend. My fear is about when I was a child. I'm not dependent on Madge for my life."

During the last year of therapy, after she left Madge, Kelly's new goal was to give herself permission to be sexual again. The partner didn't have to be the perfect person, and Kelly didn't have to do it perfectly. She had never had a normal teenage exploratory period, and she wanted it. Within several months she had the kind of sexual relationship she wanted, involved but not too involved. In her words, "The time we spend together is sweet, but I am happy to get home to my own place. After being so overly involved, where everything was so heavy and my partner would get jealous any time I saw other people, I need to live separately and keep some distance. Jeanne is here a lot, but it's no big deal to say good-bye and spend time alone. She doesn't get bent out of shape when I want to go to events without her. And I don't do it to hurt her. There are simply some times I want to go on my own or with other people."

I asked her, "Is the sex different?"

"Oh god, yes," she replied. (Kelly said that she prefers a lowercase god.) "I'm present when we're sexual. And so is she. I wouldn't settle for sex any other way. I still hold my breath when I ask for something, but it's always okay, it doesn't get heavy, and we go on. Before, sex was about manipulation or proving your love. I'd always be thinking, 'Will she think I'm good enough?' There's none of that. Also, there's no panic if I lose interest in sex for a few days or a week. Sex is not the indicator of the relationship. It's more about how we can talk and how we can play. One day she woke me up real early and said, 'Let's go skiing in the park.' That's what I like."

When I asked Kelly what had helped her most in learning these skills, she said, "I think I was suffering most from lack of education and lack of parenting around sexual issues. I never heard one positive word about sex growing up. My father's attitude toward sex was a lecherous 'Heh heh,' and my mother's attitude was 'Don't talk about it.' I was in SAA for a while but I didn't connect there very well because I was struggling to let myself be sexual. I think doing the sexual history and reading the book in our therapy group were two of the most important specific steps."

I have people in the therapy group pair up and meet on their own to do an extensive sexual history with each other. Kelly paired up with Ruth. "Ruth and I must have spent ten hours doing the sexual history together. I feel that I talked about *everything*. When we were through there was nothing I hadn't said. It was so wonderful to bond with a heterosexual woman who had a similar teenage history. After we did the history, we talked on the phone many times and she became someone I could talk to about anything."

The book Kelly mentioned, *A Kid's First Book About Sex,* was an example of how she used her wonderful assertiveness for her growth. One day Kelly, the competent one, grinning sheepishly, said to me, "What I need is for you to be my mommy and sit beside me and read a book to me about sex. And I want to be able to ask any stupid question I want without you laughing." Everyone in the group said, "Me too." I agreed to buy the book — moms are supposed to do that — and we spent a couple of sessions on it. Everyone got to play kid, and I played mom. We laughed as everyone talked and asked their secret questions about bodies and sex; tears of sadness also flowed for their having missed so basic and important an experience. (I highly recommend this book because it is about sexuality in a broad sense, not just about "plumbing" and reproduction. It teaches about touch and feelings.)

Kelly finished college, received a teaching certificate, and found a job in a school sympathetic to her values. Prior to that, she quit one of her part-time jobs where she had been scapegoated and harassed. One of the important lessons in recovery is being able to recognize harassment and abuse. So often a women who was abused as a child gets into an abusive work situation that is similar to her family system. As she comes to understand the dysfunctional nature of her family, she also begins to see the dysfunctional nature of her job situation or her work.

Four weeks before Kelly left the therapy group, she read us a list entitled "Then and Now — My Good-bye to Group." She prefaced it by saying, "I know you're supposed to say these things the last week or two, but I'm ready now." This is what she wrote:

This is a list of accomplishments and successes, progress and growth. With many items on the list, there's room for improvement, more to do, and that can be another list, but I am writing this one — all the good stuff — without interrupting myself or qualifying the positive things I have to say.

1. *This journal.* The miracle is not only the quantity of writing but that I kept coming back. It is a record of all I felt like writing in a year — and there are days, weeks, even two-month gaps. In the past I would have started a new book after each of these gaps — which explains why I have a carton full of journals with only ten to fifteen pages written. I always stopped because I did not want to document any of the pain in my life. This journal is a symbol of: I do this for me; I don't have to be perfect; I can pick up where I left off; I can be real; I can love myself — even the old me — if I look back and read something painful.

2. *I have a kind, wise, loving, grown-up woman (mother) inside of me who loves me all through the day.* At first when I came to therapy, I let Charlotte in to nurture me, and I'd hear her voice when I most needed it. She's still there, but now there's my voice, too — the part of me that, honest to god, has my best interest at heart.

3. *I am nice to myself and I still get a lot done!* All week I've been thinking about writing this good-bye list. I knew I had time on the weekend. But on Saturday I just wanted a break — a day to do nothing. On Sunday I couldn't seem to get to it either. Finally, I reminded myself that I had been anticipating this as fun and the way it would be fun would be to make a date with myself for early in the morning when I am most alert. The alarm went off at 6:30 today and when I woke up I put my arms around myself and spoke nicely to me. This is how I start most mornings. Not the old "Get to work you lazy thing." I also remember to eat well and sleep well and take time out to sit and to pray and to rub lotion on my feet. Strangely enough, I am not an ounce less competent or efficient and I have fun doing what I'm doing.

4. *About food.* These days, I eat when I'm hungry and once in a while when I'm scared. I used to eat when I was hungry and when Madge was hungry (togetherness), and when I was angry and when I was bored. And I used to not eat when I was "too busy." This morning, in the middle of writing this list, I felt hungry and looked in the fridge. I didn't see much so I decided to take myself out for breakfast and finish writing this. In the past that would have been an opportunity to deprive myself (Can't eat, gotta get this done). The sum of all of this is that food is fun and my restrictions (no meat, less sugar) are flexible. I have lost a bunch of weight without trying and my favorite summer clothes, that haven't fit for three years, fit again.

5. *I am learning to tell the truth — and that begins with going inside and letting myself know what I feel and what I want.* And I'm learning to wait for that truth to surface. While I'm waiting, I'm learning to be more alert to wrong answers that come from outside of the real me — from Hollywood and my family — and my habit of trying to manipulate other people's reactions.

6. *I am at home inside my body.* I have re-entered my body enough to really notice when I leave for a little while. I think I spend at least 90% of my time in my body. I like it and I'm learning more every day about taking care of my physical needs.

7. *I am at home in the Universe.* It's amazing and it's true. I really feel

that connection (with all beings/life/energy). Even though I keep playing with different languages and images for this, I never lose faith.

8. *I am at home at home.* Perhaps the most miraculous of all — after years of having my home environment controlled by anyone's needs but mine — home is a sanctuary and it's pretty and it's all mine. I'm very happy to let people in to visit and I get to tell them "go home now" if I need to. And the people I spend time with listen.

9. *I am making peace and having fun with my sexuality.* I have made a deliberate decision to give my sexual self attention, to learn what I never learned about sex, to question what I learned from Hollywood and my family and the Catholic Church and to believe that sexuality can be mine.

10. *About babies.* Every time I'm around them, I feel a little less of a panic about their neediness and their out-of-control bodies and how there can't possibly be enough love for me and them. Sometimes I even feel that I love them. And when I see them getting love from someone I am able to think "lucky baby," when I used to just feel rage.

11. *I know how to love and be loved and every day I welcome good things into my life.*

12. *Tangible things that have made a difference:* taking Reiki healing class, working on sexual history with Ruth, three years of Al-Anon, Charlotte's sexuality workshop, three and a half years with this group, four years with my empowerment group, going to the Sexual Violence Center and working on the rape video, finishing a degree, teaching and being good at it, starting a business to help pay the bills, writing a grant to the Women's Fund, and attending a writing workshop.

13. *I have done all of this and I am still a little cynical and a little hyper and that's OK!* I'm still Kelly. I am *more* Kelly than I used to be.

MARSHA: RECOVERY FROM CODEPENDENCY

> *"River Jordan is deep and wide, alleluia.*
> *Milk and honey on the other Side, alleluia."*
> —From "Michael, Row the Boat Ashore"

If ever a woman swam a long cold river in pursuit of her soul, it was Marsha. She didn't start out looking for milk and honey; she jumped into the river because she knew she would die if she stayed on the shore. It was a couple of years after that initial jump before she started to taste the sweetness of recovery. The first two years were sheer survival; it was all she could do just to keep paddling and breathe. Marsha started her journey with virtually no sense of herself as a human being. "I didn't exist as anyone other than a wife, a mistress to my husband, and a mother. I didn't know who I was. Someone asked me once what my favorite color was. I could tell her all of my kids' favorite colors, but I couldn't tell her mine."

Marsha, who was introduced in Chapter 3, lit the fire of her recovery the moment she blurted out to her husband, "Sex with you has felt like getting raped for twenty-five years," and then curled up and withdrew. That was her dive into the river. Marsha told me of a recent conversation about her "breakdown" when she applied for a job. "He asked me about having been in a hospital for depression. I just looked him right in the eye and said, 'Having that breakdown was the best thing that ever happened to me. It got me out of a situation I couldn't control.' He just backed down and went right on with the job interview."

To this day, Marsha does not remember making the statement about feeling raped. When I asked about her recollection of that therapy session she said, "All I remember thinking is 'If this is life I don't want it.' " She remembers only that something happened during the session with her husband, that she could no longer talk, and that when I suggested a hospital depression unit, she felt relief and wanted to go.

When I called to ask what she would like me to say in this final chapter, I found it hard to believe that this lucid, insightful woman with a wonderful sense of humor was the same person who had once thrown up a massive wall of resistance with endless platitudes and biblical quotes. Marsha took refuge in rationalizations such as, "But I've got to be sexual when he asks, the Bible says so," and "But women are meant to do this."

Since the Bible was her turf, I had decided to meet her there. I asked her to think about the spirit of Christianity instead of what she had been taught. One day when we were on the topic I asked her, "What is the spirit of the Gospels?"

"Love," she replied somberly.

"Marsha," I said, "do you believe that you get to have that love for yourself?"

There was a long pause. "Yes, but . . ." It took a few months for the answer to become yes, period.

It was just as difficult for Marsha to cease her endless "what they did to me" stories about her husband, children, and family. My customary response was "I know it's hard, I know it's not the way you want it, but what are you going to do about your situation?" The first year of therapy after her hospital stay was primarily work to reduce her massive depression and help her sort out her marriage. On a depression scale that she filled out weekly, Marsha scored in the "very high" level for nearly six months.

Reading women's books helped her. Anne Wilson Schaef's *Women's Reality* was Marsha's first contact with feminism, and it prompted her to see herself and her depression from a woman's perspective. I gave her an article on women and anger from an early feminist anthology. Whenever she read the book or the article, her depression would drop a few notches. Even so it was tough going helping her to find a support system. She would start a twelve-step CoSA or Al-Anon group, get in a hassle with someone or feel uncomfortable, and leave. She had never had female friends. Marsha had spent her whole life taking care of younger siblings, being sexually abused, then being a good wife and taking care of her husband and five sons.

As we recalled her process of recovery, I asked her about that first year of therapy. She said, "Oh, I was so mad at you. I wanted to quit so many times. I went to my sister one day to talk about Hank [her husband]. She said, 'Why don't you talk to Charlotte about it?'

"I said, 'I don't want to talk to her. I know she'll just say, "What is, is. Hank is just being Hank," and ask what am I going to do about it. I am so sick of hearing that.'

"Then my sister said, 'Well, maybe you ought to start listening to her. You can choose to go forward or you can choose to go back.'

"That really made me mad, but it sunk in. That's when I decided to let you help me."

The sister played a positive role by refusing to align with Marsha's victim side against her therapy. Codependent women frequently seek out someone to take sides with them against a therapist who sets limits, thus fueling their resistance to the hard work of recovery.

Marsha eventually decided to leave her husband. Doing so meant leaving her home and going on welfare. Learning to navigate through a demeaning bureaucracy was a major part of her therapy. She was too depressed to work and had severe back problems, but she managed to get disability coverage that would allow her to continue therapy.

Eventually I suggested that Marsha join a therapy group for survivors of childhood abuse. I was worried that she would be uncomfortable with the women, because all of them had a fairly strong feminist consciousness and three were lesbian. When I told her that there were lesbian women in the group, she choked as she said glibly, "Oh, that's fine."

"So what's the choking about?" I asked.

"Well, I've never known one."

I didn't tell Marsha then that I had also been involved with women, because it didn't feel right at that moment. I knew it would eventually come up in the group anyway. Instead I encouraged her to talk about her stereotypes of lesbian women — evil, sinful, and bad. Later, still terrified of joining the group, Marsha said, "I need a place to talk with other women about the incest, but I'm scared of being with lesbians." I encouraged her to take her time and draw her own conclusions.

Looking back, Marsha says it was a huge awakening for her to see lesbians just as other women with problems similar to her own. "Actually, it helped me because I was brought up to believe that women were slaves who bowed to men no matter what. It was just amazing to see these women who lived without men in their lives."

The bond was sealed one day in group when Angie talked about how her mother had not spoken to her for the eight years since she told her she was lesbian. When Angie's deep sorrow became apparent, Marsha suddenly said strongly, "Well, I think your mother is stupid. I'd love to have you for my daughter." Angie's tears rushed to the surface and Marsha opened her arms to her. Angie crawled into Marsha's arms and wept while Marsha stroked her hair.

As Marsha slowly became part of the group, she learned to call on women for support. She found a couple of friends outside of the group to take walks with. In her second year of therapy her headaches and insomnia began to abate. Near Christmas one year, an incident occurred that was a turning point in helping her recognize her codependency.

Marsha had found a woman who wanted to make Cabbage Patch–type dolls with her to give as Christmas presents. In her eagerness to have a new friend, Marsha had supplied most of the materials, done 80 percent of the work, and given the woman all the prettiest clothes they made, even though the woman had repeatedly asked, "But don't you want me to pay for some of this? Don't you want some of the prettier clothes?"

As Marsha recounted the story, she berated herself for being so stupid. She felt absolutely horrible. I suggested that there was a wonderful lesson to be learned from the doll affair, and she agreed to write a story about it, which she read to us the following week. It was tender, touching, and funny. At times she would interrupt herself to ask "Can you believe I did that?" She included her motives in the story, saying, "I was so lonely, and I wanted a friend so much that I gave her all the pretty clothes." The important measure of her growth was her ability to stand back from her behavior and laugh at her own game and, at the same time, to be tender toward her inner child.

The Cabbage Patch story became symbolic for her, and for the group. On several subsequent occasions, Marsha was able to remember the doll saga, and resist the impulse to give herself away or attempt to buy friendship.

Marsha had no career background when she went back to school for a two-year accounting degree. She was terrified, for she had been called stupid most of her life. When she waltzed into group waving a paper and saying, "Hey look, girls, I got an A in my first course," we all cheered. She was on the dean's list throughout school. Another benchmark was the day she arrived wearing a new pair of blue jeans. "I've just lost twenty pounds. This is my first pair of jeans in ten years!"

Over the three years I worked with Marsha she changed from a weary middle-aged housewife, forty-one going on ninety, to a lively, attractive woman. Her personhood, her humor, and her sparkle emerged like a beautiful flower coming to life.

Then came a highly upsetting jolt. Shaking with anger and crying with frustration, Marsha told us that welfare had changed her mental health coverage and had enrolled her in a group health plan that provided its own counselors. They had allotted her one session in which to terminate from our group.

After a moment of shocked speechlessness, everyone exploded in anger. These women knew what it was to battle through fear and mistrust in order to form the human bonds we had so carefully nurtured. To have that work discounted was extremely painful. Marsha told us that the new health program allowed for seventeen weeks of therapy for survivors of abuse, although one could apply for an extension. Seventeen weeks! What a travesty! Many women barely find the courage to speak during the first seventeen weeks in a survivor group. One week to terminate! I felt the protective rage of a mother bear. Fortunately, Marsha was well along in her recovery by this time, but what about the other Marshas in the world?

She decided to try the other group, and I suggested to Marsha and our members that they determine a reasonable termination period during which she could attend without paying. After we got past our sorrow at losing her, we urged Marsha to go with a positive attitude and get what she could out of the new group. She left after eight weeks. Six months later she called to say that she had graduated from school and landed an accounting job.

When I asked Marsha to identify the milestones in her process of recovery, she said that the first was learning that she was not crazy, that the problems she had had in life, particularly the chronic depression, were a result of her abuse, abandonment, and incest.

"More important," she said emphatically, "I found out that I was not the only one. Until I walked into that therapy group, I felt like the only person in the world who'd been abused like that. Knowing other women who had survived gave me hope. I saw that these women were afraid and they were angry, just like me. The other thing was that it was the first time I ever saw women cheer for each other."

Marsha also explained how important it was for her to be with women who saw her as an individual, separate from her family. Earlier family counseling had focused on her having a problem with sex and put the burden for the family's functioning largely on her shoulders. In fact, Marsha had first been referred to me because of her "sexual problems."

Another enlightening moment occurred when someone in the hospital referred to her as a survivor. "I realized that was right, I am a survivor, I've lived through a lot. I'm strong."

"How is life now?" I asked her.

"I love my life," she said, the joy emanating from a clear, beautiful voice that had once been a whisper. "I'm making a decent salary. I bought a townhouse with my brother. We have totally separate living quarters and just share a garage and a utility room. I've been off welfare for two years, and I have lady friends. We go to the movies, we go shopping, and sometimes we go out to eat together after work. This is totally new for me, just having fun with women. Can you believe, I called up a friend one Saturday morning last fall and said, 'Let's drive over to Wisconsin to see the leaves' — and we did.

There are still things I want to change. Sometimes I have a hard time at work, but," she said, laughing, "whenever I want to change my supervisor or someone else, I hear 'What is, is' going off in my head like an alarm. And most of the time, I just sit down and say to myself, 'I can't change it. I can't do anything about it.' I've also learned to talk to my boss when I feel overwhelmed. I don't just sit alone wondering how I'm going to get all this work done. I say if it is too much.

"I've also learned to trust my gut. The other day I sat down at a lunch counter and a weird man sat down beside me and tried to talk with me. I just got up and moved. Before, I would have stayed there. Either I wouldn't have trusted myself, or I wouldn't have wanted to hurt his feelings."

"What are your thoughts about religion and the church?" I asked.

"Religion is about how you live and what you do. I believe God can hear you wherever you're at. There are the church's rules and the Lord's rules. All the time I was growing up, I would see people going to church and then going home and doing awful things. I would like to find a church that fits for me, but it would have to be very different from what I grew up with."

"And sexuality?"

"I now believe sex doesn't have to be dirty. But for me right now, hugs and good communication are more intimate than sex ever was. Once sex was such a big part of life, now it's such a small part. I don't think I'd ever get married again."

I asked her to say more about how sex had been in her marriage.

"Whatever we did together involved sex. He'd take me to the movies and I'd pay with sex. We were never friends, and we were not partners. Sex always left me feeling empty. Even though I had physical feeling and orgasm sometimes, there was no real pleasure because there was no love and tenderness. But," she added after a pause, "I'm not so mad at him anymore. He didn't know anything and I didn't know anything. And as I look back, I'd bet my bottom dollar he was also abused."

Against tremendous odds, Marsha has created a rich, new life for herself. I remember Kelly's comment after Marsha had left the group. "She really helped me. I've always said, 'My mother was too old to change or leave my father.' But Marsha was over forty, she had five children, and she had to go on welfare to make it out. She has helped me see that everyone has a choice."

In closing our conversation I asked Marsha where she had found strength to keep going. What had helped her to persevere at all cost?

"I don't know exactly, but I found a strength inside I never knew I had. I remember when I got into the hospital and all those people seemed to care about me, I said to myself, 'The Lord gave me a second chance, and I'm going to grab hold and hang on for life!' "

CLAUDIA: "I HAVE TO REMEMBER EVERY DAY THAT I HAVE AN ADDICTION"

Claudia (Miss State) talked about her struggles when she was about to receive her two-year SAA medallion. When I asked if I could include her in the book, she said, "Yes, I think my story's important because I don't want women to get the idea that this is easy, or that they have to have it all together in a couple of years. A lot of women, after a couple of years, sound like everything's okay. Well, for me it isn't. I don't want women to be discouraged by stories of women who seem to get it all so quickly."

Claudia told me that she had been going through a tremendous struggle, the worst since she started recovery. When incest memories started to surface during her therapy, Claudia resumed a destructive sexual relationship that she had been out of for over a year. She also became bulimic again and put on about twenty pounds. "I'll tell you one thing," she said. "For me, when one thing goes, everything goes. When I stayed away from Karen, my weight and bulimia stayed under control. When I went back to her, everything fell apart.

"I get so angry that I have this addiction, that it's so pervasive in my life. It pisses me off that I have to spend so much of my life going to groups and therapy. Last fall I was just sick of working on it and stopped going to SAA and AA. I think that had a lot to do with my relapse. The lesson I've learned is that I'm still an addict and I need to keep going to SAA. It's too easy for me to get into my denial. The bottom line for me is that every day I don't act out is a success. It is still a minute-to-minute, hour-to-hour struggle."

Even though Claudia was telling about a difficult time, she sounded good to me. She was seeing herself clearly, she didn't seem to be beating herself up, and she still seemed hopeful. I mentioned this to her.

"I know what you mean," she said. "I do feel hopeful. I think I started the program thinking I would be celibate for a while and then have the perfect relationship. For me it's not so, and I'm learning to accept that. What's different now is that when I want to act out, I'm not so hard on myself. I keep asking 'Why? What's going on?' "

A large part of her recovery resulted from Claudia's making a dramatic shift in her work as a songwriter and lead singer in a rock band. She left the rock band and began writing a different type of song. She said, "I no longer write rock-and-roll music that has to do with sex and power. Performing that stuff triggered my addiction so much. It could be such a power trip. I could pick up that mike, start singing, and control a whole audience. There would be all these people turned on to me, desiring me. That's not good for me.

"Since then, the quality of the songs I write has totally changed. All my songs are recovery songs. One is the affirmation song — I deserve to love and be loved. All my music is soft, inner, heartfelt music. It's the only kind that feels okay. For a while I thought I could never perform again, but I'm starting to find a new way. I think I have a lot of strength, power, and initiative and I want to translate it into my music. Leaving the rock band was the best thing I could have done. Recovery has become the most important thing in my life."

She continued, "Recovering addicts are different from a lot of people because we face our problems and look at how we don't like our lives. We have a good chance to ultimately be very happy. I thank my Higher Power every day for the gift of recovery and for the strength to face my addictions."

I said to her, "You sound as if you have no doubt you are going to get through all this."

"Absolutely," she said. "I have no doubt."

RENÉE: A FAREWELL TO TWELVE-STEP GROUPS

Renée is the woman who had been outraged when I suggested an SAA group, saying, "No, I won't say I'm a sex addict. Not another addiction, not another thing wrong with me. I'm a compulsive eater on Monday, an alcoholic on Tuesday, and a codependent on Thursday. I won't go to SAA." But, during her recovery process, Renée spent two years in SAA.

She was originally referred to me from a chemical dependency treatment program where, as a college student, she had committed herself for treatment. She originally came for therapy to "work through a rape." As usual, the surface problem masked a multitude of other troubles. Renée had the symptoms of an incest survivor, but none of the memories. However, when she read the list of stages and journal work for that group she said, "These are the questions I need to be asking. This is the group I want to be in."

When she joined it was a real tossup in my mind whether or not she would stay. She was scared beyond scared. She could hardly talk, and when she did it was usually to give the "right" answer to a question. Three years later, she left as one of the most respected, liked, and powerful members of the group. Her observations were gutsy and "right on," and she was often the one who brought up risky issues. After she left, she was one of the success shadows of the group. "Remember Renée?" someone would say. "She did it!"

During her time in the group, I worked separately with Renée and her partner, a man who also attended SAA. They split up near the end of her therapy.

And where is she now?

The first thing Renée said to me when I interviewed her was "I'm not in any twelve-step groups!" We both laughed. "I have lots of respect for the way they helped," she said, "but I don't feel that I have to go to one for the rest of my life because I've rewritten and internalized the steps into a way of life. I've learned to stay on my spiritual path, ask for help, and offer help to others."

"Do you think you are truly chemically dependent?" I asked her.

There was a long pause. "No," she said simply. After another long pause she added, "I think I drank to kill the pain. I don't consider myself chemically dependent, but it's very confusing because of all the treatment propaganda. So I feel open to every possibility. If I thought I had a problem again I'd go to AA. I've had wine on a couple of occasions, and I didn't even like it, but I don't have a rigid rule about it. Before treatment I couldn't imagine why anyone would drink without getting drunk. Now I can't imagine wanting to get drunk."

I asked her if she thought she would recognize the symptoms if she began to slip. "Denial is not a problem. I've surrounded myself with people who would point it out to me."

"Tell me about your new relationship. How is it different than with Roger?"

She laughed. "How *isn't* it different? We don't live together, but we're thinking about it. I'm in no hurry." It became clear as we talked that focusing on problems was no longer central to her life.

She explained, "It's very simple in some ways. We're compatible and we can talk to each other. I don't want you to think it is totally easy; it takes work, but not deep, heavy, endless processing. I think the biggest thing is trust. I don't obsess about him because he calls when he says he'll call, he gets here when he says he will, we can handle differences, and I believe he likes to be with me."

"How is the sex part?"

She said, with a laugh, "It's wonderful. It's like something totally different. It's wonderful at moments, and then, it's back to life. It's about being close. I have this feeling now that I'm like a normal person. If sex isn't working well, we stop and talk and usually it's not about the sex. So far there hasn't been anything we can't get through."

"Do you think you were a sex addict?"

Again she pauses. "No. I think I used sex addictively, but mostly I was lonely and used sex to have people like me. I thought that was what men and women relationships were all about. One of the biggest parts of recovery was learning to see men very differently."

"How did that happen?"

"Simple little things. I started looking men in the eye, and stopped giggling around them. I started saying what was true for me."

"How were you able to do this? You used to be so scared."

"Well, of course, first I had to be away from men to get a sense of myself as a woman. Then, for a long time, I said an affirmation, 'I am the emotional and spiritual equal to everyone.' After a couple of years in recovery I joined a mixed SAA group and then a mixed therapy group where the men really got emotionally vulnerable. I kept having these flashes when men showed their feelings. 'My God, their pain is just like mine.' It was wonderful to see them reach out for touch and care. This really helped dissolve the hatred I've felt for men. Even a couple of times when I've been sexually harassed, while I didn't like it, I didn't see the men as horrible perverts. I saw them as wounded people. And their behavior scared me, but it didn't get inside and damage me like it would have before."

"Tell me about the rest of your life. What's in place and what do you still struggle with?"

"Right now I'm digging into career stuff. I'm finding so much has to do with my father. A kind of unspoken prohibition from him about work — 'Go to college, get married, and don't leave me, don't exceed me.' "

"Anything else?"

"The word *balance* is what comes to mind. I have lots of different kinds of friends — some have never been in a twelve-step group or in therapy!" We laughed together. Having therapy or being in a twelve-step group in Minnesota, the land of ten thousand treatment centers, is as common as snow in winter. "I still have program friends, but I wanted to get away from feeling identified solely with part of a subculture with a separate language. I don't want to talk about therapy and recovery all the time. Jay, my partner, has never been in a twelve-step group."

"Any other changes?"

"Oh, yes. Clothes. After I joined SAA I got rid of nearly everything I associated with the addictive time of my life. For a long time, everything I wore was baggy and boring. Just recently I bought a kind of sexy dress that I like. But it seems so different than before. It's *my* definition of sexy, which is about how I feel in the dress. It's like I'm honoring my body, respecting it, and wearing something that feels good to me."

"How is the eating going?"

"No bulimia for several years. That feels really far away. But it still gets hard sometimes. The candidiasis comes and goes. A major part of my recovery was tied to having candidiasis. It meant I had to learn to live in my body, pay attention to what I ate, and listen to what my body was telling me. I learned more and more subtle ways of reading the signals. If I was getting tired, I would check out what I was eating and adjust my diet until I felt better. I've come to respect the huge effect that eating has on my mood and general feelings."

"Anything else?"

"In general I would say I'm more grounded, more involved, more trustful. I can resonate to what's going on and respond in the moment, or at least in twenty-four hours. I keep in mind what Gandhi said, 'My commitment is to truth, not consistency.' "

GERRI: A PURPOSE IN LIFE UNFOLDS

Interlude

It's a sunny February Minnesota winter day, cold, but with a promise of spring in the air. I look out at the snow beside my front walk and wonder if the tulip bulbs are feeling any hint of spring.

On the table nearby sleeps a small black kitten I found crying in my garage a couple of weeks ago, on a 30-degree-below-zero day. I was worn out from work and from writing, but the moment I picked her up and felt her shivering little body relax against my chest, my own weariness melted away. She is a lovely little sprite and keeps me company while I write. But I know that I am stalled because I don't want to write the next segment of Gerri's story. It's not that Gerri didn't stay with recovery; she did. But the pain she suffered at the hands of our social system triggers a pain beyond words in me.

It's Not Supposed to Work This Way

A general rule of thumb for people recovering from sex addiction is to stay out of primary sexual relationships for a year or two. In Gerri's case, however, a relationship with a man provided a huge source of motivation for her to recover. Right before Gerri met Adam she had been thinking to herself, "I'm either going to commit suicide or find some meaning and purpose in my life."

Adam threw her for a loop. He seemed generally interested in getting to know her and he didn't want to be sexual right away. "Something in me was drawn to him," Gerri said. "It was not my addiction, it was my survival part that was pretty desperate for help. He was different from other men. He was interested in my intelligence and my life."

In response to Adam's genuine interest, Gerri found that she behaved differently as well. Instead of being the quick-witted, charming performer, she felt increasingly quiet inside. She was perplexed about having a relationship that didn't focus on sex. "I didn't know how to operate with someone who didn't want to be sexual. I kept asking myself, 'What am I doing wrong?' and 'Why is he still calling me?' He had a way of encouraging me to go to SAA without acting like some patronizing man trying to reform a prostitute. He genuinely cared. And I realized one day that there was nothing inside me that wanted to hurt him, as I usually did with men. I believe there is a reason he came into my life. I had really been wanting help."

As they became lovers, and eventually moved in together, Gerri's desire to be with Adam and have a new kind of bond helped crowd out her addictive impulses. As she talked about it, it seemed like the right kind of chemistry at the right time, a gift from the Universe. Recovery works best when there is something you want more than your addiction. Gerri wanted the loving bond with Adam more than her addiction.

She said, "We have a lot of ups and downs, and I continue to struggle with my addiction, but I wouldn't trade it for the world. I never bonded before in a sexual relationship. And the men always had to be rich and attractive. But with Adam I see the inner beauty, and I don't give a damn how he looks. He's really interested in being healthy and being a different sort of man."

I asked her how sex felt. "Well, once in a great while I start to perform, but it doesn't feel right anymore. And I certainly can't fake a kiss like I used to do in prostitution. It's just totally different. Sex is less frequent but it's there. It was a long process, giving up the desire to call guys or to act out. Sometimes I still dream about acting out sexually, but I don't do it."

When I asked Gerri how her son, Jimmy, was doing, the tears shone in her eyes. "Oh, Charlotte," she said, leaning closer to me, "this is the most wonderful part of recovery. I feel like I'm now able to be there for him. I'm getting to be a real mother and I know he's going to be okay. I just got a report from school saying that he is doing very well. You know, he used to be in trouble all the time, the teachers would call me saying he was starved for attention and acting out all over the place. I would feel so bad. We still go to counseling now and then." She smiled. "We've been going to a child guidance center since he was a little over two!"

The second major influence in Gerri's recovery was her SAA group. Gerri had been profoundly shamed and wounded in several chemical dependency treatment programs, which had left her terrified of any type of recovery group. Before telling about her SAA group, Gerri described her nightmarish experiences in these programs. They had been too painful to talk about when we first met. On one occasion, when she was fourteen, Gerri's treatment counselor, to "help" her face up to her seductiveness, sent her to a men's recovery group where she had been asked to stand in front of the men while they "confronted" her. It was not a confrontation at all, but a verbal stoning. The group members had hurled remarks at her, saying, "You're a slut. You're disgusting. Your boobs stick out. We're sick of mopping up after the men around here after they see you."

"After that," Gerri recalled, choking back tears, "I started having nightmares about my father raping me, and there was no one to talk to. I was so alone."

Her choking turned into sobs. I put my arm around her. Usually I keep some sense of professional distance in an interview, but something cracked open in me and I cried with her. A few minutes passed. "You don't have to tell me everything if it's too much," I said, not knowing if I said it for me or for her. "No, I want to," she said, continuing her story. "The only thing I had to comfort me after that was a little teddy bear. Then a male counselor who saw me with it said harshly, 'So this is how you get your needs met,' and took it away."

She went on to tell about another program in which she was forced to wear a sign saying GERRI BOOBS on her chest for a month. "My mother was coming for family counseling and they wouldn't let me take it off," she recounted, her voice starting to crack again. "I pleaded with them, but no. So when my mother walked in, I had to meet her wearing that sign." Once more she cried. A few minutes later she smiled at me sheepishly. "This was supposed to be an interview on recovery, and I'm talking about all this old stuff," she said.

"It's all right," I said. "In a way this is about recovery, to tell the story and have the feelings all together. I remember the first interview we had. It was like you were talking about someone else." And while this was painful, it felt like a celebration of being alive.

Gerri proceeded to talk about SAA. "There was so much love there for me. I had tried every place to get it, and finally there it was. Whenever I'd slide, people were still there for me. There was a feeling of acceptance, no matter what I did. The women would confront me in a way that wasn't shaming." She paused again, still regrouping from the pain brought up as she talked about her treatment experiences. We sat in silence a while.

"Do you want to talk about the welfare business?" I asked. "We don't have to include it. It will mean that some people will be able to identify you in the book."

"I don't care," she said. "I want it in there."

Although she had been off welfare for two years and was supporting herself by teaching in an alternative school, Gerri had been investigated for alleged welfare fraud. She had not responded to the initial written notices or appeared for questioning. "Friends told me it was a trap to go in, and I didn't want to buy in to the shame."

One day when she was teaching, two investigators came to the school saying they wanted an "identity check." While they were there, a friend who also taught at the school advised Gerri to say nothing. She stood beside Gerri, donning her most intimidating look, taking notes and asking the investigators for badge numbers. Gerri commented, "It was wonderful to have a woman there on my side." A few days later the police walked into Gerri's classroom and arrested her right in front of her class, handcuffed her, and took her off to jail on a charge of welfare fraud.

Once again Gerri had been the victim of a totally degrading assault. As fate would have it, just as the police walked in to arrest her, a guest speaker was giving a presentation on the effect of military spending on human services and poverty. As Gerri was taken out of the class, the speaker said, "Now here is an example of what I am talking about."

As Gerri recalled the horror of being taken to jail, her tears welled up. "If I hadn't had my recovery and my friends I would have tried to kill myself that night in jail. As it was, I hung on, knowing people would be there for me."

Gerri was charged with $6,000 fraud related to her going to college while on welfare. I don't know the details. I never asked. Gerri became something of a cause célèbre after that. There were editorials in the paper and a benefit to raise funds for her legal fees. There was tremendous community support from several women's organizations. Gerri remembers one woman comforting her with the words, "You didn't do anything wrong. It's not you, Gerri, it's the system. We know you chose survival." Much to Gerri's amazement no one asked her what *really* happened with the money.

Gerri, who had been alone and unprotected so much of her life, recounted her day in court. "A whole group of women went to court with me for support. My spirits were high even though I was afraid. I had been advised to plead not guilty. We heard a couple of cases before mine. A black woman got up and the judge gave her a huge bail that she couldn't possibly pay even though she said her baby was home dying of sickle cell anemia. Then we saw a man charged with arson receive a much lower bail. Something hit me at that moment. I realized how deep the hatred is for welfare women. I knew I wanted to do something about it.

"When I got on the stand, I felt an incredible sense of excitement. Other than the women who came to support me, the room was full of poor women looking scared and ashamed. All of the welfare women who went before me pled guilty. As I stood on the stand while they read the charges, I could feel the care of all the women there supporting me. When they read the charges I held my head high and said very loudly, 'Not guilty.' " Eventually her case was dropped.

"Why do you think that was?" I asked her.

"They knew that if it wasn't, there would be stories in the paper and they didn't want to be publicly embarrassed. After all, I got off welfare. I'm finishing college, and I'm a teacher and a mother. They knew how bad it would look for them to put me in the workhouse."

I thought about Gerri's plea of *Not guilty* and all it embodied. I imagined her in that courtroom with a group of women there for her at last. *Not guilty* for anything in her life. *Not guilty* for having been abused. *Not guilty* for wanting a college degree. *Not guilty* for fighting back. It seemed to me the culture should have been judged guilty for attempted murder of a soul.

Gerri talked about her subsequent work for welfare rights. "When I spoke out after my arrest, women on welfare came out of the woodwork to tell their stories. One woman with five children had spent a month in the workhouse for selling buttons on the side. Again and again I saw how women are demeaned and what harsh sentences they receive for trying to survive. As I listened to them, I could feel my own purpose in life unfolding. I never thought it would be something so unglamorous as welfare. But there it was. It was a big day for me last March when I gave a slide show presentation for the Hennepin County Welfare Department."

"How do you think this fits in with your recovery?"

"It's a big part. It is a new way for me to be powerful. Before, sex was a way to get power. It was the only way I knew. But getting involved politically and fighting back really empowered me and has brought me a lot of love. The more I'm with other women working toward change, the better I feel."

I have heard many stories of abuse and pain, and I care deeply for all my clients, yet something about Gerri touches the deepest part of my heart. I am grateful to know her. My love for her is beyond words. And while I have given her support and have been something of a mentor, it is Gerri who has filled me with an ever deepening faith in the power of the human spirit to heal.

Afterword

NAMASKARA

FEBRUARY 29, 1988. Last night I watched the closing of the 1988 Winter Olympics game, realizing that several days had gone by since I promised Kate I'd have the final pages of the book to her. I think I feel like the audience did when the torch was put out and they uttered a mournful no. Like them, I don't want the fun and excitement to be over, even though during the process of writing I would often say, "I can't wait to be done, this is such hard work."

All along, sparklers of energy came my way whenever I needed them. A woman or a man would write to say that something I had written was helpful. Friends who were reading various chapters would call to cheer me on. And there was Katrina Kenison, my editor, a virtual starburst of light energy. From the day we first met, she was tuned in to my vision for the book and immensely supportive as the book evolved with huge changes from the original plan. The enthusiastic tape-recorded messages she left on my answering machine in response to the chapters I sent her delighted me enormously. I would save the messages and play them back when I needed a lift. Likewise, Edite Kroll, my agent, has perfected the art of giving kindhearted support while finding the perfect words to say, kindly, "This doesn't work right here."

When I pondered writing this closing section last Wednesday, I considered talking about my deteriorating singles tennis game. When I thought of writing on Saturday, I envisioned telling about an interview I heard on the radio. But as I write today, my heart is in a different place, and those incidents have become old stories. The energy is gone from them, so I will close in a different way. And that's what I've learned from writing this book. Go where the energy is strong, write from that place, and let go of the preconceived plan.

The same is true when you embark on a recovery path. Each of the women followed a very strong calling to go toward the light, toward love and personal power. They didn't always know where the path would lead, but they stayed firm in their commitment to recovery. Recovery is like a marriage to oneself, one's soul, a commitment to be the wonderful gift to the universe you already are.

This brings to mind the teenage Soviet skater who, with her partner, won the Olympics pairs figure skating gold medal. She skated with brilliance and ease, joy shining in her face as if she had been born to skate. Watching her brought tears to my eyes and a tremor to my heart. The commentators described her as skating on a cloud, and that's exactly how it seemed. How many thousands of people had their spirits lifted because she took the gift her Creator gave her and lived the gift. And by living it she gave it back.

That's just what happens when women recover. In becoming themselves and fighting the good fight, they become beacons of light opening the way for others. We may not see them in the Olympics, but when a woman like Marsha, who has been called stupid all her life, comes into the room smiling and sassy and proclaims, "Hey girls, I got an A!" she is a gold medalist, too.

Last Saturday I gave a talk on sexuality and spirituality at a singles conference. I was searching for a means to help people see the soul in one another. I thought of a scene from the movie *Ironweed,* in which several homeless people find an old woman half frozen, sleeping or passed out under a tree. Someone recognizes her. As they attempt to help her, one of the men asks, "Who is she?"

"An old drunken Eskimo woman."

"She's a bum."

"She's been a bum all her life."

"No . . . Nobody's a bum all their life. She hada' been something once."

"She was a whore before she was a bum."

"And what about before she was a whore?"

"I don't know. . . . Before that I guess she was just a little kid."

"Then that's somethin'. A little kid's somethin' that ain't a bum or a whore."*

I asked the group at the conference to breathe deeply and look around at all the people in the room. Then I said, "Presto. Everyone is seven years old, a little boy or a little girl."

People laughed and the feeling in the room changed.

"How do you feel about everyone now?" I asked them.

"Everybody's so cute," one woman said.

* Dialogue adapted from *Ironweed* by William Kennedy.

"Very caring, very tender," others responded. And that's because when we pause and see the little girl or the little boy in anyone we start to see the soul, that innocent, tender essence of our being.

"Is there any child here who hasn't been afraid, or misunderstood, or lonely?" I asked.

"No."

"Is there any child here who doesn't have a dream?"

"No."

We hoped to carry that truth with us as we left the workshop, remembering to see the children within us all, and to remember our dreams.

A Hindustani word, *namaskara*, means "I salute the divinity in you." In Sanskrit the word is *namaste* (pronounced na muss´ tey). In Nepal, where many religions flourish side by side, people regularly greet each other by bowing and saying *namaste*.

I wonder what would happen if every time we encounter someone — at the office, at the checkout lane in a grocery store, when we meet our students or our teachers, as we welcome guests into our home, or as we look at ourselves in the mirror — we paused to say *Namaskara*, or I salute the divinity in you. Taking a few moments throughout the day to pause and honor the soul of another would repeatedly bring us back to our Source, our holy center. If we did this, I believe we would start moving from the dense energy of addiction to the light energy of love. We would come to know one another in the spirit of care and community.

I was delighted when one of the commentators said, at the close of the Olympics, "In talking with the athletes, we realize that most of them don't think of this in terms of medals as much as some of us on the sidelines do." And that's just right. The great people I've known don't think so much about outcome as doing things one step at a time and following their instincts and their passion.

After the torch went out at the Olympic Stadium the athletes went onto the field and started to hug and dance. They had done their best and it was time to celebrate. I too have done my best. As soon as this manuscript is mailed, it will take on a life of its own, a child gone from the nest, and I'll be on to something new. When I think of what I've learned, the words that come to mind are *acceptance, love,* and *commitment*. I feel I am doing exactly what I'm meant to be doing, and I have been so in love with writing this book that it has been easy to set priorities. Essentially I write, I play, I see friends, I exercise, and I meditate. It has been easy to stay away from situations that might upset or distract me from my purpose.

Writing this book has been like my dream of being in a play without a script. I simply had to get on the stage and start saying my lines, anything that came. Then the other players joined me, and our lines fed each other, and pretty soon we were just talking together and that became the script. And that's really how this book happened. I had my ideas, and I asked people for theirs, and I put them all together.

Namaskara. Namaskara. I salute the divinity in you.

Charlotte Davis, age nine, in a dress made by her mother just for fun.

In Appreciation of Those Who
Helped with This Book

KATE O'KEEFE

Kate has worked with me as an organizational consultant and an editor. It has been an ideal relationship. I let the words and ideas pour out, and she provides a structure and organizational framework. To get a structure for writing this book, she took a huge stack of my articles, notes, and transcripts and cut and pasted them into chapters based on the original proposal. I was dazzled. She set about to organize them as if she were making a cup of tea.

Before I started each chapter, Kate and I would get together, look over the notes, and brainstorm. Then I would write a couple of drafts and give them to her. A couple of days later I would be on the phone like an eager kid, asking, "What do you think?" She would always say the good stuff first and then gently let me know if some major overhaul seemed in order. She would argue her point strongly and I would argue mine. It was always good natured and high spirited.

When I delivered the last chapter, Kate and I sat for a moment at her dining room table. The entire manuscript was stacked before us. "How did we ever get all that done?" I thought to myself. I also felt a growing sense of euphoria as I realized the end was in sight. I told Kate how much I appreciate our working relationship, how respectful and easy it has been.

When we met, Kate was the writing consultant and editor on a state-funded project to develop a model treatment program for women. I asked if she was interested in helping me with this book. At the time she was working sixteen-hour days to meet the deadline for the Women's Treatment Program manual, so I was amazed when she sounded so interested in working with me.

When she arrived to look at my materials her wrists were swollen with terrible tendinitis. Even so, she moved right in with ideas for organization and coding the questionnaires. Within less than an hour we had agreed on a work plan, including a financial arrangement. I loved her strong energy and knew I didn't have to worry about bowling her over. We both know what it is like to be attacked for being bossy and overbearing when we experience ourselves as just being passionate and involved.

As we sat at her dining table feeling pleased with ourselves, I told her I had been thinking about what I had learned from writing this book and wondered what it had meant to her. She referred to the personal challenges she's faced during the past year and then smiled and gestured toward a small stack of articles on the other side of the table. "See those?" she said. "They're due this week. And you know what? I'm not going to have them done on time. I've worked six hours today and that's enough. I'm going to watch the Olympics tonight. I'm getting better and better at setting limits and taking care of myself."

Shortly after Kate started helping me, she came down with severe rheumatoid arthritis. For much of the year she's been in a great deal of pain, has suffered from debilitating exhaustion, and has put on some unwanted pounds. In many ways it has been the most difficult year of her life.

"That's quite a change, not meeting a deadline," I said, recalling those sixteen-hour days of a year earlier. "But I don't understand how working on this book made a difference."

"Well," she said, "something you said was very important to me."

"What was that?" I said, my ego perking up.

"One time when I called to let you know I hadn't finished editing a chapter, due to fatigue, you said. 'That's okay. I don't want anyone to be harmed working on this book. I don't want any negative energy in it.' By saying that, you gave me permission to relax and stop pressuring myself to be perfect. It made it much easier to work."

LUANN KLEPPE

I hired Luann to be a part-time personal secretary while I was writing this book. Her work for me was a stopover in her journey before she bought a camper and took off to be a wanderer for a while. Both of Luann's parents are dead and she is completely on her own in the world.

She timed her interlude with me perfectly. She typed in Kate's editorial changes on the last chapter on her last day of work. She did her job so well that she even left me with a replacement, also named Lou Ann. By typing and taking care of the myriad small tasks involved in running a therapy practice and a home, she freed me to do what I do best, just sit and write. What a treat it was to be able to do this unfettered by the clutter of life.

When Luann arrived for our interview the first words she said when she walked into my writing room were "I love all the windows and the light." I wanted to hire her on the spot. Her steadfast, calming energy was like a balm for me and it flows subliminally throughout this book. In the beginning I told her I didn't know much about having a secretary or how much time the job would take. She was a wonderful sport in helping work out a process. The job definition evolved as I would ask meekly, "Do you mind taking the cat to the vet for his shots?" Or, "Would you go buy a *Playboy* magazine for me for the Jessica Hahn story?" Or, "Please call the library to find out what ethnic groups equal about 9 percent of the population." It was gratifying for me to see that it took her eight to ten hours a week to do all the little stuff I thought I should get done in an hour or two.

When I asked Luann what being here had meant to her she said she'd thought a lot about it. "Last year when I was out in Colorado and was thinking about moving there, several people said, 'Why don't you come right away?' What's keeping you?' I don't know quite why, but I said, 'Well, I just started working for a lady who's writing a book and I want to see it through!' "

"Why did you want this job in the first place?" I asked.

"I was sick of working for projects I didn't believe in. And" — she smiled — "I really liked the thought of working in a room with a view and sunlight."

"What's it been like for you?"

"In the beginning," she admitted, laughing, "I was really afraid of you. I had been brought up to think of women as trash, and I was intimidated by the way you speak out on things. At first it was just a typing and office job. But then I'd be putting in the editing changes and a sentence or two would jump off the page. Now I can't wait to get to the typing.

"The other thing I wanted on a job was to have responsibility. But it was frightening at first. There's something comfortable about having someone tell me exactly what to do. When I'd shop for you I'd worry if I was getting the right number of carrots or if they were the right size. I'll never forget the time I came back from the co-op with a huge bag of cream of tartar and a tiny bit of baking powder and you wanted it the other way around. I was so scared you'd fire me. But you didn't. I was still there the next day, and somehow it got through to me that it was a tiny thing to mix up baking powder with cream of tartar. It wasn't a big crime. I feel I'm much stronger inside. I'm much more confident about my ability to make decisions and take responsibility."

"I'm glad," I said. "I'll miss you."

"I'll miss you, too." She laughed. "Now that I'm not afraid of you anymore."

RUBY

I named the black kitten I found in the garage Ruby, for her bright fiery energy. She was a frequent companion in my writing room for about eight weeks, until she crawled into a box under my dresser one night and gave birth to three tiny black kittens. She has been a constant source of delight in my life.

How to Contact the People
Who Worked on This Book

Kate O'Keefe
Writing consultant and editor
4700 First Avenue South
Minneapolis, MN 55409

Lenore Davis
Illustrator and artist
Box 47
Newport, KY 41072

Pat Rouse
Graphic designer
3513 Clinton Avenue South
Minneapolis, MN 55408

Note: If you are interested in workshops or trainings, please send a self-addressed, legal-sized envelope and we will send you the schedule. I love to receive letters and read them all but I cannot always respond personally and I do not have references for therapists around the country. You can write to the National Council on Sex Addiction for a list. Their address is on page 386.

Charlotte Kasl
Castle Consulting
P.O. Box 1302
Lolo, MT 59847

Resources for Help

If you are interested in starting a group or want a list of further resources for treatment and therapy, you can contact the following:

Augustine Fellowship, Sex and Love Addicts Anonymous (SLAA)
P.O. Box 119, New Town Branch
Boston, MA 02258
Phone: (617) 332-1845

Codependents of Sex Addicts

Minnesota COSA
P.O. Box 14537
Minneapolis, MN 55414
Phone: (612) 537-6904

S-Anon
P.O. Box 5117
Sherman Oaks, CA 91413
Phone: (818) 990-6910

For education, information, and referral services:

NCSA (National Council on Sex Addiction)
P.O. Box 20249
Wickenburg, AZ 85358
Phone: (602) 684-7919

Sex Addicts Anonymous (SAA)
Adult Children of Sex Addicts Anonymous (ACSA)
P.O. Box 3038
Minneapolis, MN 55403
Phone: (612) 339-0217

National Council on Sexual Addiction
P.O. Box 20249
Wickenburgh, AZ 85358
Phone: (602) 684-7919

Sexaholics Anonymous (SA)
P.O. Box 300
Simi Valley, CA 93062
Phone: (818) 704-9854

This program is not mentioned in most referral lists and is not specifically focused on sex addiction or sexual codependency. It helps people work on all their addictions simultaneously and is holistic and reasonably priced.

The Ken Keyes Center
790 Commercial Ave.
Coos Bay, OR 97420
Phone: (503) 267-6412

The program is not appropriate as primary treatment for alcoholism, drug dependency, or severe forms of sex addiction. It would be fine for people who have gone through primary treatment and are in recovery.

In choosing a recovery group it is important to find a group that fits for you. You might want to read a group's definition of its purpose and its sobriety statement. For example, SAA welcomes anyone with a sincere desire to cease compulsive sexual behavior and supports people in defining their own sobriety. By contrast, SA defines sexual sobriety as sex only within a heterosexual marriage.

Groups in general vary and take on a life of their own. If you are not sure about a group, try more than one until one connects for you. If you try several and none of them feels right you might consider looking at your own fears and resistance, or start one of your own. In any case, trust yourself.

Bibliography

American Heritage Dictionary, 2d college ed. Boston: Houghton Mifflin, 1982.

American Psychiatric Association. *Diagnostic and Statistical Manual of Mental Disorders,* 3rd ed. Washington, D.C.: American Psychiatric Association, 1980.

Andrews, Lynn V. *Flight of the Seventh Moon.* San Francisco: Harper & Row, 1984.

————. *Medicine Woman.* San Francisco: Harper & Row, 1981.

Augustine Fellowship. *Sex and Love Addicts Anonymous.* Boston: Augustine Fellowship, Fellowship-Wide Services, 1986.

Barbach, Lonnie Garfield. *For Yourself: The Fulfillment of Female Sexuality.* New York: Doubleday, 1975.

Barry, Linda. "Singles Bar." *Utne Reader* 20 (March/April 1987).

Blakely, Mary Kay. "Let Them Read Fluff." *The Newsday Magazine,* November 2, 1986.

Blank, Joani, and Quackenbush, Marcia. *A Kid's First Book About Sex.* Burlingame, Calif.: Yes Press, 1983.

Bly, Robert, trans. *The Kabir Book: Forty-four of the Ecstatic Poems of Kabir.* Boston: Beacon Press, 1977.

Boesing, Martha. *Junkie.* Presented at the Foot of the Mountain Theatre, Minneapolis, 1981.

Bradley, Marion Zimmer. *The Mists of Avalon.* New York: Ballantine Books, 1982.

Brecher, Ruth and Edward, eds. *An Analysis of Human Sexual Response.* New York: New American Library, 1966.

Brownmiller, Susan. *Against Our Will: Men, Women, and Rape.* New York: Simon and Schuster, 1975.

Bruch, Hilde, M.D. *The Golden Cage: The Enigma of Anorexia Nervosa.* New York: Random House, 1978.

Burns, David D., M.D. *Feeling Good: The New Mood Therapy.* New York: William Morrow, 1980.

Burns, Echo Bodine. *Hands That Heal.* San Diego: ACS Publications, 1985.

Butler, Sandra. *Conspiracy of Silence: The Trauma of Incest.* San Francisco: New Glide Publications, 1978.

Caldicott, Dr. Helen. *Missile Envy: The Arms Race & Nuclear War.* New York: William Morrow, 1984.

Cameron, Anne, *Daughters of Copper Woman.* Vancouver, B.C.: Press Gang Publishers, 1981.

Capra, Fritjof. *The Turning Point: Science, Society, and the Rising Culture.* New York: Bantam Books, 1982.

Carnes, Patrick. *The Sexual Addiction.* Minneapolis: Comp Care, 1983.

Castaneda, Carlos. *A Separate Reality: Further Conversations with Don Juan.* New York: Simon and Schuster, 1971.

The Century Dictionary: An Encyclopedia Lexicon of the English Language. New York: Century Co., 1889.

Cermak, Timmen L., M.D. *Diagnosing and Treating Co-Dependence.* Minneapolis: Johnson Institute Books, 1986.

Chesler, Phyllis. *About Men.* New York: Simon and Schuster, 1978.

———. *Women, Money & Power.* New York: William Morrow, 1976.

"Codependency of Sex Addiction: Some Typical Behaviors." Minneapolis: Minnesota COSA.

A Course in Miracles. Tiburon, Calif.: Foundation for Inner Peace, 1976.

Cousins, Norman. *Anatomy of an Illness.* New York: W. W. Norton, 1979.

Crook, William G., M.D. *The Yeast Connection: A Medical Breakthrough.* Jackson, Tenn.: Professional Books, 1983.

Daly, Mary. *Gyn/Ecology: The Metaethics of Radical Feminism.* Boston: Beacon Press, 1978.

Dass, Ram. *Grist for the Mill.* Santa Cruz, Calif.: Unity Press, 1977.

———. *The Only Dance There Is.* Garden City, N.Y.: Anchor Books, 1974.

Deshimaru, Taisen. *Questions to a Zen Master.* New York: E. P. Dutton, 1985.

Diamond, Jed. *Looking for Love in All the Wrong Places.* New York: G. P. Putnam's Sons, 1988.

Dodson, Betty. *Selflove and Orgasm.* 1983. Available from Betty Dodson, P.O. Box 1933, Murray Hill Station, New York, N.Y. 10156.

Dufty, William. *Sugar Blues.* New York: Warner Books, 1975.

Dworkin, Andrea. *Pornography: Men Possessing Women.* New York: G. P. Putnam's Sons, 1979.

Easwaran, Eknath, trans. *The Bhagavad Gita.* Petaluma, Calif.: Nilgiri Press, 1985.

Edinger, Edward F. *Ego and Archetype.* New York: Penguin Books, 1972.

Ellis, Albert, Ph.D., and Robert A. Harper, Ph.D. *A New Guide to Rational Living.* North Hollywood, Calif.: Wilshire Book Company, 1975.

————. *The Enquirer* 34 (June 30, 1987).

Evdokimor, Paul. *The Struggle with God.* Paulist Press, 1966.

Farrell, Warren, Ph.D. *Why Men Are the Way They Are.* New York: McGraw-Hill, 1986.

Fast, Julius, and Meredith Bernstein. *Sexual Chemistry.* New York: M. Evans and Co., 1983.

Ferguson, Marilyn. *The Aquarian Conspiracy: Personal and Social Transformation in the 1980s.* Los Angeles: J. P. Tarcher, 1980.

Finkelhor, David. *Sexually Victimized Children.* New York: Free Press, 1979.

Forward, Dr. Susan, and Joan Torres. *Men Who Hate Women and the Women Who Love Them.* New York: Bantam Books, 1986.

Frankfort, Ellen. *Vaginal Politics.* New York: Quadrangle, 1972.

Freire, Paulo. *Pedagogy of the Oppressed.* New York: Herder and Herder, 1972.

Freud, Sigmund. *Three Essays on the Theory of Sexuality.* New York: Basic Books, 1982.

Friday, Nancy. *My Secret Garden: Women's Sexual Fantasies.* New York: Pocket Books, 1973.

Gandhi, Mohandas K. *An Autobiography: The Story of My Experiments with Truth.* Boston: Beacon Press, 1957.

Gilligan, Carol. *In a Different Voice: Psychological Theory and Women's Development.* Cambridge, Mass.: Harvard University Press, 1982.

Goodman, Ellen. "A Victim's Hardened Bravado." *Minneapolis Star and Tribune,* September 29, 1988.

Grow, Doug. "Inver Grove Incident Highlights Attitudes on Sexual Harassment." *Minneapolis Star and Tribune,* December 20, 1987.

Hite, Shere. *Women and Love: A Cultural Revolution in Progress.* New York: Alfred A. Knopf, 1987.

The Holy Bible, King James Version. London: Oxford University Press, 1965.

Kanter, Rosabeth Moss, with Barry A. Stein. *A Tale of "O": On Being Different in an Organization.* New York: Harper & Row, 1980.

Kaplan, Louise J., Ph.D. *Oneness and Separateness: From Infant to Individual.* New York: Simon and Schuster, 1978.

Kasl, Charlotte. "Dear Therapist: Through the Voices of Survivors." Unpublished article, March 1986.

————. *A Feminist Perspective on Female Perpetrators of Sexual Abuse.* Paper presented at the First International Congress on Rape, Jerusalem, Israel, April 1986.

————. *Paths of Recovery: Adapted from A Quaker Feminist Perspective on Twelve-Step Programs.* Training and Resource Manual Model Treatment Program for Chemically Dependent Women, State of Minnesota, Department of Human Services, Chemical Dependency Division Grant 93635.

———. *"Psychotherapy Outcome of Lesbian Women as Related to Therapist Attitude Toward and Knowledge of Lesbianism."* Ph.D. diss., Ohio University, 1982.

———. *The Role of Addiction and Spirituality in Recovery from Childhood Abuse.* Paper presented at the First International Congress on Rape, Jerusalem, Israel, April 1986.

———. *Women and Sex Addiction.* Self-published, July and September, 1984.

Katz, Judy H. *White Awareness.* Norman: University of Oklahoma Press, 1978.

Kaufman, Gershen. *Shame: The Power of Caring.* Cambridge, Mass.: Shenkman Publishing, 1980.

Kennedy, William. *Ironweed.* New York: Viking Press, 1983.

Key, Wilson Bryan. *Subliminal Seduction.* Englewood Cliffs, N.J.: Prentice-Hall, 1973.

Keyes, Ken, Jr. *Handbook to Higher Consciousness.* Coos Bay, Ore: Living Love Publications, 1975.

———. *The Methods Work . . . If You Do!* Coos Bay, Ore: Living Love Publications, 1978.

———. *Prescriptions for Happiness.* Coos Bay, Ore: Living Love Publications, n.d.

King, Billie Jean. *Billie Jean.* New York: Viking Press, 1982.

Kinsey, Alfred, et al. *Sexual Behavior of the Human Female.* New York: Pocket Books, 1953.

Klaich, Delores. *Woman + Woman: Attitudes Toward Lesbianism.* New York: William Morrow, 1974.

Kohn, Alfie. "How to Succeed Without Even Vying." *Psychology Today,* September 1986.

Kübler-Ross, Elisabeth. *On Death and Dying.* New York: Macmillan, 1969.

Larson, Earnie. *Stage II Recovery: Life Beyond Addiction.* San Francisco: Harper & Row, 1985.

Lorde, Audre. *Uses of the Erotic: The Erotic as Power.* New York: Out & Out Books, 1978.

Loulan, JoAnn. *Lesbian Sex.* San Francisco: Spinsters Ink, 1984.

McAuliffe, Robert M., Ph.D., and Mary Boesen McAuliffe, Ph.D. *Essentials for the Diagnosis of Chemical Dependency,* vols. 1 and 2. Minneapolis: American Chemical Dependency Society.

Magid, Dr. Ken, and Carole A. McKelvey. *High Risk: Children Without a Conscience.* New York: Bantam Books, 1987.

Marshall, Paule. *Praisesong for the Widow*. New York: E. P. Dutton, 1984.

Martin, Del. *Battered Wives*. New York: Simon and Schuster, 1976.

Masters, William, and Virginia Johnson. *Human Sexual Response*. Boston: Little Brown, 1966.

Meditation Group for the New Age. *Recognition of Reality and the Dissipation of Glamour*. 3d year, set VI. Ojai, Calif.: MGNA, 1983.

Meeker-Lowry, Susan. *Economics as If the Earth Really Mattered: A Catalyst Guide to Socially Conscious Investing*. Santa Cruz, Calif.: New Society Publishers, 1988.

Miller, Jean Baker, M.D. *Toward a New Psychology of Women*. Boston: Beacon Press, 1976.

Mura, David. *A Male Grief: Notes on Pornography and Addiction*. Minneapolis: Milkweek Editions, Thistle Series, 1987.

Mussen, Paul Henry, et al. *Child Development and Personality*, 4th ed. New York: Harper & Row, 1974.

Nakken, Craig. *The Addictive Personality: Roots, Rituals, and Recovery*. Center City, Minn.: Hazelden Publishers, 1988.

Navratilova, Martina, with George Vecsey. *Martina*. New York: Fawcett Crest, 1985.

Norwood, Robin. *Women Who Love Too Much*. Los Angeles: Jeremy P. Tarcher, 1985.

Pagels, Elaine. *The Gnostic Gospels*. New York: Random House, 1979.

Peele, Stanton. *Love and Addiction*. New York: New American Library, 1975.

Perls, Frederick S., M.D., Ph.D. *Gestalt Therapy Verbatim*. New York: Bantam Books, 1969.

Pogrebin, Letty Cottin. *Growing Up Free: Raising Your Child in the 80's*. New York: McGraw-Hill, 1980.

Rahula, Walpola. *What the Buddha Taught*. New York: Grove Press, 1959.

Ray, Barbara Weber, Ph.D. *The Reiki Factor*. Smithtown, N.Y.: Exposition Press, 1983.

Ray, Sondra. *I Deserve Love*. Millbrae, Calif.: Leo Femmes Publishing, 1976.

———. *Loving Relationships*. Millbrae, Calif.: Celestial Arts, 1980.

Robinson, James M., gen. ed. *The Nag Hammadi Library*. San Francisco: Harper & Row, 1981.

Rush, Anne Kent. *Moon, Moon*. New York and Berkeley: Random House and Moon Books, 1976.

Rush, Florence. *The Best Kept Secret: Sexual Abuse of Children*. New York: McGraw-Hill, 1980.

Scarf, Maggie. *Unfinished Business: Pressure Points in the Lives of Women*. Garden City, N.Y.: Doubleday, 1980.

Schaef, Anne Wilson. *Co-Dependence: Misunderstood — Mistreated.* San Francisco: Harper & Row, 1986.

———. *Women's Reality.* Minneapolis: Winston Press, 1981.

Scheer, Robert, Barry Golson, and Jessica Hahn. "The Jessica Hahn Story." *Playboy,* November, December 1987.

Schiffman, Muriel. *Gestalt Self-Therapy and Further Techniques for Personal Growth.* Menlo Park, Calif.: Self-Therapy Press, 1971.

Schneider, Jennifer P. *Back from Betrayal: Surviving His Affairs.* New York: Harper & Row, 1988.

Siegel, Bernie S., M.D. *Love, Medicine & Miracles.* New York: Harper & Row, 1986.

Singer, June. *Boundaries of the Soul: The Practice of Jung's Psychology.* Garden City, N.Y.: Anchor Books, 1973.

Slater, Philip. *The Pursuit of Loneliness: American Culture at the Breaking Point.* Boston: Beacon Press, 1970.

Spada, James. *Grace: The Secret Lives of a Princess.* New York: Dell, 1987.

Strange, Jim de. *Visioning.* San Francisco: Ash-Kar Press, 1979.

Suzuki, Shunryu. *Zen Mind, Beginner's Mind.* Tokyo: Weatherhill, 1970.

Trungpa, Chogyam. *Cutting Through Spiritual Materialism.* Boston: Shambhala Publications, 1973.

Truss, C. Orian, M.D. *The Missing Diagnosis.* 1982. Available from The Missing Diagnosis, P.O. Box 26508, Birmingham, AL 35226.

———. "The Sexual Addiction." *The Twin Cities Reader.* Minneapolis, May 22, 1985.

"The 'Twenty Questions' of SAA." Minneapolis: Minnesota SAA.

Wagner, Sally Roesch. "Pornography and the Sexual Revolution: The Backlash of Sadomasochism." In *Against Sadomachism: A Radical Feminist Analysis,* ed. Robin Ruth Linden et al. East Palo Alto, Calif.: Frog in the Well, 1982.

Walker, Lenore E. *The Battered Woman.* New York: Harper & Row, 1979.

Woods, Margo. *Masturbation, Tantra and Self-Love.* San Diego: Omphaloskepsis Press, 1981.

Zukav, Gary. *The Dancing Wu Li Masters: An Overview of the New Physics.* New York: William Morrow, 1979.

Index

Abandonment: fear of, 48, 106, 130, 160, 163, 200, 230; of self, 192, 194
Acceptance: of self, 282, 304, 343, 360–61
Acting out, 68, 73, 100, 186, 227, 358; definition, xv
Addiction, 15, 18–19, 25–26, 27–28, 32, 75, 170–71; definition, 18; as a disease, 19–20; lessons from, 279–83, 297; limiting, 297–98, 301–2; traits of, 20, 24–25, 140–43. *See also* Codependency; Sex addiction
Addictive sex, 10–11, 50–54, 99, 318, 319; definition, 43. *See also* Sex addiction
Adult relationships. *See* Relationships
Advertising, 226–27, 330; sexual images in, 8, 9, 197–98, 256–58
Al-Anon, 31, 351
Alcohol: and sex addiction, 171, 178–80
Alcoholics Anonymous (AA), xv, 17, 28, 97, 289, 314
Alcoholism, xv, 17, 19–20, 182, 315
Anger, 189, 206, 260; in codependency, 35, 202, 251, 264, 336–37, 350; in men, 231, 234; in sex addiction, 18, 59–60, 100, 251, 255, 264. *See also* Rage
Anorexia, 184, 188
Anxiety, 19, 35, 36, 161–62; reducing, 46–47, 296–97, 306
Asexuality, 5, 60, 165
Attitudes, 149–50, 310; toward men, 249, 250, 259; toward prostitution, 99, 109; toward sex, xi, 11–12, 250

Bargaining: with addiction, 291–92, 295
Behavior, 25–28, 40, 246, 319–20, 338–40, 342. *See also* Cues (for behavior); Patterns (of behavior); specific behaviors, e.g. Compulsions
Beliefs, 77, 246. *See also* Core beliefs; Operational beliefs
Bisexuality, 56, 121, 209
Body image, 48, 49, 183, 193–94, 249–50, 258
Bonding, 55, 119–20, 146–47; between children and parents, 34, 106, 112–14, 120, 183–84, 200, 271, 327; male, 229, 243; sexual, 101, 225–26
Boredom, 18
Boundaries: personal, 312; in relationships, 259–65, 266
Buddhism, 15–16, 18, 149
Bulimia, 184, 186, 370

Cameron, Anne, 337–38
Careers, 152, 154–55, 330
Carlson, Shirley, 37–38
Celibacy, 149, 165, 240, 297
Chemical dependency, 72, 73; and codependency, 36, 37, 181–82; definition, xv; and sex addiction, 159, 171, 178–80
Child abuse, 55, 64, 108, 251, 259, 261–62, 267. *See also* Incest; Sexual abuse
Children: behavior; 112, 184, 269; in dysfunctional families, 44, 46–47, 92, 196, 203–4, 261–62, 265–67, 270–72; influence of parents on, 33, 117, 127, 271. *See also* Bond-

ing, between children and parents; Self-esteem, of children

Choices, 256; in recovery, 282, 300, 304, 306

Christianity, 16, 17, 253, 274, 362, 366; effect on sexuality, 11, 12–13, 149, 204, 255, 268

Codependency, 32, 43–44, 215, 252–53, 263, 330; definition, 31, 33, 39–40; limiting, 335–337, 341–43; in men, 226, 233, 234; stages of, 44–50; survey question replies, 160–66; traits of, 16, 33, 35–37, 39, 40, 286, 319–20

Codependency and addiction, 105–6

Codependency to addiction, 100, 104–5

Codependency with secret addictive behavior, 107

Codependents of Sex Addicts (CoSA), xii, xv, 78

Commitment: to recovery, 294–95, 306–7; in relationships, 39–40, 146

Communication, 328; in relationships, 121, 146, 148, 242, 284, 340–41

Compulsions, 25–27, 102, 171, 186

Control, 232, 244; and children, 46, 232, 261–62; by codependent women, 102, 352; lack of, 65, 140, 187, 265, 292. *See also* Power

Controlled addict, 60–63

Cooperation: in relationships, 140, 142, 148; teaching, 327–28

Core beliefs, 44–50, 141, 146, 198, 243, 310; changing, 304, 306; recognizing, 243, 302–4

CoSA. *See* Codependents of Sex Addicts

Cues (for behavior), 21, 23, 33, 58, 198, 199, 301–2

Culture, 38, 226–27, 246, 258–59; double standard in, 13, 14, 54–55, 99, 226, 233, 247–48; and sex, 5, 7–9, 26, 54, 65, 226, 227. *See also* Patriarchy

Dass, Ram, 29, 150

Daughters of Cooperwoman (Cameron), 337–38

Death: fear of, 34, 36, 44, 200, 342

Decisions: in recovery, 282, 285, 291–92, 300, 304, 306

Delusions (in addiction), 25, 179. *See also* Fantasies

Denial of problem, 25, 56, 62–63, 66, 182, 197–98, 202, 215, 303–4

Depression, 226, 249; and addiction, 36, 129–31, 164

Dodson, Betty, 250

Double standard, *See* Culture, double standard in

Eating, 194, 360

Eating disorders, 36, 184, 186, 188. *See also* Food and sex

Education, 153, 156, 311, 327–28

Ellis, Albert, 18

Emotions, 242, 310, 347; and addiction, 18–19, 25, 51, 128, 141; and codependency, 34–35, 36, 44–45, 110–11, 162, 349–50; detachment from, 54, 110–11, 142, 162, 199, 232, 252–53, 296. *See also* specific emotions, e.g. Anger

Emptiness in life, 19, 170, 198, 229; using sex to fill, 4, 20, 21, 98. *See also* Powerlessness

Energy. *See* Life force energy

Equality: in relationships, 142, 150, 213, 229, 258. *See also* Inequality

Escalation (in addiction), 21, 37

Evert, Chris, 222–23

Exhibitionism, 51, 226

Family, 246, 350–51; rejection by, 213–14, 218; role of, 195, 258, 260–62. *See also* Children; Father; Mother

Fantasies, 63–67, 197, 204, 208; adolescent, 68, 191, 231; of children, 64; in codependency, 35–36, 107, 164; male, 226, 269–70; about relationships, 66, 128, 164, 166; in sex addiction, 25, 128, 157; of suicide, 159, 205

Fast, Julius, 254

Father: and daughter, 83, 85, 214, 237, 262, 269–70; and son, 230–31

Fear, 37, 311; and addiction, 18, 24, 55, 59, 140; and codependency, 34–35, 36, 37, 55, 59, 342–43; of

and recovery, xv–xvi, 283–87, 307, 312, 315, 334, 340, 342, 343. *See also* High; Sexual energy; Spirituality

Loneliness, 48, 54, 68, 134, 186, 234, 261

Loulan, JoAnn, 7–8

Love, 6, 39, 41, 128, 129–30, 312; and sex, 29, 131, 132, 146–47, 268, 316. *See also* Self-love

Love, Medicine & Miracles (Siegel), 15, 312

Love addiction, 41, 63, 128–30

Love and Addiction (Peele), 17–18

Magid, Ken, 112

Marriage, 26, 42–43, 66, 87

Masochism, 158, 162, 193; definition, 190–91; fantasies concerning, 65, 204

Masters, William, 250

Masturbation, 157, 166, 201; fantasies concerning, 63; and recovery, 298, 319, 346

Media, 210–11, 226–27, 330; sexual images in, 8–9, 116, 192, 239, 257–58

Men Who Hate Women and the Women Who Love Them (Forward), 201–2

Miller, Jean Baker, 248–49

Minnelli, Liza, 27

Miss America, 174–75

Mistakes: acknowledgment of, 141, 146, 243, 301–2

Money problems, 152, 155

Monogamy, 5, 26, 225

Monroe, Marilyn, 106–7

Mother: and child, 46, 85; and son, 230, 231, 234–37

Mother love, 125, 230, 231

Motivation, 40–41, 230; in addiction, 21, 51, 59, 115

My Secret Garden (Friday), 197

Nakken, Craig, 25

Navratilova, Martina, 222, 223

Needs, 120, 121, 229, 250, 296

Negativity (attitude), 25

Norms: of sexuality, 43, 65, 192, 227

Norwood, Robin, 39, 40

Obsessions, 25, 63, 67–68, 157, 166, 186, 187, 194

Operational beliefs, 47–50, 295, 296, 348–52

Orgasm: myth of, 250

Patriarchy, 149, 203, 211, 223, 247, 248, 252

Patterns (of behavior), 26, 33–34, 51, 101–7, 136, 141, 179, 286

Peel, Stanton, 17–18

Peer groups: and recovery, 292, 296–97, 303, 335–36, 337–38, 351

Pornography, 8–9, 190, 239, 254, 257; effect on children, 231, 268–69, 328–29, 356–57; in therapy, 252; use of, 51, 57–58, 147–48, 162, 201, 250

Post-traumatic stress syndrome, 266–67

Power, 229, 239, 251, 282, 302, 322; feeling of in addiction, 47, 49, 50, 110, 143; feeling of in codependency, 161, 344; and responsibility, 259, 325, 337; source of, 38, 51, 141, 186, 231, 256; surrender of, 140, 243, 244; of women, 14, 178, 210, 211, 221–23, 226, 249, 250, 351. *See also* Life force energy

Powerlessness, 47, 65, 229; in addiction, 20, 24, 27, 75, 140, 187, 265, 292; of children, 32–33, 46, 200, 232, 261–62, 263–64, 303; in codependency, 32, 35–36, 38, 43, 49

PRIDE (People Reaching Independence, Dignity, and Equality), 108

Prostitution, 51, 99, 108–11, 201, 257, 330

Psychic numbing, 197. *See also* Emotions, detachment from

Rage, 54, 60, 182, 201, 230, 350. *See also* Anger

Rape, 247–48, 252, 253–56, 257

Rational Emotive Therapy model, 18

Rationalization, 25, 56–57, 162–63, 190, 265, 295, 339–40

Recovery: for men, 240–45; steps to, 288–89

Reiki healing, xv–xvi. *See also* Life force energy, and recovery
Rejection, 213–14, 218; fear of, 37, 142, 227, 272
Relationships, 113–17, 139–40, 155, 347–48, 371; fantasies about, 66–67; fear of, 60, 114, 142–43, 152–53, 303–4; long-term, 5, 55–56, 121, 227, 268; stages in, 117–21, 127–31, 132–33, 137, 139–40, 179; traits in addictive, 140–43; with women, 56, 100, 101, 121, 211–12, 220. *See also* Healthy relationships; Intimate relationships
Religion, 17, 274, 311, 378; effect on sexuality, 11–13, 107, 149. *See also* Buddhism; Christianity
Responsibility: in families, 38, 261, 262–64, 265, 266; for others, 259–60; for self, 24, 35, 116, 325, 337
Resurrection (movie), 13
Rigidity (of behavior), 24, 25, 298
Rituals, 27, 171, 299–300
Rivera, Geraldo, 228
Role models, 8, 13, 33, 35, 60, 116–17, 239, 249, 268
Role of sex, 3–4, 147, 257
Roles: in addictive relationships, 120, 251; of children, 237, 265–66; in codependency, 38, 43, 59, 63, 87, 107; inequality in, 115, 238–39, 249–50, 254, 335–36; for men, 234, 237, 239–40; for women, 38–39, 101, 178, 191, 213, 222–23, 255, 351
Romance addiction, 63, 107, 179, 185

SAA. *See* Sex Addicts Anonymous
Sadomasochistic behavior, 193, 201, 204
Sadomasochistic relationships, 51, 158, 162, 199, 269
Safety problems: in addiction, 154; in codependency, 108–9, 156–57
Schaef, Anne Wilson, 362
Security: addiction to, 33, 50, 59, 99, 107, 124, 251; search for, 47, 48, 125
Self-abuse, 51, 158, 191–97, 199–201, 202–3, 206, 249–50. *See also* Masochism; Suicide

Self-esteem, 118, 205, 272; in addiction, 165; of children, 35, 46, 261–62, 264, 272; in codependency, 35, 50, 255, 268, 333, 335; influences on, 130, 141, 163, 264–65, 282; of men, 227
Self-knowledge, 10, 33, 35, 115, 188; and fantasies, 64; and recovery, 68–69, 335–36, 352
Self-love, 7, 300, 346; search for, 19, 30, 185, 234, 240, 255
Self-Love and Orgasm (Dodson), 250
Self-worth. *See* Self-esteem
Sensuality: and sexuality, 5–6
Sex, 315–19, 320; as a commodity, 4–5, 257; talking about, 8, 163, 208, 250, 359. *See also* Love; Prostitution
Sex addiction, 44, 51, 100, 251; definition, 43; and pornography, 58; stages of, 21–24, 44–50; survey question replies, 157–60, 165–66; traits of, 20–21, 24–25, 319–20. *See also* Addictive sex; Codependency
Sex addiction and codependency (simultaneous), 106–7
Sex addiction to codependency, 100, 102–4
Sex Addicts Anonymous (SAA), xii, xv, 62, 74, 77–79, 97, 98, 372–73
Sex education, 268, 269, 328, 329
Sexual abuse, xi, 238–39, 259; effect on adult relationships, 10, 60, 185, 235–36; perpetrators of, 14, 226, 234–37, 238. *See also* Incest
Sexual Chemistry (Fast), 254
Sexual energy, 9, 13–14, 66, 68, 186, 243, 264, 270
Sexual experience, 50–56
Sexual harassment, 259–60
Sexuality, xi, 8, 44, 194–95; and codependency, 344–46; power of, 14, 210, 226, 250
Sexual preference, 108–9, 219–21
Sexual sobriety, 65, 301; in codependency, 333–34, 346–48; guidelines for, 297–300, 333–44; for men, 240–41, 242. *See also* Celibacy

About the Author

Charlotte Davis Kasl received her Ph.D. in counseling psychology from Ohio University and works as a psychologist and healer in Minneapolis, Minnesota. In the last fourteen years she has done extensive work with survivors of childhood abuse and with addicted women. She has conducted numerous workshops here and abroad, and lectures on childhood abuse, addiction, codependency, sexuality, and spirituality.